Managing Information Technology in Small Business: Challenges and Solutions

Stephen Burgess
Victoria University, Australia

 **Idea Group Publishing**

 **Information Science Publishing**

Hershey • London • Melbourne • Singapore • Beijing

Acquisition Editor: Mehdi Khosrowpour
Managing Editor: Jan Travers
Development Editor: Michele Rossi
Copy Editor: Maria Boyer
Typesetter: LeAnn Whitcomb
Cover Design: Tedi Wingard
Printed at: Integrated Book Technology

Published in the United States of America by
        Idea Group Publishing
        1331 E. Chocolate Avenue
        Hershey PA 17033-1117
        Tel: 717-533-8845
        Fax: 717-533-8661
        E-mail: cust@idea-group.com
        Web site: http://www.idea-group.com

and in the United Kingdom by
        Idea Group Publishing
        3 Henrietta Street
        Covent Garden
        London WC2E 8LU
        Tel: 44 20 7240 0856
        Fax: 44 20 7379 3313
        Web site: http://www.eurospan.co.uk

Library of Congress Cataloging-in-Publication Data

Burgess, Stephen, 1958-
   Managing information technology in small business : challenges and solutions /
Stephen Burgess.
        p. cm.
Includes bibliographical references and index.
  ISBN 1-930708-35-1 (cloth)
     1. Small business--Electronic information resources--Management. 2. Information
technology--Management. 3. Small business--Management. I. Title.

HD62.7 .B835 2002
658--dc21   2001051713

British Cataloguing in Publication Data
A Cataloguing in Publication record for this book is available from the British Library.

NEW from Idea Group Publishing

- **Data Mining: A Heuristic Approach**
  Hussein Aly Abbass, Ruhul Amin Sarker and Charles S. Newton/1-930708-25-4
- **Managing Information Technology in Small Business: Challenges and Solutions**
  Stephen Burgess/1-930708-35-1
- **Managing Web Usage in the Workplace: A Social, Ethical and Legal Perspective**
  Murugan Anandarajan and Claire Simmers/1-930708-18-1
- **Challenges of Information Technology Education in the 21st Century**
  Eli Cohen/1-930708-34-3
- **Social Responsibility in the Information Age: Issues and Controversies**
  Gurpreet Dhillon/1-930708-11-4
- **Database Integrity: Challenges and Solutions**
  Jorge H. Doorn and Laura Rivero/ 1-930708-38-6
- **Managing Virtual Web Organizations in the 21st Century: Issues and Challenges**
  Ulrich Franke/1-930708-24-6
- **Managing Business with Electronic Commerce: Issues and Trends**
  Aryya Gangopadhyay/ 1-930708-12-2
- **Electronic Government: Design, Applications and Management**
  Åke Grönlund/1-930708-19-X
- **Knowledge Media in Healthcare: Opportunities and Challenges**
  Rolf Grutter/ 1-930708-13-0
- **Internet Management Issues: A Global Perspective**
  John D. Haynes/1-930708-21-1
- **Enterprise Resource Planning: Global Opportunities and Challenges**
  Liaquat Hossain, Jon David Patrick and M.A. Rashid/1-930708-36-X
- **The Design and Management of Effective Distance Learning Programs**
  Richard Discenza, Caroline Howard, and Karen Schenk/1-930708-20-3
- **Multirate Systems: Design and Applications**
  Gordana Jovanovic-Dolecek/1-930708-30-0
- **Managing IT/Community Partnerships in the 21st Century**
  Jonathan Lazar/1-930708-33-5
- **Multimedia Networking: Technology, Management and Applications**
  Syed Mahbubur Rahman/ 1-930708-14-9
- **Cases on Worldwide E-Commerce: Theory in Action**
  Mahesh Raisinghani/ 1-930708-27-0
- **Designing Instruction for Technology-Enhanced Learning**
  Patricia L. Rogers/ 1-930708-28-9
- **Heuristic and Optimization for Knowledge Discovery**
  Ruhul Amin Sarker, Hussein Aly Abbass and Charles Newton/1-930708-26-2
- **Distributed Multimedia Databases: Techniques and Applications**
  Timothy K. Shih/1-930708-29-7
- **Neural Networks in Business: Techniques and Applications**
  Kate Smith and Jatinder Gupta/ 1-930708-31-9
- **Managing the Human Side of Information Technology: Challenges and Solutions**
  Edward Szewczak and Coral Snodgrass/1-930708-32-7
- **Cases on Global IT Applications and Management: Successes and Pitfalls**
  Felix B. Tan/1-930708-16-5
- **Enterprise Networking: Multilayer Switching and Applications**
  Vasilis Theoharakis and Dimitrios Serpanos/1-930708-17-3
- **Measuring the Value of Information Technology**
  Han T.M. van der Zee/ 1-930708-08-4
- **Business to Business Electronic Commerce: Challenges and Solutions**
  Merrill Warkentin/1-930708-09-2

Excellent additions to your library!

Managing Information Technology in Small Business: Challenges and Solutions

Table of Contents

Preface i
>   Stephen Burgess, Victoria University, Australia

Chapter I
Information Technology in Small Business: Issues and
Challenges 1
>   Stephen Burgess, Victoria University, Australia

Part I: Small Business and Information Technology

Chapter II
Adoption and Use of Computer Technology in Canadian
Small Businesses: A Comparative Study 19
>   Linda Duxbury, Carleton University, Canada
>   Yves Decady, Statistics Canada, Canada
>   Angel Tse, Carleton University, Canada

Chapter III
Information Systems Development Outcomes: The Case
of Song Book Music 48
>   M. Gordon Hunter, University of Lethbridge, Canada

Chapter IV
Information System Check-Up as a Leverage for
SME Development 63
>   Aurelio Ravarini, Cattaneo University, Italy
>   Marco Tagliavini, Cattaneo University, Italy
>   Giacomo Buonanno, Cattaneo University, Italy
>   Donatella Sciuto, Politecnico di Milano, Italy

Chapter V
Modeling Technological Change in Small Business: Two
Approaches to Theorizing Innovation 83
>   Arthur Tatnall, Victoria University, Australia

Chapter VI
Unique Challenges for Small Business Adoption of
Information Technology: The Case of the Nova Scotia Ten 98
    M. Gordon Hunter, University of Lethbridge, Canada
    Monica Diochon, St. Francis Xavier University, Canada
    David Pugsley, St. Francis Xavier University, Canada
    Barry Wright, St. Francis Xavier University, Canada

Chapter VII
Franchising and Information Technology: A Framework 118
    Ye-Sho Chen, Louisiana State University, USA
    Robert Justis, Louisiana State University, USA
    P. Pete Chong, Gonzaga University, USA

Chapter VIII
Use of Decision Support Systems in Small Businesses 140
    Yanqing Duan, University of Luton, UK
    Russell Kinman, University of Luton, UK
    Mark Xu, University of Portsmouth, UK

Chapter IX
Computer Security in Small Businesses–An Example
from Slovenia 156
    Borut Werber, University of Maribor, Slovenia

Part II: Small Business, the Internet and Electronic Commerce

Chapter X
Factors Inhibiting the Collaborative Adoption of
Electronic Commerce Among Australian SMEs 178
    Kristy Lawrence, University of Tasmania, Australia

Chapter XI
Web Initiatives & E-Commerce Strategy: How Do
Canadian Manufacturing SMEs Compare? 193
    Ron Craig, Wilfrid Laurier University, Canada

Chapter XII
The Role of SMEs in Promoting Electronic Commerce
in Communities 209
    Celia Romm, Central Queensland University, Australia
    Wal Taylor, Central Queensland University, Australia

Chapter XIII
Strategies for Consultancy Engagement for E-Business
Development–A Case Analysis of Australian SMEs 227
 Shirley Bode, Edith Cowan University, Australia
 Janice Burn, Edith Cowan University, Australia

Chapter XIV
Building the Professional Services E-Practice 246
 Dieter Fink, Edith Cowan University, Australia

Chapter XV
How a Procedural Framework Would Assist SMEs in
Developing Their E-Business Strategy 261
 Anthony Stiller, University of the Sunshine Coast, Australia

Chapter XVI
Management's Contribution to Internet Commerce
Benefit–Experiences of Online Small Businesses 279
 Simpson Poon, Charles Sturt University, Australia, and
  The University of Hong Kong, Hong Kong

Chapter XVII
Options for Business-to-Consumer E-Commerce in
Developing Countries: An Online Store Prototype 299
 Robert Klepper, Southern Illinois University–Edwardsville, USA
 Andrew Carrington, Southern Illinois University–Edwardsville, USA

Chapter XVIII
Electronic Commerce Opportunities, Challenges
and Organizational Issues for Australian SMEs 316
 Mohini Singh, RMIT University, Australia

Chapter XIX
Training for E-Commerce Success in SMEs 334
 Yanqing Duan, University of Luton, UK
 Roisin Mullins, University of Luton, UK
 David Hamblin, University of Luton, UK

About the Authors 349

Index 358

Preface

In many countries, small businesses comprise over 95% of the proportion of private businesses and approximately half of the private workforce, with information technology (IT) being used in a majority of these businesses. Governments around the world are placing increasing importance upon the success of small business entrepreneurs and are providing increased resources to support their success. There are a number of key differences in the use of IT between small and larger businesses. These include: small businesses generally have fewer resources available to devote to IT, they have very little control over forces that are external to the organisation, they generally do not have their own separate IT department and small businesses generally have less formalised planning and control procedures for the adoption and use of IT. Small business entrepreneurs are thus often placed in the situation of knowing that IT can support their business in some way, but they lack the expertise and resources to know how it can be effectively applied.

Up until a few years ago, research into the use of IT in small businesses was almost non-existent when compared with the amount of research being carried out for medium and large-sized businesses. Recently, an increasing amount of research has been conducted into this important, emerging field.

The main purpose for **Managing Information Technology in Small Businesses: Challenges and Solutions** is to showcase the wide variety of research being carried out in the area of small business and IT. In doing this, the book examines the challenges facing small businesses in their use of IT and the solutions that are being proposed. The book is separated into two major parts, research that deals with IT and small business in general, and research that deals with the rapidly expanding field of e-commerce.

Chapters in each part fit into one or more sub-themes. The first sub-theme relates to **Studies** that are breaking new ground in the field. Even though the amount of work being done in the area is rapidly increasing, we still do not know enough about the manner in which small businesses use IT. The second sub-theme is **Frameworks and Models.** Much work is being done to provide frameworks and guidelines that will allow us to direct small businesses to use IT effectively. The final sub-theme is **Challenges and Solutions,** examining some of the current challenges facing small businesses in the use of IT and the available solutions.

A brief overview of the book follows.

The first chapter, by the editor, provides an introduction to many of the areas covered in the book.

Part One: Small Business and Information Technology

Chapter Two, by *Linda Duxbury, Yves Decady* and *Angel Tse,* examines the impact of company size on the adoption, use and perceived impact of computer technology in Canadian businesses. It also compares and contrasts small, medium and large businesses with respect to their use of computer technology and its perceived impacts.

Chapter Three, by *M. Gordon Hunter*, analyses an information systems development project which is considered by the users to be "completed," yet unsuccessful. It concludes with a discussion of how the framework may be useful in understanding information system success or failure within a small business context.

Chapter Four, by *Aurelio Ravarini, Marco Tagliavini, Giacomo Buonanno* and *Donatella Sciuto,* suggests that small businesses could benefit from a tool that supports the business in monitoring information systems adequacy and making competent choices about information systems development. The purpose of the chapter is to provide such a tool.

Chapter Five, by *Arthur Tatnall*, suggests that the introduction of a new information system into a small business, or the upgrading of an existing system, should be seen as an innovation and so considered through the lens of innovation theory. The chapter considers the well-known innovation diffusion theory, but argues that another approach, that of innovation translation, has more to offer in the case of innovations that take place in smaller organisations.

Chapter Six, by *M. Gordon Hunter, Monica Diochon, David Pugsley* and *Barry Wright,* explores the unique issues faced by small businesses regarding the adoption of information technology by examining 10 small businesses in Nova Scotia. The discussion is presented relative to major themes which emerged during interviews with the 10 small business managers. A series of recommendations are made for the major stakeholder groups.

Chapter Seven, by *Ye-Sho Chen, Robert Justis* and *P. Pete Chong,* looks at small businesses involved in franchising. The chapter suggests how IT can be used to help develop the working knowledge that is disseminated throughout the franchise system. This is achieved by organising previous studies into a framework to provide a comprehensive view of the franchising business operations and the role IT plays in enhancing the effectiveness and efficiency of the franchise system.

Chapter Eight, by *Yanqing Duan, Russell Kinman* and *Mark Xu,* is concerned with current practice in relation to decision support systems (DSSs) in small businesses. The authors identify managers' needs for computer-based support, and explore if and how computer-based DSS could be better developed and utilised to meet these needs. Factors that hamper the utilisation of DSS in small firms are also discussed.

Chapter Nine, by *Borut Werber*, examines basic computer security problems and the use of IT in 122 small Slovenian businesses. The purpose of the study was to assess why some Slovene small businesses do not use IT, what kind of security measures are used, how many and what kind of problems they had with computer hardware and software and how they managed to solve those problems.

Part Two: Small Business, the Internet and Electronic Commerce

Chapter Ten, by *Kristy Lawrence*, discusses the advantages of electronic commerce and the potential of collaborative, or industry-based, practices to encourage the adoption of electronic commerce technologies among small businesses. The Tasmanian Wine sector was investigated in order to identify issues that may inhibit the development of collaborative, industry-wide electronic commerce adoption programs.

Chapter Eleven, by *Ron Craig*, examines small and medium-sized manufacturing businesses in Canada, specifically in their use, and potential use, of the Internet and electronic commerce. The following questions were examined. Do they lead or lag larger firms? Is an e-commerce strategy important for them, and what reasons do they see for pursuing it? Are firms that pursue an e-commerce strategy more successful than those that do not?

Chapter Twelve, by *Celia Romm* and *Wal Taylor,* looks at whether small businesses should consider national or global business as the main reason for getting themselves 'e-commerce enabled.' The authors promote local e-commerce, particularly as it pertains to regional, rural or remote communities, and propose the Action, Reaction, Integration (ARI) model, which considers the role that SMEs can play in promoting Internet technologies in their communities.

Chapter Thirteen, by *Shirley Bode* and *Janice Burn*, examines the role of consultants in the development of small business Web sites. The chapter incorporates an analysis of 10 Western Australian online small businesses who contracted Web site design consultants to produce their sites. The following questions were addressed. Do small businesses have explicit e-business strategies prior to development of a Web site? Are Web site consultants engaged through a formal engagement process, aligning business and web development strategies? To what extent do small businesses feel their individual e-business needs are understood and met by Web site design consultants?

Chapter Fourteen, by *Dieter Fink*, provides an outline for small professional services practices with an understanding of how to enter the 'e-age' by building an 'e-practice.' It proceeds by mapping the progress that needs to be made in moving from a previous stage of organisational development to one that is suitable for the 'virtual age.' In the transition to the mature stage of development, they need to re-engineer their practices to offer online services and to maximise their intellectual capital through technology-enabled knowledge management. Much of the content of the chapter is based on research carried out in small and medium accounting firms.

Chapter Fifteen, by *Anthony Stiller*, looks at the provision of a procedural framework for small business managers to follow when designing their e-business plan and revenue model so they can remain in charge of the process (and not be pushed into a particular template designed by a consultant to suit their hardware and software platform). The aim of the framework is to give the small business owner control over the entire process until they are at the stage to either develop their own online presence, or have sufficient information to take to a web consultant who can develop a model which reflects the e-business strategy and is in harmony with the traditional business and marketing plan.

Chapter Sixteen, by *Simpson Poon*, examines the following questions through a study of 224 Singaporean small businesses. Is there any difference between traditional IT applications and e-commerce? Can we apply what we have learned from earlier small business IT experiences to e-commerce? Does the largely external nature of e-commerce systems mean that management needs to play a different role than in the past? The purpose of the study was to bridge the knowledge gap between traditional small business IT systems and e-commerce systems, with the idea of helping management to rethink how they can secure e-commerce benefits.

Chapter Seventeen, by *Robert Klepper* and *Andrew Carrington*, considers some of the challenges faced in establishing an electronic commerce store in a developing country, particularly techniques for reducing costs that otherwise would be a barrier to entry. The described prototype store utilises many low-cost (or free) technologies. A discussion of some of the technical issues involved in developing the prototype is available at the end of the chapter.

Chapter Eighteen, by *Mohini Singh*, discusses the findings of an Australian study that identified the objectives, opportunities and challenges of e-commerce experienced by small businesses that were mostly early adopters of the Internet as a medium of trade. E-commerce issues presented in this chapter include research findings, supported by theory from literature. The chapter concludes with a series of recommendations and strategies for small businesses wishing to adopt e-commerce.

Chapter Nineteen, by *Yanqing Duan, Roisin Mullins* and *David Hamblin*, contends that training is often seen as the most effective way to help small businesses to cope with the increasing demand on improving their skills, while not increasing staffing. The chapter reports the results and summarises the findings from empirical studies conducted across five countries. A pilot project supported by the European Commission's Leonardo Da Vinci programme was set up to address training issues and provide on-line training and support for SMEs in participating countries. To provide the training in the most needed areas and at the most appropriate levels, surveys and focus group discussions were conducted. Guidelines for the development of the on-line training system are derived from the findings.

Acknowledgments

Primarily, I would like to thank the authors in this book. All of them are 'pioneers' of sorts in the area of small business and IT. Their dedication to this task is highlighted by the final version of this book being very similar to the vision for the book I had after the initial call for chapters was sent out in late 2000. Virtually all of the authors made the transition from being 'potential' contributors to being 'actual' contributors. This meant that they stuck through the review process (each chapter was blind reviewed by two of their peers) and tolerated requests from the editor to alter 'this focus' or 'that paragraph' on a number of occasions. Once again, I thank them for their significant contributions to the final result.

I particularly want to thank the following groups and individuals, who have in some way contributed to and nurtured by interest in this area:

- My employer, the School of Information Systems at Victoria University (VU), Australia, especially my colleagues who have tolerated my varying moods over lunch after some heavy 'reading sessions.'
- John Breen, Head of the Small Business Research Unit in the Faculty of Business and Law at VU.
- The staff of Small Business Victoria, now a section of the Department of State Development in the State Government of Victoria, Australia – especially Geoff Lee for assistance in recent years.
- Members of the Small Business Counselling Service, an 'arm' of Small Business Victoria. This group specifically helped to add the 'reality' to my research.
- The Owner/Managers of the many small businesses who have answered surveys, tolerated interviews or complained about how things should be! They all helped to supply another piece to the puzzle and provide the 'practical' aspect that is vital to this type of research.

Special thanks to Idea Group Publishing for inviting me to edit this book, and to Michele Rossi (Development Editor from Idea Group Publishing) for her assistance, encouragement and prompt replies!

Stephen Burgess
Victoria University
Melbourne, Australia

Chapter I

Information Technology in Small Business: Issues and Challenges

Stephen Burgess
Victoria University, Australia

INTRODUCTION

Research into the use of information technology (IT) in small businesses is extremely diverse. It encompasses the many different characteristics of small businesses, including size, culture, business strategy, attitudes to IT, industry and location, to name a few. The authors in this book have contributed chapters that address many of these characteristics of small businesses. This chapter provides an introduction to many of the areas covered in the book.

A VIEW ON RESEARCH INTO IT AND SMALL BUSINESS

There is some anecdotal evidence to suggest that the use of information technology in small businesses has been the subject of an increasing amount of research over the last 10 to 15 years. The 'evidence' often occurs in the form of a general comment at the commencement of a published paper, which mentions the 'explosion' of recent research in the area or 'increased interest' in the area. As one means of examining this, a review of the business article research reference tool, ABI/Inform,[1] was conducted in March 2001. ABI/Inform is a global business database that covers areas such as marketing, advertising, economics, human resources, taxation, computers and companies. It contains a large component of mainly full text articles. A count of the number of peer review articles was made under the search topic (Computers or "Information Technology") for information technology and ("small business" or SME) for small businesses (refer to Table 1). The number of peer-reviewed articles listed that had the combined defined search topics (small business and information technology) listed in the citation or abstract reached its highest level in the three years 1997-1999, with the highest number of 23 articles being in 1999. Whether or not this means that there has been more research in the area is difficult to claim, as it depends upon a number of factors, including the number of journals listed in the service each year. For instance, if there had been an addition to the number of journals being referenced in the service, it may look like there has been an increase in the research output of a number of topics. Perhaps a better comparison is that of the amount of articles listed in the combined research area with the peer-reviewed articles available in each separate area. The number of peer-reviewed articles related to small business and IT has hovered around two-thirds to one percent of the total number of peer-reviewed articles in the general area of IT over the last decade and a half. There has been some weak evidence of an increase in the percentage since 1993. There is no evidence presented to conclude that the number of peer-reviewed articles related to small business and IT has increased at all when compared with those listed for small business in general.

Perhaps then, this idea of an increasing amount of research in the area is more

Table 1: The number of peer-reviewed articles related to small business and information technology listed in ABI/Inform 1986-1999

Year	Number of Peer-Reviewed Articles in the Area of Computing and Small Business	% Related to Peer-Reviewed Articles in the Area of Information Technology	% Related to Peer-Reviewed Articles in the area of Small Business
1999	23	1.35	4.8
1998	12	0.95	2.9
1997	15	0.62	2.1
1996	10	0.64	2.5
1995	11	1.17	3.1
1994	10	0.89	3.2
1993	10	0.95	3.5
1992	6	0.61	2.8
1991	6	0.69	3.9
1990	6	0.82	7.6
1989	8	0.86	7.3
1988	4	0.54	4.3
1987	5	0.81	4.8
1986	5	0.76	6.0

due to interest in the separate areas of small business and information technology than the combined area.

✓ISSUES

One of the difficulties facing small business researchers is to generalize their research findings across the small business base so that they can be useful to a wider audience. This is (almost) impossible, as it is very difficult to generalize results for such a diverse range of businesses. Most small business researchers overcome this by selecting a particular niche of small businesses to examine, or by reporting at a very general level. This section looks at some of the issues facing researchers as they attempt to investigate the use of IT in small businesses. Many of the chapters in this book also address these issues to varying degrees.

What Is Small?

When studying the use of IT in small business, the range of definitions used to describe 'small business' is interesting to say the least. This range can make it extremely difficult for researchers to 'match up' different small business studies.

In Australia, an annual study examining the use of computers and electronic commerce in small and medium businesses (Telstra Corporation and NOIE, 2000) defines a small business as having 1-19 employees and a medium sized business as having 20-200 employees.

A 1997 study of 174 small and medium businesses (Bridge and Peel, 1999) used the European definition of 'small' being 10 to 99 employees and 'medium' as 100 to 499 employees.

In a study of 244 Canadian 'small' businesses, El Louadi (1998) targeted businesses with up to 300 employees and ended up with the sample having an average of 28 employees per business.

Pollard and Hayne (1998) have identified a number of studies that set the upper limit of employees for a business to be classed as small as 50, 100, 200, 250 or 500! They themselves have decided that any business with up to 200 employees can be classed as small.

Despite a number of requests from the authors of this book to provide guidelines in relation to a definition of 'small business,' I have asked them to use their own definitions for 'small business.' This is for the purpose of making the book a reflection of research in the area as it is currently being carried out. When pressed, I did tell them that my preferred definition (a rather parochial, 'Australianized' definition) was that a small business was any business with one to 20 employees. A micro business has up to five employees (refer to next section). Medium businesses? I don't really care! Actually, I would be prepared to accept any number up to 50, 100 or 200. But that is only so I can compare them with small businesses! I do not use any other method for measuring business size (such as annual turnover) because I have found that it is much easier to get a small business to tell you how many employees that they have than to ask them any financial information.

Medium and Micro

A 'micro' business is a special type of small business—one that is *very* small. Bridge and Peel (1999) have defined a micro business as having up to nine employees. As mentioned in the previous section, I prefer to define a micro business as one with up to five employees.

A somewhat wider grouping (that includes small businesses) comes in the form of '**SME.**' SME is a general acronym that stands for Small and Medium Enterprises. It is commonly used to describe research that is carried out into a combination of small and medium sized businesses. The problem occurs when the different definitions of the size of the businesses are taken into account. Although I personally do not like it, 'SME' is here to stay. It is part of the vocabulary, certainly of much of the small business research community. I have encouraged authors in this to book to use it where they are comfortable with it.

So, what is classed as 'small' in one study (say 120 employees) may be 'medium' in another study and 'large' in yet another study, depending upon the chosen method of classification! My advice to anybody attempting to interpret research that is carried out in the small business area (and in this book) is to make sure that you look at the definition that the researchers have used for 'small' and take that into account in your interpretation of the results.

Size Is Important!

Why is it so important to consider the size of the business?

A number of studies suggest that there is a relationship between the size of a business and its level of adoption of IT (McDonagh and Prothero, 2000). A 2000 study of Australian small businesses revealed that 79% of businesses with 1-2 employees used computers, with this percentage increasing as the size of the businesses increased: 3-9 employees (90%), 10-19 employees (93%) and more than 20 employees (100%). Similar business size trends were evident in levels of Internet usage and adoption of Web sites (Telstra Corporation and NOIE, 2000).

There is also a relationship between the size of a business and the different characteristics it will have that can lead to the successful use of IT (Igbaria et al.,

1997; Pollard and Hayne, 1998). As such, research findings based upon traditional 'MIS' in larger businesses are not necessarily directly applicable to small businesses. Some of these are investigated in this book.

Barriers and Opportunities

The literature around the area of small business and information technology is rife with what is now a fairly accepted list of 'barriers' to the successful implementation of IT in small businesses. These barriers typically include (Management Services, 1997; Igbaria et al., 1997; Pollard and Hayne, 1998; McDonagh and Prothero, 2000):

- The cost of IT
- Lack of time to devote to the implementation and maintenance of IT
- A lack of IT knowledge combined with difficulty in finding useful, impartial advice
- Lack of use of external consultants and vendors
- Short-range management perspectives
- A lack of understanding of the benefits that IT can provide, and how to measure those benefits
- A lack of formal planning or control procedures.

One advantage that small businesses (especially innovative ones) have is that they are flexible. They are able to preserve labor relationships, bring a 'personal touch' to operations, cater to niche markets and they have small capital requirements. The fact that they are under constant pressure can also spur them to be inventive and innovative in their business operations (International Trade Forum, 1999) These are all factors that can help them to overcome the barriers mentioned earlier in this section.

Success Factors

Having identified some of the barriers to the successful use of IT, there is also a fairly common list of factors that are listed in the literature that appear to indicate a greater chance of successful implementation of IT in small businesses.

Some of these factors are (Swartz and Walsh, 1996; Naylor and Williams, 1994; Zinatelli et al., 1996; Yap and Thong, 1997):

- The involvement of Owner/Managers in the implementation of IT
- The involvement of users (employees) in development and installation
- The training of users
- The selection of applications chosen for computerization
- The use of disciplined planning methodologies in setting up applications
- The number of analytical/strategic (versus transactional) applications being run

- The level of IT expertise within the organization
- The role of the external environment (especially consultants and vendors).

The idea behind introducing this list (and the barriers listed earlier) is that you will see these points raised again and again in the following sections and in the chapters throughout the book.

Owner/ Managers

One of the key factors leading to successful use of IT in small businesses identified in the previous section was the involvement of small business owners/managers in the IT implementation.

It is perhaps incorrect to link owners and managers of small businesses together. As businesses become larger it is less likely that the owner (*or owners*) will be manager(*s*), and the manager will tend to take on a description such as CEO or the like as the business get larger! Having said this, the 'joint' term is often used in studies, so readers should be aware of it.

There is some evidence to indicate that managers in small businesses are less likely to know how to use IT effectively or to keep up with the latest trends in IT than their counterparts in larger businesses (Pollard and Hayne, 1988). In a 1997 survey of United Kingdom small businesses, small business managers described themselves as failing to exploit IT to its potential. The reasons given were a lack of proper resources to manage the information properly and the belief that the costs of IT outweigh the benefits (Management Services, 1997).

Igbaria et al. (1997) cite a number of references to support the view that management support can promote the acceptance of IT. They found that the support of management positively affected the perceived ease of use and the perceived usefulness of IT within the small business. In their case, management support could take the form of encouragement to use IT, provision of a wider selection of easy-to-use specialist software, offering training programs, using IT in a variety of applications to support business tasks and encouraging experimentation.

Uses

These days, the vast majority of small businesses in most countries have computers.

The issue, however, is not whether small businesses have computers, but how well they use them.

(El Louadi, 1998)

It has been well reported in the literature that small businesses that use computers mainly use them for administrative and operational purposes (such as accounting, budgeting, payroll, inventory control and the like) (Pollard and Hayne, 1988; El Louadi, 1998; Bridge and Peel, 1999).

Much of the software that is used by small businesses is purchased 'off the shelf' (McDonagh and Prothero, 2000), although there is some evidence to suggest that small businesses with particular (specialized) needs are prepared to invest in customized software (Burgess, 1997).

The literature also suggests that some small businesses are beginning to realize that IT can be used to gain competitive advantages (Pollard and Hayne, 1998). Bridge and Peel (1999) divided UK small businesses into groupings of 'high planners' and 'low planners.' These classifications related to the degree of detail with which strategic plans (of longer than one year) were worked out by the business.

…SMEs which engaged in more intensive (detailed) strategic planning were significantly more likely to utilize business software (spreadsheets, database, MIS and statistical packages) related to decision-making.

(Bridge and Peel, 1999)

Location

Why is 'location' important when considering the use of IT in small business? The major answer to this is a combination of *resources* and *distance*. The further you are away from resources, the longer it takes and the more it costs to get them. This can particularly be the case with hardware and software purchases, training and support. What is the point of having a 24-hour, seven-day-a-week on-site warranty provided by your computer vendor if it takes them two days to reach you? How much will it cost to get them to provide such a service anyway? Is it cheaper to just buy two computers? When one breaks down you can just take it in to get fixed on your 'next visit to town'!

Another reason for examining location is *culture*. Some countries, and even different regions within countries, have their own traditions and their own established ways of doing things. This can influence the behavior of small businesses and the manner in which they use IT (refer to the next few sections).

The main aim of this section is to examine some of the issues facing small businesses using IT in developing countries and rural areas.

Developing Countries

Small businesses make up a major portion of businesses in developing countries (in some countries the percentage is higher than in developed countries). Recognizing their importance, many governments are providing support programs for small businesses (for the types of support programs provided, the reader is referred to the section on Government Support later) (International Trade Forum, 1999).

One of the major barriers faced by small businesses in developing countries is access to information, especially information used in decision-making. Another problem is the lack of data sources from which to obtain the type of information required. Problems with the technological infrastructure of developing countries only exacerbate this (Sawyerr et al., 2000). As such, businesses in developing countries are limited in their ability to perform research and development and have difficulties in accessing trade information (Belisle and Czinkota, 1999). The political environment of a country can also affect the ability of a business to set up systems to obtain external information for use in decision-making. Sawyerr et al. (2000) quote the case of Nigeria, which has been recently characterized by frequent changes of power, as an example of this. Small businesses can find the task of any long-term planning to be difficult in such an environment.

New technologies (including information technologies) can provide these businesses with an opportunity to catch up with the rest of the world (Belisle and Czinkota, 1999; Mehta, 1999). Although, electronic commerce (e-commerce) will be discussed in a later section, some points need to be mentioned in relation to developing countries. To be able to access some of the benefits of e-commerce, such as faster service and shipments and precise transmittal of orders, it is necessary to have an efficient telecommunications structure, a problem area in many developing countries (Belisle and Czinkota, 1999). A starting point can be to increase the number of available telephone lines. After this, the quality of the transmission needs to be addressed as this has been cited as causing difficulties in the ability to obtain information from foreign sources and to effectively use the Internet (Sawyerr et al., 2000).

Today, the cost of installing a national telecommunications structure has fallen. When combined with reduced costs of international transport, it is easier for small businesses in many developing countries to gain access to international markets (International Trade Forum, 1999). Uptake of the Internet in developing countries has been on the increase since 1996, the level of growth (again) being hindered by problems with the telecommunications infrastructure (Gallagher, 1999). According to Belisle and Czinkota (1999), it is a matter of when, not if, such an infrastructure will be available in developing countries that desire it. There will, however, be vast areas of the world that will *not* have access to the Internet soon. For businesses in these areas, access to the Internet will remain secondary to other concerns, such as personal and business survival through sustained tenure, secure food and water supplies, and access to business institutions and credit (Mehta,

1999). In addition to this, there are some countries where use of the Internet is discouraged. According to Gallagher (1999), the Internet is unlikely to have a major impact for small businesses in these countries in the next few years.

Rural Small Businesses

Some of the problems facing rural small businesses are similar to those facing small businesses in developing countries.

A study of small businesses in the rural areas of the United Kingdom (Management Services, 2001) indicated a wide and growing use of computers and the Internet, but a lack of ISDN or other broadband services had restricted access in some remote areas. It was felt that there was a lack of opportunity to develop familiarity with computers. It was thought that there could be a possibility of using local schools for acquiring these skills, but difficulties related to clashes with working time, distance, travel time and the relevance of the courses offered needed to be addressed.

One of the benefits that the Internet may provide is remote access to many desired IT resources, such as training. Access to the Internet can also provide small, rural businesses with greater opportunities to trade across borders though the reduction of transactions costs (Gallagher, 1999).

Skilful use of the Internet can create opportunities by giving farmers, small business people and communities the capacity to present a regional image to the world, create focal points for inquiries about local businesses and their offerings, create global businesses and develop new products and services.

(Gallagher, 1999)

Interestingly, a year 2000 survey of Australian small businesses revealed that 29% of metropolitan small businesses had a Web site, compared to 20% of rural small businesses. The main reason given by rural small businesses for not having a Web site was that they did not have access to the skills needed to design, build and maintain a Web site (Telstra Corporation and NOIE, 2000).

Industry

There is some relationship between the industry that small businesses are involved in and the types of IT that they use. In exploring this, it should be remembered that some types of industries tend to locate in urban areas, while others will be in rural areas. In a 1997 study of Australian businesses (Burgess, 1997), there was a high percentage of Wholesale/Retail, Finance/Property/Business Services and Professional businesses located in the central business district (CBD). Wholesale/Retail businesses were mainly based in shops. Professional and Building/Construction businesses were based at home or (as they grew larger) in offices.

Finance/ Property and Business-based services were located almost primarily in offices. Manufacturing business tended to be based in other premises (such as factories and farms).

Perhaps not surprisingly, Professionals and Finance/ Property/ Business Services small businesses are the ones that use the 'latest' IT. The Building/ Construction industry is typically the least enthusiastic to use IT at all, let alone the latest IT (Burgess, 1997). A later Australian study revealed consistent results. Computer penetration was highest in the Business Services industry (94%) and lowest in the Building/Construction industry (77%). Similar industry trends were evident in usage of the Internet and adoption of Web sites (Telstra Corporation and NOIE, 2000).

There is also some evidence that different software is used by different industries. For instance, the building/construction industry uses scheduling, drafting/design and project management software. Manufacturing firms use software for scheduling, operating machinery and monitoring operations. Wholesale/Retail firms use point-of-sale software (as well as bar code scanners) (Burgess, 1997).

CHALLENGES

This section examines some of the areas that small business researchers are targeting in their recommendations for how the use of IT in small businesses can be improved. These are areas that small businesses often neglect or, even worse, know nothing about.

Planning

One of the barriers identified earlier that hinder the effective use of IT in small businesses is a lack of formal planning and control methodologies. Again, this relates to a lack of knowledge of how to plan effectively, lack of time and money to seek this knowledge, lack of time to apply it even if they have the knowledge and a lack of understanding that they even need the knowledge! Small businesses are, however, concerned with issues relating to how they can operate more effectively and efficiently and/or how they can grow (El Louadi, 1998). One of the problems is that management practice in small businesses is often based on the short term and is informal and ad hoc. Much of the time is spent 'surviving,' so that little time can be devoted to examine IT projects (Pollard and Hayne, 1988). Having said this, the relationship between successful strategic use of IT by 'high planners' (refer to Uses section earlier) should encourage small businesses to take the time out to relate their use of IT to their overall business plans.

A similar trend is occurring in relation to small business and their use of the Internet. Although usage of the Internet by small businesses is on the increase, little is known about the relationship (if any) between the overall strategic goals of small firms and their Internet strategies. Many small businesses appear to have Web sites because it is the "thing to do" (Dandridge and Levenburg, 2000).

Working Out the Benefits of IT

Another barrier to the successful use of IT in small businesses is a lack of understanding of the benefits that IT can provide, and how to measure those benefits. The success of IT implementations relate to the extent to which the system contributes to achieving organizational goals (Yap and Thong, 1997). There have typically been three methods used to evaluate the success of IT systems in small businesses. These are (Naylor and Williams, 1994; Zinatelli et al., 1996):

- Measures of system usage
- Impact upon organizational performance
- Measures of user satisfaction.

System usage is often measured using data automatically collected from the system. For instance, this may be the number of transactions that have been entered, reports being requested from the system and so forth. The impact of IT upon organizational performance is difficult to assess, as so many other factors can directly or indirectly effect organizational performance (Naylor and Williams, 1994).

The most common way used to determine the level of IT success is to measure small business user satisfaction with information technology. Such measures of user satisfaction have one major problem–they are linked with user expectations (Naylor and Williams, 1994). For instance, an owner/manager understanding the strategic benefits that IT can provide may be less satisfied with a simple transactional system than an owner/manager who is unaware of these strategic benefits. This is despite the possibility that they may be reviewing systems that perform in a similar manner. Again, the problem falls back to a lack of proper knowledge about the advantages that IT can provide. Interestingly, a 2000 survey of UK small and medium businesses (Management Services, 2000) revealed that over half of the businesses felt that the Internet and IT had no effect on their business at all!

Igbaria et al. (1997) have suggested that another measure of success could be user acceptance of IT. The voluntary use of computers can potentially play a role in enabling small businesses to compete successfully and provide better customer service. Individuals in small businesses are more likely to use a computer system if it is easy to use and if they feel that they can use it to improve their performance and productivity.

Training

How important is training to the users of IT in small businesses? Factors relating to 'a lack of knowledge of IT' or 'lack of understanding of the benefits of IT' have been mentioned a number of times already in this chapter and are mentioned many times throughout this book. Appropriate training in IT has been mentioned earlier as one of the factors leading to successful use of IT in small businesses. Many small and medium businesses feel that they are unsure of how to use the technology they have, let alone increase their investment in it (Management Services, 2000).

Igbaria et al. (1997) found that the amount of training that users had received from other users or IT specialists within the firm had an effect on the perceived usefulness of the system. External training had a positive effect on the perceived ease of use of IT, which they theorize may enhance computer skills and reduce 'negative attitude' barriers to the acceptance of IT. A lack of training was a cause of user frustration.

It has already been suggested that the Internet may help to solve some of the problems facing small businesses in remote areas via the provision of online training.

External Information

Small business managers perceive more uncertainty in their environment than their counterparts in larger businesses. Effective management of external information can help them to reduce the level of uncertainty that they feel (El Louadi, 1998). There are two facets to the external environment that relate to IT and small businesses.

The first is the use of IT to assist with obtaining and using external information that is useful to business in an effective and efficient manner. A number of surveys of small businesses (El Louadi, 1998) have found that they are more preoccupied with external information than larger businesses, looking for information relating to their customers, their competitors, regulatory information and how they can grow their business or make it more efficient. Traditionally, the sources of much of this information are the personal contacts and networks developed by the small business manager. The ability to gather trade information and intelligence on competitors requires not only the ability to research the market and analyze information, but also experience with IT, which can provide difficulties for many small businesses (International Trade Forum, 1999).

The second facet involves gaining external information and support in relation to the IT operated by the business. Three important ways of gaining these are through training programs (refer previous section), vendors and consultants, and through government support programs.

Vendors and Consultants

In many instances, small businesses have to rely on the IT expertise of vendors and/or consultants because of a lack of internal IT expertise. Igbaria et al. (1997) have found that good external support provided by vendors and/or consultants such as technical support, training and a harmonious working relationship can reduce the risk of IT failure in small businesses.

There is a view, however, that vendors and consultants do not understand the small and medium business market and that the level of support provided by them is only adequate or less than adequate (Management Services, 2000). Careful selection of vendors and/or consultants as providers of hardware or software, to integrate the IT into the business and/or to fill the IT knowledge gap within the organization, is therefore vital to the successful use of IT in many small businesses.

Government Support

Governments worldwide are beginning to realize the importance of the small business community. The role of government in developing countries has already been touched upon in this chapter. IT is one of the areas that are the subject of increased government resources, through improved information programs, increased training opportunities and technology support grants and awards.

It is one thing providing these programs. It is another thing having small businesses take advantage of them. In the United Kingdom, less than 15% of small businesses use advice available from government bodies. Their main sources of IT information are their own small business communities and computer magazines (Management Services, 1997).

To be able to take advantage of government programs, two events have to occur. First of all, small businesses have to know about them. This means that governments have to be proactive in informing small businesses of the programs *in the communities within which small businesses operate.* Secondly, small businesses must be convinced that their investment of resources into the program will provide identifiable benefits to their businesses.

The Internet and Electronic Commerce

There is no doubt that a rapidly increasing number of small businesses are using the Internet (McDonagh and Prothero, 2000). Gallagher (1999) claims that the level of Internet use is growing faster than any other technology in history! The level of this growth is such that almost half of this book is devoted to chapters that address the use of the Internet or e-commerce in small businesses.

Many small businesses are establishing a presence on the Internet, be it through the development of a Web site or through the use of email. Two primary uses of Internet technologies in small businesses are the use of email for communication and the Internet to gather information (McDonagh and Prothero, 2000; Dandridge and Levenburg, 2000). Part 2 of this book is devoted to the use of the Internet and e-commerce in small businesses.

A 2000 study of Australian and medium small businesses revealed higher levels of connection to the Internet in businesses where (Telstra Corporation and NOIE, 2000):

- There was a culture of innovation.
- There was a willingness to adopt new technologies.
- Competitors and those in like industries had success using the Internet
- Businesses had access to relevant skills and knowledge and were willing to use those skills.
- Customers and/or suppliers wanted or demanded contact by email or online transactions.
- Businesses had a strategic sense of how to move forward.
- There was an awareness of the financial benefits available.

In a 1999 survey of Irish small and medium businesses (McDonagh and Prothero, 2000), 32% of small businesses had established Web sites. In this survey, security issues (concerns about customer transactions, misuse of information or fear of hackers) were cited as major fears related to the use of e-commerce. This is not only from the viewpoint of the customer, but also of the business dealing with partners and suppliers. In a survey of United States 'small' businesses of less than 100 employees (The Yankee Group, 1999, referenced in Dandridge and Levenburg,(2000), 31% had a Web site. A 2000 study of Australian small businesses revealed that 25% of small businesses (up to 20 employees) had a Web site. This was more likely in 'proactive' small businesses, who saw a Web site as (Telstra Corporation and NOIE, 2000):

- an essential part of their promotional and advertising mix,
- a means of providing business and product information to clients, and
- a basis for developing an order and payment facility.

CONCLUSION

This chapter has introduced a number of issues related to the use of IT in small businesses. When looking at small business research, it is important to determine what the researcher's view of 'small' actually is. This is so that proper comparisons can be made across studies.

Barriers, opportunities, applications and success factors in relation to the use of IT were identified for small businesses as being common areas covered in the literature. The importance of owner/manager involvement, the location of the business and industry involvement were other issues that were discussed.

A number of challenges facing small businesses were also identified. The need for planning, to be able to measure success, to provide effective training and have access to important external sources of information were discussed. Finally, the effect of e-commerce and the Internet on small businesses was introduced.

This purpose of this chapter has been to introduce a book that brings together the work of many different authors in the area of IT and small business. I have endeavoured to introduce some of the many characteristics of small businesses that suggest that the way in which they use IT is significantly different to that of larger businesses. In doing so, there are still a number of issues given a cursory coverage in this chapter that are mentioned in greater detail throughout the book, such as political and business culture, and security issues. It is hoped that the reader has been encouraged to delve further into many of these issues by reading through the rest of the chapters in the book and further exploring the use of IT in small businesses.

ENDNOTE

1 Copyright © 2000 Bell & Howell Information and Learning Company.

REFERENCES

Belisle, J. D. and Czinkota, M. R. (1999). Trade must extend to poorer countries. *International Trade Forum*, (3), 11-13.

Bridge, J. and Peel, M. J. (1999). Research note: A study of computer usage and strategic planning in the SME sector. *International Small Business Journal*, July-September, 17(4), 82-87.

Burgess, S. (1997). Information technology and small business: A categorized study of the use of IT in small business. *Detailed Survey Report*, Small Business Victoria, Melbourne, June.

Dandridge, T. and Levenburg, N. M. (2000). High tech potential? An exploratory study of very small firms' usage of the Internet. *International Small Business Journal*, January-March, 18(2), 81-91.

El Louadi, M. (1998). The relationship among organization structure, information technology and information processing in small Canadian firms. *Canadian Journal of Administrative Sciences*, June, 15(2), 180-199.

Gallagher, P. (1999). E-commerce trends. *International Trade Forum, Geneva*, (2), 16-18.

Igbaria, M., Zinatelli, N., Cragg, P. and Cavaye, A. L. M. (1997). Personal computing acceptance factors in small firms: A structural equation model. *MIS Quarterly*, September, 21(3), 279-305.

International Trade Forum. (1999). *Export Strategies for Small Firms*, (1), 9-12.

Management Services. (1997). Computers fail to click with small businesses. *Enfield*, 41(9), 4.

Management Services. (2000). Nearly half of SMEs believe that the Internet and IT has no impact on them. *Enfield*, 44(10), 6.

Management Services. (2001). Impact of information and communication technologies in EU rural areas. *Enfield*, February, 45(2), 4.

McDonagh, P. and Prothero, A. (2000). Euroclicking and the Irish SME: Prepared for e-commerce and the single currency? *Irish Marketing Review*, 13(1), 21-33.

Mehta, L. (1999). From darkness to light? Critical reflections on the world development report 1998/99. *The Journal of Development Studies*, October, 36(1), 151-161.

Naylor, J. B. and Williams, J. (1994). The successful use of IT in SMEs on Merseyside. *European Journal of Information Systems*, 3(1), 48-56.

Pollard, C. E. and Hayne, S. C. (1998). The changing faces of information systems issues in small firms. *International Small Business Journal*, April-June, 16(3), 70-87.

Sawyerr, O. O., Edbrahimi, B. P. and Thibodeaux, M. S. (2000). Executive environmental scanning, information source utilization and firm performance: The case of Nigeria. *Journal of Applied Management Studies*, June, 9(1), 95-115.

Swartz, E. and Walsh, V. (1996). Understanding the process of information management in small firms: Implications for government policy. *19th ISBA National Conference Proceedings*, 387-399.

Telstra Corporation and NOIE (The National Office for the Information Economy). (2000). *Small Business Index: Survey of Computer Technology and E-Commerce in Australian Small and Medium Businesses*. Melbourne, Australia: Pacific Access Pty. Ltd.

The Yankee Group. (1999). *Many Companies Still Doubt Web's Strategic Value, NetMarquee, Inc.* Available on the World Wide Web at: http://www.yankeegroup.com/yg.nsy. Accessed January 5, 1999.

Turner, C. (1997). SMEs and the evolution of the European information society: Policy themes and initiative. *European Business Journal*, 9(4), 47-52.

Yap, C.-S. and Thong, J. Y. L. (1997). Program evaluation of a government information technology program for small businesses. *Journal of Information Technology*, (12), 107-120.

Zinatelli, N., Cragg, P. B. and Cavaye, A. L. M. (1996). End user computing sophistication and success in small firms. *European Journal of Information Systems*, (5), 172-181.

Part I

Small Business and Information Technology

Chapter II

Adoption and Use of Computer Technology in Canadian Small Businesses: A Comparative Study

Linda Duxbury
Carleton University, Canada

Yves Decady
Statistics Canada, Canada

Angel Tse
Carleton University, Canada

INTRODUCTION

This chapter examines the impact of company size on the adoption, use and perceived impact of computer technology in Canadian businesses. Such research is critical for several reasons. First, while there is a large body of research that examines the adoption, use and impact of computer technology, most studies either ignore workplace size or focus exclusively on medium and large workplaces. That research which is available would suggest that small businesses differ in many key ways from larger organizations. They are, for example, more likely to: (1) have simple and highly centralized structures, (2) experience severe financial constraints on growth, (3) lack trained personnel resources, and (4) take a short-range management perspective imposed by a volatile competitive environment (Welsh and White, 1981). These differences may mean that organizational theories and practices on firm adoption and use of computer technology which have been developed from research on large businesses may not be applicable to those who operate in the small business sector. As Igbaria et al. (1997) note, the differences between the computing environments of small and large organizations make it necessary to develop an IT implementation model specifically for small businesses. Welsh and White (1981) concur and observe that small businesses are simply "not a little big business."

Second, most research on computer use in small business has grouped businesses of various sizes (that is under 99 employees, under 200 employees) into one category for study, with the assumption that all small businesses have similar computing applications needs and adoption practices (e.g., Malone, 1985; Nickell and Seado, 1986). Little is known, therefore, about the implications of relative company size on the use of computer technology.

Third, our previous research with small businesses would suggest that owners of Canadian small businesses are becoming more interested in computer technology (Duxbury and Higgins, 1999). This interest originates in an increased awareness that the appropriate use of computer technology may play an important role in small business success or failure. Kagan et al. (1990) also report that small business executives have become more concerned about the importance of information technology. They attribute this increased interest to the following: (1) their competition is adopting technology and using it effectively, (2) the cost of IT has decreased and the perceived benefits have increased, (3) more user-friendly systems are being developed that can be implemented by small business firms without a high degree of computer expertise. In addition, the deregulation of telecommunications (and lower cost) has created new dynamics and strategic opportunities for small firms to deploy technology to mask their size from their external partners (e.g., electronic data interchange) (Lin et al,. 1993).

Finally, research in this area is critical because of the increasing economic importance of this sector to the Canadian economy. The following data illustrates this assertion. There were approximately two million businesses (with employees) in Canada in 1993. Of these businesses, 97% had fewer than 50 employees, and 99% had fewer than 100 employees (Industry Canada, 1995). Data for 1993 (the last year such detailed data are available) show that while there were 25% more businesses in 1993 than 1983, 99% of these new businesses were small or medium enterprises (SMEs) (Industry Canada, 1995). A second measure of the vitality of this sector is its contribution to the Canadian GDP. SMEs were estimated to contribute to some 57% of total private sector GDP in 1993, up 3.8% from the level reported in 1983 (Industry Canada, 1993).

OBJECTIVES

As noted above, there is little Canadian empirical research that links the adoption of computer technology to company size. Nor is there research that compares and contrasts small, medium and large businesses with respect to their use of computer technology and its perceived impacts. The research that is available is limited by the fact that much of it was done in the 1980s and early 1990s (that is, it is dated), and uses small, industry-specific samples. Comparisons between those studies that do exist are further complicated by the fact that researchers have defined small business in a number of different ways. The research study summarized in this chapter was undertaken to fill these gaps by addressing the following questions:

1. Is the adoption of information technology (hardware and software) associated with company size?
2. Is the use of information technology by workers (hardware and software) associated with company size?
3. How do workers acquire the skills they need to work with information technology? Does skill acquisition vary with company size?
4. What factors impede the implementation of new technologies in the workplace? Do barriers to the implementation of technology vary with company size?
5. What have been the effects of the implementation of information technology on the organization? Do these effects vary with company size?

BACKGROUND

Adoption of Information Technology and Company Size

A number of studies suggest that firm size has a direct positive relationship to the adoption and successful use of management information systems (MIS). Winston and Dologite (1999) attribute these differences to the fact that larger organizations have more opportunities to use IT, a more developed infrastructure and a more developed strategic planning function, findings which are consistent with earlier research by Ein-Dor and Segev (1978) and DeLone (1981). Raymond (1985) reported that firm size (in term of number of employees) was not significantly associated with either user satisfaction or system utilization, but was significantly related to many of the organizational characteristics of computer usages such as EDP experience, development of IT, application used and MIS ranking in the organization. Raymond also stated that larger firms tend to have greater Electronic Data Processing (EDP) experience, develop a greater proportion of their applications internally, implement a greater number of administrative applications and have MIS functions situated at a lower organizational level. Malone (1985) offers a dissenting view and postulates that small businesses are, in many ways, uniquely advantaged with respect to IT implementation. Advantages he notes include a more flexible environment, increased capacity to respond rapidly and a more open personal working environment (Malone, 1985).

Use of Information Technology and Company Size

A number of researchers (such as Montazemi, 1988; Glynn and Koenig, 1995; Thong et al., 1996; Burrows, 1994) suggest that there are some major differences between small and large firms with respect to their use of IT. These differences include the fact that small firms tend to use computers more as tools and less as a communications medium and have fewer resources available to implement IT solutions. Larger businesses, on the other hand, were more likely than smaller businesses to use communication packages such as e-mail and make greater use of database and expert system applications.

The concept of "sophistication" of information technology has also been used to compare computer use in small businesses to larger firms. Raymond and Pare (1992) define technological sophistication as the number or diversity of information technologies used by a firm (that is, computer graphics, CAD/ CAM, local and wide area networking). They operationalize information sophistication, on the other hand, by looking at the companies' application portfolios.

Researchers have operationalized IT sophistication in a number of ways. Some (such as Ein-Dor and Segev, 1982; Cheney, 1983; Lehman, 1985) used the number of workstations along with the level of hardware decentralization in the organization to indicate IT sophistication of the organization. Others choose to assess IS sophistication by the diversity of programming languages (that is, 3rd and 4th generation) and development tools (for example, graphics) used (Lehman, 1985), the types of applications used (Raymond, 1985; Kagan et al., 1990) and hardware/software capability (Raymond, 1985).

Kagan et al. (1990) developed an IT sophistication score based on the results of a rating of computing applications used by 30 industrial and academic computers. They took these ratings and constructed the following continuum of computer sophistication (the higher the score, the greater the sophistication): word processing = 1.65, payroll applications = 3.26, ordering applications = 4.03, pricing applications = 4.08, employee scheduling = 4.19, spreadsheet applications = 4.26, inventory control = 4.64, data applications = 5.16, telecommunications = 5.74, database = 6.13 and decision models = 8.78.

Early studies (Cheney, 1983; Farhoomand and Hryeyk, 1985; Malone, 1985; Baker, 1987) of small firm computing showed IS sophistication to be relatively low, with a typical firm having only one microcomputer, and accounting systems being the most common application. In recent years, however, the development of the PC has led to the introduction of affordable user-friendly software. As a result, computing efforts in small businesses in recent years have become more sophisticated and the number of applications used have diversified (Berry and Wood, 1998; Cragg and Zinateli, 1995; Raymond and Pare, 1992).

In addition to the cost reduction of the PC, many other factors have influenced the evolution and sophistication of IS in small firms. According to Cragg and King (1993), important motivators included enthusiasm from the owner as well as perceived benefits to individuals and the organization. Important inhibitors to growth include low IS knowledge and skills, lack of managerial time, lack of funds and technical complexity.

While only a few studies could be found which described the penetration of hardware and software within the small business environment, those studies that are available report quite consistent results. Malone (1985) reported that small business managers rated accounting and inventory control functions as the most important computer applications. Farhoomand and Hryeyk (1985) observed that small business firms use computers to support accounting applications, for word processing activities and for spreadsheet analysis. Nickell and Seado (1986) determined that 68% of the 121 small businesses studied had computers which they used for accounting, budgeting, inventory control and word processing.

Barriers to Implementation of Computer Technology and Company Size

Despite the many programs and efforts of governments and information providers, the literature indicates small business adoption of IT is still relatively slow (Palavi, 1996). The estimates of small business use of computers range from 27% to 68% depending on location, size, and nature of the businesses surveyed. The literature suggests a number of reasons why small businesses are less likely to adopt computer technology. Malone (1985) determined that many owners have reservations regarding information systems usage that can be attributed to a lack of the resources needed for MIS implementation, a lack of formalized systems and the short management time frame characteristic of the small business environment. Doukidis, Smithson and Kybereas (1994), on the other hand, suggest that many small business do not implement computer technology because their owners do not believe that information technology is necessary in their business and perceive that technology is changing too fast. Cragg and King (1993) identified four factors that they felt discouraged the use of information systems in small business: lack of IS knowledge, limited financial resources, lack of computer expertise and lack of managerial time. They also note that user resistance and lack of acceptable software may also inhibit the use of information technology in small firms. Details on each of these barriers are given below.

No specialists: Studies (DeLone, 1988; Gable, 1991) have found that small businesses typically do not have the appropriate technical skills available in-house to maintain computer information systems. This means that if they want to implement computer technology, they either have to train existing staff or purchase appropriate skills from the marketplace. Work by Thong et al. (1996) also suggests that due to their small size, limited number of senior positions and fewer alternative career paths, small businesses have a more difficult time attracting and retaining skilled information systems staff.

Financial constraints: Although IT has dropped in price, it still represents a considerable investment for small business. According to Welsh and White (1981), small businesses operate in a highly competitive environment, watch their cash flow carefully and tend to have a short-range management perspective. Under these circumstances it is often difficult to justify the cost of information systems. Even when the costs of IT are justified, many small businesses choose the lowest cost information system available–one which may be inadequate for their purposes (Thong et al., 1996).

Time constraints: The time required for the installation and implementation of a computer system may absorb a considerable amount of the business owner/senior manager's time. According to Doukidis et al. (1994), many owners of small businesses are too busy in day-to-day operations to invest time in such a project.

User resistance: Past research (Cheney, 1983; Malone, 1985) has shown that the primary problem with the implementation of IT in small businesses is user resistance to computer systems. This can be attributed to perceived threats to job security and a lack of understanding and confidence in the new technology. The main reason for the misunderstanding is because small businesses do not have the resources to provide formal training for the user of the computers, and the training provided by the vendor is often considered inadequate (Gable, 1991). Without proper training, the small business user often finds the systems to be difficult to use and are consequently dissatisfied with them.

Lack of acceptable software: Small firms also often suffer from difficulties in acquiring acceptable software. Research by DeLone (1981) indicates that many small business find the available software packages to be either inflexible or inadequate for their needs.

The Effects of Information on Small Businesses

Studies (DeLone, 1981; Doukidis et al., 1994; Thong et al., 1996) have suggested a number of ways that information technology can benefit small business. These include better decision making, enhanced competitiveness, increased accuracy in customer statements, faster billing of customers, timelier reporting and more management information. According to Thong, Yap and Raman (1996), information technology can help small businesses develop their markets, increase sales turnover, raise profitability, secure their positions within their industries and gain a competitive edge. Doukidis, Smithson and Kybereas (1994) attribute the following benefits to small businesses who use information technology: (1) improved productivity and performance within the enterprise; (2) greater internal control of operations; (3) the possibility of new ways of managing activities; (4) greater extension and penetration of markets; (5) the possibility of new organizational forms (for example, networked organizations); (6) the delivery of a valued and high quality package of product and service; and (7) the redefinition of existing businesses or the spawning of whole new businesses.

METHODOLOGY

What is a small business?: The research literature is divided on how to define a "small" business (some use revenues, some use number of employees, some use a combination of the two). The issue is further complicated by the fact that those who determine "small" based on the number of employees (as we do in this research) have used a variety of thresholds for this determination. For example, while some classify a businesses with less than 50 employees as being "small" (Cragg and King, 1993), others have used 100 employees (Doukidis et al., 1994), 200 employees (Kagan et al., 1990; Harrison et al., 1997), and 300 employees (DeLone, 1988).

The large amount of data available to us through the WES (Work Environment Survey–refer to the next section) allows us to take an innovative and comprehensive approach to defining small business.

We start with the premise that a "small business" includes any firm with fewer than 100 full-time paid employees. We then divide small businesses into three sub-groups:

- Micro businesses: two to nine employees (that is, no entrepreneurs)
- Mid-sized small businesses: 10 to 49 employees

- Larger small businesses: 50 to 99 employees

This study compares small businesses to medium (100 to 500 full-time employees) and large (more than 500 employees) organizations. All but approximately 2,000 of the more than 2.1 million businesses in Canada fall within the self-employed or SME (small and medium enterprise) categories (Industry Canada, 1995).

The Sample: The Workplace and Employee Survey

The Workplace and Employee Survey (WES) is a new undertaking by Statistics Canada. WES is a dual survey that starts with a sample of establishments and then draws a sample of employees within that establishment. Employees and employers are administered separate questionnaires covering a broad range of issues. This permits researchers to study 'both' sides of the market. The WES was designed to be a *longitudinal survey* which will track both establishments and workers over time. The second phase of the WES was collected at the same time this chapter was being written. The collection and analysis of a cross-sectional integrated survey such as the WES is very complex and beyond the scope of this chapter. Complete discussions of the WES can be found in Krebs et al. (1999) and Patak et al. (2000). Relevant details are given below.

The Methodology of the WES

The Workplace and Employee Survey uses two distinct sampling units, workplace and employee. The workplace is defined as a physical location where employer-employee data are linked directly. WES is implemented as a stratified two-stage design. A sample of the workplace was selected in stage one and a sample of employees from the selected workplaces in the second. The target population of the employer (that is, workplace) component was defined as *all workplaces operating in Canada with paid employees* (several types of organizations, such as those operating in the Canadian North, were excluded from the study as discussed in Krebs et al., 1999). This population was partitioned into non-overlapping groups based on the workplace's industrial activity and geographic region. A stratum was defined as the crossing of industry, region and employment size. Overall, 252 strata were formed. A sample of workplaces was then drawn independently in each stratum using simple random sampling without replacement. Several strata containing very large workplaces were sampled exhaustively.

The target population for the *employee* sample was defined as all persons drawing pay for services rendered and for whom the employer had to complete a Revenue Canada T-4 Supplementary form. Once a selected workplace was contacted, a list of employees was created. This list contained all employees at the workplace including all paid on-site or off-site employees. Depending on the size of the workplace, a systematic sample of three, six, nine or 12 employees was drawn from the list (see Krebbs et al., 1999).

Weighting and Estimation

The population of workplaces in Canada is dominated by small work-places. A process of simple random sampling from this population would therefore generate a similarly distributed sample and would not include suffi-cient workplaces to permit reliable inferences to be drawn for such groups. This is corrected by applying differential sampling weights to the sampled units prior to the analysis. In order to obtain unbiased population estimates, weights must be applied to all analysis of the WES to accommodate the WES sample design. To obtain accurate estimates of the reliability (precision) of the survey data, it is also necessary to account for the features of the WES sample design in the calculation of standard errors and the application of significance tests.

At the first stage of the sampling, the frame is stratified by region, industry and employment size. Sampling fractions vary by size so that larger employers have a greater probability of being included in the sample. At the second stage, employees are only sampled if their workplaces have already been selected for the workplace sample. The effect, in both cases, is to increase sampling errors when compared with simple random sampling with replacement designs. Standard methods of estimating the sampling error associated with estimates from WES are not reliable. In order to take proper account of the complex design of WES, STATA, a statistical package which provides a family of commands for the analysis of complex surveys, was used. Within STATA, differences were calculated using Scheffe's Cross Tab procedure (frequency data) and Student t (mean data). Differences that are statistically significant at the 5% level are delineated in Tables 4 though 9 with a *; those that are statistically significant at the 10% level are shown as ** (significance require-ments were relaxed to compensate for smaller sample sizes in some cells). These data, while not shown, are available from the authors upon request.

Description of the Achieved Sample

In total, Statistic Canada sampled 9,144 locations. Of these, 257 organi-zations refused to participate in the research and 2,536 were non-respondents (out-of-scope, unable to locate and so forth).

Among the 6,531 responding workplaces, 5,815 had at least one re-sponding employee (for a total of 24,597 responding employees) and 536 had none. Information on the sample used in these analyses are shown in Tables 1 through 3. Table 1 shows the number of firms of different sizes that participated in this research, as well as the number of employees participating per firm and the mean number of employees working in Canadian micro (4), mid-sized (24) and large (72) small businesses and medium (223) and large (1,623) businesses. Table 2 gives the data on technology adoption by company size while Table 3 looks at computer usage.

One section of the WES was designed to enable researchers to focus on the adoption of computer-based technologies by Canadian companies. To conserve space and promote readability, the questions from the WES used in this analysis are presented in the appropriate sections below.

DISCUSSION OF RESULTS

Is the Adoption of Information Technology Associated with Company Size?

Employers were asked to consider the time period of April 1, 1998, and March 31, 1999, and indicate if their workforce had implemented:

- a major software and/or hardware application, where 'major' was defined as follows: "not an upgrade but rather a new application. To be major an application must affect at least half of the users in the workplace or department within the workplace."
- computer-controlled or computer-assisted technology (that is, retailing, scanning technology, manufacturing robots, optical, laser, audio/photo-

Table 1: Firms and employees by firm size: Workplace and employee survey (1999)

FIRM SIZE	NUMBER OF FIRMS OF THIS SIZE IN SAMPLE	TOTAL NUMBER OF EMPLOYEES WORKING IN THESE FIRMS	MEAN NUMBER OF EMPLOYEES INTERVIEWED PER FIRM	MEAN NUMBER OF EMPLOYEES IN THIS SIZE FIRM
<10	2,155	8,361	2.0	3.9
10-49	1,668	40,751	3.8	24.4
50-99	792	56,678	5.0	71.6
100-500	1,249	278,491	5.5	223.0
500 +	486	788,790	6.7	1,623.0
Total	6,350	1,173,071	4.0	184.2

Table 2: Adoption of technology of information: By firm size and type of technology

FIRM SIZE	NEW SOFTWARE	CAD/CAE	OTHER	ADOPTERS	NON-ADOPTERS	TOTAL
<10	478	70	74	556	1,599	2,155
10-49	575	129	102	682	986	1,668
50-99	323	74	40	380	412	792
100-499	550	175	117	665	584	1,249
500 +	238	89	55	294	192	486
Total	2,164	537	388	2,577	3,773	6,350

Table 3: Computer usage and firm size

Firm Size	EMPLOYER DATA			EMPLOYEE DATA		
	USE COMPUTER	NO COMPUTER	TOTAL SAMPLE	USE COMPUTER	NO COMPUTER	TOTAL SAMPLE
<10	1488	667	2155	2421	1815	4236
10-49	1571	97	1668	3821	2528	6349
50-99	782	10	792	2410	1515	3925
100-499	1240	9	1249	4424	2386	6810
500 +	479	7	486	2369	901	3270
Total	5560	790	6350	15445	9145	24590

graphic technologies, hydraulic or other mechanical technologies) (that is, CAD).

• any other major implementation of other technology.

Respondents who implemented any of the above forms of technology were also asked, "What was the approximate cost of implementing _____ in the workplace?" Total costs associated with implementing technology were obtained by adding costs associated with the three implementations noted above. Cost per employee was calculated by dividing total costs by number of employees in the firm. Responses to these questions are shown in Table 4.

Approximately one in three Canadian firms had a major software or hardware implementation during this timeframe. The likelihood of having a major implementation was significantly associated with company size with larger small businesses (that is, 50 to 99 employees) and medium businesses being more likely to implement than smaller or larger firms.

Far fewer Canadian firms implemented computer-controlled technology (6%) or other major technologies (4%) during this timeframe. Medium and large companies were significantly more likely to adopt both of these forms of technology. Interestingly, mid-sized small businesses (that is, 10-49) were also more likely to say that they had implemented another major technology.

Canadian firms spent approximately $9 billion Canadian on major technological implementations in 1998/99. This works out to approximately $1,000 per Canadian employee working in the SME and large business sectors. While micro and larger small businesses spent less money on computer implementations than other sized companies, these differences were not significant when the analysis was done with the weighted sample. Costs of adoption per employee were, however, higher for those operating in the medium business sector ($1,600 per employee).

Is the Use of Information Technology Associated with Company Size?

Employees who participated in the WES were asked the following questions:

- Do you personally use a computer in your job? By computer we mean a PC, a microcomputer or a laptop that can be programmed to perform a variety of operations.
- How many hours per week do you normally spend using a computer at your job? By this we mean using or developing computer applications

Table 4: Is the adoption of information technology associated with company size?

Data from April 1, 1998, to March 31, 1999, collected from the employer	Company Size					
	Under 10	10 to 49	50 to 99	100 to 500	500 +	Total
% who installed new software application	32.06	36.08	43.69 *	52.53 *	34.26	34.23
% who implemented CAD	5.3	6.87	6.92	13.06 *	11.1 *	6.04
% who had "other" major technology implementation	2.78	7.53 *	4.21	8.43 *	8.58 *	4.37
Total cost of technology implemented (in $ Canadian)	1.040×10^9	2.163×10^9	9.655×10^8	2.693×10^9	2.276×10^9	9.14×10^9
Cost of technology implemented per employee	$ 1115.96	$1,007.45	$ 823.43	$1603.22 *	$1007.43	$1086.08

rather than just having the computer turned on.
- What types of applications do you use? (asked to select from a list)
- Which of these applications do you use the most? (top three applications identified)
- How many hours per week do you spend using these three applications?
- Since you started your job, has the technological complexity of your work: (1) stayed the same, (2) increased or (3) decreased.

Responses to these questions are shown in Table 5 and discussed below. The majority of Canadian employees (almost two-thirds) use computers in their work. Further, the data would indicate that those employees who use computers in their work are highly reliant on this technology, spending approximately half of their work week (19 hours out of 37) on the computer.

While the percent of the workforce using computers increases with company size (approximately half of those in micro businesses use computers compared to almost three-quarters of those in large businesses), the differences were not significant when the weighted sample was used. The amount of the work week spent using a computer is, however, significantly associated with company size, with employees in micro businesses and large businesses spending significantly fewer hours per week on the computer (that is, lower levels of reliance).

What applications do Canadians use? The most commonly used applica-

Table 5: Is the use of information technology associated with company size?

Data from April 1, 1998 to March 31, 1999 collected from the employer	Company Size					
	Under 10	10 to 49	50 to 99	100 to 500	500 +	Total
% of workforce using computers	52.88	57.23	61.51	61.37	72.23	62.81
Mean number of hours per week spent using computer on job	17.93	19.87 *	20.68 *	20.15 *	17.16	19.07
% Using the following applications:						
⇨ Word processor (1)	52.35	52.80	56.44	61.90	64.31	57.50
⇨ Spreadsheet (2)	28.32 *	40.50	44.81	46.97	40.98	40.30
⇨ Databases (3)	26.51	29.11	31.89 *	31.59 *	31.12 *	30.00
⇨ Communications (4)	19.91 *	29.12	27.70	35.56	41.48	31.43
⇨ General Mgt. Applications (5)	11.02	8.68	8.75	8.86	7.84	8.92
⇨ Graphics (6)	6.91 *	10.18	10.39	15.00	16.36	11.96
⇨ Development Tools (7)	2.35	2.49	3.11	4.31 *	5.40 *	3.55
⇨ Office Applications (8)	38.21	39.80	32.60	31.53 *	27.90 *	34.39
⇨ Data Analysis (9)	3.65	4.91	6.56 **	7.21*	8.16 *	6.07
⇨ CAD/CAE (10)	3.94	5.66	3.81	4.91	4.27	4.70
⇨ Expert Systems (11)	1.71 *	3.70	2.38 *	3.95	4.13	3.35
Which applications used most frequently (Q22d - top three)	1,8 &3	1,8&2	1,8&2	1,8&2	1,8&2	1,8&2
Average hours per week using these three technologies	14.51	15.07	15.37	14.51	12.25 *	14.31
Changes in technological complexity	1.58	1.63	1.65	1.69 *	1.69 *	1.65

tions are word processing (used by 58%), spreadsheets (used by 40%), office applications such as payroll and scheduling (used by 34%), communications (used by 31%) and databases (used by 30%). In others words, most Canadian employees can be considered to use applications with moderate to low sophistication. Only 3% of Canadians use expert systems (high end of sophistication continuum).

The results show that application use is associated with company size. Micro businesses make significantly less use of spreadsheets, communications applications, graphics and expert systems, reinforcing the literature which suggests that their use of computers is not as sophisticated as that found in larger businesses.

The data would suggest that in many ways employees working for larger small businesses use similar applications to their counterparts in medium and large businesses. Employees in all three of these sizes of companies make greater use of database and data analysis applications than their counterparts in smaller firms. Employees in larger small business are, however, less likely to use expert systems while employees in medium and large firms are more likely to use development tools and less likely to use office applications. This last finding suggests that many of the office applications currently available do not meet the needs of larger firms.

With respect to application use, all Canadian firms, regardless of their size, rely heavily on word processing and office application packages (all firms indicated that these were the two sets of applications they used most frequently). The third most used application varies significantly with company size, with micro businesses making more use of database applications and firms with 10 or more employees making more use of spreadsheet packages.

Finally, the data indicates that while the majority of Canadian employees perceive that the technological complexity of their work has increased over time, those in medium and large companies are significantly more likely to hold this view than those in small businesses.

Does Information Technology Skill Acquisition Vary with Company Size?

Employers who participated in the WES and who answered that they had implemented new software, new CAD or other new technologies were asked the following questions:

- How many of your employees received training directly related to this implementation?
- What was the usual duration of this training?

Employees who participated in the WES were asked to think about the

Table 6: Is the acquisition of skills associated with company size?

Employer Survey	Company Size					
	Under 10	10 to 49	50 to 99	100 to 500	500 +	Total
% of workforce who received training for:						
⇨ New software	53.46	39.31 *	22.27 *	43.63	21.86 *	46.72
⇨ New CAD	40.74 *	30.73 *	21.88	18.51	6.76	35.30
⇨ Other new technology	44.17	45.32	17.23 *	11.01 *	9.33 *	42.77
⇨ Total who received training	55.21	45.50	23.93 *	42.28	20.74 *	50.12
Day in training per employee for new implementations:						
⇨ New software	1.39	0.78	0.17 *	0.19 *	0.02 *	0.93
⇨ New CAD	1.77	0.75	0.11 *	0.08 *	0.03 *	1.17
⇨ Other new technology	3.37	0.84	1.12	0.14	0.02	1.55
⇨ Total days in training per employee for new technology	1.91	0.91 *	0.23 *	0.20 *	0.03 *	1.21
EMPLOYEE SURVEY						
% who indicated they learned the application through:						
⇨ self learning	46.53	43.77	45.25	48.17	43.98	45.28
⇨ employer paid formal	14.39 *	20.18	21.10	26.25	29.25	22.52
⇨ self paid formal	3.78	2.41	2.87	2.84	4.60	3.30
⇨ on job training	43.26	46.32	48.51	44.38	39.46	44.15
⇨ university or college	8.34	6.56	6.97	6.27	6.34	6.80
% who found the following type of training most useful:						
⇨ self learning	38.02	38.81	41.15	37.99	36.13	38.16
⇨ employer paid formal	13.06	8.68	10.67	17.39	15.51	13.11
⇨ self paid formal	1.98	1.66	3.24	0.60	8.79 *	3.41
⇨ on job training	41.43	45.56	42.67	40.56	35.17	40.97
⇨ university or college	3.45	3.11	2.20	2.73	3.60	3.10
% who said they learnt more:						
⇨ on company time	62.6	64.6	65.9	65.5	59.2	63.34
⇨ on own time	13.3	14.4	11.2	12.4	18.9 *	14.50
⇨ company and own time equal	24.1	21.0	22.9	22.1	21.9	22.16

computer application they used the most in their work and indicate how they had learned this application, what method they found the most helpful in learning, and whether or not they had learned the application on company time or on their own time. Responses to this question are given in Table 6.

The data would suggest that Canadian employees receive little training on how to use new computer or information technologies, regardless of the size of company they worked for. Only half of those employees who went through a major technological implementation in 1998/99 received training on how to use the new technology. Those that did receive training on the new system received just over one day of training.

While the likelihood of receiving training and the time in training is associated with the type of implementation, training was not the norm for any of the three types of implementation examined in this study and ranged from a high of 47% receiving training on how to use new hardware or software to a low of 35% who received training for new CAD. Time in training ranged from a high of 1.6 days training for other major technical implementations to a low of one day for those receiving training for new hardware/software.

The likelihood of receiving training and the actual days in training per employee are both associated with company size. While the literature would suggest that many small businesses do not have the funds to train their employees, our data says that this stereotype only applies to larger (that is, 50-99) small businesses. Employees who worked for micro businesses were more likely to receive training on new hardware/software, on CAD systems and overall. Those who worked for mid-sized small businesses were more likely to receive CAD training and training overall. They also received more days of training. Employees who worked for a larger small business, on the other hand, were less likely to receive training for new software/hardware, other major implementations and in total. They also spent substantially less time in training. Large companies, on the other hand, were significantly less likely to provide employees with training for new technologies.

Company size appears to have little impact on how employees learn the computer applications that they use, their preferred method of learning and when they learn. The majority of Canadian employees, regardless of company size, learn new applications through self-learning (45%) and through on-the-job, experiential training (44%). Not coincidently, these are also the types of training they find most useful (perhaps because these are the only types they have access to). One in five Canadians indicated that they had learned through formal training funded by their employer (13% indicated that they preferred to learn this way). Employees who worked for micro businesses were less likely to say that they had received employer-funded formal training.

Almost two-thirds of Canadian employees said that they had learned how to use work-related computer applications on company time and another 22% learned on their own time as well as the employers' time. Only 15% learned more on their own time. Consistent with the employer data on training presented above, employees who worked for larger businesses were more likely than employees in other sized businesses to say that they had learned the application on their own time.

Do the Perceived Barriers to the Implementation of Computer Technology Vary with Company Size?

Employers who participated in the WES were given a list of nine factors and asked which of these factors had impeded the implementation of new technology in their workplace. As can be seen in Table 7, lack of financial resources is by far the largest perceived barrier to the implementation of computer technology within Canadian firms (34% gave this response). Medium and large sized firms were more likely than small businesses to give this response, suggesting that the costs associated with implementing computer technology increases with company size (that is, more complex software, great need for training, reduced ability to purchase turn-key solutions).

Table 7: Are the perceived barriers to the implementation of computer technologies associated with company size?

% of Employers giving each of the following:	Company Size					
	Under 10	10 to 49	50 to 99	100 to 500	500 +	Total
Lack of financial resources	32.99	36.96	26.94	51.21 *	75.73 *	33.96
Lack of skilled personnel	8.74	15.71 *	23.87 *	19.87 *	10.97	10.56
Lack of information on technologies	6.29	7.32	9.19	10.41	3.37	6.59
Lack of information on markets	4.42	3.35	2.23	2.89	0.80 *	4.14
Deficiencies in the availability of external technical services	3.06	3.28	10.66	4.03	12.10 *	3.26
Internal resistance to change	8.02	10.83	17.07	24.50 *	14.09	8.95
Barriers to cooperate with: ⇨ other firms ⇨ scientific/educational institutions	1.76 0.64	1.72 0.60	0.60 * 0.04	3.45 4.56	3.10 1.35	1.76 6.63
Government standards and regulations	4.17	4.89	2.09	12.86 *	22.56 *	4.36

The second greatest barrier to the implementation of computer technology within Canadian firms is a lack of personnel with the appropriate skills (cited by one in 10 employers). Employees in micro businesses and large businesses were significantly less likely to perceive this barrier. Those in mid-sized and large small businesses and medium business were more likely to experience this barrier. Approximately 10% of the sample felt that internal resistance to change acted as a barrier to the implementation of computer technology. Medium businesses were more likely to identify this barrier. Two other barriers were cited by approximately 7% of the employers: lack of information on available technologies and difficulties cooperating with scientific/educational institutions. Neither of these responses was associated with company size.

The other factors were identified by less than 5% of the total sample. There were some interesting size differences, however, with respect to these other barriers. Large businesses were less likely to feel that a lack of information on markets was a barrier to the implementation of computer technology but more likely to perceive difficulties associated with deficiencies in the availability of external technical services (cited by 12% of large businesses) and government standards and regulations (cited by 23% of large businesses). Medium businesses were also more likely to perceive government standards and regulations to be a barrier. Larger small businesses were less likely to identify barriers to cooperate with other firms as something that prevented them from implementing computer technology.

Do the Perceived Effects of Implementing Information Technology Vary with Company Size?

Employers who participated in the WES were asked to think of the implementation of the new technology with the largest approximate cost and indicate what effects this implementation had on each of 19 factors. Their response choices included no effect (a new technology was implemented but it had no effect), a positive effect or a negative effect. Those who had not implemented a new technology indicated 'not applicable.' Employers were also asked to indicate what the result of the implementation of this technology had been on the number of non-management employees in the workplace, the number of management employees in the workplace and the skill requirements of employees. The following two questions were also used in this phase of the analysis to assess innovation (question one) and performance (question two):

- Between April 1, 1998, and March 31, 1999, has your workplace introduced: New goods or services? Improved goods or services? New processes? Improved processes? (yes/no response)
- Compared to your competitors, how would you rate your workplace performance between April 1, 1998, and March 31, 1999, in each of the following areas: productivity, sales growth, profitability, overall (response choices ranged from 1 = much worse, 3 = about the same, 5 = much better)

Perceived Benefits and Drawbacks: What do Canadian employers perceive to be the benefits of implementing computer technology? As can be seen from the data in Table 8, the benefits identified most frequently are associated with the overall effects of technology: technological capabilities (82% cite as benefit), quality of products or services (77% cite as benefit), working conditions (69% cite as benefit), lead times (67% cite as benefit), the range of products or services offered (59% cite as benefit) and profit margins (56% cite as benefit). Seventy percent also cited increased shares in foreign markets as a key benefit. These benefits of technology are consistent with those reported in the literature. Very few companies perceived that technology has had a negative impact in any of these areas (see Table 9) with employers who do not perceive a positive impact, reporting that technology has had no overall impact at all.

Table 8: Are the perceived effects of implementing computer technologies associated with company size? Positive impacts.

% of Employers Experiencing Positive Effects	Company Size					
	Under 10	**10 to 49**	**50 to 99**	**100 to 500**	**500 +**	**Total**
OVERALL EFFECTS						
Profit margins	56.51	58.71	40.95 **	53.70	50.01	56.28
Quality of products or services	79.89	73.36	67.80	72.97	76.76	77.00
Technological capabilities	81.12	82.66	76.75	83.25	85.47	81.54
Working conditions	66.48	75.38**	64.79	67.75	60.75	69.30
Lead time	66.07	70.84	49.41**	63.93	72.25	66.78
Range of products or services	59.57	63.48	36.21*	45.50*	59.64	59.16
Factors of Production						
Labour requirements	29.93	41.39**	29.44	43.76*	40.96	34.39
Energy requirements	27.15	27.55	15.03**	26.39	11.66*	26.47
Capital requirements	23.94	30.02	15.79	27.64	16.70	25.57
Material requirements	28.67	32.00	18.43**	31.11	20.34	29.23
Design costs	17.85	23.98	33.73	31.40*	19.00	21.04
MARKET SHARE						
Shares in local market	18.07	24.17	20.66	42.69*	28.22	20.94
Shares in national markets	4.32	17.86 *	10.63**	27.67 *	23.41*	10.03
Shares in foreign markets	68.74	72.69	66.14	81.50*	79.45**	70.41
INTERACTIONS: OUTSIDE PARTNERS						
Interactions with customers	17.56	25.29	13.16	29.21	22.70	20.28
Interactions with suppliers	22.47	37.0**	23.67	40.64*	32.65	28.45

A minority of employers (between 20% and 34%) feel that technology has had positive impacts with respect to factors of production. The most commonly cited benefits in this regard include labour requirements (35% cite as benefit) and material requirements (29% cite as benefit). While the majority of respondents feel that technology has had no impact on factors of production, a substantive minority do perceive drawbacks in this area. This group perceives

Table 9: Are the perceived effects of implementing computer technologies associated with company size? Negative impacts

% of Employers Experiencing Negative Effects	Company Size					
	Under 10	10 to 49	50 to 99	100 to 500	500 +	Total
Overall Effects						
Profit margins	8.32	6.63	10.56	8.31	8.57	7.90
Quality of products or services	0.00	0.75*	2.47	1.49*	0.13*	0.40
Technological capabilities	0.00	0.00	2.25	1.12**	0.00	0.17
Working conditions	2.73	3.88	2.85	3.81	0.0**	3.13
Lead time	1.39	2.97	3.04	3.76	1.43	2.06
Range of products or services	0.00	0.40	0.50	2.16	0.40	0.41
Factors of Production						
Labour requirements	4.67	7.18	1.92**	10.05*	7.03	5.59
Energy requirements	6.31	10.08	10.58	20.80 *	15.88*	8.31
Capital requirements	23.06	35.67*	33.71	30.00	50.00*	28.20
Material requirements	8.54	9.18	8.36	13.00	23.89**	8.98
Design costs	7.51	19.20*	14.53**	19.87*	15.65**	11.85
MARKET SHARE						
Shares in local market	1.42	0.10	0.60	0.10	0.00	0.92
Shares in national markets	0.00	0.00	0.61	0.07*	0.00	0.04
Shares in foreign markets	0.68	0.09	2.06	1.28	0.00	0.56
INTERACTIONS: OUTSIDE PARTNERS						
Interactions with customers	0.41	1.11	0.68	0.26	0.32	0.65
Interactions with suppliers	3.86	0.03	0.38	0.17	0.34	0.25

that technology has had a negative impact on their capital requirements (28% cite as a drawback), their design costs (12% cite as a drawback), their material requirements (9% cite as a drawback) and their profit margins (8% cite as a drawback). While the likelihood of reporting that technology has had negative impacts on profit margins and capital requirement is not associated with company size, larger businesses are more likely than small businesses to feel

Table 10: Are the perceived effects of implmenting computer technologies associated with company size? Impact on growth of company and skill requirements of employees

Data from the Employer Survey	Company Size					
	Under 10	10 - 49	50 to 99	100 to 500	500 +	Total Sample
Impact on number of non-managers:						
⇨ Increased	7.22	10.49	11.02	11.09	11.65	8.56
⇨ Decreased	2.17	2.98	2.04	4.74	7.97	2.54
Impact on number of managers:						
⇨ Increased	3.63	4.32	5.18	5.60	4.77	4.00
⇨ Decreased	1.12	2.61	0.73	2.30	5.69	1.62
Impact on skill required of employees:						
⇨ Increased	46.81	55.77	49.24	46.66	71.18 *	49.71
⇨ Decreased	0.34	1.49	0.03	0.86	0.81	0.69

that technology has negatively impacted their material and energy requirements.

While most employers perceive that technology has had a positive impact on their ability to access foreign markets, they are not as likely to perceive that it has helped them with respect to national markets (10% cite as benefit) and local markets (21% cite as benefit). That being said, few see that technology has had a negative impact in these areas. Rather, they perceive that technology has had no impact at all.

Impact of Firm Size on Perceived Benefits and Drawbacks: Firm size has an interesting impact on the perceived benefits and drawbacks of technology. Surprisingly, it is the businesses at both ends of the size spectrum that have the most similar views of the benefits of technology. With the exception of perceived impact on regional and foreign markets shares (larger businesses were significantly more likely than micro businesses to perceive a positive impact in these areas) and energy requirements (large businesses were less likely than micro businesses to perceive that technology had provided benefits in these areas), micro small businesses and large businesses had very similar perceptions regarding the benefits of technology: perceptions that were essentially the same as those reported for the total sample. Large businesses were, however, significantly more likely than micro businesses to report disadvantages with respect to four of the five factors of production considered in this analysis (that is, half cite disadvantages with respect to capital requirements, one-quarter cite disadvantages with respect to material requirements and 16% cite disadvantages with respect to both energy requirements and design costs).

Mid-size small businesses were significantly more likely than other sized firms to recognize benefits with respect to working conditions, labour requirements, shares in national markets and interactions with suppliers. Unfortunately, companies in this size group were also more likely to perceive drawbacks with respect to capital requirements (36% cite as drawback) and design costs (19% cite as drawback). Overall, however, the data would suggest that mid-sized small businesses perceive that the benefits of implementing technology outweigh the drawbacks.

Larger small businesses, on the other hand, were less likely than larger or smaller firms to perceive that technology has had positive impacts on any of the factors included in the overall effects of technology and market share groupings of factors. They were significantly less likely to cite benefits with respect to profit margins, lead time, range of products or services and shares in regional or national markets. Large small businesses were also significantly less likely to perceive a positive impact on energy requirements and material requirements and significantly more likely to perceive a negative impact on design costs. This would indicate that larger small businesses are less likely to receive benefits from IT in the area of factors of production.

Finally, the data would suggest that the medium sized companies experience a quite different set of benefits from the implementation of computer technology than other sized firms. This type of firm was more likely to cite benefits with respect to factors of production (labour requirements, design costs) and market share (shares in local markets, shares in regional markets, shares in foreign markets) and less likely to recognize benefits with respect to the range of products or services that could be offered. Interestingly, this group was also significantly more likely to say that the biggest drawbacks of computer technology are associated with labour requirements and design costs. Future research could examine why some medium businesses perceive that computer technology provides benefits with respect to labour requirements and design costs while others feel that it has had a negative impact. While it may be that these differences are due to firm sector, they could also be due to the fact that the companies experiencing benefits are using the technology differently.

Perceived Impact on Company Size and Skill Requirements of Employees: The majority of Canadian companies perceive that computer technology has not affected either the number of non-managers or the number of managers they have working for their firm. This perception is not associated with company size (see Table 11). Employers do, however, perceive that computer technology has meant that the skills required of their employees has increased. Large firms are significantly more likely to hold this view than medium or small firms.

Table 11: What distinguishes companies that adopt new technology from those that do not?

Data from Employer Survey	Company Size					
	Under 10	10 to 49	50 to 99	100 to 500	500 +	Total
New goods or services:						
⇨ Adopter	44.40	59.33 *	54.75	36.76	52.82	48.87
⇨ Non-adopter	26.93	38.52 *	53.51 *	34.47	16.97	31.15
Improved goods or service:						
⇨ Adopter	48.24	65.40 *	64.51 *	46.42	55.60	54.10
⇨ Non-adopter	31.77	45.01 *	40.30	47.84 *	87.04 *	35.20
New processes:						
⇨ Adopter	35.57	47.91 *	41.69	45.03	54.31 *	40.01
⇨ Non-adopter	16.43	24.79 *	20.89	31.79*	22.27	18.56
Improved processes:						
⇨ Adopter	42.10	60.51 *	57.32 *	48.63	64.92 *	48.70
⇨ Non-adopter	19.08 *	30.16	30.04	44.88	87.55 *	22.21
Rating of Performance (1 = much worse to 5 = much better)						
Productivity:						
⇨ Adopter	**3.68**	**3.77**	3.62	**3.37 ***	**3.56**	3.69
⇨ Non-adopter	**3.45**	**3.58 ****	3.37	**3.63 ***	**3.19 ****	3.48
Profitability:						
⇨ Adopter	3.31	**3.43**	3.93	**3.18**	3.37	3.49
⇨ Non-adopter	3.17	**3.24**	3.25	**3.41 ***	3.14	3.19
Sales growth:						
⇨ Adopter	**3.46**	**3.68 ***	3.55	3.35	3.62	3.53
⇨ Non-adopter	**3.31**	**3.47 ***	3.39	**3.54 ***	3.85 *	3.35
Overall:						
⇨ Adopter	**3.48**	**3.63 ****	3.55	**3.30 ***	3.52	3.57
⇨ Non-adopter	**3.31**	**3.43 ***	3.34	**3.52 ***	3.40	3.34

Note: * signifies significant differences across rows, Bold signifies significant differences between adopters and non-adopters

Innovation: The data would suggest that firms that have implemented new technology are also more likely to have introduced new goods or services, improved goods or services, new processes and improved processes (see Table 12). In other words, the adoption of new computer technology is associated with an increased tendency towards innovation.

The likelihood of a firm demonstrating innovation with respect to product or processes is associated, with company size with mid-sized small firms (both adopters and non-adopters) being significantly more likely to demonstrate innovation in both of these areas. Larger small businesses that adopted computer technology were also more likely to have introduced improved goods/services and processes, while large firms that adopted technology were also significantly more likely to have introduced new and improved processes. While micro and medium businesses who adopted new technology were more likely to be innovative than similarly sized firms that did not adopt new technology, they did not differ significantly from the total sample of adopters with respect to their degree of innovation.

Perceived Performance: The following observations can be made with respect to the impact of the adoption of computer technology on perceived performance (see Table 9):

- Micro businesses that adopted computer technology rated their productivity, their sales growth and their overall performance significantly more positively than their counterparts that did not adopt technology.
- Mid-sized small businesses that adopted computer technology rated their productivity, their profitability, their sales growth and their overall performance significantly more positively than their counterparts that did not adopt technology.
- Large small businesses that adopted technology did not differ from those that did not adopt technology with respect to any of the four dimensions of perceived performance examined in this study.
- Medium business that adopted technology rated their productivity, their profitability and their overall performance more negatively than their counterparts that did not adopt technology.

Large businesses that adopted technology rated their productivity more favourably than their counterparts that did not adopt new technology.

These data would suggest that small and mid sized companies that adopt computer technology enjoy greater productivity, sales growth and performance than companies of this size that do not adopt computer technology, while medium sized companies that adopt computer technology have the opposite experience. It is, however, impossible to determine the direction of causality of these findings. Two alternative explanations are possible. First, it may be that more profitable companies are more able to adopt technology. Alternatively, it may be that the adoption of technology makes a firm more competitive and profitable. It is hoped that this question can be resolved with the second wave of the WES.

CONCLUSIONS AND RECOMMENDATIONS

Access to WES data collected by Statistic Canada has allowed a more comprehensive analysis of computer use and company size than has been possible in the past. The sampling process (representative stratified random sampling of businesses in Canada) and the analysis of the data using appropriate weighting factors allow us to extrapolate the findings from this survey to the Canadian population as a whole. The WES data allow us to distinguish between those aspects of the adoption and use of computer technology that vary with company size (see Table 12) and those which do not.

While the differences are interesting and important, researchers, business owners, vendors (hardware, software, training) and those who set policy in this area also need to be aware of the issues that are shared. The following aspects of computer technology adoption and use were not found to be associated with company size: amount spent on technology, high reliance on word processing and office applications, percent of the workforce using computers in their work, an increase in technological complexity of jobs over time, the amount of information technology training Canadian employees receive (limited for all), how employees learn the computer applications that they use (self-learning, experiential training), their preferred method of learning (self-learning, experiential training), when they learn (on company time), and the impact of technology on the number of employees working for the company (none). Lack of financial resources is by far the largest perceived barrier to the implementation of computer technology within Canadian firms regardless of size and, in general, businesses of all sizes perceive that they realize more benefits from implementing technology than drawbacks. These advantages are most likely to be associated with the overall impacts of technology (that is, profits, quality and range of products and services, lead times, working conditions, technological capabilities) and the ability to compete in foreign markets. Despite the advantages of technology touted in the literature, the majority of Canadian businesses, regardless of size, perceive that technology has had no impact on factors of production, market share and interactions with customers and suppliers. Why benefits in these areas are not being realized is an area requiring future research. For all sized firms, the disadvantages of implementing technology are all associated with money: capital requirements, design costs, material requirements and profit margins were cited by all sized firms as the major negative impact of implementing technology. The likelihood of perceiving these drawbacks are, however, associated with company size as shown in Table 12.

The following key conclusions can be drawn from the data summarized in Table 12:

- Small businesses are not just little big businesses. With respect to the implementation of computer technology, there are a number of important differences that are associated with company size (see Table 12). This would suggest that small business owners need to be cognizant of how their companies' size can affect the adoption and use of computer technology. Best practices in these areas need to be identified for the small business sector, as this study indicates that the practices that work in larger companies may not transfer to smaller businesses.
- All small businesses are not the same–in other words, small is not small.

Table 12: Summary of Differences by Company Size

Differences	Company Size				
	Under 10	10 - 49	50 to 99	100 to 500	500 +
Major hardware/software implementation 1998/99	No difference	No difference	More likely	More likely	No difference
Penetration of CAD/CAE	None	None	None	Greater	Greater
Employees' reliance on computer	Lower	Higher	Higher	Higher	Lower
Cost per employee of implementing technology	No difference	No difference	No difference	Higher	No difference
Third most frequently used application	Database	Spreadsheet	Spreadsheet	Spreadsheet	Spreadsheet
Performance compared to non-adopters of same size	Better	Better	Better	Worse	Better except sales growth
Employees perceive technological complexity of their jobs have increased over time	Less likely	Less likely	Less likely	More likely	More likely
Sophistication of software	Lower	Moderate	Moderate	Higher	Higher
Likelihood of receiving employer funded formal computer training	Lower	No difference	No difference	No difference	No difference
Innovation compared to non-adopters of same size	Higher	Higher	Higher	No difference	Higher for new, lower improved
Innovation compared to adopters of different sizes	Same	Higher – all four types	Higher improvements	Same	Higher improvements
Main barriers to implementing technology compared to total sample	None	Lack of skilled personnel	Lack of skilled personnel	Lack of skilled personnel and finances Govt regulations Internal resistance	Lack of finances and of external technical services Govt regulations
Overall, does this size firm experience more benefits or drawbacks from technology	Overall neutral	Benefits	Least likely to benefit	Depends on sector	Overall, hard to say
Main benefits of technology compared to total sample	None	Working conditions Labour requirements National market share Interaction: suppliers	None (less likely to see benefits associated with lead time, profit margins and products)	Factors of production and market share	Market share
Main drawbacks of technology compared to total sample	None	Capital requirements and design costs	Design costs	Factors of production	Factors of production

*"No differences" comparison is with the total sample

There is a wide degree of variation within what has traditionally been thought of as the small business sector at least with respect to the adoption and use of computer technology. This means that one cannot assume that with respect to technology, what works for micro small businesses will apply to larger small businesses and vice versa.

• The greater availability of user-friendly, low-cost software applications appears to have leveled the playing field with respect to the sophistication of software used within Canadian businesses. The data collected for this analysis suggest that larger firms with a greater need for more specialized software and hardware are having more difficulties with respect to the availability of appropriate technology.

This research should help in the development of an IT model which incorporates the impact of company size as it points out how small businesses are similar to, yet different from, medium and large businesses. The small business size breakdown used in this analysis should also prove useful as a model to use in future research in this area.

The data also indicates that the adoption of new computer technology is associated with an increased tendency towards innovation and improved performance. Unfortunately, without longitudinal data is it hard to determine if companies that are more innovative are more likely to adopt technology which in turn increases performance or if the adoption of computer technology provides organizations with more opportunity to be innovative. It is hoped that this important question can be resolved with the second wave of the WES (the second wave of data is now being collected). Finally, it should be noted that additional data analysis (not shown) suggests that along with company size, sector plays a large role in the adoption and use of computer technology. Future research in the area of computer use and company size should include sector as a possible moderating variable. The WES will also allow this type of analysis.

REFERENCES

Baker, W. H. (1987). Status of information management in small businesses. *Journal of (B), J. R. Innovation: The Key to Success in Small Firms*, Statistic Canada.

Berry, R. and Wood, J. (1998). *A Survey of Information Technology Use by Small Business*.

Burrows, P. (1994). Giant killers on the loose. *Business Week*, (3372), 108-110.

Cheney, P. H. (1983). Getting the most out of your first computer system. *American Journal of Small Business*, 7(4), 476-485.

Cragg, P. B. and King, M. (1993). Small-firm computing: Motivators and inhibitors. *MIS Quarterly*, 17(1), 47-60.

Cragg, P. B. and Zinateli, N. (1995). The evolution of information systems in small firms. *Infomation & Management*, 29, 1-8.

DeLone, W. H. (1981). Firm size and the characteristics of computer use. *MIS Quarterly*, 5(4), 65-77.

DeLone, W. H. (1988). Determinants of success for computer usage in small business. *MIS Quarterly*, 12(1), 51-61.

Doukidis, G. I., Smithson, and Kybereas. (1994). Trends in information technology in small businesses. *Journal of End User Computing*, 6(4), 15-25.

Duxbury, L. and Higgins, C. (2000). *Human Resource and Work-Life Practices in Canadian Small Businesses*. London: Ivey Institute for Entrepreneurship, Innovation and Growth, University of Western Ontarion.

Ein-Dor, P. and Segev, E. (1978). Organizational context and the success of management information systems. *Management Science*, 24(10), 1067-1077.

Ein-Dor, P. and Segev, E. (1982). Organizational context and MIS structure; Some emprical evidence. *MIS Quarterly*, 6(3), 55-68.

Farhoomand, F. and Hryeyk, G. P. (1985). The feasibility of computers in small business environment. *American Journal of Small Business*, 9(4), 15-22.

Gable, G. G. (1991). Consultant engagement for computer system selection: A pro-active client role in small business. *Information & Management*, (20), 83-93.

Glynn, K. and Koenig, M. E. D. (1995). Small business and information technology. *Annual Review of Information Science and Technology*, 30, 251-280.

Harrison, D. A. et al. (1997). Executive decisions about adoption of information technology in small business: Theory and empirical tests. *Information Systems Research*, 8(2), 171-195.

Igbaria, M. et al. (1997). Personal computing acceptance factors in small firms: A structural equation model. *MIS Quarterly*, 279-305.

Industry Canada. (1995). *Small Business in Canada: A Statistical Overview*. Entrepreneurship and Small Business Office: Ottawa.

Kagan, A., et al. (1990). Information system usage within small business firms. *Entrepreneurship Theory and Practice*, Spring, 25-37.

Krebs, H., Patak, Z., Picot, G. and Wannell, T. (1999). The development and use of a Canadian linked employer-employee survey. In Haltiwanger, J. et al. (Eds.), *The Creation and Analysis of Employer-Employee*

Matched Data. Amsterdam: North-Holland.

Lehman, J. (1985). *Organization Size and Information Systems Sophistication. Working Paper#85-18*, MIS Research Center, University of Minnesota.

Lin, B. et al. (1993). Information technology strategies for small business. *Journal of Applied Business Research*, 9(2), 25-29.

Mahmood, M. A. and Mann, G. J. (1993). Impact of information technology investment: An empirical assessment. *Journal of Accounting, Management and Information Technology*, 3(1), 23-32.

Malone, S. C. (1985). Computerizing small business information systems. *Journal of Small Business Management*, April, 10-16.

Montazemi, A. R. (1988). Factors affecting information satisfaction in the context of the small business environment. *MIS Quarterly*, 12(2), 239-256.

Nickell, G. S. and Seado, P. C. (1986). The impact of attitudes and experience on small business computer use. *American Journal of Small Business*, 10(1), 37-48.

Palvia, P. C. (1996). A model and instrument for measuring small business user satisfaction with information technology. *Information & Management*, 31, 151-163.

Palvia, P. C. and Palvia, S. C. (1999). An examination of the IT satisfaction of small-business users. *Information & Management*, 35, 127-137.

Patak, Z., Hidiroglou, M. and Lavallée, P. (2000). *The Methodology of the Workplace and Employee Survey*, Statistic Canada Internal Document.

Raymond, L. (1985). Organizational characteristics and MIS success in the context of small business. *MIS Quarterly*, 9(1), 37-52.

Raymond, L. and Pare, G. (1992). Measurement of information technology sophistication in small manufacturing businesses. *Information Resource Management Journal*, 5(2), 1-13.

Thong, J. K. L. et al. (1996). Top management support, external expertise and information systems implementation in small businesses. *Information Systems Research*, 7(2), 248-267.

Welsh, J. A. and White, J. F. (1981). Small business is not a little big business. *Harvard Business Review*, 59(4), 18-32.

Winston, E. R. and Dologite, D. G. (1999). Achieving IT infusion: A conceptual model for small businesses. *Information Resources Management Journal*, 12(1), 26-38.

Chapter III

Information Systems Development Outcomes: The Case of Song Book Music

M. Gordon Hunter
University of Lethbridge, Canada

INTRODUCTION

When is an information system development outcome considered a success and when is it considered a failure? What factors contribute to a conclusion of either success or failure? How does the situation arise to create the environment which contributes to the above conclusions? Generally, an information system is considered a success when it does what it is supposed to and/or the user is satisfied with the system's performance in support of the information-providing and decision-making responsibilities. Naturally, this area is fraught with the problems inherent in divergent interpretations of "what it is supposed to do," "satisfaction," and "systems performance." Suffice it to say, when the systems developer and user are in positive agreement about these interpretations, the information system development outcome may be considered successful.

Negative information system development outcomes can be classified as either "completed" or "abandoned" projects. First, "completed" projects result in the implementation of an information system, but either the information system fails to attain initially stated goals or attains the goals after the expenditure of more time and effort. According to Laudon and Laudon (1998), 51% of all corporate software development projects result in costs of two to three times more than the initial budget amount, and eventually may require up to three times longer than originally estimated to complete. Ewusi-Mensah (1997) reports similar statistics, suggesting, as reported in a study by the Standish Group, that almost one-third of all information system projects are terminated before completion. As well, "... 52.7% of the projects completed are 189% over budget..." (Ewusi-Mensah, 1997:74). Thus, is the project a failure, or was the original estimation simply in error? Should these outcomes be regarded as failures or eventual successes? The answer seems to depend upon the perspective taken by the decision-maker. User satisfaction has been employed to provide a relative measure of an interpretation of success or failure as perceived by users. Second, "abandoned" projects are those projects which are never completed. Unfortunately, while they do not even result in the implementation of an information system, they are the cause of the ineffective consumption of company resources.

This chapter analyses an information systems development project, which is considered by the users to be "completed," yet unsuccessful. Initially, the literature available in the area is presented and reviewed. This review is followed by a description of the McComb and Smith (1991) system failure risk framework, which has been adopted as a means of analyzing the case presented in this document. Then the specific situation is presented with a description of the project and the results. The chapter concludes with a discussion of how the framework may be useful in understanding information system success or failure within a small business context.

Before proceeding further it is important to differentiate between the terms "entrepreneur" and "small business." In effect, these terms define businesses from two different perspectives. An entrepreneur, in general, represents an attitude towards business operations. Thus, an entrepreneur will tend to be innovative and take action, which will promote growth of the organization. An administrator, in contrast to an entrepreneur, will tend to carry out assigned duties within the scope of a job description. The term "small business" represents an economic entity (Kao, 1989) of a certain size defined by such factors as annual revenue, size of investment, or number of employees. So, either an entrepreneur or an administrator could operate a small business. A further differentiating factor for a small business is the lack of resources, both human and financial. Malone (1985) has suggested this factor also serves to differentiate how small businesses regard employing technology relative to larger businesses.

BACKGROUND

Research into information system development outcomes can be categorized as relating to Users, Systems Analysts, or the interaction between the two groups. First, a series of research projects is reported on, which have attempted to identify factors contributing to successful information system development outcomes. Then a series of projects is presented, which discuss aspects leading to negative outcomes.

The research described in the following paragraphs investigated successful information system development outcomes. The identified factors relate to some aspect of users and their relationship to the information system development project.

Barki and Hartwick (1994) investigated the relationships among user participation, user involvement, and user attitude, and their contribution to the development of successful information systems. To conduct their research into user–information system relationship, the authors have developed the following definitions:

- **User Participation**–"…refers to the assignment, activities, and behaviors that users … perform during the systems development process" (Barki and Hartwick, 1994:60).
- **User Involvement**–"…a psychological state reflecting the importance and personal relevance of a new system to the user" (Barki and Hartwick, 1994:62).
- **User Attitude**–"…a psychological state reflecting the reflective or evaluative feelings concerning a new system". (Barki and Hartwick, 1994:62).

They determined that user participation influenced both involvement and attitude, and all three contribute to the development of successful information system.

Robey et al. (1993) investigated the relationships among participation, influence, and conflict resolution during information system development, with success as an outcome variable. They found, among other factors, that conflict resolution leads to project success. They suggest that, "… the success of a project is largely dependent on the extent to which incompatible goals are resolved by consensus among project members" (Robey et al., 1993:135-136). They also discovered that user participation did not contribute as much to project success as did influence and conflict resolution. Relevant definitions in this case are as follows:

- **Participation** – "… extent to which members of an organization are engaged in activities related to system development" (Robey et al., 1993:125).
- **Influence** – "… extent to which members affect decisions related to the final design of an information system". (Robey et al., 1993:125).
- **Conflict** – "… Manifest disagreement among group members [which]

implies incompatible goals among group members". (Robey et al., 1993:125).

It is interesting to note that while Robey et al. have used the same definition for "participation" as Barki and Hartwick, the concept of "involvement," as defined by Barki and Hartwick, has not been included as a differentiating aspect of the user–information system relationship.

Byers and Blume (1994) investigated the relationship between critical success factors (CSFs) and information system development. They suggest the process of identifying CSFs leads to increased user involvement and a better understanding of the business functions on the part of information system personnel. These two factors lead to the creation of a partnership between information system development staff and the functional area, which supports the focus on those aspects critical to the business.

In general then the above research suggests that information system development outcomes will tend to be considered successful with the existence of increased user participation or user involvement, and some mechanism, which may be employed for conflict resolution. The following paragraphs describe unsuccessful information system development outcomes. The factors identified here relate to project management and organizational context of the information system development project.

Using Cognitive Dissonance Theory, Szajna and Scamell (1993) investigated the ability to predict information system failures based upon an assessment of user expectations. They determined the existence of an association between realistic user expectations and their perceptions. However, they were unable to establish a relationship between expectations and perceptions, and users' actual performance.

Keil and Mixon (1993) investigated the concept of "escalating commitment" to runaway information system development projects. While the authors have considered several theories, such as self-justification theory and the sunk cost effect of prospect theory, they have developed their research program through studies grounded in escalation theory as a framework to attempt to explain why decision-makers tend to delay project cancellation decisions. They have adapted Brockner's (1992) concept of "escalating commitment to a failing course of action" to attempt to explain runaway projects. This concept suggests that individuals will remain committed to a prior decision in spite of information which suggests the decision was incorrect. They discuss some theories (self-justification theory, prospect theory, and escalation theory) as a framework to attempt to explain why decision-makers tend to delay project cancellation decisions.

Ewusi-Mensah and Przasnyski (1991) discuss development project abandonment as one aspect of information system failure. Survey results indicate project abandonment was a complex issue relating to a combination of factors such as cost overrun, schedule slippage, technological inadequacies, as well as issues related to behavioral, political, and organizational factors, which emerged from the research as the most dominant. Ewusi-Mensah (1997) confirmed the earlier results obtained by Ewusi-Mensah and Przasnyski (1991) and suggested factors contributing to the cancellation of projects relate to project goals, project management and control, technical know-how, infrastructure, senior management involvement, and escalating cost and time.

Lederer and Nath (1991) suggest information system failures are the result of the individuals involved not sufficiently recognizing that information system development actually represents organizational change. They suggest that systems developers consider, "...such commonly practiced organizational change activities as the redesign of worker responsibilities to improve efficiency, the instituting of new management styles, the restructuring of management reporting relationships, or the reduction of interpersonal conflict..." (Lederer and Nath, 1991:23) as a means to put in context the development process. They suggest a framework which promotes developer-user interaction and includes such components as cultivation of a project champion, recognition of resistance to change, resolution of conflict, recognition of human sub-system issues, collaboration, and team building. Unfortunately, the article does not include a detailed discussion of the operationalization of the framework and its components. It does, however, serve to support the contention of the importance of the human aspects of information system development practices and their impact on outcomes.

Davis et al. (1992) provide a diagnostic framework and interpretative process for analyzing information system failures. Based upon one episode of an information system failure, they have developed the social and technical dimensions of their framework. Each dimension is divided into four characteristics, creating 16 components which highlight useful considerations for analyzing information systems failures. The framework is proposed as a model to be used when approaching the analysis of a specific information system failure. While taking an individual information system perspective, this framework seems to be more related to, and thus, more appropriate for the investigation of information system development outcomes in larger organizations.

The next research reported on here presents a framework which emphasizes the interaction between stakeholders. For this reason (stakeholder interaction), this framework seems to be an appropriate method for analyzing the case discussed here, because of the focus upon individuals performing within the context of a small business.

THE FRAMEWORK

This framework also incorporates factors determined by other researchers, which were presented in an earlier section. Factors contributing to successful information system development outcomes include user participation and involvement (Barki and Hartwick, 1994); participation, influence, and conflict (Robey et al., 1993); and involvement and understanding (Byers and Blume, 1994). Factors contributing to unsuccessful information system development outcomes include user expectations (Szajna and Scamell, 1993); escalating commitment (Keil and Mixon, 1993); organizational change (Lederer and Nath, 1991); and a series of issues relating to costs, schedule, technological in adequacies, project goals, project management, infrastructure, and senior management involvement (Ewusi-Mensah and Przasnyski, 1991; Ewusi-Mensah, 1997). Also, the framework proposed by Davis et al. (1992) provides further support for the use of the McComb and Smith (1991) framework. While Davis et al. proposed a framework with similar dimensions to the McComb and Smith framework, the Davis et al. proposal seems to relate more to the environment encountered in larger organizations. As presented later in the Results and Discussion section, the McComb and Smith framework presents dimensions of information system outcomes more suited to the environment encountered by small business.

McComb and Smith (1991) identified patterns within less successful information system development projects. They identified two categories relating to planning and executing, and two factors within each category of human and technical. Based on their findings they propose an analytical framework to assist in the identification of potential problems, which may contribute to the prevention of project failures. Figure 1 presents the McComb and Smith system failure risk framework.

McComb and Smith suggest that Figure 1 "...provides an analytical framework for linking observed systems failures to behavioral factors. Common planning and execution behaviors are traceable to both the technical and human sides of systems development that have resulted in systems failures. Any given project may be traceable to one or more of these factors" (McComb and Smith, 1991:25-26).

Thus, the authors organize their framework along two continua. The first continuum, the Planning-Executing dimension, differentiates factors relative to deciding what to do (Planning) and then carrying out the activities (Executing). The Planning dimension includes such factors as estimating (developing time and costs resource requirements) and compression (deciding whether to apply additional time and monetary resources). The Executing dimension includes change management (methods employed to monitor and control modification to specifications during system development) and workarounds (innovative methods used to resolve inconsistencies between planned and actual activities).

The second continuum, the Technical-Human dimension, serves to differentiate the factors relative to the physical components (Technical) of an information system rather than the personal (Human) components. The Technical dimension includes such aspects as ensuring data accuracy and system reliability, response time, and ensuring current technology is appropriate, or investigating the application of new technology. The Human dimension revolves around aspects relating to interpersonal relations and includes staffing, feedback, motivation, and involvement.

A further description of each factor is included in Figure 2.

These factors are discussed later in this chapter with specific reference to the case reported on in the next section.

RESEARCH METHOD

A case study research approach was employed to investigate the specific situation of implementing an integrated information system for a small sheet music store, which will be referred to as Song Book. As Yin (1994) suggests,

Figure 1: A system failure risk framework

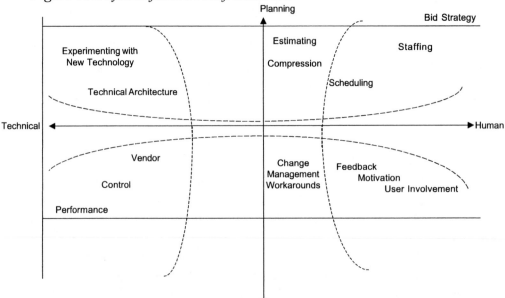

Figure 2: Interpretation of framework factors

FACTORS   INTERPRETATION
Planning
    Estimating: independent of the method used, the more accurate the estimate, the
        less risk
    Compression: adding staff to complete a task may actually increase the time
        required

Planning-Human
    Bid Strategy: methods use to acquire and assess external services
    Staffing: assigning and retaining the appropriate skills of those involved in the
        project
    Scheduling: the logical sequencing of activities

Executing-Human
    Feedback: unbiased reporting of performance
    User Involvement: participation in the design and training related to the system
    Motivation: commitment of those involved to solving the problem

Executing
    Change Management: methods used to control specification modification
    Workarounds: ingenious ways to resolve inconsistencies

Executing-Technical
    Vendor: reliability and credibility of external service organization
    Control: methods for ensuring accuracy of data and reliability of the system
    Performance: system response time

Planning-Technical
    Experimenting with New Technology: attempt to use unproven physical
        components
    Technical Architecture: ensure the physical components address functional
        requirements

case studies are appropriate when investigating contemporary events where the researcher does not have control of the events which transpire within the area of investigation. More specifically, research projects which ask, "How and why questions are likely to favor the use of case studies…" (Yin, 1994:7). Further, Stake (1994) suggests, "… a particular case is examined to provide insight into an issue or refinement of theory" (Stake, 1995:237). Further, more specifically related to the study of information systems, Galliers (1994) has suggested that case studies provide an opportunity for capturing reality in detail in order to describe existing relationships. Thus, case studies allow researchers to investigate an information system in its natural setting. This approach permits the researcher to thoroughly investigate the nature and complexity of the existing process, and the interactions among stakeholders. The data-gathering process employed the Narrative Inquiry method, which documents for subsequent analysis research participants' interpretations of personal experiences from an event or series of events. The interviews gathered comments from the research participants about the major events which transpired in the planning and development of a specific information system.

The following paragraphs present a brief overview of the company and the implementation project.

In the summer of 1994, Ruth and Ellen (fictitious names) purchased Song Book Music from the absentee owner. Ruth, a music teacher, had managed the store since September 1993. Ellen, who had an Administration degree, brought small business accounting experience to the partnership.

For the first two years, the new owners continued operations as before. Eventually, they decided it would be necessary to implement a more effective inventory control system. This decision was made in response to problems concerning knowing what inventory was on-hand, what had to be ordered, and where to acquire both existing and new items. The inventory problem was also creating poor customer service because product might not be available or it could be difficult to process special orders. The owners also thought it would be helpful to include order entry and sales processes into an integrated inventory control system.

Initially, the owners investigated various alternatives. They interviewed a ski shop owner and attended a seminar presentation of an accounting system, which included an inventory control module. They determined in each case that the systems did not meet their needs.

Because most of the owners' time was taken up in managing and running the store, they decided to acquire the services of a consultant to help them resolve this business problem. So, in July 1996 they contacted Buck, the sole proprietor of Buffalo Consulting. Buck not only developed custom software, he built his own computers. He had been working as an independent consultant with local industry for quite some time. Buck provided the owners with a very impressive list of former clients. As stated by the owners, because the list was so impressive, they did not consider contacting any of the former clients. They also concluded that no other bids would be necessary, again because of the names of former clients. The owners accepted this list as fact. However, they discovered later that, while it was a list of former clients, the services provided were not related to the information system development effort to be acquired, in this instance, by the owners.

The owners met with Buck and explained their situation to him in detail. After two or three subsequent visits, Buck made a verbal proposal on July 9, 1996, and presented a bill for $240 for consulting services. Buck suggested a custom-designed system, which he would develop. The system would include software developed by him and two networked computers entirely constructed by him. It was the owners' interpretation that the system would be completely developed and implemented by the end of August 1996. Based on data in the project file, Figure 3 represents the owners' interpretation of what Buck had committed to accomplish over the period of July and August 1996. It should be noted that this data is based upon the owners' recollections and there was never a written document exchanged regarding these dates.

Thus, Phase 1, software development and hardware construction, was to be carried out from July 9 to July 24. Phase 2, system testing, would be conducted from July 24 to 31. During the month of August, the system would be implemented, as Phase 3. This is the period of time when all product data would be entered into the system. On August 31 Phase 3 would be completed with the installation of the system. This was the plan; however, what transpired was quite different.

The owners were not involved in Phase 1. During this time Buck spent his time constructing the hardware and developing the software according to his interpretation of the requirements of the system as outlined by the owners.

Figure 3: Project plan

DATE	ACTIVITY
July 2, 1996	First meeting with Buck
July 9, 1996	Proposal (Total $11,500)
	Committed to Phase 1 ($5,000)
	Development of software and construction of software
July 24, 1996	Phase 2 ($3,000)
	System Testing
July 31, 1996	Phase 3 ($2,000)
	Implementation
August 31, 1996	Completion of Phase 3 with the installation of the system

There was very little interaction between the owners and Buck. When queried, his response was invariably polite with an indication that all was proceeding, as it should.

During Phase 2, system testing, some problems started to arise. At this time, not all of the system was available to test. It was still being developed. Also, the part which was available could not handle all of the required data elements.

In early August the situation began to deteriorate drastically. Even though the system was not completely installed, Buck began to demand full payment for his services. The Song Book store's lawyer recommended withholding payment. Buck began to behave unprofessionally, regularly missing appointments. Data entry proceeded very slowly. It had to be re-started in November because of a system crash with no back-up in place. Testing was eventually completed in April 1997 and a physical inventory was taken. Thus, the project, which had been planned to be complete in two months, actually took eight months.

At that time Buck was paid in full at the recommendation of Song Book's lawyer and he was informed his services were no longer required. The husband of one of the owners is currently carrying out maintenance of the system. While the system is being used, it regularly causes problems and must be reprogrammed when errors are discovered. The overall reaction of the owners to the experience is negative. They are not satisfied and classify the system as a failure. They feel it is simply a matter of time before they will replace the system.

RESULTS AND DISCUSSION

The literature reviewed earlier in this document suggests aspects contributing to negative information system development outcomes can be related to technical and human-oriented factors.

First, several technical factors contributed to the negative outcome at Song Book. The most significant was the schedule overrun. Originally, it was expected that the project would be completed in two months. However, the project actually took eight months. While no cost overruns were generated, the timing of the delivery of the information system functional components and the "demand" for payment did not match. This situation increased the users' frustration with the overall process and the information system specifically. There was no conflict resolution mechanism in place, which Robey et al. (1993) suggest would have contributed to the potential for a successful IS development outcome. Another technical factor related to technological inadequacies. Both users are not technical experts. Indeed, they recognized this fact with the decision to obtain the services of a consultant. The consultant, however, was also found lacking in this aspect. Buck experienced problems with his knowledge of the software and understanding its capability regarding the development of the required functionality. He also encountered problems with the hardware. He assembled the computers himself. The construction process was not the best. This caused the machines to operate inconsistently. He had a great deal of trouble trying to have the two machines communicate with each other.

Second, a number of human-oriented aspects also contributed to the negative information system development outcome. Both users felt that they participated and were involved in the development process. However, their participation was limited to data entry and their involvement was, at best, a superficial interaction with Buck regarding the current status of the project. Perhaps the more important factors relate to expectations and commitment. There seems to be a major difference in the interpretation of the expectations for the functionality of the information system. Both parties seemed to not understand the others' description of the information system requirements. This situation was even further confounded by the lack of written documentation. Also, the users reported a feeling of escalating commitment to the project even though they thought the process was not going to produce the kind of information system they expected. The users felt that they had committed the greater portion of available funds to the project too early in its existence. Their interpretation was that it would have been difficult or impossible to extricate themselves from the situation.

All of these factors led to deterioration in the interaction between Buck and the users. By the end of the project, the two parties were even having difficulty discussing aspects of the information system.

In this case, perhaps the most important factor contributing to the negative information system development outcome relates to the fact that both parties are involved in the operation of relatively small companies. This fact creates a unique situation with regards to the development and implementation of an information system to support the business functions. In the following paragraphs the Song Book case is discussed relative to the McComb and Smith (1991) framework, presented in Figure 1.

Small business managers tend to be action oriented and would then fall closer to the "Executing" than the "Planning" continuum. In this case both the Song Book owners and Buck would tend to converge toward the "Executing" end. Thus, both parties would subsequently tend to ignore those aspects associated with Planning. This would create a potential for risk with regards to the unsuccessful completion of the information system project. This was indeed the situation here. There was little evidence of planning, especially in relation to what should have been conducted relative to the early stages of a system development life cycle.

Further, the two parties involved can be associated with different ends of the continuum relative to "Technical" versus "Human." Buck is obviously technically oriented. His education and work experience was specifically related to the more technical aspects of computers. His interpersonal skills were also lacking as indicated earlier when the project started to deteriorate. The two owners, on the other hand, are more "Human" oriented. They possess excellent interpersonal skills. They work in a people-oriented business. The technical aspects of computers and information systems are of little interest. This divergent situation would tend to create difficulties in the relationship between these two groups, which would result in another area where the information system would be more susceptible to failure.

EPILOGUE

Approximately 18 months after the initial case study, reported above, was documented, another interview was conducted with Ruth and Ellen in order to determine their current interpretation of the outcome of installing the information system.

Since the initial contact the business has grown. Revenues have increased and the geographical marketplace has become more extensive. Indeed, potential customers from as far away as Ontario and Texas have contacted Song Book.

With regards to the information system, many changes have been made. New, faster computers have been installed. Some program logic has been revised mainly in order to correct mistakes. A number of new programs have been added which provide more reporting capability regarding invoices, payments, and unreconciled inventory. Overall, about another 300 hours have been spent resolving the above problems and adding the new reporting capability. Fortunately, this work has been carried out, in effect, for free by Ruth's husband who works as a systems analyst for a large company.

So, the owners feel the system is 'useable,' but they retain a very negative impression of the information system and the overall experience. In general, they are satisfied. They will continue to use the information system only because they cannot find anything better. In its current form the system supports the owner's information requirements. They both now know how to interact with the system.

CONCLUSION

This chapter has reported a case of two small organizations attempting to develop and implement an information system. The result of the project has been interpreted by the users as negative. The outcome of this project has been affected by technical factors such as schedule overrun and technological inadequacies of the parties involved. Also, human-oriented factors, such as user expectations and commitment, have negatively affected the outcome. Perhaps the most important factor affecting this specific case relates to the small business perspective of the parties involved.

In general, individuals running small businesses (with the exception of information system development firms) will tend to associate more easily with the "Executing-Human" ends of the McComb and Smith (1991) continua. Thus, they will be more susceptible to potential system failure from aspects relating to Planning and Technical factors. It is therefore incumbent upon small business managers who intend to develop and implement information systems to respond to these factors. From a technical perspective, they must at least know the capabilities of computers and related communications facilities. Further, small business managers must ensure that time is taken early in an information system development project to devote to planning.

Small business information system development firms, however, will more easily associate with "Executing-Technical" ends of the McComb and Smith (1991) continua. Thus, Planning and Human factors will tend to contribute to an interpretation of information system failure. In responding to these factors, information system development firms must address communication in general through concentrating on user involvement, motivation, and feedback. Further, extensive planning early in the project will contribute to both a better understanding of what has to be done and an improved estimate of how long it will take to complete the task.

Finally, these are the areas where small businesses are most susceptible to negative information system development outcomes. Concentrating on these factors will increase the potential for a successful information system development outcome.

REFERENCES

Barki, H. and Hartwick, J. (1994). Measuring user participation, user involvement, and user attitude. *MIS Quarterly*, March, 59-82.

Brockner, J. (1992). The escalation of commitment to a failing course of action: Toward theoretical progress. *Academy of Management Review*, 17(1), 39-61.

Byers, C. R. and Blume, D. (1994). Tying critical success factors to systems development. *Information and Management*, 26, 51-61.

Davis, G. B., Lee, A. S., Nickles, K. R., Chatterjee, S., Hartung, R. and Wu, Y. (1992). Diagnosis of an information system failure–A framework and interpretive process. *Information and Management*, 23, 293-318.

Ewusi-Mensah, K. (1997). Critical issues in abandoned information systems development projects. *Communications of the ACM*, September, 40(9), 74-80.

Ewusi-Mensah, K. and Przasnyski, Z. H. (1991). On information systems project abandonment: An exploratory study of organizational practices. *MIS Quarterly*, 67-86.

Galliers, R. (1994). Choosing information systems research approaches. In Galliers, R. (Ed.), *Information Systems Research–Issues, Methods and Practical Guidelines*. Henley-on-Thames, UK: Alfred Waller Ltd.

Kao, R. (1989). *Entrepreneur and Enterprize Development*. Toronto: Holt, Rinehart and Winston.

Keil, M. and Mixon, R. (1993). Laboratory studies of IS failures as escalating commitment to a failing course of action: Overcoming the obstacles. In Degross, J. I., Bostrom, R. P. and Robey, D. (Eds.), *Proceedings of the Fourteenth International Conference on Information Systems*, 382. New York: ACM.

Laudon, K. C. and Laudon, J. P. (1998). *Management Information Systems–New Approaches to Organization and Technology*. Upper Saddle River, NJ: Prentice Hall, Inc.

Lederer, A. L. and Nath, R. (1991). Managing organizational issues in information systems development. *Journal of Systems Management*, November, 23-39.

Malone, S. (1985). Computerizing small business information systems. *Journal of Small Business Management*, 23(2), 10-16.

McComb, D. and Smith, J. Y. (1991). System project failure: The heuristics of risk. *Journal of Information Systems Management*, 8(1), 25-34.

Robey, D., Smith, L. A. and Vijayasarathy, L. R. (1993). Perceptions of conflict and success in information systems development projects. *Journal of Management Information Systems*, 10(1), 123-139.

Stake, R. E. (1994). Case studies. In Denzin, N. K. and Lincoln, Y. S. (Eds.), *Handbook of Qualitative Research*. Thousand Oaks, CA: Sage Publications, Inc.

Szajna, B. and Scamell, R. W. (1993). The effects of information system user expectations on their performance and perceptions. *MIS Quarterly*, December, 493-516.

Yin, R. K. (1994). *Case Study Research–Design and Methods*. Thousand Oaks, USA: Sage Publications, Inc.

Chapter IV

Information System Check-Up as a Leverage for SME Development

Aurelio Ravarini, Marco Tagliavini and Giacomo Buonanno
Cattaneo University, Italy

Donatella Sciuto
Politecnico di Milano, Italy

INTRODUCTION

The widespread adoption of information and communication technology (ICT) has been involving both large companies and smaller ones. However, while large enterprises usually own the managerial competence and financial resources to face innovation, a lot of research has been highlighting the typical weakness related to small and medium enterprises[1] (SMEs) (Burns, 1996; Raymond, 1985, 1992). In fact, their typical focus on production activities, together with their limited investment budget, very often lead SME entrepreneurs to exclude information systems (IS) issues whenever planning organizational development. As a result, SMEs usually devote minimal resources to the IS department and, whenever they do, IS staff competence are strictly narrowed to technical issues (Soh, 1994; Palvia, 1994; Zinatelli, 1996). The consequent lack of internal expertise limits ICT specification and selection policies (Monsted, 1993; Schleich, 1990), and inevitably leads SMEs to develop an IS which is inadequate to the organizational needs (Cragg, 1995; Lai, 1995; Lang, 1997).

From the fast pace of ICT innovations arises the issue of the worth of IS management: among SMEs it is definitively questionable whether IS has been developed according to efficiency and effectiveness requirements, and whether it is aligned with the business strategy. Even more critically, it is questionable whether anyone in the company does consider IS efficiency, effectiveness and strategic alignment as issues. As a consequence, SMEs could greatly benefit from a tool supporting the ICT manager (or the person in charge of the IS) and the entrepreneur in monitoring the IS adequacy and making competent choices about IS development.

On the other hand, the previous remarks suggest that, in order to be applicable within SMEs, any managerial tool should be low in time and cost consumption and should not require specific skills to be used. Therefore, the purpose of this chapter is to provide a tool fulfilling the aim of IS management support, while respecting such requirements.

The chapter presents a detailed analysis of the literature on this subject, carried out to identify the existing approaches. Then, the identified approaches are compared and their adequacy to SME characteristics is assessed. The last section describes a tool specifically developed for SMEs and discusses its application within a set of Italian companies.

IS MANAGEMENT PROCESS AND
IS CHECK-UP TOOLS

Similar to any other managerial process, it is possible to represent the Information System Management Process as a sequence of three main phases (planning, development, maintenance). Moreover, in order to keep IS characteristics coherent with the company needs along time, it is essential to add a fourth phase (check-up) providing feedback to the ongoing outcomes of the process itself (Figure 1).

Figure 1: The information system management process

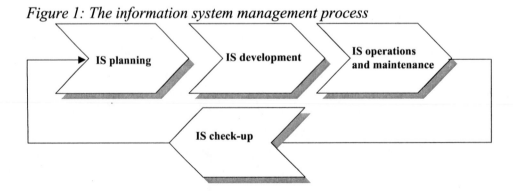

More precisely, IS check-up (similar to other check-up activities) can be further separated into a three-step process: an *analysis* phase, aimed at identifying possible IS malfunctions, a *diagnosis* phase, to detect their causes, and a *therapy* phase, providing suggestions about the actions to be undertaken. To guarantee the best results, these steps should be carried out by considering the IS support to business activities at two different levels: the relationship between the IS and strategic choices and the organizational characteristics of the company (*strategic level*); and the impact of the IS on company efficiency and effectiveness (*operating level*).

The topic of the evaluation of ICT influence on company performance has been a concern for both IS researchers and practitioners since the first business applications: even in 1961, the International Federation of Information Processing decided to devote its first conference to evaluation issues (Frienklin, 1961). Since then, a large part of the IS literature has been debating the issue, following at least three main approaches.

1. A major set of research has been focusing on ICT investment evaluation, that is, on the analysis and diagnosis steps of the described check-up process. Within this field of research, many tools and models have been developed: all of them aim at describing the state of the art of the IS in order to infer general statements about the actual business opportunities derived by ICT innovations. More precisely, some of them focus on ICT effectiveness and thus its implications on strategic performance (Bharadwaj, 1999; Harvey, 1996; McFarlan, 1984; Brynjolffson, 1993). Other research has investigated ICT efficiency, emphasizing its consequences on companies' productivity (Strassmann, 1990; Brynjolfsson and Hitt, 1996; Prattipati, 1997).

2. Another well-developed subject has been the evaluation of IS investments at the proposal stage (Renkema and Berghout, 1997). In this case, researchers have built methods and techniques aimed at supporting the choice between alternative and already defined IS projects. This approach involves all the three steps of the check-up process, but its application is limited to IS projects that are going to be implemented in the future.

3. The subject of this study is the IS check-up defined as the analysis and the evaluation of the current state of a company IS (therefore, of the whole set of past implemented IS projects) and the consequent definition of future projects (Eason, 1988; Ahituv, 1989; Ein-Dor, 1991). Although this topic has been seldom explored in the academic literature, the available IS check-up models can be classified into two main categories, which essentially differ by the characteristics of their outcomes.

    • A first set of tools fulfills the completeness of the check-up process: these models (Nolan, 1982; Bracchi 1985) require the evaluation of a large set of indicators to compare the performance improvements achieved through ICT with the related costs. A first set of indicators measure the extent and quality of ICT support to the company activities. Other *economic* indicators (such as the absolute value of ICT expenses, the percentage of such value with respect to the sales and the costs per manpower) aim at evaluating the amount and distribution of ICT expenses and investments. However, none of these tools provide suggestions about how to derive a general evaluation from the multiple assessments, and therefore make it difficult to design any IS development plan.

• In order to remove this limitation, more recent check-up models (Miller, 1987; Broadbent, 1993; Borovits, 1993) privilege synthesis rather than completeness. All such tools require the evaluation of two main indicators, computed as weighted means of a limited number of parameters (that are a selected subset of the previously mentioned functional and economic indicators). To enable a diagnostic overview of the IS, these models suggest to plot the results of the analysis within a matrix in which rows and columns correspond to the main indicators.

However, even these models that allow carrying out a complete IS check-up process do not appear suitable for SMEs. All of them assume the availability of a large amount of data with a high level of precision: their application requires either to assess the value of a large number of variables from a quantitative point of view, or to involve a lot of people in the evaluation process. As a consequence, their application is appropriate within large companies but is difficult within SMEs, where they could turn out to be extremely time and cost consuming.

A MODEL FOR IS CHECK-UP WITHIN SMES

The outcomes of the literature analysis highlight the need for an *ad hoc* tool for IS check-up within SMEs. Therefore, this chapter presents an original model that has been developed, taking into account the typical SME requirements for any managerial tool, both in terms of cost/time and of skills needed for the application. Nevertheless, the previous models represent an essential frame of reference for identifying the indicators and developing the methodology.

The IS check-up model for SMEs (described from here on as "the check-up model") can be described as a two-step process: a preliminary data-acquisition phase, followed by an evaluation procedure (Figure 2).

The model is structured according to a threefold framework:

• The model assumes that check-up is carried out by the ICT manager, supported by the entrepreneur or a high-level manager. In fact, only top managers have the knowledge and competence necessary to provide information related to the company strategy.

- The model is based on a *functional* representation of the company: SMEs are typically characterized by a functional structure, and, in any case, they more easily depict themselves through the traditional functional separation.
- The model makes use of both quantitative and qualitative evaluations. Given the requirements of low time/costs, the model makes large use of qualitative measures.

The Phases of the Model

Data collected in the preliminary phase represent the input of the evaluation process. This is based on two different check-up levels: the *strategic* check-up and the *operating* check-up, and can be separated into three main steps:

1. *strategic alignment assessment*, which aims at verifying if the IS support to each organizational unit is proportional to the strategic importance of such unit;
2. *positioning of the organizational units into an evaluation grid*, which highlights the inefficiencies of each unit and identifies the actions required to improve the IS performance;
3. *evaluation of the IS development trend*, which compares subsequent applications of the model to verify whether the IS has been developing correctly.

The characteristics of the model will be described through a practical application within an Italian medium sized enterprise working in the manufacturing industry, that we will call "CM."

Preliminary Data Acquisition

The check-up model makes use of both quantitative and qualitative evaluations. The preliminary phases aim at collecting input data necessary to carry out the following steps.

The *first preliminary phase* requires the identification of the company organizational units and their arrangement in a decreasing order of strategic importance. Of course, this evaluation requires the involvement of the entrepreneur or a high-level manager with a deep knowledge of the organization. The following table describes the organizational units selected by CM ordered according to their strategic importance.

The *second preliminary phase* requires, for each organizational unit "i", the evaluation of three main indicators:

1. IS Coverage Level CL_i
2. ICT Investment Level IL_i
3. Organizational Impact Level OIL_i

Figure 2: The IS check-up model of small and medium enterprises

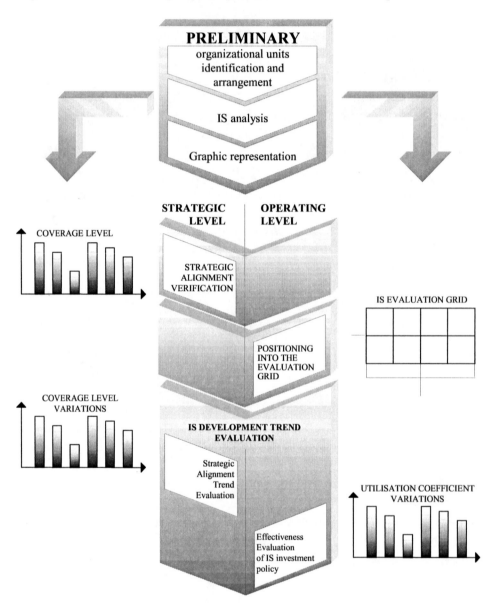

Table 1: Strategic importance of CM organizational units

	Organizational Unit
1	Technical Support
2	Sales
3	Service
4	Management Control
5	Accounting
6	Pay roll
7	Purchasing
8	Planning and Control
9	Logistics

IS Coverage Level

The **IS coverage level** CL_i evaluates the extent of the support provided by the IS to the activities carried out in each unit. CL_i depends on the values of three quantitative indicators, defined for each organizational unit as follows:

1. POTENTIAL COVERAGE RATIO: $Pot.Cov._i = 100 * D_i^*/D_i$
2. IS UTILIZATION COEFFICIENT: $UC_i = 100 * DA_i/D_i^*$
3. ACTUAL COVERAGE RATIO: $Act.Cov._i = UC_i * Pot.Cov._i$

where D_i^* represents the number of activities of a given organizational unit that *could be supported* by the existing IS, DA_i is the number of activities *actually* supported by the IS in that unit, and D_i represents the whole number of activities carried out within the unit.

The Actual Coverage Ratio $Act.Cov._i$ provides a qualitative evaluation of the actual IS dimension because it considers both the IS characteristics and the user capability of completely exploiting them. Nevertheless, the different values of the Actual Coverage Ratio cannot be compared, since they could be extremely different from one organizational unit to another. Therefore, in order to make these values homogeneous (thus comparable), they are transformed for each unit into *IS Coverage levels* through a comparative assessment within a range of values (Figure 3): the *Maximum Level of Possible Automation, MLPA(i)*, and the *Minimum Acceptable Level of Automation, MALA(i)*.

MLPA(i) is a technological limit which cannot be exceeded considering the state-of-art ICT. In fact, some organizational units (such as marketing, research and development) can only be partially supported by the IS, because they require thought processes or managing relationships activities that can only be carried out by humans and not machines. Therefore, the benefits derived by ICT investments for these units are more easily subject to saturation; any further investment beside a certain level does not lead to any meaningful improvement.

MALA(i) is settled by the requirements of efficiency characterizing each organizational unit. A qualitative assessment of this indicator can be performed by answering the following question: *which is the minimum level of automation for each organizational unit necessary to avoid serious inefficiencies (in terms of time and money)?*

MLPA(i) increases according to the technological progress (substantially exogenous to the choices of a small or medium enterprise). On the other hand, *MALA(i)* depends on the characteristics of the industry that the company belongs to, and on the strategic/organizational decisions, hence it represents a variable which managers can potentially control.

Figure 3 shows the Actual Coverage Ratios of CM organizational units together with the related values of *MALA(i)* and *MLPA(i)*. For each organizational unit i, the **IS Coverage Level CL(i)** is computed by comparing the Actual Coverage Ratio $Act.Cov._i$ with the arithmetic mean of *MALA(i)* and *MLPA(i)*: if $Act.Cov._i$ is greater than this arithmetic mean, then the IS Coverage Level *CL(i)* will be high, otherwise it will be low.

ICT Investment Level

The **ICT Investment Level IL_i** is an estimation of the financial efforts devoted to business automation. The quantitative evaluation of *ICT investments* of each organizational unit provides a first measure of this effort, but is affected by a number of factors. First of all, each organizational unit could require different ICT investment: the entrepreneur is asked to assess, for each organizational unit i, a threshold value above which the investment level will be considered "high." Figure 4 shows the values of ICT investments within CM organizational units.

Moreover, the efforts necessary to raise the coverage levels are not the same for all the organizational units; therefore, the model suggests to consider the *Average Cost per Coverage Unit ACpCU_i*, a qualitative measure of the average financial effort needed to increase the Coverage Level related to a specific organizational unit. A comparative evaluation between ICT investment values and corresponding $ACpCU_i$ values leads to convert investment *values* into **ICT Investment Level IL_i**, thus making comparable ICT investments in different units.

Organizational Impact Level

The **Organizational Impact Level OIL_i** is a subjective qualitative evaluation of time savings and overall increase of activities performance due to the

Figure 3: Assessment of the IS coverage level (i)

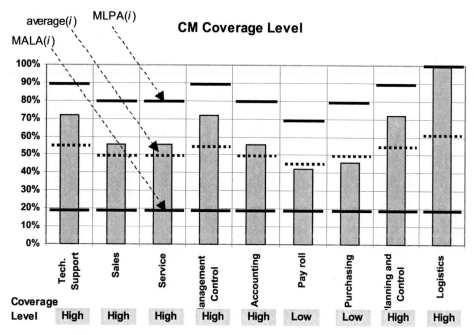

Figure 4: ICT investments within CM organizational units

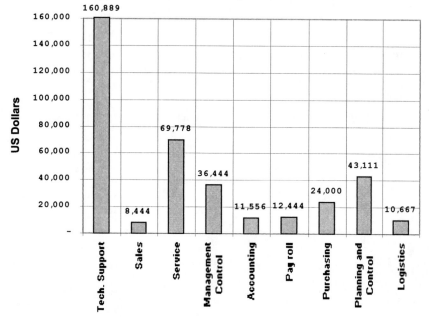

introduction of the IS in each organizational unit. Such evaluation should be performed by end-users, using a 5-value Likert scale, showing the extent of organizational impact. Within CM the end-users of each organizational unit filled in a brief questionnaire on the IS organizational impact: the arithmetic mean of their answers (all expressed in terms of values ranging from 0 to 5) provided an estimation of the IS Organizational Impact Level OIL_i, which will be considered "high" whenever the arithmetic mean turns out to be greater than 2.5.

Strategic Alignment Verification

The IS *strategic alignment* is achieved when the strategic importance assigned to an organizational unit is proportional to the support provided by the information system to that unit (Porter, 1985; Henderson and Venkatraman, 1992; Miller, 1993). The described procedure used to determine the IS Coverage Level CL_i vouches that such an indicator can be considered a measure of the IS support to each organizational unit. Therefore, the strategic alignment is verified whenever the strategic importance of each organizational unit shows a direct proportionality to the corresponding coverage level.

Positioning into the Evaluation Grid

This phase of the model (as shown in Figure 2) aims at integrating the information gathered for each organizational unit. The values of the three main indicators (Coverage Level, Investment Level and Organizational Impact Level) have been converted through a qualitative assessment according to a two-level scale (high and low levels). Combining the binary values of the three indicators, it is possible to draw an eight-box grid (Figure 6); each organizational unit can be positioned within the grid by means of the corresponding values of the indicators.

Table 2: Organizational impact level of CM organizational units

Organizational unit	Mean of end-users assessments	Organizational Impact Level
Tech. Support	2.1	Low
Sales	3.4	High
Service	2.4	Low
Management Control	1.8	Low
Accounting	1.9	Low
Pay roll	2.3	Low
Purchasing	2.2	Low
Planning and Control	1.9	Low
Logistics	2.1	Low

Figure 5: Verifying CM strategic alignment

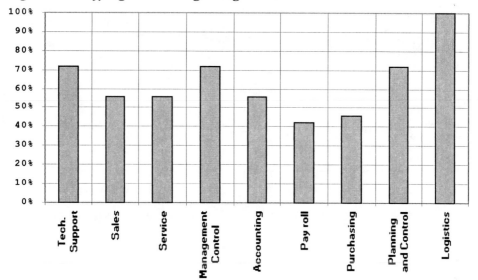

Further support on interpreting the meaning of each position in the grid is provided by the IS Utilization Coefficient (UC_i). According to our experience, we assume that the values of UC_i are correlated to the level of system service, the amount of training activities and the solicitation toward the system utilization, as well as negatively influenced by the end-users' resistance to change and the turnover rate of specialized personnel.

As detailed below, from the positioning of an organizational unit into each grid box, it is possible to infer a synthetic description of the main IS management issues related to that unit and therefore the possible actions aiming at improving its performance in terms of IS effectiveness and efficiency.

Position 1: Optimal Position

An organizational unit positioned into this box highlights *optimal* condition of ICT support: it represents the achievement of good results in terms of efficiency and effectiveness, with low expenses.

Position 2: Good Position

This position can still be considered a *good* result: the high investments in ICT are fully exploited. In such a situation, SME managers seem to have correctly considered the IS organizational impact, achieving high IS performance.

Figure 6: The information system evaluation grid

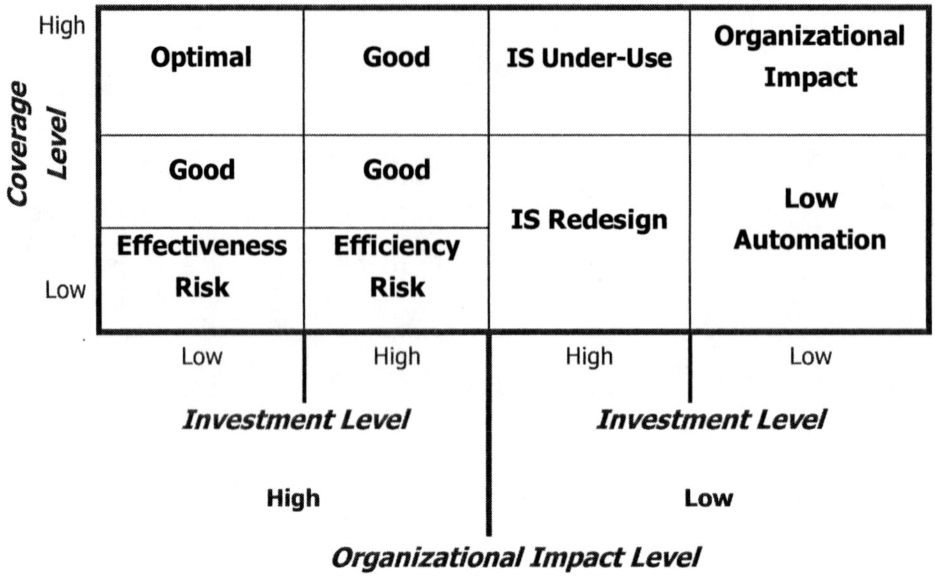

Optimal	**Good**	**IS Under-Use**	**Organizational Impact**
Good	**Good**	**IS Redesign**	**Low Automation**
Effectiveness Risk	**Efficiency Risk**		

(Coverage Level: High to Low; Investment Level: Low, High | High, Low; High Organizational Impact Level | Low)

Position 3: IS Under-Use

This position is characterized by a high amount of ICT investments, possibly aiming at automating most activities. Nevertheless, the potential of such resources does not seem to be completely perceived and exploited by the IS users.

Position 4: Underestimated Organizational Impact

This box represents an intermediate position between positions 1 and 3: since a lower effectiveness is achieved, the situation it represents is far from being optimal (Position 1) but, unlike Position 3, these levels can be justified by the limited ICT investments. In that case, the management may have underestimated the organizational impact of the IS.

Position 5: Low Automation

The presence of an organizational unit into this box can be interpreted in two different ways. The first is similar to Position 2: the low ICT investment level causes insufficient IS performance.

Conversely, low Coverage Level and Organizational Impact Level values could be ascribed to planning inefficiencies and/or low user information satisfaction. The analysis of the Utilization Coefficient UC_i should help understanding whether to detail the analysis (low value of UC_i), or to consider the current situation as correct (high value of UC_i).

Position 6: IS Redesign

Units positioned into this box show a discrepancy between their Coverage Level and the Investment Level. This situation highlights mistakes in assessing both the ICT effectiveness and organizational impact: the low Organizational Impact Level is coherent with the consequent low service level.

Such a situation may be caused by low technical competencies of the IS staff or by an improper management of relationships with hardware and software suppliers, who often provide SMEs with an essential support to the entire IS development process.

Position 7: Good Position/Low Efficiency Risk

The positioning of an organizational unit into this box can be interpreted in two different ways, depending on the value of the Utilization Coefficient. If UC_i is high, then the high Investment Level could be explained by an expensive training activity aimed at fully exploiting the functions of a restricted IS; hence, if the strategic alignment condition is satisfied, this result can be considered good. On the other hand, a low value of UC_i could lead to a *risky* situation, because of the difference between the actual and the perceived quality of the IS. In fact, the high Organizational Impact Level shows that users are satisfied with their system, while the real problem (like in Position 6) is the IS inefficiency, pointed out by the discrepancy between the low Coverage Level and the high investment effort. In such a situation, if the inefficiency is not detected, the system performance may decrease with an uncontrollable trend.

Position 8: Good Position/Low Effectiveness Risk

As before, the value of Utilization Coefficient leads to two different interpretations. If UC_i is high the limited automation effort–confirmed by the low Investment Level–is consistent with the low Coverage Level, while the high Organizational Impact Level is possibly determined by an actual adequacy of the IS to users' information needs. Therefore, if the considered unit does not require higher values of CL_i for strategic alignment reasons, this position could be considered acceptable.

On the other hand, when UC_i is low, the high Organizational Impact Level is in contradiction with the limited performance of the IS (as the other two indexes highlight). In this case, the value of AIL_i may depend on an incorrect evaluation: users may declare to be satisfied in spite of the small IS dimension (if the Potential Coverage was low anyway) or scarce use (if the Potential Coverage was high).

Evaluation of the IS Development Trend

The check-up procedure described so far is based on a single application of the model (static use). On the other hand, a comparative study between the previous and current applications of the model allows to assess the IS development trend (dynamic use). This kind of analysis can be performed both from a *strategic* and an *operating* point of view.

Strategic Level: Strategic Alignment Trend

This phase aims at verifying the changes that have occurred in the strategic alignment referring to the previous application period. A correct trend would be pointed out by decreasing coverage level values $CL(i)$ related to organizational units of decreasing strategic importance.

The presence of ICT investments aimed at aligning the organizational units according to their strategic importance is a demonstration that the company is aware of the discrepancy between business goals and IS characteristics, and has taken correct decisions to solve the problem. The discrepancy between the present and correct trends measures the extent of actions yet to be taken.

Operating Level: Trend of the ICT Investments Policy Effectiveness

From the operating point of view, the evaluation of ICT investment effectiveness for each organizational unit requires comparison of the poten-

Figure 7: Positioning CM organization units within the IS evaluation grid; the association between numbers and organizational units is shown in Table 1

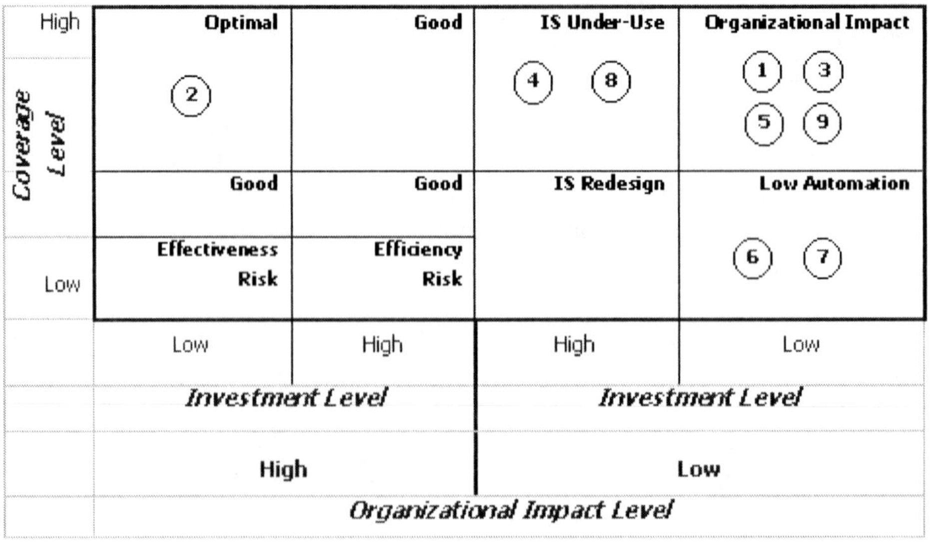

tial and actual coverage levels since the last application of the model. The ideal situation is obtained when ICT investments determine:

- a growth of the Coverage Level in all the corresponding organizational units; the ideal situation is represented by the IS supporting all firm activities, but the lack of financial resources imposes the need to assign priorities to different units.
- a growth of the Utilization Coefficient in all the organizational units, towards its maximum value (100%): the higher the value of $UC(i)$, the more effective will be any ICT investment.

Therefore, the analysis of the "Coverage Level Variations" and the "Utilization Coefficient Variations" highlights the effectiveness of ICT investments and the IS overall performance.

The IS Evaluation Grid allows further details: comparing the positioning of each unit between two subsequent applications of the model enables an evaluation of how much the change of the Investment Level of each unit has induced the desired effects, possibly suggesting the proper therapy.

THE OUTCOMES OF THE MODEL

After a test on a preliminary sample of eight SMEs and consequent refinement, a *questionnaire* was submitted to CEOs and CIOs of 55 self-selected Italian SMEs, mainly placed in the Northern part of Italy. Together with the questionnaire, all the companies of the sample received an *application manual* describing in detail the characteristics of the model and providing comprehensive instructions about its application.

All of the questionnaires were filled-in via direct interviews, taking about half a day each. The most time-consuming part of the analysis has been the detailed collection of data regarding ICT investments that often have been managed by different roles over time. Figure 8 shows the distribution of the sample according to the company size and industry.

The analysis of collected data confirmed some of the basic issues coming from the literature.

- Small companies seldom make use of internal IS staff, but normally outsource IS management; this probably means that, regardless of the experiences of larger companies, they still do not consider the IS management strategic enough to develop internal competencies.
- There seems to be an inverse proportionality between company turnover and strategic alignment. Thus, if small companies attached enough strategic importance to the IS area, probably they would more easily support their strategy and raise their competitiveness.

Figure 8: Distribution of the sample according to company size and industry

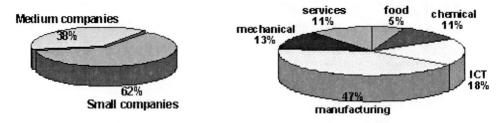

- The applications of the check-up model showed that IS support to a meaningful percentage of organizational units is considered satisfactory; the other units emphasize problems mostly related to automation issues. Again, this probably means that SME managers think of IS support only in terms of automating the business activities, without considering it as a way to support or even redefine the business strategy.

In summary, the survey results show how companies of all sizes should consider the ICT strategic and organizational impact. One of the most interesting outcomes is that companies entrusting IS management only to internal staff provide a more effective support to the business strategy than those companies (with similar turnover and number of employees) making use of external consultants. This suggests that SME organizational structures should include a function with the technical and managerial competencies needed to effectively manage the IS, thus enabling a real support to the company strategic goals.

However, 'on-the-field' applications highlighted the need for caution in interpreting the model outcomes. Whenever the model has been perceived by the ICT manager only as a tool to evaluate its own competence, the analysis has been carried out with a general lack of objectivity (for example, the limits affecting IS have been charged to previous managers). In such a situation, the results of the model are distorted. Moreover, this approach, not allowing the detection of an inappropriate IS assets distribution before it becomes structural, can lead to a high risk of future failures.

On the other hand, whenever carried out with objectivity, the check-up model provides the ICT manager with a comprehensive evaluation of the business information system. At the same time, it can provide top managers with an understandable report about the adequacy of the ICT investments supporting the business objectives.

Finally, it is worth noting that the application of the model forces SME managers to highlight problems not directly related to IS, like knowledge of the company's strategies and their connection to the organizational development. The reticence in admitting such problems shows that they can be underestimated. This side-effect result increases the usefulness of the model.

CONCLUSIONS AND FUTURE WORK

Nowadays, in order to be competitive in a constantly changing market, companies of any size must deal with ICT management. The complexity of information systems (even within very small firms) determines the need for specific tools supporting the ICT manager in the difficult task of planning and managing the IS development. The available methods for the IS evaluation and management have been designed for large enterprises, and they are seldom useful to SMEs for a number of different reasons.

This chapter describes a tool for the IS check-up expressly designed for SMEs' specific requirements: it is easy to understand, it requires minimal data, and it does not need particular technical skills to be applied. At the moment, the model makes use of a unique approach for all of the different types of SMEs. The high differentiation of SME features suggests that it is possible to develop the model by applying it within specific subsets of companies, identified by dimension or industry. The analysis of the peculiarities of each subset could enable explicating in deeper detail the positioning of the organizational units within the evaluation grid and the corresponding suggested therapies.

ENDNOTE

1 This chapter will refer to current definition of SMEs provided by the European Community (EU DGXII's Press Releases, 1996), which identifies those companies with less than 250 employees, a turnover lower than 40 million ECU, and which are owned for less than 25% by non-SMEs, except banks or venture capital companies.

REFERENCES

Ahituv, N. (1989). Assessing the value of information: Problems and approaches. *Proceedings of the Tenth International Conference on Information Systems*, December 4-6, Boston, MA.

Bharadwaj, A. S. (1999). A resource-based perspective on information technology capability and firm performance: An empirical investigation, *MIS Quarterly*, March, 1-44.

Borovits, I. and Chmura, A. (1993). Cost/utilization: A measure of computer information system performance. In Goldberg, R. and Lorin, H. (Eds.), *The Economics of Information Processing*. New York: John Wiley & Sons.

Bracchi, G. and Motta, G. (1985). *Sistemi Informativi e Imprese (in Italian, Information Systems and Firms)*. Italy: Franco Angeli, Milano.

Broadbent, M. and Lofgren H. (1993). Information delivery: Identifying priorities, performance and value. *Information Processing Management*, 29(6), 683-701.

Brynjolffson, E. (1993). The productivity paradox of information technology: Review and assessment. *Communications of the ACM*, December.

Brynjolfsson, E. and Hitt, L. (1996). Paradox lost? Firm level evidence on the returns to information systems spending. *Management Science*, 42(4), 541-558.

Burns, P. and Dewhurst, J. (Eds.). (1996). *Small Business and Entrepreneurship* (2nd Ed.). MacMillan Business.

Cragg, P. B. and Zinatelli, N. (1995). The evolution of information systems in small firms. *Information and Management*, 29(July), 1-8.

DG XII's Press Releases. (1996). *A New Common Definition For SMEs–But Not Before the 5th Framework Programme Brussels*.

Eason, K. (1988). *Information Technology and Organizational Change*. Taylor & Frances.

Edoho, F. (1994). Demystifying strategic management: The need for strategic management in small business firms. *Proceedings of the 1994 Annual Conference of the USA Association for Small Business and Entrepreneurship*.

Ein-Dor, P. and Jones, C. R. (1991). *Information Systems Management: Analytical Tools and Techniques*. New York: Elsevier.

Frienklin, A. B. (Ed.). (1961). *Auditing Automatic Data Processing*. Amsterdam: Elsevier.

Harvey, D., Islei, G. and Willcocks, L. (1996). *Measuring the Performance of Corporate Information Technology Services*, BI/OXIIM Report, Business Intelligence, London.

Henderson, J. C. and Venkatraman, N. (1992). Strategic alignment: A model for organizational transformation through information technology. In Kochan, T. A. and Useem, M. (Eds.), *Transforming Organisations*. New York: Oxford University Press.

Lai, V. (1994). A survey of rural small business computer use: Success factors and decision support. *Information & Management*, 26, 237-304.

Lang, J. R., Calatone, R. J. and Gudmundson, D. (1997). Small firm information seeking as a response to environmental threats and opportunities. *Journal of Small Business Management*, 35(1), 12-18.

McFarlan, F. W. (1984). Information technology changes the way you compete. *Harvard Business Review*, May/June.

Miller, J. (1993) Measuring and aligning information systems with the organization: A case study. *Information & Management*, 25.

Miller, J. and Doyle, B. (1987). Measuring the effectiveness of computer-based information systems in the financial services sector. *MIS Quarterly*, March, 107-124.

Monsted, M. (1993). Introduction of Information Technology to Small Firms: A Network Perspective, Entrepreneurship and Business Development. Klandt, H. Avebury (Ed)., Aldershot.

Nolan, R. L. (1982). *Managing the Data Resource Function*. St. Paul, MN: West Publishing Co.

Palvia, P., Means, D. B. and Jackson, W. M. (1994). Determinants of computing in very small businesses. *Information & Management*, 27, 161-174.

Porter, M. and Millar, V. (1985). How information gives you competitive advantage. *Harvard Business Review*, July-August, 149-160.

Prattipati, S. and Mensah. (1997). Information systems variables and management productivity. *Information & Management*, 33-43.

Raymond, L. (1985). Organizational characteristics and MIS success in the context of small businesses. *MIS Quarterly*, March, 37-52.

Raymond, L. (1992). Computerization as a factor in the development of young entrepreneurs. *International Small Business Journal*, 11(1), 34.

Renkema, T. J. W. and Berghout, E. W. (1997). Methodologies for information systems investment evaluation at the proposal stage: A comparative review. *Information and Software Technology*, 39, 1-13.

Soh, P. P. C., Yap, C. S. and Raman, K. S. (1994). Impact of consultants on computerization success in small business. *Information & Management*, 22, 309-319.

Schleich, J. F., Carney, W. J. and Boe, W. J. (1990). Pitfalls in microcomputers system implementation in small business. *Journal of System Management*, 41.

Strassmann, P. A. (1990). *The Business Value of Computers*. The Information Economics Press, USA.

Subramanian, A. and Nilakanta, S. (1994). Measurement. A blueprint for theory-building in MIS. *Information & Management*, 26, 13-20.

Zinatelli, N., Cragg, P. B. and Cavaye, A. L. M. (1996). End user computing sophistication and success in small firms. *European Journal of Information Systems*, 5, 172-181.

Chapter V

Modeling Technological Change in Small Business: Two Approaches to Theorizing Innovation

Arthur Tatnall
Victoria University, Australia

INTRODUCTION

Many small businesses are quite entrepreneurial in their operation, and are prepared to consider the advantages conferred by information technology. On the other hand, some are still quite happy to continue to do things in the same way they always have, and see no need to investigate use of this technology. How and why these businesses differ in this way, and why they adopt some technologies and not others, is investigated in this chapter.

The introduction of a new information system into a small business, or the upgrading of an existing system, should be seen as an innovation and so considered through the lens of innovation theory. The most widely accepted theory of how technological innovation takes place is provided by innovation diffusion, but most of the research based on this model involves studies of large organizations or societal groups. This chapter argues that another approach, that of innovation translation, has more to offer in the case of innovations that take place in smaller organizations–those employing less than 20 people (Burgess, Tatnall, & Darbyshire, 1999).

INNOVATION AND SMALL BUSINESS

There are some important differences in the processes by which small and large enterprises choose to adopt, or reject, computers and information technology (IT). Most small businesses have few spare resources available, and generally do not have a separate IT department. This means that they typically have less formalized planning and control procedures and, in many cases, the owner/manager does not have the time, the resources, or the expertise necessary to formalize the evaluation of IT projects. Often, a reliance on whatever internal IT expertise may be available has meant that small businesses are only aware of the cost savings that can be provided by computers and not of other potential benefits that innovative use of IT may provide (Burgess, Tatnall, & Darbyshire, 1999).

The link between entrepreneurship and the commercial success of small enterprises is generally acknowledged (Guzman-Cuevas & Santos-Cumplido, 1999), but the term 'small business entrepreneur' is used differently by various writers. In the context of this chapter, it will be used to denote those dynamic individuals who may be seen as responding to, or creating, new conditions and applying new knowledge (Nystrom, 1999)–individuals who are considered to be innovative.

The *Shorter Oxford English Dictionary* defines innovation as "the alteration of what is established; something newly introduced" (Oxford, 1973). The *Macquarie Dictionary* adds "introducing new things or methods" (Macquarie Library, 1981), and *Roget's Thesaurus* offers the synonyms 'newness' and 'change.' As the introduction or improvement of an information system in an organization *necessarily* involves change, it should be considered as an innovation.

Changing the way things are done is a complex affair and one that is difficult to achieve successfully. Success in innovation is always doubtful because people who are prepared to support the innovator can be difficult to find and to convince. Although writing of *political* change almost 500 years ago, Niccolò Machiavelli summed this up as follows: "There is nothing more difficult to handle, more doubtful of success and more dangerous to carry through than initiating changes ... The innovator makes enemies of all those who prospered under the old order, and only luke-warm support is forthcoming from those who would prosper under the new. Their support is lukewarm partly from fear of their adversaries, who have the existing laws on their side, and partly because men are generally incredulous, never really trusting new things unless they have tested them by experience" (Machiavelli, 1995 :19)

The dominant paradigm by far in innovation research is that of *innovation diffusion*, and no discussion of innovation would be complete without a consideration of this approach. Another approach, however, that of *innovation translation* informed by actor-network theory, is also worthy of consideration. Innovation diffusion has had considerable success in describing how innovations move, or diffuse, through large populations. There are occasions, however, when diffusion does not occur despite the excellence of the idea or the technical quality of the innovation, and the diffusion model finds these instances difficult to explain. In the translation model, on the other hand, the key to innovation is the creation of a powerful enough consortium of actors to carry it through, and when an innovation fails to be taken up, this can be considered to reflect on the inability of those involved to construct the necessary network of alliances amongst the other actors. This chapter will compare these two models of technological innovation.

INNOVATION DIFFUSION

Innovation diffusion is based on the notion that the adoption of an innovation involves the spontaneous or planned spread of new *ideas*, and Rogers defines an innovation as "... an idea, practice, or object that is, perceived as new" (Rogers, 1995:11).

Rogers, perhaps its most influential advocate, approaches the topic of innovation diffusion by considering a variety of case studies on topics including: controlling scurvy in the British Navy, diffusion of hybrid corn in Iowa, diffusion of the news, bottle feeding of babies in the third world, how the refrigerator got its hum, Xerox PARC and Apple Computer, black music in white America, Minitel in France, the non-diffusion of the Dvorak keyboard, and causes of the Irish potato famine. The prime concern in all these studies is the identification of factors that affect the speed with which an innovation is adopted, or that cause it not to be adopted at all.

In diffusion theory the existence of an innovation is seen to cause uncertainty in the minds of potential adopters (Berlyne, 1962) causing a lack of predictability and of information. Rogers (1995) asserts that a technological innovation embodies information, and that this has the potential to reduce uncertainty. Diffusion is thus considered to be an information exchange process among members of a communicating social network driven by the need to reduce uncertainty. There are four main elements of the theory of innovation diffusion: characteristics of the innovation itself, the nature of the communication channels, the passage of time, and the social system through which the innovation diffuses (Rogers, 1995).

Characteristics of the Innovation Itself

Rogers argues that the attributes and characteristics of the innovation itself are important in determining the manner of its diffusion and the rate of its adoption, and outlines five important characteristics of an innovation that affect its diffusion:

- **Relative advantage**–or the degree to which an innovation is perceived as better than the idea it supersedes. Rogers contends that an innovation's relative advantage is positively correlated with its rate of adoption.
- **Compatibility**–the degree to which an innovation is perceived by potential adopters as being consistent with existing values and past experiences. Rogers asserts that the perceived compatibility of an innovation is positively related to its rate of adoption.
- **Complexity**–the degree to which an innovation is perceived as difficult to understand and use. The more complex the innovation, the less likely it is to be quickly adopted.
- **Trialability**–the amount that a particular innovation may be subjected to limited experimentation. If 'playing' with the innovation is possible, adoption is more likely.
- **Observability**–the more the results of an innovation are visible to others, the more likely the innovation is to be adopted.

The attributes of the potential adopter are also seen as an important consideration in the adoption of an innovation. Rogers maintains that these attributes include social status, level of education, degree of cosmopolitanism, and amount of innovativeness.

Nature of the Communications Channels

Acts of communication are a necessary part of any change process, and to reach a potential adopter, the innovation must be diffused through some communications channel. Channels involving mass media are often the most rapid and efficient means of spreading awareness of an innovation, but interpersonal channels are generally more effective in persuading someone to accept a new idea.

The Passage of Time

In common with earlier researchers, Rogers found that different individuals in a social system do not necessarily adopt an innovation at the same time. Borrowing from the work of Deutschmann and Fals Borda (1962), he proposes that adopters can be classified in their degree of 'innovativeness' into five categories: innovators, early adopters, early majority, late majority, and laggards, and that if the number of individuals adopting a new idea is plotted over time, it usually follows the familiar bell-shaped, normal curve.

The Social System

In this paradigm, diffusion occurs within a social system in which the social structure constitutes a boundary inside which the innovation diffuses. Rogers argues that the system's social structure affects diffusion through the action of social norms, the roles taken by opinion leaders and change agents, the types of innovation decisions that are taken, and the social consequences of the innovation.

INNOVATION TRANSLATION

An alternative view is that of innovation translation which draws on the sociology of translations, more commonly known as actor-network theory (ANT). The core of the actor-network approach is translation (Law, 1992), which can be defined as: "... the means by which one entity gives a role to others" (Singleton & Michael, 1993:229).

Research in technological innovation is often approached by focusing on the technical aspects of an innovation and treating 'the social' as the context in which its adoption takes place, assuming that outcomes of technological change can be attributed to the 'technological' rather than the 'social' (Grint & Woolgar, 1997). At the other extreme, social determinism holds that more or less stable social categories can be used to explain change, and concentrates on investigation of social interactions, relegating the technology to context, to something that can be bundled up and forgotten. This bundling means that fixed and unproblematic properties or 'essences' can be assigned to the technology and used in explaining change (Tatnall & Gilding, 1999).

Problems with Essentialism and Innovation Diffusion

Diffusion theory asserts that a technological innovation embodies 'information': some essential capacity or 'essence' instrumental in determining its rate of adoption (Rogers, 1995). A significant problem with an essentialist paradigm like this arises if a researcher tries to reconcile the views of all parties involved in the innovation on what *particular* essences are significant. The difficulty is that people often see *different* 'essential attributes' in any specific technological or human entity, making it hard to identify and settle on the ones that allegedly were responsible for the diffusion.

To illustrate this difficulty, consider the case of a small business deciding, some years ago, whether to purchase their first computer. Researchers using an innovation diffusion model would begin by looking for innate characteristics of the PC that would make a potential adopter more likely to accept it. They would consider the relative advantages of a PC over alternatives like a typewriter and filing cabinet. An examination of the compatibility, trialability, and observability of a PC with this older office technology would show good reasons for acceptance. An examination of the PC's complexity would, however, bring out some reasons for reluctance in its adoption. The researchers would then investigate characteristics of the potential adopters, considering factors like their educational background, innovativeness, and how they heard about the innovation.

If, however, you *ask* small business people why they purchased their first PC, the answers sometimes do not match with this view. In some straightforward cases, the PC was purchased for a specific business application and the reasons for adoption fit well with a diffusion model. In the example that follows, however, this is not the case.

Many small businesses are family related concerns with several family members working in the business (Burgess et al., 1999). My investigations suggest that one common reason why a small business first acquired a PC is that it was, at least partly, intended for family use. In this regard one reason that the PC was obtained was in the belief that it would assist with their children's education. Once obtained, other uses are almost always also found for the technology, but the question remains: would the characteristics of the PC and of the people involved in its adoption have been identified by a diffusion model?

Grint and Woolgar (1997) contend that most views of technology attribute an essential inner core of technical characteristics to the non-human elements, while portraying the human elements as secondary and transitory. Objecting to any implicit endowment of inherent properties in the technology, they propose that many other factors, including our attitudes towards technology, our conceptions of what technology can and cannot do, and the various ways in which technology is represented in the media and in organizations, need to be taken into account in order to understand this impact. They contend that contemporary ideas of technology often still rely on the idea of an essential capacity within a technological entity which accounts for its degree of acceptance or rejection–the concept of 'a god within the machine'–and argue for an anti-essentialist view of technological innovation in which technology is attributed no influence that can be gauged independent of human explanation. This philosophical stance is taken up in actor-network theory by the innovation translation model.

Actor-Network Theory: The Sociology of Translations

Rather than recognizing in advance the essences of humans and of social organizations and distinguishing their actions from the inanimate behavior of technological and natural objects, ANT adopts an anti-essentialist position in which it rejects there being some difference in essence between humans and non-humans. ANT considers both social and technical determinism to be flawed and proposes instead a socio-technical account (Callon & Latour, 1981; Latour, 1986; Law & Callon, 1988) in which neither social nor technical positions are privileged. It offers the notion of heterogeneity to describe projects such as the use of a programming language, database management system, barcode scanner, human programmer and operator in the construction of a small business accounting system. To address the need to properly consider the contributions of both human and non-human actors, actor-network theory attempts impartiality towards all actors in consideration, whether human or non-human, and makes no distinction in approach between the social, the natural, and the technological (Callon, 1986b).

In ANT, change results from decisions made by actors and involves the exercise of power. Latour (1986) argues that the mere 'possession' of power by an actor does not automatically confer the ability to cause change unless other actors can be *persuaded* to perform the appropriate actions for this to occur. The notion that power is an attribute that can be *possessed* by an actor is an essentialist one, and Latour contends that rather than this, it is the number of other people who enter into the situation that indicate the amount of power that has been exercised. He maintains that in an innovation translation model, the movement of an innovation through time and space is in the hands of people, each of whom may react to it in different ways. They may accept it, modify it, deflect it, betray it, add to it, appropriate it, or let it drop. In this case the adoption of an innovation comes as a consequence of the actions of everyone in the chain of actors who has anything to do with it. Furthermore, each of these actors shapes the innovation to their own ends, but if no one takes up the innovation then its movement simply stops. Instead of a process of transmission, we have a process of continuous transformation (Latour, 1996), where faithful acceptance involving no changes is a rarity requiring explanation.

McMaster et al. note that innovations do not wait passively to be invented or discovered, but are instead created: "... from chains of weaker to stronger associations of human and non-human alliances. ... Each actant *translates* and contributes its own resources to the shape ..." (McMaster, Vidgen, & Wastell, 1997:4) of the innovation.

The key to innovation is the creation of a powerful enough consortium of actors to carry it through, and when an innovation fails to be taken up, this can be considered to reflect on the inability of those involved to construct the necessary network of alliances among the other actors. Getting an innovation accepted calls for strategies aimed at the enrollment of others.

Mechanisms of Translation in an Actor-Network

An actor-network is configured (Grint & Woolgar, 1997) by the enroll-ment of both human and non-human allies, and this is done by means of a series of negotiations in a process of re-definition in which one set of actors seeks to impose definitions and roles on others (Callon, 1986b). Translation can be regarded as a means of obliging some entity to consent to a 'detour' (Callon, 1986a) that takes it along a path determined by some other entity.

The process of translation has four aspects or 'moments' (Callon, 1986b), the first of which is known as *problematization*. In this stage, a group of one or more key actors attempts to define the nature of the problem and the roles of other actors so that these key actors are seen as having the answer, and being indispensable to the solution of the problem. In other words, the problem is re-defined (translated) in terms of solutions offered by these actors (Bloomfield & Best, 1992).

The second moment is *interessement* and is a series of processes that attempt to impose the identities and roles defined in the problematization on the other actors. It means interesting and attracting an entity by coming between it and some other entity (Law, 1986). Here the enrollers attempt to lock the other actors into the roles proposed for them (Callon, 1986b) and to gradually dissolve existing networks, replacing them by a network created by the enrollers themselves. If the interessement is successful, then the third moment, *enrollment*, will follow through a process of coercion, seduction, or consent (Grint & Woolgar, 1997), leading to the establishment of a solid, stable network of alliances. Enrollment, however, involves more than just one set of actors imposing their will on others; it also requires these others to yield (Singleton & Michael, 1993). Finally *mobilization* occurs as the proposed solution gains wider acceptance and an even larger network of absent entities is created (Grint & Woolgar, 1997) through some actors acting as spokespersons for others.

To illustrate how this mechanism operates, consider the case of a small business deciding whether, or how, to make use of the combination of mobile phone technology and the World Wide Web (mCommerce). There are many different possible problematizations of Web use, ranging from travel bookings, genealogy, and email to advertising and business-to-business eCommerce applications. A problematization that will interest one small business and lead to adoption of this technology may not interest another. Suppose that a small business is thinking in terms of business-to-business mCommerce, an innovation translation model would then look at how this Web and mobile phone problematization began to convince the actors involved with the business of its advantages over other ways of doing business (interessement). The business may then be enrolled, and work to mobilize this technology and widen the network by enrolling others.

INNOVATION TRANSLATION COMPARED WITH INNOVATION DIFFUSION

Latour (1986) remarks that instead of seeing *transmission* of the same token which may perhaps have been slightly deflected or slowed down, the translation model posits the continuous *transformation* of this token into new forms by all those who touch it. The essentialist tenets of innovation diffusion–that there is some property in the innovation, the society, or the potential adopter that facilitates diffusion–differs radically from the translation view in which it is the potential adopters who hold the key in their actions.

There are occasions when diffusion does not occur despite the excellence of the idea or the technical quality of the innovation, and the diffusion model finds these difficult to explain. The non-diffusion of the Dvorak keyboard is just such an example and Rogers (1995) suggests that the Dvorak keyboard failed, despite its 'obvious superiority' over the QWERTY keyboard, because of 'vested interests' supporting its rival. Actor-network theory, on the other hand, would argue that the Dvorak keyboard was not adopted because there were just too many things attached to use of the QWERTY keyboard; it had too many associations to make it feasible for the Dvorak keyboard to un-attach them.

Consider the adoption of a PC-based mailing system for postal distributing of advertising material by a small business. An innovation diffusion approach would, in outline, begin with a consideration of the characteristics of a PC-based mailing system including its ease of use, its functionality, its compatibility with the old manual system used before, and so on, and how these characteristics might help or hinder its adoption. It would then look at the channels through which information about the innovation reached the small business: the business press, university or training courses or friends from other companies, and how effective these were in delivering the message. Next it would consider aspects of the 'culture' of the small business: things like whether it was a family business, how much money it was prepared to spend, and the type of work it does.

On the other hand, innovation translation would concentrate on issues of network formation. It would investigate the human and non-human alliances and networks built up by the small business, their customers, the technology, and other actors involved in the implementation. It would concentrate on the negotiations that allow the network to be configured by the enrolment of both human and non-human allies, and would consider the mailing system's characteristics only as network effects resulting from association. Actor-network theory would suggest that it is not any innate properties of these systems that are important, but rather network associations such as the extent to which the business has been enrolled in the time-saving possibilities of the new system. It would look at the process of re-definition in which the small business tried to seek compromises from the mailing system, and how this system sought to impose on them definitions of mailing, and how advertising material should be addressed; how it 'interested' the business and then got them to follow its interests, so becoming indispensable to them. What is finally adopted for this task is not the mailing system originally examined as such, but a translation of this in which it becomes a tool for their particular business use.

Another situation in which innovation translation appears to offer ex-planatory advantages over a diffusion model is in the employment of IT consultants by some small businesses. IT consultants are employed for a variety of reasons, but the most common include advice on the choice of hardware, software, and implementation. Although innovation diffusion would see these consultants as 'change agents,' and attempt to apply attributes of successful change agents in judging the likely outcome, I would argue that translation offers a more plausible explanation of their influence.

In a translation model consultants are seen as new actors who offer different problematizations of the small business situation, and so act to destabilize existing networks. They bring their influence to bear by offering interessements in which the new technologies are seen to offer better ways of solving problems than the existing alternatives.

Example: Adoption of a Slide Scanner by a Small Publishing Company

To illustrate the use of the two innovation models, consider the case of DP Pty Ltd–a small publishing company where four people work on the publication of information systems and computing textbooks. DP is very small business with a relatively low turnover, but a well-established market. Members of the company do much of the writing, and all of the work involved in publication of their books, but then send their work off to an outside printer for printing and binding. Most of DP's print runs are quite small and so the company makes use of a printer with access to Xerox printing technology rather than the more traditional offset printing. All those involved in the work of the company are highly computer literate and make good use of information technology. None of them, however, has much knowledge of computer graphics. The company is well known to the author of this chapter.

Several years ago the company decided it needed to improve the appearance of the covers on its new textbooks, and several options were considered until someone thought of using a photograph as the cover background. The brother of one of the directors is a professional landscape photographer and he was able to provide a suitable color photograph for the next book to be published. The photograph was supplied in print form, and a problem arose in how to convert the photograph (or its negative) into a suitable format to print on the cover along with the cover text. A digital image seemed to be the answer. The photograph was scanned (using a flat-bed scanner), the image imported into Adobe PhotoShop for cropping and editing, and the digital image inserted into Microsoft Word so that text could easily be added. The final result was then converted into an Acrobat file and sent off to the printer for printing along with the contents of the book. This process, however, proved to be quite a lot of bother.

Today the company makes use of a Nikon slide and negative scanner, considerably improving the quality of the covers, but also making the process of producing them much simpler. This device is capable of producing digital images of slides, negatives, and APS (Advanced Photo System) film at various resolutions, and of manipulating these images in many different ways. The question is: why did DP decide to adopt this particular item of technology?

Consider first the application of a diffusion model. Using a diffusion explanation the company would have been mainly influenced by attributes and characteristics of the technology itself. The directors would have considered the relative advantage, compatibility, complexity, trialability, and observability of this technology compared with the alternatives of using a flat-bed scanner, getting an outside printer to do the scanning, or not using a cover of this type at all. As the second and third alternatives were seen as undesirable by the company and only suitable as fall-back positions, I will consider just the first alternative. Two of the directors of the company certainly did see some relative advantage in using the slide scanner, particularly as they both had large numbers of color slides that they had taken over the years. There was, however, one major disadvantage of this technology and that was its high cost: the slide scanner was around four times as expensive as a good flat-bed scanner. The slide scanner also did not come out well on compatibility or complexity as it was quite different, and much more complex to use than the flat-bed scanner alternative. It was possible for the company to arrange trial use of the scanner, which was lucky as it had proved difficult to find anyone else using one and so its observability was low. On this basis it is difficult to see why DP would have adopted the slide scanner at all.

It is interesting then to look at how DP learned about this innovation. When the need to digitize cover images was initially identified, the first reaction of the directors was to consider the purchase of a digital camera. They were dissuaded after discussions with the landscape photographer who suggested that the cost of this technology was too high (at that time) if adequate quality was to be maintained. He showed them a magazine article describing slide and negative scanners and suggested that, although he had no personal experience of using this technology, a device like this might provide a better solution. The main communication channel by which the company found out about the technology was thus interpersonal rather than mass media and, at first sight, this seems to fit well with a diffusion explanation in which interpersonal channels of communication are regarded as the most influential for adoption decisions. Further investigation, however, highlighted that the photographer had just pointed out the possibility of using this technology: he did not endorse it or attempt to persuade them of its advantages as the diffusion model would suggest.

When a translation model is applied, the situation is seen quite differently. The socio-technical network consisting of the publishing company personnel, their computers, and their books was destabilized by the need to find a new way of producing book covers. The addition of a new actor, the landscape photographer, introduced new possibilities that worked to further destabilize this network. The slide scanner (also seen as an actor seeking to enter the network) offered a new problematization in which existing (and future) slides and negatives could easily be turned into digital images. Part of this problematization was that *any* of the directors' old slides could easily be turned into digital images, not just those required for book covers. As well as the main application of producing book covers, both directors quickly saw advantages in a device that could also easily convert the old slides and negatives they had each taken of their children and of their holidays into digital format; this seemed to provide a good alternative to their aging slide projectors, and produced a strong interessement in favor of this technology and against flat-bed scanners and slide projectors. It was thus a combination of factors, some business-related and others rather more personal, that the translation modes suggests could be seen as leading to the enrollment of this technology and hence its adoption.

It should also be pointed out that a significant translation occurred from the slide scanner advertised by Nikon in the magazine article and on their Web page to the device adopted by the publishing company. DP was not interested in using the scanner in all the ways that Nikon offered, and was not interested in using all of its features. The company wanted a device to digitize slides and negatives for two reasons: the easy creation of attractive book covers, and the conversion of their own color slides into a format that could easily be displayed on a video monitor. They did not adopt the scanner advertised by Nikon, but a device for creating book covers and formatting their slides for video display.

CONCLUSION

The translation approach to innovation details the construction of networks and alliances to support and embed changes in order to make them durable. Innovation diffusion and innovation translation are based on quite different philosophies, one stressing the properties of the innovation and the change agent and routed in essentialism, and the other emphasizing negotiations and network formation.

I contended that in the study of technological innovation in small business, an innovation translation approach has more to offer than innovation diffusion in providing a useful explanation of the process of change. It has more to offer as it provides a method of highlighting those aspects of the innovation that actually influenced the adoption decisions, and not just those identified by someone as being 'important' attributes or characteristics of the technology. The question is: important to whom? Innovation translation identifies this shortcoming of diffusion theory and offers, I believe, a better way of visualizing the innovation process as it occurs in a small business.

Innovation translation is more attuned to the human and political issues involved in small business decision making, and so offers a useful approach to modeling innovation in small business. Although most current writings on technology uptake and innovation employ either no theoretical model at all, or else use a diffusion model, I suggest that future research should further investigate the use of a translation model to explain the adoption of information technology in small business. I would encourage future researchers to consider this approach.

REFERENCES

Berlyne, D. E. (1962). Uncertainty and epistemic curiosity. *British Journal of Psychology*, 53, 27-34.

Bloomfield, B. P. and Best, A. (1992). Management consultants: Systems development, power and the translation of problems. *The Sociological Review*, 40(3), 533-560.

Burgess, S., Tatnall, A. and Darbyshire, P. (1999). Teaching small business entrepreneurs about computers. Paper presented at *EuroPME–Entrepreneurship: Building for the Future*, September 30-October 2, Rennes, France.

Callon, M. (1986a). The sociology of an actor-network: The case of the electric vehicle. In Callon, M., Law, J. and Rip, A. (Eds.), *Mapping the Dynamics of Science and Technology*, 19-34. London: Macmillan Press.

Callon, M. (1986b). Some elements of a sociology of translation: Domestication of the scallops and the fishermen of St. Brieuc Bay. In Law, J. (Ed.), *Power, Action & Belief. A New Sociology of Knowledge?* 196-229. London: Routledge & Kegan Paul.

Callon, M. and Latour, B. (1981). Unscrewing the Big Leviathan: How actors macro-structure reality and how sociologists help them to do so. In Knorr-Cetina, K. and Cicourel, A. V. (Eds.), *Advances in Social Theory and Methodology Toward an Integration of Micro- and Macro-Sociologies*, 277-303. London: Routledge & Kegan Paul.

Deutschmann, P. J. and Fals Borda, O. (1962). *Communication and Adoption Patterns in an Andean Village (Report)*. San Jose, Costa Rica: Programa Interamericano de Informacion Popular.

Grint, K. and Woolgar, S. (1997). *The Machine at Work–Technology, Work and Organization*. Cambridge, MA: Polity Press.

Guzman-Cuevas, J. and Santos-Cumplido, F. J. (1999). A theoretical approach to the quality of the entrepreneur: An application to the Province of Seville. Paper presented at *EuroPME–Entrepreneurship: Building for the Future*, September 30-October 2, Rennes, France.

Latour, B. (1986). The powers of association. In Law, J. (Ed.), *Power, Action and Belief. A New Sociology of Knowledge? Sociological Review Monograph*, 32, 264-280. London: Routledge & Kegan Paul.

Latour, B. (1996). *Aramis or the Love of Technology*. Cambridge, MA: Harvard University Press.

Law, J. (1986). The heterogeneity of texts. In Callon, M., Law, J. and Rip, A. (Eds.), *Mapping the Dynamics of Science and Technology*, 67-83. UK: Macmillan Press.

Law, J. (1992). Notes on the theory of the actor-network: Ordering, strategy and heterogeneity. *Systems Practice*, 5(4), 379-393.

Law, J. and Callon, M. (1988). Engineering and sociology in a military aircraft project: A network analysis of technological change. *Social Problems*, 35(3), 284-297.

Machiavelli, N. (1995). *The Prince* (Bull, George, Trans.). London: Penguin Classics.

Macquarie Library. (1981). *The Macquarie Dictionary*. Sydney, Australia: Macquarie Library.

McMaster, T., Vidgen, R. T. and Wastell, D. G. (1997). Towards an understanding of technology in transition. Two conflicting theories. Paper presented at the *Information Systems Research in Scandinavia, IRIS20 Conference*, August 9-12, Hanko, Norway.

Nystrom, H. (1999). Creativity and entrepreneurship: An integrated economic and psychological approach. Paper presented at *EuroPME–Entrepreneurship: Building for the Future*, September 30-October 2, Rennes, France.

Oxford. (1973). *The Shorter Oxford English Dictionary* (3rd Ed.). Oxford: Clarendon Press.

Rogers, E. M. (1995). *Diffusion of Innovations* (4th Ed.). New York: The Free Press.

Singleton, V. and Michael, M. (1993). Actor-networks and ambivalence: General practitioners in the UK cervical screening program. *Social Studies of Science*, 23, 227-264.

Tatnall, A. and Gilding, A. (1999). Actor-network theory and information systems research. Paper presented at the *10th Australasian Conference on Information Systems (ACIS)*, Wellington.

Chapter VI

Unique Challenges for Small Business Adoption of Information Technology: The Case of the Nova Scotia Ten

M. Gordon Hunter
University of Lethbridge, Canada

Monica Diochon, David Pugsley and Barry Wright
St. Francis Xavier University, Canada

INTRODUCTION

The global nature of product and service markets, technology and competition has increased business requirements for flexibility, quality, cost-effectiveness and timeliness. As a key resource for meeting these requirements, information technology (IT) has been revolutionizing business practice. While there has been considerable research into the way in which large businesses use this technology, there has been far less attention paid to the adoption of information technology among small businesses. This is surprising considering that the innovative capacity of a nation's economy to meet changing demands in the global economy has been linked to the flexibility and responsiveness of small businesses.

According to Berman (1997), improvements in both IT and communication equipment have been a major contributor to the growth of small businesses. Indeed, the small business sector represents an important component in the Canadian economy. For example, there are over 2.3 million small businesses with fewer than 100 employees, accounting for over 50% of the private sector employment and for 43% of total economic output (Industry Canada, 1997). In viewing the small business sector as a catalyst to faster economic growth (Balderson, 2000), governments have been attempting to offer financial and nonfinancial programs to assist small businesses (Smith, 1984). Yet, without a better understanding of the use of IT among small businesses, there will be little basis for developing effective programs.

If research is to contribute to a better understanding of this issue, it is important to recognize the differences in business practice between small and large firms. Evidence suggests that some of these key differences often get overlooked when it comes to IT research. For example, Cragg and King (1993) note that much of the research into the use of IT among small firms aims to confirm findings from studies set in large firms. Arguably, if the IT needs of small businesses are to be better understood and served, it is important to explore how the unique aspects of small business practice might impact on this sector's use of IT.

This issue is important to several stakeholders. First, it is important to small businesses themselves that aim to use IT to gain a competitive advantage. Second, it is important to IT consultants whose aim it is to help small businesses add value through the use of IT. Third, it is important to vendors who aim to target this burgeoning market by being better able to service its needs. Finally, it is important to government policymakers in their effort to support the growth of the small business sector through the use of IT.

The objective of the research reported here is to document and explore the unique issues faced by small businesses regarding the adoption of information technology. Generally, the term small business is used to describe an economic reality (Kao, 1989). However, there is considerable variation in the criteria used to define this reality. For example, ACOA (1996) uses the number of employees, Statistics Canada uses annual revenue, while other federal departments (Government of Canada, 1985) define a small business by the size of investment. For the purposes of our investigation, a small business is defined as an owner-managed independent firm with less than 100 employees. Indeed this criterion is the one most widely used (Longnecker, Moore & Petty, 1997).

The chapter begins with a discussion of how small businesses and large businesses differ. This section will indicate those factors that make small business practice unique and contribute to the distinct way small businesses consider information technology adoption. The following section will report on the currently available literature regarding research into small business adoption of information technology. Next, the research method and project will be presented. Then a discussion is included regarding the findings of the research project. This discussion will be presented relative to the major themes, which have been identified as emerging from the data gathered during interviews with the 10 small business managers. Subsequently, a series of recommendations will be made for the major stakeholder groups. Finally, some general conclusions will be presented regarding information technology adoption by small businesses.

UNIQUE CHARACTERISTICS OF SMALL BUSINESS

In presenting our definition of a small business, the previous section highlights many factors that could be employed to differentiate small business from large business, including revenue, capital investment or number of employees. However, to gain insight into the adoption of information technology, it is more appropriate to explore this issue as it relates to business practice. Stevenson (1999) provides a useful conceptualization by considering business practice along a continuum ranging from a 'promoter' approach at one end to a 'trustee' approach at the other.

As outlined in Table 1, the strategic orientation of 'promoters' involves pursuing opportunities without regard to resources they control, while 'trustees' are concerned with the efficient use of existing resources. Indeed, managers of innovative small firms, commonly referred to as entrepreneurs, tend to be oriented toward the 'promoter' end of the spectrum. In contrast, managers of large businesses, often noted for their administrative capacity, tend to have a 'trustee' orientation.

One key aspect of business practice concerns the use of resources. With a 'promoter' approach to management, resource commitments are multi-

Table 1: Approaches to business practices

ASPECTS OF BUSINESS PRACTICE	PROMOTER ◄————————►	TRUSTEE
Strategic orientation	Capitalize on an opportunity	Focus on efficient use of current resources to determine the greatest return
Resource commitment and control decisions	Act in a very short timeframe	Long timeframe, considering long-term implications
	Multi-staged	One-time, up-front commitment
	Minimum commitment of resources at each stage	Large-scale commitment of resources at one stage
	Respond quickly to changes in competition, market and technology	Formal procedures of analysis such as capital allocation systems

staged in nature. In aiming to use the minimum possible amount of resources, the concern is with controlling rather than owning the resources needed to pursue business goals. In contrast, a 'trustee' approach typically involves a single-stage, one-time commitment of resources, with the ownership of required resources a key concern.

In general, when a 'promoter' approach is adopted in relation to resources, this reduces risk and/or increases flexibility in a number of ways (Stevenson, 1984): the amount of *capital* required is smaller, therefore reducing the financial exposure and dilution of the owner's equity; it reduces the risk of obsolescence; a lack of resource ownership increases the firm's flexibility and speed of response to market opportunities; and fixed costs are lowered, thus favorably affecting breakeven. Although variable costs might rise, if the product or service has a high gross margin, it will likely be able to absorb this rise.

As one of many resources a business might use, information technology typically involves not only a significant investment of effort, time and capital, it can also be a potentially high maintenance activity. On the one hand, when viewed in terms of a company's flexibility, such an investment could pose a serious constraint when it demands a permanent commitment to a certain technology or software. On the other hand, such an investment has tremendous potential to increase the speed at which business can respond to customers and market opportunities.

SMALL BUSINESS ADOPTION OF INFORMATION TECHNOLOGY

Research undertaken by Lin et al. (1993) determined that the deregulation of the telecommunications industry would allow more small businesses to compete with large businesses. It was felt that the impending widespread use of the Internet would make E-commerce concepts more attractive to small business. Beyond these technologies, research (Berman, 1997; Canadian Federation of Independent Business, 1999) also found that momentum for the adoption of information technology by small businesses came from a number of sources. First, small businesses were reacting to actions of competition in adopting information technology. Second, because of the aforementioned deregulation and the prevalent use of information technology, the cost to implement was becoming within the reach of small businesses. Third, the technology was becoming more reliable and powerful. Fourth, small businesses started to see the adoption of information technology as a way to compete with larger companies (Timmons, 1999).

Although some studies (Bridge & Peel, 1999; Fuller, 1996) have found small and medium sized firms (SMEs) are using IT mainly for operational and administrative tasks, others (Bennett & McCoshan, 1993; Chen & Williams, 1993; Pollard & Hayne, 1998; Timmons, 1999; Van de Ven, 1993) suggest IT is playing a more strategic role. These somewhat conflicting results suggest that the extent to which small businesses are utilizing information technology for strategic purposes is unclear. Indeed, much of the research that has been conducted relates mainly to *plans* small businesses have with regard to IT. For example, El Louadi (1998) found that small businesses were prepared to invest more resources in information technology. However, the nature of the actual investment is not clear. Thus, the research reported below investigates *how* the technology is currently being employed by small businesses.

RESEARCH METHOD

To gain an understanding of how small businesses use IT, it is necessary to adopt methods that allow research participants to talk about their perceptions and processes and what their experiences mean to them (Gartner et al., 1992). This study therefore employed an interpretive approach based upon a qualitative research methodology. Where quantitative approaches traditionally isolate, define and determine the relationship of variables to each other prior to collecting the data, qualitative approaches serve to isolate and define categories during the data collection process. Since a qualitative approach allows the researcher to examine a much wider range of relationships than would be practical using a quantitative approach (Bryman, 1988), it was judged the most appropriate, given the exploratory nature of the area under investigation. Specifically, we adopted grounded theory as a theoretical guide. Grounded theory was developed as a data-driven analysis method to support the gathering of research participants' interpretation of reality in social situations (Glaser & Strauss, 1967). In this case the domain of discourse relates to the specific small business manager and the adoption of information technology.

Research participants were identified as small businesses (owner-managed independent firms with less than 100 employees), which had been in operation for at least five years within the Canadian province of Nova Scotia. In our sample the mean organizational size was 28 full-time employees; the smallest organization had eight employees while the largest had 96 full-time employees. A 'purposeful sample' (Lincoln & Guba, 1985) of 10 small businesses was selected. This selection was based on recommendations from professionals providing either IT or business advisory services. Because prior knowledge is required to select cases exemplifying IT 'best practice,' these professionals were found to have the most reliable knowledge of the business community. Care was taken to ensure sufficient variety regarding business sectors and geographic regions within the province.

Initial contact was made with each small business by contacting the person who was identified as the 'owner.' Approval was obtained from this person to proceed with interviewing one individual within the organization who the owner considered the most knowledgeable of the small business's information technology operations. It is interesting to note that all small business owners and information technology representatives agreed to participate in the project and the interviews. This agreement not only indicates a willingness to contribute to the objectives of the research project, but also serves to indicate the high level of importance these individuals attribute to information technology within the context of small business.

The interview technique was based upon McCracken's (1988) 'long interview technique.' This technique allows research participants to reflect upon the domain of discourse in a relatively unbiased and free-flowing manner. McCracken suggests two main types of questions for the interview technique. First, 'grand tour' questions are asked, which are general and non-directive and allow the research participant to specify the substance of the response. Second, 'planned prompt' questions may be asked near the end of the interview, which allows the researcher to delve into subjects gleaned from the literature. On average the interviews lasted about 40 minutes. Each interview was taped with the permission of the research participant and the guarantee that the firm's identity would not be revealed. The interviews were transcribed and the transcriptions were analyzed to identify emerging themes.

Each author reviewed the resulting transcripts. The data were investigated to identify emerging themes, first within a specific interview and then across a number of interviews. This identification of emerging themes is a common approach to analyzing qualitative interview data (Miles & Huberman, 1994). The process involves a continual interaction between the data and the emerging themes. Further, in this case, the interplay was extended to include discussions and reflections among the researchers. Eventually, a consensus was achieved concerning the interpretation of the interview data relative to the identification of emerging themes.

RESULTS

The results of the interviews and subsequent analysis of the data suggests the adoption of information technology by small businesses present many challenges. Two major themes emerged from the interview data: dependency and efficiency. The discussion that follows is not meant to indicate a relative level of importance of these two themes. Indeed, the relative importance would be contingent upon the situation unique to each small business. In order to elaborate upon each theme, quotations from the interview transcripts are employed and respondents are identified as R-1 through R-10. This process again reflects the method suggested by Miles and Huberman (1994) which recommends the continual interplay between the data and the emerging themes.

Theme 1: Dependency

The adoption of information technology increased dependency within the businesses. It was determined from the interview data that dependency related to either reliance on an internal individual (network administrator or information technology champion) or an external entity (consultants, customers, suppliers, competitors). The increase in dependency tends to increase the risk to the firm as noted in the discussion of the findings, which follow.

Internal Dependency

In response to how decisions are made to add new IT– *"As far as that goes, that's XXXXX's side of things and she would look into that."*
From one employee– *"I handle all of that (IT), I keep things going."*

In most of the firms interviewed, an internal 'champion' or key information technology employee was responsible for the majority of information technology usage, upgrades and maintenance. Previous research (Montazemi, 1988; Thong et al., 1994) has shown that internal expertise in information systems is preferred to external for small firms. However, respondents in the current study noted inhibitors such as high salaries and limited need for internal expertise to be problems. In the majority of the firms interviewed, the internal 'champion' tended to be an individual who took on the role as an ancillary task since a full-time individual could not be justified. In one instance, an administrative assistant had taken some upgrading courses to allow performance of basic network administration, while in another firm a full-time engineer would spend a day or more per week dealing with information technology issues and administration.

It may be surmised that information technology is seen as an ancillary task, related primarily to administration decisions. Consequently, it may receive sub-optimal attention by the owner in a busy work environment. This organizational structure may reduce the effectiveness of information technology in the firm but, as importantly, it makes the owner very dependent upon staff regarding the design and operation of the information system. The typical reliance on one individual (in our findings this was rarely the owner/manager) increases the risk to the firm if that individual were to leave. Being placed in this precarious position presents a challenge to the owner/manager's self-reliance. Much of the success enjoyed by small businesses stems from the owner/manager's knowledge, skills and/or abilities in the specific area of operation or activity. If information technology begins to play a key role in the operation of the business, it may mean that the owner/manager no longer has intimate knowledge of all aspects of the business.

External Dependency

In most instances, the decision regarding hardware or software applications tended to be based upon the advice or influence of a competitor, customer, supplier or outside consultant. There was little evidence to indicate that a systematic assessment was made of how well the available offerings could meet the business's specific needs as described by R-1 and R-6 respectively:

"We had some learning curves. We went to a co-ax system...and discovered that it didn't work the best...There was some software that we probably had bought that we thought we would use and we didn't use it either because it wasn't the application we thought it was or was hard to use, for whatever reason."

"If somebody comes in with something and really proves to us that it's going to really make changes or pay for itself or we can justify it, it's pretty well instantly approved."

The use of a particular information technology application by a major competitor often made it necessary, as interpreted by the manager, for the small business to follow suit in order to retain the current customer base or potentially attract new business as explained by R-2 and R-3 respectively:

"One of our major customers adopted [ABC] software on a trial basis. The cost was $15,000 for us so we hoped to put off the investment until [Client C] had finalized their decision. Soon after we found out that [Competitor A who did similar work for the client] had purchased the software and was in the process of training. We didn't have much choice unless we wanted to risk losing [Client C]."

"Our competitors are doing the same thing. They were starting to do it [using the software for remote sales demonstrations] and we started doing it a lot more."

This illustrates a dependency on information technology which can result in risky expenditures. Previous research has concluded that competitive forces had little effect on the adoption or extent of use of information technology in small firms (Thong et al., 1994). However, our research suggests that in at least some small firms, competition is driving information technology adoption.

Pressure from customers often resulted in a similar situation as R1 describes:

> *"We're pretty much following what they [customers] need. Our software typically matches theirs, maybe one step ahead... Certainly sometimes the decisions are made for us. Like when [Client A] said, we're now using [X] as software...and we suggest you use it as well. As they're an important client, we would hear them. We would buy that..."*

For many small firms, the adoption of information technology is perceived to be a necessity in order to maintain relations with suppliers as explained by R-6 and R-7:

> *"... they [suppliers] really depend on the Internet for delivering service. We're missing out on that right now...I think the Internet's going to help us an awful lot..."*

> *"Our suppliers required us to do it."*

In several instances the firms had made significant capital expenditures in order to maintain supply chain relationships and not risk the loss of major customers.

Previous research has suggested that information technology provides the ability to "compete on a more equal footing with large organizations through leveraging gains IT offers" (Pollard & Hayne, 1998). However, our research identified only one firm–R-3–that was capitalizing on this opportunity:

> *"It levels the playing field for us...But now with IT we can send out our message with email and design just as nice a Web page [as a large company can...] We can look like a large multi-site location and still operate on the size of our budget...Sometimes it's hard to believe where we win some of the jobs because five or 10 years ago we would have never gotten in touch with those people."*

Generally, there was little evidence that the key decision-makers were fully aware of the scope of products available and the extent to which product performance might vary in meeting a specific business need. Moreover, in no case was there any long-term information technology strategy. On the one hand, this could be viewed as a weakness, but on the other it could be viewed as a way to increase the firm's capacity to respond to customer needs. Since small business owner/managers were found to either contract out or delegate responsibility for maintaining the information system or determining future requirements, they are very dependent upon the quality of the advice they receive from others. In some instances this advice may not lead to the optimal decision for the business. For example, respondent R-9 describes his choice of accounting package:

"Our accountant recommended [X] accounting package a few years ago because that is what he used. We thought it would be easiest if we went with the same package, so we had it installed a short while later ...It works pretty well for us although it has some limitations that we weren't aware of and [our secretary] does a lot of extra work on spreadsheets to keep track of all of the information we need."

The limitations of the software in this example are the lack of a job-costing module in the software for an engineering firm that has hundreds of jobs in progress at any given time. A number of suitable alternative software packages are available within the price range, but the owner was not aware of a single alternative software package. This example is consistent with the findings of Thong et al. (1994) that small businesses tend to overestimate external consultants' ability to achieve information technology success and underestimate the requirement for information technology awareness by key decision-makers within the firm.

Overall, dependency of small firms in relation to information technology seems to be widespread as discussed in this section. As stated, the dependency itself is not completely negative, as it allows the small business to focus on its niche. However, failure to ensure adequate knowledge of information technology and at least some strategic vision does cause the risks inherent in these dependency relationships to become greater.

Theme 2: Efficiency

Despite all the technological advances and calls for the strategic use of information technology by small business (Pollard & Hayne, 1998), it is still being employed primarily at the transactional/operational level. The findings of this research project suggest very little strategic use of information technology, as small business managers were primarily interested in using information technology as an operational tool. This term is referred to in this document as efficiency, indicating that small businesses are still focused on getting things done as opposed to effectiveness or doing the right things. Information technology effectiveness is defined as the extent to which a given information system contributes to the achievement of organizational goals (Bridge and Peel, 1999; Thong

For the majority of small businesses, the key benefit from information technology is the reduction of resources required to perform operational tasks–

accounting, design, inventory management, invoicing, estimating and marketing/sales as explained by R-4, R-6 and R1 respectively:

> " ... *the accounting... It would take two of us the whole weekend and until Wednesday of the next week to do that. Now, it's there all the time. Two people, five days work is freed up.*"

> "*Our invoicing and time-keeping and inventory and all that are done by computer.*"

> "*There are two main areas of [IT use]. One would be production [drafting] and the other is the communications area [email].*"

Overall, the research participants reported obtaining considerable time and cost savings as reported by R-6:

> "*It could take you a day or two or more by hand... this way, you can get up and running very quickly, it's cheaper for the customer and you can get more work out and get the job done quicker.*"

Generally, these efficiencies have been gained in response to specific needs or problems encountered in daily operations and not as a result of a deliberate search for an information system that could integrate all facets of the business. R-6 describes the firm's information technology decision-making as follows:

> "*I would think any upgrades are going to be on an as-needed basis...It was a situation where our old software was no longer going to be upgraded. And this new software came along with a very good deal to switch and that's what we did.*"

Interestingly, while Pollard and Hayne (1998) reported that the number one issue facing Canadian small businesses was 'using information technology for competitive advantage,' our findings suggest that this view of employing information technology is different from what is transpiring. Although the majority of respondents indicated they were pleased with the results of their information technology expenditures, there was no indication of plans to capitalize on the benefits of information technology more broadly in other areas of the firm. It could be, as suggested by others (Thong et al., 1994), that 'resource poverty' is the overriding factor in this situation. Resource poverty refers to a lack of financial and human resources in small businesses. Resource poverty combined with the action-oriented nature of small business owners would result in focusing on the most critical areas first (transactional and operational to capture data) and not having the resources or desire to take the project further. Cragg and King (1993) found these parameters tend to limit the rate of computerization in small businesses.

Alternatively, the general absence of strategic information technology deployment might be explained by the nature of resource commitments made in small firms. Arguably, if information technology were to be deployed to all functional areas of a firm, this would involve a large, one-time commitment of financial and other resources (for example, training of personnel). While such an investment is consistent with the business practices of large firms, it is not characteristic of the way in which resource commitments are made by small firms. As indicated previously, our findings support the contention that small businesses tend to make minimal and multi-staged commitments. Arguably, large, one-time commitments may make it difficult to use information technology strategically, as the rapid changes in hardware and software applications could render incremental implementation virtually impossible. Moreover, it is possible that the current under-utilization of information technology for strategic advantage may result from owner/managers not having the experience or knowledge base to be able to fully recognize opportunities for doing so. Clearly, in order to shift from a focus on efficiency to that of effectiveness, the challenges associated with committing resources to information technology will need to be dealt with. The next section contains suggestions that attempt to address this situation.

RECOMMENDED STAKEHOLDER RESPONSES

In light of the emerging themes identified above, it is evident that the nature of small business practice presents some unique challenges in regard to the adoption of information technology. This section presents a number of recommendations for various stakeholders–small business managers, consultants, vendors and government–intent on increasing the strategic use of information technology within the small business sector. These suggestions take into consideration the themes identified in this research project and data gleaned from other sources.

Small Business Manager

In light of the characteristics of small business practice, the following suggestions relate to making decisions and obtaining advice.

First, to overcome the limitations of being dependent upon others' expertise, for information technology to be successfully leveraged, the owner/manager needs to gain an understanding of information technology in much the same way as (s)he needs to have an understanding of financial statements. While there is no need to know how to prepare financial statements, a basic understanding of what these statements mean is required for sound financial decision-making. Similarly, while an owner/manager does not need to know how to design or develop information technology, (s)he does need to understand how the technology might be used as a key resource in adding value to the firm's core business products or services.

Unlike large firms where managerial knowledge tends to be specialized in a particular area, a small business owner/manager is a generalist with intimate knowledge of the various areas of the firm. Clearly this knowledge could not be gained without an open attitude to learning. However, since small business managers typically use informal rather than formal means of learning, it is important to ensure that enough credible sources are accessed to acquire a level of understanding that is appropriate for the type of business (s)he is in.

Second, the small business manager should establish a relationship with a specific individual regarding a source for advice. The following steps are suggested. To begin, the manager should 'shop around' to find an individual with whom (s)he may feel comfortable working with and taking advice. In order to find this person, the manager should rely upon his or her informal network. Thus individuals could be contacted who are in a similar business sector or who may be using the same technology. Then, it is important to ensure that those contacted in both the informal network and those who will provide the advice do not have a vested interest in a particular product. That is, the small business manager should not rely upon hardware or software vendors alone for advice. The recommendation is for the manager to establish a relationship with someone who is independent of a specific solution and who will be prepared to play a strategic role taking a long-term perspective. Further, the small business manager must re-assess this relationship periodically. It is incumbent upon the manager to review the relationship to ensure that the recommendations being proffered are appropriately contributing to the long-term success of the firm. This advice is consistent with that of Stevenson and Sahlman (in Timmons 1999) who suggest doing two seemingly contradictory things when seeking to hire a consultant: seek out the best advisors, involving them early and more thoroughly than in the past. At the same time, be more sceptical of their credentials and their advice.

In addition, under the dependency theme, since the small firm is very focused on the 'bottom-line,' it would be advisable to avoid being an early adopter of new hardware and/or software applications. Deferring adoption until the hardware and/or software has a proven performance capacity will help minimize financial risk. Unsuccessful forays into the information technology area can be expensive. A recent example, albeit a large company in Nova Scotia, is Sobeys Inc. which abandoned an $89.1 million system due to incompatible application problems (Mearian & Songini, 2001). Thus small business owners may wish to wait to find out whether a particular information technology will add value or just add expense.

One final recommendation, to overcome the focus on efficiency exclusively, small business managers should take a more proactive approach toward the adoption of information technology. This would involve actively seeking out ways to leverage information technology to create or improve products or services offered to customers. While information technology in itself is not a source of competitive advantage, as it is readily available and easily duplicated, the way in which it is utilized may be difficult for other businesses to copy. For example, if the small business provides a very specialized service, it might use the web to collaborate with other firms that provide complementary services but who may be spread out across the country or the globe. By being able to 'bundle' their services, this 'virtual' firm now has a collective capacity to provide an offering that might be difficult for others to match in terms of quality or cost. Because no one firm has to develop and maintain multiple areas of expertise, the overhead is lower and pricing competitive. What this would mean for the individual firm is that it would not be as dependent upon a single (or few) key customers. Such action, therefore, would increase efficiency and effectiveness, as well as the firm's capacity for flexibility and responsiveness to the needs and demands of the market.

Consultants

In facing issues where expertise is lacking, such as those relating to the use of information technology, hiring a consultant is a common practice (Timmons, 1999). However, currently there is little evidence to suggest that consultants fully understand and consider the implications of how business practices vary between small and large firms. For example, Atlantic Progress (Strowbridge, 1999) prepared a feature article where two major consulting firms were commissioned to analyze the operations of two Atlantic Canadian small businesses and recommend technologies that could help the firms accomplish key business objectives. Indeed, their recommendations would require a large-scale commitment of resources at one point in time, which is akin to the resource commitments of large corporations and not in-line with the 'resource poverty' perspective that most small businesses face.

Clearly, it is important for consultants to recognize that in regard to the nature, timing and acquisition of resources, the small businessperson generally aims to minimize the amount of resources used at each stage of the firm's growth. As the findings reported on here indicate, the resources allocated for information technology are consistent with this practice. Since small business people are concerned with being able to use a resource rather than owning it, this suggests there may be opportunities for expanding currently available leasing options. Such an approach could reduce some of the risk in pursuing opportunities. For example, if less capital is required, the financial exposure and risk is reduced. Moreover, it could increase flexibility since commitment and decommitment can be achieved quickly when a resource is not owned.

In aiming to meet the needs of the small business sector, Timmons (1999, p. 331) provides the following advice concerning the desirable qualities in a consultant: "a shirtsleeve approach to the problems, an understanding attitude toward the feelings of managers, a modest and truthful offer of services and an ability to produce results, a reasonable and realistic charge for services, and a willingness to maintain a continuous relationship."

Generally, consultants need to be able to provide opportunities for small businesses to 'phase in' information technology in stages. Doing so will accommodate small business practice and form the foundation for a potentially ongoing relationship.

Vendors

In this context, vendors are regarded as those entities which supply hardware and software to small businesses. The recommendations for this stakeholder group relate to commitment, functionality and decisions.

The first suggestion is that vendors make a visible commitment to small business. Far too often vendors provide products or services based upon a geographic distribution. Vendors should consider the establishment of a more sector-oriented approach. Thus, the establishment of a division or even a separate entity specifically directed at small business is recommended. This act would address, to some extent, the concerns of the small business manager, regarding priority of service. As noted in our introduction, the small business sector is a large and important one; target marketing this sector makes good business sense.

Second, vendors should develop solutions with the functionality of small business in mind. Software vendors must ensure that an application performs the necessary functions for small business. This requires the identification of what the small business does and the interpretation of that into the appropriate functionality of the application. Again, the important word here is 'appropriate.' Thus, it is incumbent upon the vendor to ensure the hardware or software addresses the appropriate functionality of the small business. A solution with too much capacity will not be helpful. A solution which provides an unrequired capability will also not be helpful.

Finally, the vendor representative should investigate who makes or helps make the decisions in the small business. There will be, usually, one individual within the small business who has responsibility for information technology decisions. But, as suggested above, there should also be an advisor (or consultant) who will provide input. Information about proposed solutions also should be supplied to this second individual. Indeed in some cases this person may be the more important decision-maker.

Government

Focusing on the research findings, if government aims to encourage the growth of the small business sector through the use of information technology, they cannot ignore the financial constraints small business faces. Government can help overcome the resource poverty small businesses cope with by providing information technology advice to small businesses and by providing financial incentives.

While Canadian small businesses have been found to use outside professional services, many small businesses report that the fees for this service are excessive (Zinger et al., 1996). As securing advising relationships on information technology is important for the small business owner, providing specific, cost-effective, IT assistance would indeed be a valuable service.

As well, when faced with competing operational needs, tradeoffs are invariably required. If information technology is not perceived to be essential, it is unlikely opportunities to use information technology will be explored. Fundamentally, if government aims to encourage the growth and development of the small business sector, the role of tax and other financial incentives may need to be considered in encouraging both the use of information technology to improve how things are done (efficiency) and what things are done (effectiveness).

Finally, although there are a number of services which have been established to provide support to small business, often they are underutilized by small businesses (Zinger et al., 1996). Therefore, it is recommended that government services be provided on a more pro-active basis. By initiating relationships with small business managers, individuals representing government services can more effectively support these managers by tapping into their informal networks to provide and exchange required information.

CONCLUSIONS

While the findings of this research project indicate that information technology has increased the efficiency of various aspects of daily operations, they also indicate that the capacity of information technology to increase the business's effectiveness was being underutilized. Generally, the evidence suggests that information technology expenditures are being made in reaction to needs or problems.

Based on the in-depth experiences of 10 businesses, the results of this investigation indicate that the current use of information technology follows a pattern that is very consistent with the way in which other resources are used by small businesses. There was little evidence of a willingness or ability to make a large, one-time financial commitment to integrate information technology into all aspects of the firm. Arguably, even if a firm had the financial wherewithal to make such a commitment, doing so would compromise the flexibility and responsiveness that is the hallmark of the small business sector. While further research is needed before these results could be generalized, they do suggest that the greatest challenge associated with the adoption of information technology presents itself not to the small business sector, but to its constituents–consultants, vendors and government.

If the aim is to support the growth and development of the small business sector, then the onus is on others–for example, vendors to design software that can be adopted modularly–to provide products and/or services that are conducive to doing so. If the adoption of information technology would complement rather than conflict with small business practice, it is likely that it would be more enthusiastically embraced and strategically used by small businesses. Moreover, this would encourage small business owner/managers to seek out opportunities for leveraging information technology so that dependency situations could be minimized.

If the small business manager is pro-actively committed to capitalizing on information technology, he or she will be more likely to seek out opportunities for strategic impact. For example, by keeping abreast of information technology developments, managers can use this knowledge to determine ways of using information technology to add value by creating unique products or services. If multiple sources of reliable, objective information technology information are used as a basis for decision-making, there is a greater likelihood that the information technology adopted will be more suited to the needs of the firm. At a minimum, greater knowledge of information technology among small business managers will increase their ability to assess the quality of the advice or proposals they receive. Indeed, the respondents we interviewed seemed poised for learning about how to capitalize on the Internet.

In summary, this investigation has found that although there are some key differences in how information technology is used by small business, these differences are very much in keeping with how resource decisions are made by small businesses. In light of the increased dependency and the focus on efficiency, recommendations were proposed to address how various stake-holders might better meet the challenges associated with the adoption of information technology within the small business sector.

REFERENCES

Atlantic Canada Opportunities Agency. (1996). *The State of Small Business and Entrepreneurship in Atlantic Canada–1996 (CAT # C89-1/3-1996E)*. Moncton, NB: Programs and Development Branch, Atlantic Canada Opportunities Agency.

Balderson, D. W. (2000). *Canadian Entrepreneurship and Small Business Management*. Toronto: McGraw-Hill Ryerson.

Bennett, R. and McCoshan, A. (1993). *Enterprise and Human Resource Development*. London: Paul Chapman Publishing Ltd.

Berman, P. (1997). *Small Business and Entrepreneurship*. Scarborough, Ontario: Prentice Hall.

Bridge, J. and Peel, M. (1999). Research note: A study of computer usage and strategic planning in the SME sector. *International Small Business Journal*, July-September, 82-87.

Bryman, A. (1988). *Quantity and Quality in Social Research*. London: Unwin Hyman.

Canadian Federation of Independent Business. (1999). *Results of Members' Opinion Surveys #37-42*. http://www.cfib.ca/research/98internet.asp (August 29, 2000).

Chen, J. C. and Williams, B. C. (1993). The impact of microcomputer systems on small business: England, 10 years later. *Journal of Small Business Management*, July, 96-102.

Cragg, P. and King, M. (1993). Small-firm computing: Motivators and inhibitors. *MIS Quarterly*, 47-60.

El Louadi, M. (1998). The relationship among organizational structure, information technology and information processing in small Canadian firms. *Canadian Journal of Administrative Sciences*, 15(2), 180-199.

Fuller, T. (1996). Fulfilling IT needs in small businesses: A recursive learning model. *International Journal of Small Business*, 14(4), 25-44.

Gartner, W. B., Bird, B. J. and Stan, J. A. (1992). Acting as if: Differentiating entrepreneurial from organizational behavior. *Entrepreneurship Theory and Practice*, 16(3), 13-31.

Glaser, B. and Strauss, A. (1967). *The Discovery of Grounded Theory: Strategies for Qualitative Research*. Chicago: Aldine.

Government of Canada. (1985). *Consultation Paper on Small Business*. Ottawa: Regional Industrial Expansion.

Industry Canada. (1996-1997). *Your Guide To Government of Canada Services and Support For Small Business: Trends and Statistics (Catalogue No. C1-10/1997E)*. Ottawa: Canadian Government Publishing Centre.

Kagan, A., Lau, K. and Nusgart, K. (1990). Information systems usage within small business firms. *Entrepreneurship Theory and Practice*, Spring, 25-37.

Kao, R. (1989). *Entrepreneurship and Enterprise Development*. Toronto: Holt, Rinehart and Winston of Canada Ltd.

Lin, B., Vassar, J. and Clack, L. (1993). Information technology strategies for small business. *Journal of Applied Business Research*, 9(2), 25-29.

Lincoln, Y. and Guba, E. (1985). *Naturalistic Inquiry*. Beverly Hills, CA: Sage Publications.

Longnecker, J., Moore, C. and Petty, J., (1997). *Small Business Management*. Cincinnati, OH: South-Western College Printing.

Malone, S. (1985). Computerizing small business information systems. *Journal of Small Business Management*, 23(2), 10-16.

McCracken, G. (1988). *The Long Interview*. New York: Sage Publications.

Mearian, L. and Songini, M. (2001). Retailers hit installation bumps with SAP software. *ComputerWorld*, February, 36.

Miles, M. B. and Huberman, A. M. (1994). *Qualitative Data Analysis*. Thousand Oaks, CA: Sage Publications.

Montazami, A. R. (1998). Factors affecting information satisfaction in the context of small business environment. *MIS Quarterly*, 12(2), 239-256.

Nickell, G. and Seado, P. (1986). The impact of attitudes and experiences on small business computer use. *American Journal of Small Business*, 10(1), 37-48.

Pienda, R., Lerner, L., Miller, M. and Phillips, S. (1998). An investigation of factors affecting the information-search activities of small business managers. *Journal of Small Business Management*, 36(1), 60-71.

Pollard, C. and Hayne, S. (1998). The changing faces of information systems issues in small firms. *International Small Business Journal*, 16(3), 70-87.

Rue, L. and Ibraham, N. (1994). The relationship between planning sophistication and performance in small business. *Journal of Small Business Management*, 11(2), 24-32.

Smith, D. (1984). *Why Small Business Is So Important*. (Budget Brochure, Ministry of State for Small Business and Tourism, Government of Canada.

Stevenson, H. H. (1999). A perspective of entrepreneurship. In Stevenson, H. H., Grousebeck, H. I., Roberts, M. J. and Bhide, A. (Eds.), *New Business Ventures and the Entrepreneur*, 3-17. Boston, MA: Irwin McGraw-Hill.

Stevenson, H. H. (1984). A new paradigm for entrepreneurial management. *Proceedings from the 7th Anniversary Symposium on Entrepreneurship*. Boston, MA: Harvard Business School.

Strowbridge, L. (1999). Wired. *Atlantic Progress*, 6(7), 41-50.

Timmons, J. A. (1999). *New Venture Creation* (5th Ed.). Boston, MA: Irwin McGraw-Hill.

Thong, J., Yap, C. and Raman, K. (1994). Engagement of external expertise in information systems implementation. *Journal of Management Information Systems*, 11(2), 209-223.

Van de Ven, A. (1993). The development of an infrastructure for entrepreneurship. *Journal of Business Venturing*, 8, 211-230.

Zinger, J. T., Huguette, B., Zanibbi, L. and Mount, J. (1996). An empirical study of the small business support network–The entrepreneurs' perspective. *Canadian Journal of Administrative Sciences*, 13(4), 347-357.

Chapter VII

Franchising and Information Technology: A Framework

Ye-Sho Chen and Robert Justis
Louisiana State University, USA

P. Pete Chong
Gonzaga University, USA

INTRODUCTION

According to Justis and Judd (1998), franchising is defined as "a business opportunity by which the owner (producer or distributor) of a service or a trademarked product grants exclusive rights to an individual for the local distribution and/or sale of the service or product, and in return receives a payment or royalty and conformance to quality standards. The individual or business granting the business rights is called the *franchisor*, and the individual or business granted the right to operate in accordance with the chosen method to produce or sell the product or service is called the *franchisee*." Although the business of the franchisor is usually larger than the "satellite small businesses" of the franchisees, most franchisors manage mostly small and medium-size enterprises (Stanworth, Price, and Purdy, 2001). The U.S. Small Business Administration (SBA) recognizes this fact and sponsors various seminars in franchising, for example, business plan and raising capital, through regional Small Business Development Centers (Thomas and Seid, 2000). In addition, SBA sets up programs specifically designed for franchises (for example, Franchise Registry Web site: www.franchiseregistry.com) to streamline the review process for SBA loan applications (Sherman, 1999) and provide special incentives for franchisees to open locations in economically depressed areas (Thomas and Seid, 2000).

Franchising has been accepted as a growth strategy for small businesses (Barber, Mand so forthalfe, and Porteous, 1989; ACOST, 1990; Justis, Catrogiovanni, and Chan, 1994). Two main schools of thoughts support this growth strategy: Resource Scarcity and Agency Theory. The Resource Scarcity school argues that the primary barrier for small business to grow is the lack of working capital, and this barrier can be overcome through franchising as franchisees bring in some capital for growth (Norton, 1988; Hall, 1989; Lafontaine and Kaufmann, 1994). The Agency Theory school argues that the agency costs, such as the costs of monitoring managers, can be reduced through franchising, since the incentives for the agent (franchisee) and principal (franchisor) are very closely aligned through the contract (Brickley, Dark, and Weisbach, 1991; Lafontaine 1992). Franchising is also believed to be an important forum to transfer technology and import entrepreneurial activity into developing economies (Stanworth, Price, and Purdy, 2001). For example, emerging markets such as Internet business (Jupiter Report, 2001) are reported recently to be among the fastest growing markets through international franchising (Paswan, Young, and Kantamneni, 2001; Welsh and Alon, 2001). Franchising is not only a way for small businesses to succeed but also a model by which small businesses may learn the structure needed to become successful.

The use of franchising as a small business growth strategy has its share of problems (Kirby, Watson, and Waites, 2001). For example, in the early stages of franchise development, "the strains normally associated with small business growth are, in fact, likely to be magnified and concentrated, rather than reduced" (Stanworth, 1995, p.60); "expenditure will almost certainly exceed income" (Ayling, 1987, p.114); and it could take three to five years for a business to break even (Mendelsohn, 1992). Understanding and solving the problems are of the greatest interest to the franchise community. In their study on U.S. franchisor entry and survival, Lafontaine and Sun (2001) identify the following four important factors on franchisor survival: (1) business experience, that is, the number of years of experience of a firm before it becomes involved in franchising; (2) corporate units, that is, the number of company-owned outlets in the chain when it begins franchising; (3) franchisee units, that is, the number of franchised units it established in its first year; and (4) capital, that is, the amount of capital required to open an outlet. They also suggest: "mostly that firms significantly increase their chances of being successful in franchising if they face good post-entry macroeconomic conditions. Thus firms may want to use forecasts of GDP growth from well-established sources to adjust the timing of their entry and maximize their likelihood of success." Other factors on franchisor survival in the literature also include contract design, especially the provision of exclusive territories (Azoulay and Shane, 2001) and media certification (Shane and Foo, 1999).

The 'franchisor survival' literature, discussed in the previous paragraphs, provides readers with the understanding of issues at the macro level. Justis and Judd (1998), on the other hand, examined issues at the micro level–that is, specific franchise systems at different levels of growth in various industries. They identify the franchisor-franchisee relationship as a vital key for a franchise system to survive and grow. They also found that organization learning is the key for developing this relationship, and this learning process consists of five stages (Cormack, Hammerstein, and Justis, 2001): (1) Beginner–learning how to do it; (2) Novice–practicing doing it; (3) Advanced–doing it; (4) Master–teaching others to do it; and (5) Professional–becoming the best that you can be. Through this organization learning process, both franchisor and franchisee gradually build a "family" relationship composed of five crucial elements: (1) Knowledge–proven abilities to solve business problems; (2) Attitude–positive and constructive ways of presenting and sharing the working knowledge; (3) Motivation–providing incentives for learning the working knowledge; (4) Individual Behavior–understanding and leveraging the strengths of the participants to learn and enhance the working knowledge; (5) Group Behaviour–finding the best collaborative way to collect, disseminate, and manage the hard-earned working knowledge.

It is obvious that working knowledge is the base of the "family" relationship (Chen, Chong, and Justis, 2000b; Cormack, Hammerstein, and Justis, 2001). Through the process of learning, working knowledge is disseminated throughout the franchise system, and this chapter is about how information technology (IT) can be used to help develop this working knowledge. With the authors' collective academic and consulting experiences in franchising (Justis and Judd, 1998; Cormack, Hammerstein, and Justis, 2001) and IT in small business (Chen, Chong, and Chen, 2001; Chen, Ford, Justis, and Chong, 2001; Chen, Chong, and Justis, 2000a & b), we attempt to organize previous studies into a framework to provide a comprehensive view of the franchising business operations and the essential role IT plays in enhancing the effectiveness and efficiency of the franchise system. We will first describe the franchise working environment, then discuss the issues and solutions in working knowledge management and the proper IT to use. Finally, we will discuss how Application Service Providers (ASPs) can be used to reduce the cost of IT investment.

THE FRANCHISE BUSINESS ENVIRONMENT

In his best seller, *Business @ the Speed of Thought*, Bill Gates (1999) wrote: "Information Technology and business are becoming inextricably interwoven. I don't think anybody can talk meaningfully about one without talking about the other." Indeed, IT is useful only when the solutions IT provides help develop good relationships between the franchisor and the franchisees, and this relationship is developed while a franchisee learns how the business operates from the franchisor. In this section we will describe the franchise business environment for the franchisor headquarter, the franchisee unit, and the franchise community as a whole. As we will see, their diverse functions incur diverse needs and thus require different IT solutions.

The Franchisor Headquarter: A Small Business Supporting Many "Satellite" Small Businesses

Unlike large businesses, a franchisor headquarter is typically small. Stanworth, Price, and Purdy (2001) note that few franchisors in America and Europe are truly qualified as large. Operations in a franchisor headquarter consist of four major activities: helping and supporting business units, marketing and advertising to prospective franchisees for franchise development, managing people who perform franchise support and franchise development, and dealing with financial issues such as accounting and finances.

These daily operations in the franchisor headquarter usually involves the following four entities (Figure 1):

- *Business units owned by franchisees or companies*. Since business units are where the tires meet the road, they should be the center of attention for all these activities. There are three types of business units: startup franchisees, established franchisees, and company units. Among these three a franchisor headquarter should do its best to support startup franchisees. Established franchisees are the ones the franchisor headquarter needs to provide incentives to encourage expansion. Company units are the ones owned by the company, and the company likes to use them as role models for the franchisees.

- *Prospective franchisees*. Prospective franchisees may contact the franchisor headquarter in three different formats. The first is the referrals from, for example, franchisees, for their associates, friends, and relatives to contact the franchisor headquarter about franchise opportunities. The second is from current customers who are interested in owning and running franchise units. Finally, it may be leads generated from various marketing channels, including advertisement, web site promotion, community services, and public relationships.

Figure 1: The business environment of the franchisor headquarter

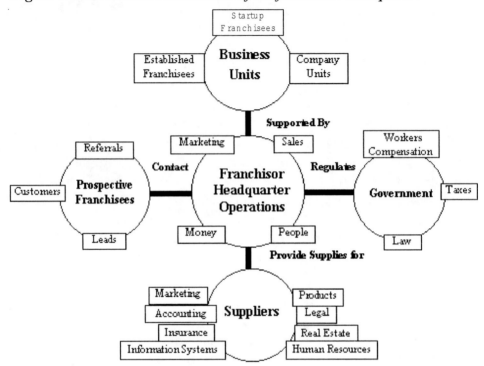

- *Suppliers.* Suppliers to a franchisor headquarter provide more than just the raw materials for business units to produce goods and services. Business service providers such as marketing agents, accountants, insurance providers, attorneys, information systems vendors, real estate agents, human resource management companies, and so forth should be considered as suppliers as well.
- *Government.* The franchisor headquarter is subject to the regulations of the government, including taxes and various business laws, such as workers compensation.

The Franchisee Unit: A "Satellite" Small Business

A franchisee unit, without a doubt, is a small business. However, this small business is highly dependent on its franchisor. Stanworth, Price, and Purdy (2001) call the franchisee unit a "satellite" to the franchisor. Be this "satellite" unit domestic or international, its operation must consider the following four crucial parties (Figure 2):

- *Customers.* The operation of a franchisee unit consists of making sales to customers, managing people who make sales to the customers, marketing and advertising to customers, and dealing with financial issues such as accounting and finances. It is obvious that customers should be the center of the attention, and we can classify customers into frequent customers, infrequent customers, and potential customers. Frequent customers are the ones a unit should do its best to keep, infrequent customers are the ones a unit needs to provide incentives to encourage them to purchase more, and potential customers are the ones a unit likes to have start buying.

- *Franchisor headquarter.* To support operations in franchisee units, a franchisor headquarter provides help desk services on issues happening during the unit operations, personal demonstrations from visiting field representatives, and training and continued education from the management group of the franchisor.
- *Suppliers.* As mentioned earlier, suppliers provide more than just the raw materials for producing goods and services to the franchisee unit. This group includes marketing agents, accountants, insurance providers, attorneys, information systems vendors, real estate agents, human resource management companies, and so forth as part of the suppliers.
- *Government.* The franchisee unit, similar to that of the franchisor headquarter, is subject to the regulations of the government, including taxes and various business laws.

Figure 2: The business environment of the franchisee unit

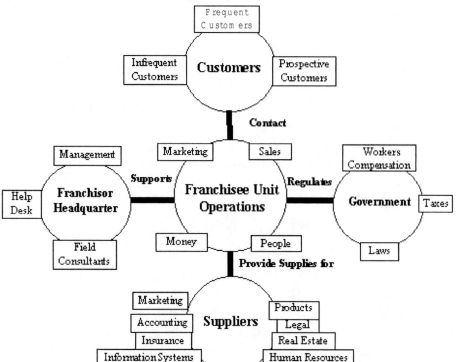

Building Franchisor-Franchisee Relationship in the Franchise Community

Figures 1 and 2 show typical activities at a franchisor headquarter and franchisee units, respectively. Figure 3, adapted from McKenna's virtual community in electronic commerce (McKenna, 1999), is a visual depiction of the franchise community where the franchisor-franchisee relationship is developed and built. In a franchise community there are three interrelated groups of relationships:

- *Relationship management within the franchise system*, where a franchisor builds up relationships with the board of directors, franchisees, prospective franchisees, franchisor management and employees, and most importantly the franchise advisory council (Justis and Judd, 1998). The council is formed to deal with issues associated with relationships. One of the "hottest" issues for relationship management today, for example, is encroachment–the expansion of the franchisor having negative impacts on the market share of the franchisees (Hellriegel and Vincent, 2000). Learning how to deal with those hot issues is proven to be the key to the survival of the franchisor.

- *The relationship with consumers*, including customers, investors, competitors, media, and government. In their recent article, Shane and Foo (1999) report that gaining media certifications is a very important survival strategy for new franchisors. A positive relationship with the media will indeed have a positive impact on the franchisor-customer relationship.

- The relationship with suppliers, including the International Franchise Association (IFA), law firms, co-branding partners, goods distributors, real estate agents, information system consultants, accounting firms, and marketing agents. The IFA (www.franchise.org) is formed with the mission of protecting, enhancing, and promoting franchising. Franchisees will enjoy additional support and positive impacts on their businesses when the relationship between their franchisor and IFA is good.

WORKING KNOWLEDGE MANAGEMENT USING IT

In this section we will use Figures 1 to 3 as a guide to discuss ways IT can be used to manage working knowledge, the foundation of the "family" relationship (Chen, Chong, and Justis, 2000b; Cormack, Hammerstein, and Justis, 2001). The working knowledge management includes four parts: developing, preserving, disseminating, and leveraging. We start with a real-life example of

Figure 3: The networked franchise community

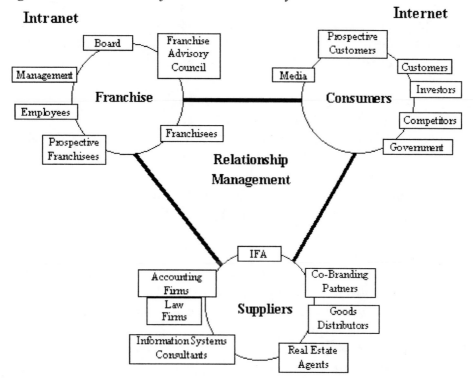

working knowledge in action.

Working Knowledge in Action: An Example

We will use an example, "Steps to Becoming a Franchisee at Smoothie King®" (www.smoothieking.com) to illustrate how IT and working knowledge are used in real-life practices (see Table 1). Smoothie King® is a franchise of Juice Bars that provide Food/Quick Service to customers. The company has been in business since 1987 and became franchised in 1988. Currently Smoothie King® has more than 200 franchised units. Recently Entrepreneur Magazine (www.entrepreneur.com) ranked Smoothie King® 164 among the Top 500 Franchises and number 1 in the Juice Bars category.

Step 1: Obtain Franchisee Information Packet–A franchise information package can be requested simply by submitting an inquiry.

Step 2: Submission of Information Forms, Financial Statements, and Resume–Complete and submit the forms in the packet to Smoothie King®. Our executive staff will review the information. Upon preliminary approval, you will be notified of our interest. This information will be kept confidential.

Step 3: Interview/Presentation–A Franchise Development Representative schedules an interview with you at our headquarters in Kenner, LA. During this visit, you will get an in-depth introduction to the Smoothie King operation, receive your Uniform Franchise Offering Circular (UFOC[1]), meet the executive staff, and have an opportunity to visit several existing franchise locations.

Step 4: UFOC Reviewed by Prospect–The UFOC contains valuable information to help you analyze our franchise system.

Step 5: Meet with Existing Franchisees–After careful review of the UFOC and your visit to headquarters, you may wish to interview some of our existing Smoothie King franchisees.

Step 6: Information Review–Your information forms, financial statements, credit forms, and background information are analyzed and evaluated. Upon a mutual decision to proceed, you may be scheduled for a second interview if necessary.

Step 7: Second Interview–A Franchise Development Representative schedules a second interview with you at Smoothie King headquarters. At this meeting, you will meet our corporate franchise support staff and visit our training center in Metairie, LA.

Step 8: Enter into Franchise Agreement–By this point, you should have enough information about Smoothie King to make a prudent decision. If approved, you may sign a franchise agreement.

Step 9: Orientation–As soon as possible, you will attend a one-day orientation class. At this class you will be oriented on all of the steps involved in opening your store. This will include budgeting, financing, planning, site selection, ordering, construction, and much more. After orientation, our real estate department will work with you to find the perfect site.

Step 10: Training–You and your management staff attend training at our training center.

Step 11: Complete Construction–Upon completion of construction, store set-up and on-site training begins.

Step 12: Open for Business.

In Table 1 we highlighted three profiles in bold faces: Personality Profiles, Site Profiles, and Customer/Product Profiles. These three profiles are very important examples of working knowledge in franchising (Justis and Judd, 1998):

• *Site Profiles.* Selecting a good site is perhaps the most important decision in the franchise business. A well-run franchise system will have the working knowledge in the form of site profiles to help prospective franchisees select good business sites. The profiles enlist vital elements of

Table 1: Smoothie King®–Steps to becoming a franchisee

Step	Activities	Information Technologies Used
1	Obtain Franchisee Information Packet	Web Pages on Company's Web Site
2	Submission of Information Forms, Financial Statements, and Resume	Web Pages on Company's Web Site Email
3	Interview/Presentation	Appointment Software Presentation Programs
4	UFOC* Reviewed by Prospect	Web Pages on Company's Web Site Email Desktop Publishing Word Processing
5	Meet with Existing Franchisees	Email
6	Information Review	**Personality Profiles** Email
7	Second Interview	Appointment Software Presentation Programs
8	Enter into a Franchise Agreement	Email
9	Orientation	Presentation Programs Training Software **Site Profiles**
10	Training	Presentation Programs Training Software
11	Complete Construction	Project Management Site Management
12	Open for Business	Help Desk Management **Customer/Product Profiles**

value and risk for sites, which are identified based on several years' experiences. For example, sales data at each site may be analyzed daily to determine the best and worst performers on the previous day immediately. Long-term analyses of such data can exhibit vital value and risk elements of sites, which in turn become the working knowledge of site selection of the franchise.

- *Personality Profiles*. A successful franchisor knows that franchisees must have a strong work ethic, high self esteem, relationship extension abilities (the desire to become friends with the customers), a commitment to service, team orientation, and exactness and cleanliness (Webb, 1999). The information on the best and worst franchisees can be identified through comprehensive analyses of sales and performance reports with respect to these traits. The analyses over the years will exhibit the vital value and risk elements of personality, which in turn become the working knowledge for franchisee recruitment.

- *Customer/Product Profiles*. According to the well-known 80/20 Principle (Koch, 1999), we may observe that (1) 80% of sales come from 20% of total products; and (2) 80% of business comes from 20% of customers. Immediate implications of the principle are that in order to be successful, we need to: (1) be market-led in those few right products, and (2) be customer-centered for those few right customers. Thus, we need to build product profiles that focus on the vital few product groups, that is, 20% of the total products that generate 80% of product sales, and customer profiles that focus on the vital few customer groups, that is, 20% of customers generating 80% of total sales.

Developing Working Knowledge Using IT

The working knowledge profiles are developed over a long and complicated process. As a startup franchise, the franchisor is either a beginner or novice. That is, in the first several years, the people at the franchise headquarter are either learning or practicing the various activities in Figure 1. The focus at this stage of learning is on operational efficiency and productivity, since these are the bases for future expansion. As the system continues to grow, the franchisor reaches the advanced and master level. That is, the people at the headquarter are able to do the typical activities in Figure 1 efficiently and productively. They are also able to teach the essential tasks outlined in Figure 2 to franchisees. Along with the increase of the franchisee units comes the challenge of managing the franchisor-franchisee relationship. For example, both sides must deal with the hot issue of encroachment (Hellriegel and Vincent, 2000), as shown in Figure 3. Since the process of relationship management is time consuming and resource intensive, a franchisor at this stage typically chooses to slow down the growth in the number of units and focus on solving the internal operational issues on hand.

Thus, the major goal of IT for the growing startup franchise is to assist with the development of working knowledge solutions to increase franchise efficiency and productivity for the activities listed in Figures 1 and 2. In addition, improved working knowledge can help resolve the new and, especially, hot issues associated with the franchisor-franchisee relationship management shown in Figure 3. General IT frameworks to assist the franchisor headquarter, the franchisee unit, and the franchise community are discussed below and shown in Tables 2, 3, and 4, respectively.

- Based on the business environment illustrated in Figure 1, useful ITs for franchisor headquarter operations can be categorized into five major areas (Table 2): (1) Franchise Support System, supporting business units using applications software for tasks such as help desk, performance tracking, marketing, and auditing; (2) Franchise Development System, contacting and building relationship with prospective franchisees using applications software for tasks such as marketing, contact management, and real estate management; (3) Franchisor Headquarter Management System, helping the franchisor deal with office issues using applications software for tasks such as human resource management, accounting, and financing; (4) Suppliers/Government Contact Management System, contacting and building relationship with suppliers/government using applications software for tasks such as scheduling and reminders; and (5) Communication System, helping the franchisor communicate efficiently and effectively with business units, prospective franchisees, suppliers, and government.

- Based on the business environment illustrated in Figure 2, useful ITs for the franchisee unit operations can be categorized into three major areas (Table 3): (1) Front Office Operation System, serving customers using applications software for tasks such as business transactions and marketing; (2) Back Office Operation System, dealing with office issues, using applications software for tasks such as accounting and financing; and (3) Communication System, helping the franchisee communicate efficiently and effectively with customers, franchisor headquarter, suppliers, and government.

- Based on the business environment illustrated in Figure 3, useful ITs for the franchise community can be categorized into three major areas (Table 4): (1) Internet for Business-to-Consumer (B2C) collaborations (Mehta, Stewart, Kline, and Maniam, 2001); (2) Intranet for Intra-Enterprise collaborations (Dickey and Ives, 2000; Dickey and Murphy, 2000); and (3) Extranet for Business-to-Business (B2B) collaborations. This community of franchise firms, consumers, and suppliers can be virtually networked for collaboration (Paswan, Loustau, and Young, 2001).

Using the IT framework shown in Tables 2 to 4, working *knowledge* is generally accumulated from *information* that is deciphered from *data* analyses. A franchise system generates voluminous data every day from various applications systems such as the Front Office Operation System at the franchisee unit shown in Table 3. Every business transaction–billing, customer tracking, inventory control, and labor–adds to the enormous amount of data generated each day. At the end of day, a report is sent through the Communication System to the franchisor headquarter to summarize the daily business transactions such as total sale, total cost of raw materials, and total cost of labor. If the report is not received after a pre-determined time, a message is triggered to request prompt actions. Once daily sales reports are received from

Table 2: General IT framework for the franchisor headquarter

	Business Units: Franchisee and Company	

Prospective Franchisees: Customers, Referrals, and Leads	**Franchisor Office**
	• Franchise Supports
	   • Help Desk
	   • Performance Tracking
	   • Marketing
	   • Auditing
	• Franchise Development
	   • Marketing
	   • Prospective Franchisees Contact Management
	   • Real Estate Management
	• Office Management
	   • Human Resources
	   • Accounting
	   • Financing
	• Communications with Business Units, Prospective Franchisees, Suppliers, and Government
		Government: Local, State, and Federal

	Suppliers: Products, Legal, Real Estate, and so forth	

Table 3: General IT framework for the franchisee unit

	Customers: Current and Prospective	

Franchisor Headquarter: Help Desk, Field Consultants, and Management	**Franchisee Store**
	• Front Office Operations
	   • Point-of-Sale Transactions
	      ○ Billing
	      ○ Customer Tracking
	      ○ Inventory Control
	      ○ Labor
	   • Marketing
	• Back Office Operations
	   • Accounting
	   • Financing
	• Communications with Customers, Franchisor Office, Suppliers, and Government
		Government: Local, State, and Federal

	Suppliers: Products, Legal, Real Estate, and so forth	

Table 4: General IT framework for the franchise community

Information Technologies	Business Transactions	Examples
Internet	Business-to-Consumer (B2C)	• Customer Relationship Management • Business Intelligence • Franchise Sales and Marketing
Intranet	Intra-Enterprise	• Enterprise Resource Planning • Online Training and Manuals • Knowledge Management
Extranet	Business-to-Business (B2B)	• Supply Chain Management

all the business units, they are converted into information using a variety of analytical methods. For example, a company may use statistical data modelling, including regression analysis, correlation analysis, time series analysis, forecasting, Pareto analysis, and quality assurance. Recently, data mining modelling (including decision tree analysis, cluster analysis, market segmentation analysis, cross-sell analysis, and association analysis) is also becoming popular. These statistical data analyses can also help generate many business intelligence reports. For example, a business unit may receive its performance ranking report along with the report of the top 10 best-performing business units. This information generation process may also incorporate some sort of reward system. For example, the owner of a business unit may receive a free trip to Hawaii if s/he has been on the top-10 list for a number of consecutive times. The information contained in the daily business intelligence reports becomes the foundation upon which a franchise system builds its working knowledge.

Table 5 gives some examples of how these three types of IT software applications are used at the franchisor headquarter (shown in Table 2), the franchisee units (shown in Table 3), and among the franchise community (shown in Table 4). Working knowledge in franchising is presented in the form of profiles. Three examples (Personality, Site, and Customer/Product Profiles) are presented in Table 1.

Preserving Working Knowledge Using IT

A franchise system has to learn to survive in the business world, but it also must learn to organize working knowledge profiles effectively to help the other four crucial elements of the "family" relationship–Attitude, Motivation, Individual Behaviour, and Group Behavior–discussed in the Introduction section. Using selection of franchisee business site as an example, Tables 6, 7, and

Table 5: IT software applications classified by type: Data, information, and knowledge

	Data	Information	Knowledge
Applications at the Franchisor Headquarter (Table 2)	• Contacts with franchisees • Contacts with prospective franchisees	• Daily sales analysis of franchisee units • Performance of support staff	• Site Profiles • Franchisee Profiles
Applications at the Franchisee Units (Table 3)	• Point of sales • Employee work schedule	• Inventory statistics • Hot products statistics	• Customer Profiles • Product Profiles
Applications Among the Franchise Community (Table 4)	• Daily online news • New government regulations	• Stock performance in the franchise industry • Yearly Franchise 500 reports	• Competitor Profiles • Supplier Profiles

Figure 4 illustrate the Value-Cost-Risk (VCR) methodology for organizing Site Profiles. The same principle can be effectively applied to organizing other working knowledge profiles as well. The values of the attributes on the left column of Tables 6-7, the weights and rates in Table 6, and the cost numbers in Table 7 can be assessed from the collective knowledge of the franchisor and franchisees at a certain stage of the franchise development. The collective knowledge can be easily preserved and refined continuously as the franchise grows and expands. Figure 4, on the other hand, visualizes the collective knowledge in a very easy-to-understand way which empowers the franchise team to make site selection decision efficiently and effectively. For example, Site 1 shall be chosen since it has the highest value, the lowest risk, and the lowest cost.

Disseminating Working Knowledge Using IT

Once the working knowledge of the entire organization is preserved, the next challenge is to disseminate it over the company's intranet to those who can benefit form the knowledge. Table 8 shows a proposed Franchise Knowledge Repository Framework, which contains two important classifications: (1) user skill levels, including beginner, novice, advanced, master, and professional; and (2) knowledge level for the collaborative team, the franchisee unit, the franchisor headquarter, and the franchise community. The foundation of the framework is the working knowledge for the collaborative team whose goal is to train its members to practice the five crucial elements–Knowledge, Attitude, Motivation, Individual Behaviour, and Group Behaviour (acronym: KAMIG)– for building the "family" relationship. The working knowledge profiles shown in Table 8 are modularized according to the level of the user. A curriculum of working knowledge modules can then be designed to effectively train the user.

Table 6: Evaluating candidate sites using values and risks

	Weight (1)	% of Weight (2)	Site 1 Rate (3)	Site 1 (2)x(3)	Site 2 Rate (4)	Site 2 (2)x(4)	Site 3 Rate (5)	Site 3 (2)x(5)
Values								
Buying Power Index	10	15.9%	5	79.5%	2	31.8%	3	47.7%
Sales Potential	9	14.3%	4	57.2%	2	28.6%	1	14.3%
Population in 1 Mile Radius	8	12.7%	4	50.8%	2	25.4%	2	25.4%
Ingress/Egress of Site	10	15.9%	4	63.6%	3	47.7%	1	15.9%
Parking	9	14.3%	4	57.2%	2	28.6%	3	42.9%
Total				**3.08**		**1.62**		**1.46**
Risks								
Work Force Inventory	9	14.3%	1	14.3%	1	14.3%	3	42.9%
Suppliers Services	8	12.7%	1	12.7%	2	25.4%	2	25.4%
Total	63	100%		**0.27**		**0.4**		**0.68**

Table 7: Estimating the total cost (x1000) for each candidate site

	Site 1	Site 2	Site 3
Land cost	20	30	27
Design/building cost	15	10	15
Utilities/communications cost	10	15	15
Equipment purchase cost	10	12	10
Safety cost	10	16	30
Periodic site management cost/month	10	25	20
Miscellaneous cost	5	15	9
Total	**80**	**123**	**126**

Figure 4: The value-cost-risk diagram for comparing candidate sites

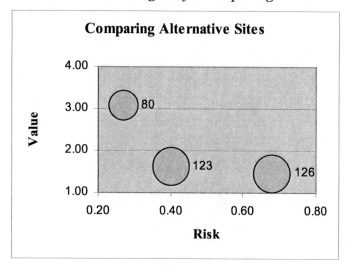

Table 8: Franchise knowledge repository framework

| | | User Skill Levels | | | |
		Beginner	Novice	Advanced	Master	Professional
Franchisee Unit	Collaborative Team	Beginner guide to KAMIG	Practicing KAMIG	Doing KAMIG	Teaching others KAMIG	Improving KAMIG
		Beginner guide to working knowledge profiles for running the Franchisee Unit	Practicing working knowledge profiles for running the Franchisee Unit	Doing working knowledge profiles for running the Franchisee Unit	Teaching others working knowledge profiles for running the Franchisee Unit	Improving working knowledge profiles for running the Franchisee Unit
Franchisor Headquarter		Beginner guide to working knowledge profiles for running the Headquarter	Practicing working knowledge profiles for running the Headquarter	Doing working knowledge profiles for running the Headquarter	Teaching others working knowledge profiles for running the Headquarter	Improving working knowledge profiles for running the Headquarter
Franchise Community		Beginner guide to working knowledge profiles for relationship management with the community	Practicing working knowledge profiles for relationship management with the community	Doing working knowledge profiles for relationship management with the community	Teaching others working knowledge profiles for relationship management with the community	Improving working knowledge profiles for relationship management with the community

Leveraging Working Knowledge Using IT

The final challenge in managing the working knowledge is to take advantage of the successful brand names, and leverage and market the working knowledge of the franchise business. The new products or services created from such leveraging may transform the business into a more, sometimes surprisingly, profitable enterprise. For example, McDonald's real estate business, Franchise Realty Corporation, became a real moneymaking engine. In the book *McDonald's: Behind the Arches*, Love states (1995, p.152): "What converted McDonald's into a money machine had nothing to do with Ray Kroc or the McDonald brothers or even the popularity of McDonald's hamburgers, French fries, and milk shakes. Rather, McDonald's made its money on real estate and on a little-known formula developed by Harry J. Sonneborn." Ray Kroc, founder of McDonald's, further commented months before he died (Love, 1995, pp.152-153): "Harry alone put in the policy that salvaged this company and made it a big-leaguer. His idea is what made McDonald's rich."

APPLICATION SERVICE PROVIDERS (ASPS) IN FRANCHISING

Although IT can add many benefits to the franchise system, the immediate question is "at what cost?" The implementation of IT could be very complicated and expensive, and most franchise companies, especially small ones, find it unaffordable (Kennedy, 1998). However, a new type of service in IT called Application Service Providers (ASPs) promises to make IT more economical and affordable to the franchise community. According to the ASP Industry Consortium (2001), ASP delivers and manages applications and computer services from remote data centers to multiple users via the Internet or a private network. The ASP concept has significant appeal in the franchising industry. An ASP providing excellent services to its client can duplicate the success to other similar franchises quickly and inexpensively. For franchising companies, an ASP can offer the benefits of: (1) reducing focus on the IT issues; (2) reducing total cost of ownership of IT; (3) reducing time to deploy applications; (4) reducing the risks to develop, implement, and maintain the applications; and (5) reducing cost of recruiting, training, and retaining skilled information technology staff.

Using Table 5 as a guide, we recommend franchise companies to outsource IT for data and information applications to ASPs. There are five major reasons for doing so:

- These are not core processes in a franchise business, activities related to the working knowledge of the franchise are:
- These are routine and time-consuming functions.
- It is more cost effective.
- It is more professional.
- And most importantly, a successful ASP focusing on specific industries in franchising will be able to provide its clients valuable statistics such as industry averages, benchmarks, and so forth. Those statistics are most likely obtained from its customer base. Through the statistics the franchise company will be able to answer several key questions; for example, (1) are we over or under spent on certain investments? and (2) where do we stand in terms of the industry competition?

Keeping working knowledge applications in-house makes good sense, although some of the IT supporting the knowledge repository, for example, distance learning facilities, can be outsourced also.

CONCLUSION

Franchising has been popular as a growth strategy for small businesses; it is even more so in today's global and e-commerce-centered world. Although IT is quite important in franchising, IT researchers have largely ignored this arena. One major reason is that few IT researchers are vested in the knowledge of how franchising functions, and without this intimate knowledge it is difficult to implement effective IT systems. Based on years of collective academic and consulting experiences in franchising and IT, the authors propose a framework of IT in franchising. At the heart of the framework is to manage working knowledge and use IT to build up the "family" relationship between franchisor and franchisees. As cost is a major concern for both franchisor and franchisees; we recommend using ASP as part of the IT strategy to keep down the cost while improve efficiency. In addition to the attractive concept of subscribing rather than purchasing IT, an ASP that provides excellent services to its client can duplicate its success to other similar franchises quickly and inexpensively in franchising industry. As a result, the average cost to clients may even decline further. However, ASP is not the panacea for everything. Among the three types of IT applications (data, information, and knowledge), we recommend outsourcing the data and information applications to an ASP but keeping the knowledge applications in house. We also recommend for the franchise system to build an Intranet-based knowledge repository to leverage the hard-earned working knowledge.

ENDNOTE

1 UFOC is a federal regulation requiring a franchisor to disclose extensive documentation to prospective franchisees (International Franchise Association, 2001).

REFERENCES

A.C.O.S.T. (1990). The enterprise challenge: Overcoming barriers to growth in small firms. *HMSO*.

ASP Industry Consortium. (2001). *All About ASP: Definitions, Reports and Links, 2001*. Available at www.aspindustry.org/faqs.cfm.

Ayling, D. (1987). Franchising has its dark side. *Accountancy*, 99(1112): 113-114.

Azoulay, P. and Shane, S. (2001) Entrepreneurs, contracts, and the failure of young firms. *Management Science*, March, 47(3).

Barber, J., Mand so forthalfe, J. and Porteous, M. (1989). *Barriers to Growth in Small Firms*. London: Routledge.

Brickley, J., Dark, F. and Weisbach, M. (1991). An agency perspective on franchising. *Financial Management*, 20(1), 27-35.

Chen, Y., Chong, P. and Chen, J. (2001). Small business management: An IT-based approach. *Journal of Computer Information Systems*, 41(2), 40-47.

Chen, Y., Ford, C., Justis, R. T. and Chong, P. (2001). Application service providers (ASPs) in franchising: Opportunities and issues. *Proceedings of the 15th Annual International Society of Franchising Conference*, Las Vegas, Nevada, February 24-25.

Chen, Y., Chong, P. and Justis, R. T. (2000a). Information technology solutions to increase franchise efficiency and productivity. *Proceedings of the 2000 Franchise China Conference and Exhibition*, Beijing (November 6-7), Guangzhou (November 9-10), and Shanghai (November 13-14), China. The Conference Web site is located at www.franchise.globalsources.com.

Chen, Y., Chong, P. and Justis, R. T. (2000b). Franchising knowledge repository: A structure for learning organizations. *Proceedings of the 14th Annual International Society of Franchising Conference*, San Diego, California, February 19-20.

Cormack, C., Hammerstein, S. B. and Justis, R. T. (2001). *Franchisor: The Professional Guidebook*. Available on the World Wide Web at: http://www.bus.lsu.edu/ei/franchiseclass/pages/ForBook/title.html.

Dickey, M. H. and Ives, B. (2000). The impact of intranet technology on power in franchisee/franchisor relationship. *Information Systems Frontiers*, 2(1), 99-114.

Dickey, M. H. and Murphy, L. (2000). Intranets as a source of increased virtuality in franchise organizations: Observations and research directions. *Proceedings of the 2000 Americas Conference on Information Systems*, Long Beach, CA, 1719-1722.

Gates, W. (1999). *Business @ the Speed of Thought*. Warner Books.

Hall, G. (1989). Lack of finance as a constraint on the expansion of innovatory small firms. In Barber, J., Mand so forthalfe, J. and Porteous, M. (Eds.), *Barriers to Growth in Small Firms*. London: Routledge.

Hellriegel, J. E. and Vincent, W. S. (2000) The encroachment handbook: The problem, the history, the solution. *Proceedings of the 14th Annual International Society of Franchising Conference*, San Diego, California, February 19-20.

International Franchise Association. (2001). What is the federal trade commission franchise rule? *ABCs of Franchising*. Available on the World Wide Web at: http://www.franchise.org/resourcectr/faq/q11.asp.

Jupiter Report. (2001) *Asia Pacific to Outpace U.S. Online Population by 2005, But US Sites Turn Blind Eye Toward Globalization*, January 11. Available on the World Wide Web at: http://www.businesswire.com/cgi-bin/f_headline.cgi?bw.011101/210112033&ticker=JMXI.

Justis, R. T., Catrogiovanni, G. J. and Chan, P. (1994). Franchisor quick-start.

In Swerdlow, S. (Eds.), *Understanding and Accepting Different Perspectives: Empowering Relationships in 1994 and Beyond*. Minneapolis, Minnesota: University of St. Thomas, Institute for Franchise Management, Paper No. 8.

Justis, R. T. and Judd, R. J. (1998). Franchising. *DAME*.

Kennedy, T. (1998). *Information systems in franchising. Franchising*, In Justis, R. T. and Judd, R. (Eds.), *DAME*.

Kirby, D.A., Watson, A. and Waites, J. (2001). Franchising as a small business development strategy: A qualitative study of problems faced by franchisors. *Proceedings of the 15th Annual International Society of Franchising Conference*, Las Vegas, Nevada, February 24-25, 2001.

Koch, R. (1999). *The 80/20 Principle: The Secret to Success by Achieving More with Less*. Doubleday.

Lafontaine, F. (1992). Agency theory and franchising: Some empirical results. *Rand Journal of Economics*, 23(2), 263-283.

Lafontaine, F. and Kaufmann, P. (1994). The evolution of ownership patterns in franchise systems. *Journal of Retailing*, 70, 97-113.

Lafontaine, F. and Sun, S. (2001). The effect of macroeconomic conditions on U.S. franchisor entry and survival. *Proceedings of the 15th Annual International Society of Franchising Conference*, Las Vegas, Nevada, February 24-25.

Love, J. (1995). *McDonald's: Behind the Arches*. Bantam Books.

McKenna, R. (1999). *Real Time*. Boston, MA: Harvard Business School.

Mehta, S. S., Stewart, W. T., Kline, D. M. and Maniam, B. (2001). The franchising industry's use of Internet technology. *Proceedings of the 15th Annual International Society of Franchising Conference*, Las Vegas, Nevada, February 24-25.

Mendelsohn, M. (1992). *The Guide to Franchising*. Cassell.

Norton, S. (1988). Franchising, brand name capital, and the entrepreneurial capacity problems. *Strategic Management Journal*, 9, 105-114.

Paswan, A. K., Loustau, J. and Young, J. A. (2001). Modeling franchise network organization. *Proceedings of the 15th Annual International Society of Franchising Conference*, Las Vegas, Nevada, February 24-25.

Paswan, A. K., Young, J. A. and Kantamneni, S. P. (2001). Public opinion about franchising in an emerging market: An exploratory investigation involving Indian consumers. *Proceedings of the 15th Annual International Society of Franchising Conference*, Las Vegas, Nevada, February 24-25.

Shane, S. and Foo, M. (1999). New firm survival: Institutional explanations for new franchisor mortality. *Management Science*, 45(2).

Sherman, A. J. (1999). *Franchising & Licensing*. AMACOM.

Stanworth, J. (1995). Penetrating the mists surrounding franchise failure rates– Some old lessons for new businesses. *International Small Business Journal*, 13(2), 59-63.

Stanworth, J., Price, S. and Purdy, D. (2001). Franchising as a source of technology-transfer to developing economies. *Proceedings of the 15th Annual International Society of Franchising Conference*, Las Vegas, Nevada, February 24-25.

Thomas, D. and Seid, M. (2000). *Franchising for Dummies*. IDG Books.

Welsh, D. and Alon, I. (2001). International franchising in emerging markets: A review and summary. *Proceedings of the 15th Annual International Society of Franchising Conference*, Las Vegas, Nevada, February 24-25.

Webb, W. (1999). Personality profiles: Next best thing to "cloning." *Franchise Times*, 24.

Chapter VIII

Use of Decision Support Systems in Small Businesses

Yanqing Duan and Russell Kinman
University of Luton, UK

Mark Xu
University of Portsmouth, UK

INTRODUCTION

The research outlined in this chapter is concerned with current practice in relation to decision support systems (DSSs) in small businesses. The purpose of this research (based on a survey approach) was to identify managers' needs for computer-based support, and to explore if and how computer-based DSS could be better developed and utilized to meet these needs. Factors that hamper the utilization of DSS in small firms are also discussed.

There have been different measures of what small business is, and different views on what a DSS ought to be. For the purposes of the research, the DSS and small business are defined as follows:

Decision Support System (DSS)

Early DSSs were developed in parallel with Management Information System (MIS) in the 1970s. An MIS is developed to primarily generate management information from operational systems, while DSSs as defined by Gorry and Scott Morton (1971) are information systems that focus on supporting people in the unstructured and semi-structured decision-making process. A typical DSS consists of four main components: the database, the model base, the user interface and the users. Central to the DSS are the models and analytical tools that assist managers in solving decision problems. The most common models include: the optimization model (where mathematical models are used to calculate optimal solutions); the "what if?" model, and goal-seeking scenarios (where mathematical models of decision problems are manipulated by varying inputs and observing changes in the outputs). Concomitant with advances in the technology of computing, most DSSs provide easy access to data and flexible control models with a friendly user interface design. Some DSSs also incorporate a variety of analytical tools and report / graphic generators. The main purpose of DSSs is not to replace managers' ability to make decisions, but to improve the effectiveness of their decision-making.

DSS in practice can hardly be separated from other types of computer-based systems, as it is often integrated with those systems, for example, operational databases, spreadsheets, report generators, and executive support systems. Thus the boundary of DSS has now been extended, and DSS broadly refers to any computer-based information system that affects or potentially affects how managers make decisions. This includes data- and model-oriented systems, reporting systems, executive support systems, expert systems and group decision support systems. In light of this view, DSS in this research is defined broadly to encompass any decision-making activity that is supported by computers. These activities include: planning and scheduling (capacity planning, production planning, materials planning, personnel planning and capital budgeting); controlling (inventory control, production control), analysis and forecasting (job estimating, cost analysis, labor productivity analysis, sales/market analysis, sales/profit forecasting), as well as R & D of new products.

Small Business

The success and continued growth of small- and medium-sized enterprises (SMEs) are critically important to local and national prosperity, but their problems are not always accorded the same importance as those of larger organizations. Compared to the research devoted to large organizations on the use of information systems, SMEs have attracted much less attention. It is also the case that the problems inherent in providing support for small business management are more commonly studied from a social or economic viewpoint. Very few studies indeed have addressed decision support needs in the context of the use of information technology.

There is a common tendency to apply experience and techniques gained from large organizations directly to small businesses, without recognizing the differing decision support needs of the small business. Managers of small businesses have often been disappointed with software packages because of the inability of these to adapt well to their needs (Heikkila et al., 1991). There are dangers in seeing small businesses as miniature versions of large businesses; many problems differ, and even similar problems require differing solutions. Small enterprises normally have limited resources and less skilled managerial staff. They have higher failure risks and commonly do not have suitable access to the information they need (Raymond, 1985). The distinctive characteristics of the smaller business, indicated by Raymond et al. (1989, cited by Naylor and Williams (1994)) include: a low level of organizational maturity so that planning and control processes are generally less formalized; decision-making, often the sole responsibility of the owner-manager; a lack of (academically) qualified managers, staff training facilities and adequate staff development funding; a lack of good access to information needed for decisions; and "resource poverty" in many other areas.

The term "small business" has been used throughout this chapter for the purpose of convenience. The sample used for this research is small and medium manufacturing firms with between 10 and 250 employees. According to the size definition used in the UK, many would describe these firms as "small and medium-sized enterprises."

LITERATURE REVIEW

The need for this research was triggered by the extensive growth in the DSS market as reported by a survey of large UK companies (Business Objects UK, 1997). The survey shows that on average, 11% of the corporate information technology budget is spent on DSS (ranging from minimum 2% to maximum 55%), and some major UK companies are "placing enormous importance on establishing a DSS strategy." It is probable that small business will represent a productive domain for attempts to introduce greater levels of computer-based decision support. Research by Ray et al. (1994) shows that small business managers and their staff have positive attitudes towards the use of computers in business. Other surveys show that many have plans to increase their use of computer applications (Cragg and King, 1993). The wish for better information was identified as the motivating force in all case studies conducted by Cragg and King (1993). In the majority of the firms studied by Khan and Khan (1992), managers believed that a computerized system improved their performance in selected areas, but that there is still room for significant further development.

Gordon and Key (1987) point out that if small business managers' problem-solving skills are deficient in any of the critical areas of management decision-making, then they must improve those skills through the use of appropriate educational programs, consultants, decision support tools or some combination of these. Unfortunately, the owner-manager (because of involvement in the day-to-day operation of the firm) has not the time, resources or expertise needed to evolve, an appropriately analytical approach (Raymond et al. (1989), cited by Naylor and Williams (1994)). There would seem to be as strong a case for the potential benefits of DSS to the smaller business as for its larger counterpart, provided suitable software is available and it is effectively used by the managers concerned.

Much of the limited research into small businesses has investigated the success factors for information technology (including DSS), based upon the current use of IT/DSS (Delone, 1988; Heikkila, et al., 1991; Lai, 1994; Raymon, 1985; Raymond and Bergeron, 1992), or the design and development of specific DSSs for SMEs (Chaudhry et al., 1996; Houben, et al., 1999). Little work has been done specifically to identify those areas that have not been adapted to DSS, but show potential for its introduction for the small business. Most research (for example, see Cragg and King, 1993; Khan and Khan, 1992; Lai, 1994; Levy, 1999) indicates that computer use is still confined to operational activities, although a few studies (Levy et al., 1998; Naylor and Williams, 1994) found that some SMEs have realized the value of their information systems as decision support tools and had begun to use them for more complex activities. Other researchers suggest there to be many areas in which DSSs can be better developed and utilized to help managers in critical decision-making processes, such as marketing, sales promotion, cash-flow management and customer services (Heikkila et al., 1991; Khan and Khan, 1992; Lai, 1994). It has been argued that small businesses can improve their organizational performance and increase their competitiveness with appropriate information systems (Chau, 1994; Levy et al., 1999). The increasing emphasis on competitiveness in small business has led to a new focus on the competitive advantage promised by appropriate use of information technology (Levy et al., 1999; Lin et al., 1993). This promise cannot be realized, however, without an adequate understanding of current practice in DSS use, and better identification of users' needs. As is stressed by Lin et al. (1993), a lack of such understanding may lead to inappropriate use of information technology, inadequate resource allocation, and ineffective use of information technology for strategic advantage. A better understanding of managers' needs would help systems developers recognize the emerging opportunities for creative use of information technology, and implement necessary changes. Within this context, the following research questions are developed and outlined.

RESEARCH QUESTIONS

In order to reveal the current practice of the usage of DSS in small business and the associated problems, the research focuses on the following questions:

- the extent of use of DSS to support managers' decision-making activity;
- the extent of managers' satisfaction with current DSS support for decision-making;
- factors that hold small business back from adopting DSS for decision-making activities;
- the methodology used for developing the DSS;
- managers' perception on the effectiveness of DSS in support decision-making; and
- the perceived important decision activities that require DSS support.

RESEARCH METHOD

The research was conducted in the manufacturing sector in the county of Bedfordshire, UK. The target population was small and medium manufacturing companies with employee numbers between 10 and 250. This working definition of small businesses is in line with that used by the Department for Trade and Industry (DTI) in its SME Statistics for the UK (DTI, 1998), and its 1998 Spectrum Business Survey on the use of Information and Communication Technologies in SMEs (DTI, 1999). Of all Bedfordshire companies, manufacturing companies account for 17%. Within Bedfordshire manufacturing industry, 96% are small firms, according to the definition used. All 592 manufacturing firms falling within this definition in Bedfordshire were surveyed. Business contact addresses were obtained from Business Link Bedfordshire (a business service centre run by the county council) which has a large, regularly updated database containing information on virtually all firms in the county. To ensure a reasonable response rate, a follow-up mailing was carried out. A further psychological boost to responses was provided by the use of stamped, addressed return envelopes. The localized nature of the survey was also expected to help increase the response rate.

No suitable validated questionnaire was found for the purpose of the research. Several researchers, such as Davis (1989), Lai (1994), Raymond and Bergeron (1992) and Sanders and Courtney (1985), have developed instruments to measure various parameters related to the extent of use of DSSs, types of DSSs used and users' perceptions of DSS; unfortunately, all of these have been validated in other countries or in different industrial sectors. To obtain the most benefit from these existing instruments, suitable parts of the questionnaires were adapted for inclusion. Additional questions were added to investigate issues which were not covered. The resultant questionnaire was constructed in three parts: 1) general information on the respondents; 2) general information on the firm; 3) current use of DSS, their development methods, managers' satisfaction with the current DSS and managers' desired levels of future DSS support.

Questionnaires were sent to 592 firms in the first mailing, and 97 replies were received, 85 of which were counted as valid. The follow-up mailing with a duplicated questionnaire and a modified covering letter was sent to the 482 companies that did not respond to the first mailing. This resulted in a further 48 valid responses (from 55 replies). The overall response rate was 26% (total of 153 responses from 592 firms). The total usable questionnaires were 133. Additional evidence was collected from 40 respondents (about 30% of all respondents) who gave their personal comments on different issues related to the survey. The comments cover issues such as: the problems experienced with DSS; factors affecting successful implementation of DSS; advice and help needed for running the DSS.

Evaluating content validity is basically a question of judgment (Raymond, 1987). The initial questionnaire design was based on the literature analysis and reported case studies. This was tested with external and internal scholars to assess content validity. The revised questionnaire was then sent to six companies for a pilot test. Criticism was received about the length of the questionnaire, the terms used, ambiguous questions and the format of the questionnaire, which was duly refined.

Internal reliability tests on users' perceptions of DSS were undertaken by applying coefficient alpha analysis to the individual items and to the overall measure. The results showed that the coefficient alphas of the seven individual items adopted from Sanders and Courtney (1985) ranged from 0.8566 to 0.8856. The overall reliability coefficient alpha was 0.8906. The internal consistency of a test is deemed acceptable when the reliability coefficient exceeds the 0.80 level (Raymond, 1987).

The decision-making activity was measured by 18 actual decision activities at different levels (operational, tactical and strategic). These are "capacity planning," "production scheduling," "production control," "inventory/stock control," "job estimating/quoting," "job costing/cost analysis," "material requirements planning," "labor productivity analysis," "cash management," "short-term sales forecasting," "sales market analysis," "budget preparation," "project management," "personnel planning," "long-range sales forecasting," "long-range profit forecasting," "capital budgeting," "R&D of new products." Respondents were encouraged to add to the list where necessary. The extent of

DSS support on these activities was measured by a Likert scale of 1 to 5, 1 for "none" and 5 for "extensive." Managers' satisfaction with DSS support on the listed decision-making activities was measured by a 1 to 5-point scale, 1 for "very dissatisfied" and 5 for "very satisfied." The DSS development methods were listed and explained to the respondents as follows: "user–developed by managers as users"; "in-house–developed by your own specialists"; "off-the-peg – purchased commercial package"; "bespoke–designed for you by a software house". Five factors that may hamper the usage of DSS by small business were drawn from literature and exposed to respondents, and open space was provided for respondents to add more factors that affect their firms. Some of Sander and Courtney's (1985) instruments were used to measure the perceived effectiveness of the DSS. A 5-point scale was used to measure the extent of DSS effectiveness where 1 means "strongly disagree" and 5 means "strongly agree." A 5-point scale, 1 for "none" and 5 for "extensive," measured the desired level of DSS support on the decision activities.

Descriptive statistics were used to conduct the data analysis: the frequency, mean score and the standard deviation. Significant tests were not carried out due to concerns of the small size and the local nature of the sample.

SURVEY RESULT AND DISCUSSION

Profile of Participant Firms And Respondents

The profile of the participant companies and respondents is given in Table 1. The data shows that 70% of the firms employed 10 to 49 people. Seventy-four percent had been in existence for less than 25 years. Average annual turnover was £4.0 million, ranging from £0.2 million to just over £34 million. Sixty-two percent of the respondents were general managers or managing directors, and 38% were managers, such as financial managers, IT/IS managers, and so forth. Those who reported using computers personally had used them on average for 10 years; 36% had more than 10 years' experience and 25% less than six years. Most managers expressed general satisfaction with the computer systems used in the firm, being either satisfied (43%) or moderately satisfied (34%); only 2% were very dissatisfied with their systems while 10% were very satisfied. This high level of managerial satisfaction with current computer systems may suggest that information technology is supporting these companies effectively, although the satisfaction may also act to prevent managers from seeking further improvement, as one of the managers noted: *"we feel we have the optimum."* The relatively low levels of computer literacy reported (less than 20% of managers indicating "good" or "high" levels) might also suggest that there is limited understanding of the potential benefits to be offered by computing systems, and DSS in particular.

The Use of DSS for Decision-Making Activities

Table 2 shows the extent of the use of DSS applications in participating firms at the time of the survey, and the managers' reported levels of satisfaction with these systems. As can be seen from the table, the extent of DSS use is generally limited, ranging from 1.62 (little use) for personnel planning to 3.27 (moderate use) for inventory/stock control. High standard deviations for most applications suggest that the extent of DSS use varies considerably among the firms surveyed. However, even where there was a reported low level of DSS use, managers' satisfaction was relatively high. The applications with which managers were most satisfied were: cash management (3.53), budget preparation (3.51) and materials requirements planning (3.47).

Despite the relatively low usage of DSS generally, 79% of respondents indicated that they use computers personally to aid business decisions; this suggests that there is, at least, widespread use of desktop computing in

Table 1: Profile of the participant firms and respondents

	Number	%		Number	%
1. Number of employees			4. General knowledge of IT		
10-19	35	27%	1 – none	2	1%
20-49	56	43%	2 – little	17	13%
50-99	18	13%	3 – some	64	49%
100-249	22	17%	4 – good	38	29%
			5 – extensive	10	8%
2. Annual turnover			5. Level of satisfaction with computer systems used in the firm		
< 1 million	30	24%	1 - very dissatisfied	3	2%
1 - 2 million	27	22%	2 – dissatisfied	15	12%
2 - 5 millions	35	29%	3 - moderate satisfied	43	34%
5 - 10 millions	17	14%	4 – satisfied	54	43%
>10 millions	14	11%	5 - very satisfied	13	10%
3. Job title			6. General level of computer literacy of most managers in the firm		
MD/GM/Owner	80	62%	1 - no literacy	7	5%
Finance/Accounts Manager	15	12%	2 - little literacy	44	34%
IT/IS Manager	4	3%	3 - some literacy	54	42%
Marketing/Sales Manager	6	5%	4 - good literacy	22	17%
Production/Operation Manager	5	4%	5 - high literacy	3	2%
Works/Quality Manager	8	6%			
Administration Clerk	6	5%			
Others	4	3%			

managers' offices. It would be interesting to investigate this finding more deeply, to establish just what decision-making tasks are supported, and in what ways.

Table 3 presents the results of a question about inhibitors to the greater use of DSS. A lack of staff time to analyze needs and identify solutions is the most significant factor identified. Lack of finance for systems purchase or development, lack of experience of systems development and lack of information on available DSS packages were other factors commonly cited.

DSS Development Methods

DSS for small businesses can be developed and implemented in different ways. Four routes were identified for the purposes of the survey:

- *Off-the-peg*–purchase of a commercially developed package
- *Bespoke*–designed by a software house for the specific application
- *In-house*–developed by the firm's own specialist staff
- *User*–developed by managers as users

The results show (see Table 4) that the majority of DSS were purchased as commercially developed packages (56%); other systems were developed

Table 2: The extent of the use of DSS applications and managers' satisfaction

Decision-Making Activity	Extent of DSS use (1-none, 5-extensive)		Managers' satisfaction with DSS (1-very dissatisfied, 5-very satisfied)	
	Mean	Std. Dev.	Mean	Std. Dev.
inventory/stock control	3.27	1.51	3.20	1.13
budget preparation	3.23	1.46	3.51	1.00
job costing/cost analysis	2.90	1.53	3.14	1.09
cash management	2.90	1.62	3.53	1.00
job estimating/quoting	2.70	1.60	3.24	1.11
material requirements planning	2.42	1.62	3.47	1.01
production control	2.39	1.49	3.18	1.09
production scheduling	2.37	1.47	3.24	1.04
long-range profit forecasting	2.32	1.42	3.18	0.97
short-term sales forecasting	2.28	1.29	3.36	0.87
capacity planning	2.24	1.41	3.30	0.94
project management	2.16	1.37	2.96	1.00
capital budgeting	2.15	1.41	3.29	0.86
long-range sales forecasting	2.14	1.43	3.17	0.97
sales market analysis	2.06	1.27	3.33	0.99
labour productivity analysis	2.05	1.40	3.18	1.11
R & D of new products	1.78	1.28	3.00	0.94
personnel planning	1.62	1.13	3.20	0.95

Table 3: Factors holding a business back from adopting or making further use of DSS

Factors	Percentage
lack of staff time to analyse needs and identify solutions	60%
lack of finance for systems purchase or development	44%
lack of experience of systems development	34%
lack of information on available DSS packages	20%
appropriate software is not available	8%
others	9%

by managers as users (17%), developed by in-house specialists (14%) or developed as bespoke systems by software houses (13%). In view of the normally limited resource base for IT development (Heikkila, et al., 1991), it is not surprising that most small firms choose to purchase commercially developed, ready-to-use DSS software.

By breaking down the development methods into three decision-making levels (see Table 5), it can be seen that commercial packages are more commonly used at the operational level (60%) than at strategic level (51%). In contrast, user-developed DSSs are more commonly used at the strategic level (25%) than at the operational level (13%).

The advantages and disadvantages of commercial packages and tailored software are discussed by Heikkila et al. (1991), but research on *in-house* and *user* development methods in small firms is scarce. The evidence from this survey suggests that small business managers are capable of developing their own DSSs, and that a certain proportion do so. There is, of course, no way of evaluating the quality of these systems from the survey results. Research in Canada by Raymond and Bergeron (1992) found that user-developed DSSs in small businesses are more successful than any developed by other means. A study by Lai (1994) in the USA, however, revealed no link between the method of system development and DSS success. This area might also prove productive for future enquiry.

The survey attempted to investigate how DSSs for different decision-making activities were implemented. It was found that capital budgeting, cash management, material requirements planning and inventory control, were most commonly purchased *off-the-peg*. *User* and *in-house* development methods were used to support research and development of new products, personnel planning, sales forecasting, long-range profit forecasting, project management and labor productivity analysis; in these applications DSSs are evidently less amenable to standard specification, and need to be more flexible to fit individual needs. *Bespoke* software was most commonly developed for applications such

Table 4: DSS development methods at different decision-making levels

Decision-making levels	Off-the-peg	User	In-house	Bespoke
Operational	60%	13%	11%	16%
Tactical	51%	18%	20%	11%
Strategic	51%	25%	13%	11%
All three levels	56%	17%	14%	13%

as: inventory control, production control, budget preparation and job estimating/quoting. Tasks supported by bespoke DSSs are few, presumably because of the cost of the software.

By far the most commonly used DSSs in small manufacturing firms are commercial packages purchased off the shelf for operational decision-making. The readiness of small business managers to purchase commercial packages, coupled with their recognition that DSSs provide valuable support suggest that small businesses represent a market for software developers that will continue to grow. That many managers are developing their own systems to support strategic decisions might also suggest there to be a market opportunity here.

Users' Perception on the Effectiveness of DSS

The survey adapted some of the instruments developed by Sanders and Courtney (1985) to identify DSS users' personal perceptions on the effectiveness of the systems. Among 133 respondents, 59 (45 %) who had personally used DSS for their decision-making responded to this question. The results in Table 5 show that the majority of managers agreed, or strongly agreed with statements describing the benefits of DSS. Only a very small number of users (less than 4%) strongly disagreed with these statements.

The Extent of DSS Support Required by Managers

It is believed that no research has attempted to identify the gaps between the current provision of DSS and small business managers' desired levels of DSS support. Respondents were asked to indicate their current and desired level of DSS support for each decision-making activity listed in the survey. These activities were categorized into three decision-making levels in organizations–operational, tactical and strategic. Table 6 presents the analysis of the responses. The findings reveal that:
- the current level of DSS usage is low;
- although DSSs usage is limited, managers are generally satisfied with DSS they are using;
- the desired level of support is much higher than current provision;
- the high standard deviations for current DSS use and desired levels of

Table 5: End users' perceptions on the effectiveness of DSS

	strongly disagree	disagree	uncertain	agree	strongly agree	mean	std.dev.
I have come to rely on DSS in performing my job.	3%	24%	2%	52%	19%	3.59	1.16
DSSs are extremely useful to the firm.	2%	0%	17%	54%	27%	4.05	0.78
Utilization of DSS has enabled me to make better decisions.	2%	9%	20%	39%	31%	3.88	1.00
As a result of DSS, I am better able to set my priorities in decision-making.	3%	10%	35%	41%	10%	3.35	0.94
Use of data generated by DSS has enabled me to present my arguments more convincingly.	4%	11%	23%	51%	12%	3.58	0.96
As a result of DSS, the speed at which I analyse decisions has increased.	2%	9%	21%	51%	18%	3.74	0.92
As a result of DSS, more relevant information has been available to me for decision-making.	2%	5%	11%	60%	23%	3.96	0.84

support indicate high variations among responses. The standard deviation of levels of satisfaction is lower than the other two variables; this suggests that there is less disagreement on this issue.

Differences found between the three decision-making levels provide support for arguments in the literature that current DSSs in small businesses are geared to operational rather than strategic decision-making (Khan and Khan, 1992; Lai, 1994; Raymond, 1982). From the current study, it is evident that the low level of DSS use found by Raymond (1982) has not changed significantly. The desired level of support at operational level is also much higher than that at the strategic level. Users appear to expect that DSSs will provide most benefit for operational decisions. This is perhaps as well, given the nature of the decision-making tasks at the strategic level, involving complex and changing environments, high levels of uncertainty and the need to include decision-makers' personal intuition and judgment. The lower level of DSS use and desired support for strategic decision-making does not mean that there is no space for further improvement, however. Indeed, the fact that many managers are "going it alone" could be seen to suggest that professional support will enhance strategic planning. Levy et al.'s (1998) study found that one of their case study firms had been successful in integrating information systems into its business strategy and gained competitive advantages. However, computer support for strategic decisions is still a challenging area for future research, and much effort is being expended to overcome the difficulties (Duan and Burrell, 1995; Li et al., 2000), albeit, yet again, in the context of the larger business.

A comparison was made between the current usage of DSS and managers' desired level of DSS for decision-making activities. The result presented in Table 7 shows the 10 decision-making tasks that have the largest gap in responses between the current DSS provision and the desired DSS provision. Gaps perceived by respondents are greater in areas of operational and tactical decision-making rather than strategic. Further research is needed to establish whether this effect is a function of a preoccupation of managers with the tactical, rather than a lack of conviction that greater use of DSS will assist in strategic planning.

CONCLUSION

Decision support systems are designed to assist managers to make more effective decisions. Potentially, they could provide great benefits to SME managers and enhance managers' decision-making capability. However, this research reveals that current study of the use of decision support systems in small business is very limited. More research is necessary to investigate the current practice of DSS usage in small firms and to establish managers' decision support needs. The research reported in this chapter sought to make some contribution to these issues by conducting questionnaire surveys. One feature of this study was that the issues were explored using a detailed examination of individual decision-making tasks as well as taking a broader organizational view. The purpose was to help small enterprises and their managers make more effective use of IT and DSS.

The research reveals that the extent of DSS implementation in small manufacturing business is still low in general, although there is significant variation between different firms. The literature review of previous studies indicated that the situation has not changed significantly since Raymond's investigation in 1982, and the present study confirms this. Lack of staff time to

Table 6: DSS in three decision-making levels

Decision-Making Level	Level of Current DSS Use (1-no use, 5-extensive use)		Manager's Satisfaction with Current DSS (1-very dissatisfied, 5-very satisfied)		Desired DSS Support Level (1-none, 5-extensive)	
	Mean	Std. Dev.	Mean	Std. Dev.	Mean	Std. Dev.
Operational	2.69	1.11	3.33	0.90	3.59	0.88
Tactical	2.49	1.20	3.40	0.88	3.05	1.13
Strategic	2.20	1.20	3.16	0.88	2.75	1.19
Overall	2.56	1.02	3.34	0.80	3.29	0.88

Table 7: Decision-making activities which respondents believe need DSS support most

	Decision-making activity	Current DSS level Mean (1-none, 5-extensive)	Desired DSS level Mean (1-none, 5-extensive)	Gap between current and desired levels Mean differences
1	production control	2.39	3.73	1.34
2	labor productivity analysis	2.05	3.30	1.25
3	production scheduling	2.37	3.54	1.17
4	job costing/cost analysis	2.90	4.03	1.13
5	capacity planning	2.24	3.25	1.01
6	sales market analysis	2.06	3.07	1.01
7	material requirements planning	2.42	3.41	0.99
8	job estimating/quoting	2.70	3.66	0.96
9	cash management	2.90	3.84	0.94
10	inventory/stock control	3.27	4.18	0.91

analyze needs and identify solutions is the most significant factor holding firms back from adopting, or making further use of DSS. Use of DSS at the operational decision-making level is higher than at the strategic level. Small business managers are satisfied with the DSSs they are using and are hoping for much better DSS support in the future. DSS development, particularly DSS for strategic decisions in small business, still represents both a challenge and an opportunity for DSS professionals and researchers.

DSSs are most commonly implemented by purchase of a commercial package, and only rarely by bespoke development. Most DSSs are used for operational rather than strategic decision-making. A quarter of those firms that do use DSSs to support strategic decisions rely upon user-developed models.

Although DSS applications are still relatively few in number, most DSS users report satisfaction with their systems. A high demand is indicated for more, and more effective DSS support. To reduce the gaps between current DSS provision and the managers' indicated needs, a greater focus on small business by DSS researchers and practitioners is needed. Systems most likely to appeal to small business managers will have to be appropriate to their sector's needs, and capable of implementation with minimal user training. The current study appears to indicate that not much has changed since Doukidis wrote that "[the current situation in relation to DSS in small business] *is full of potential but requiring further professional support*" (Doukidis, 1994, p. 24).

Further investigation is indicated by the present study in a range of areas affecting DSS usage in small business: the effectiveness of different DSS development methods; factors affecting the success of commercially provided

DSS packages; the quality of user-developed DSS in meeting business needs; aspects of strategic planning in small business amenable to DSS support; and the relationship between the extent of DSS utilization and business performance.

REFERENCES

Business Objects UK Ltd. (1997). Business plans to spend more on decision support. *Computer Personnel,* July.

Chau, P. Y. C. (1994). Selection of packaged software in small business. *European Journal of Information Systems*, 3(4), 292-302.

Chaudhry, S. S., Salchenberger, L. and Beheshtian, M. (1996). A small business inventory DSS: Design, development, and implementation issues. *Computers & Operations Research*, 23(1), 63-72.

Coakes, E. and Merchant, K. (1996). Expert systems: A survey of their use in UK business. *Information & Management*, 30(5), 223-230.

Cragg, P. B. and King, M. (1992). Information system sophistication and financial performance of small engineering firms. *European Journal of Information Systems*, 1(6), 417-426.

Cragg, P. B. and King, M. (1993). Small-firm computing: Motivators and inhibitors. *MIS Quarterly*, 17(2), 47-59.

Davis, F. D. (1989). Perceived usefulness, perceived ease of use, and user acceptance of information technology. *MIS Quarterly*, 13(2), 319-340.

Delone, W. H. (1988). Determinants of success for computer usage in small business. *MIS Quarterly*, 12(1), 51-61.

Doukidis, G. I., Smithson, S. and Lybereas, T. (1994). Trends in information technology in small businesses. *Journal of End User Computing*, 6(4), 15-25.

Duan, Y. and Burrell, P. (1995) A hybrid system for strategic marketing planning. *Marketing Intelligence and Planning,* 13(11), 5-12.

Freedman, D. H. (1996). Through the looking glass. *The State of Small Business*, 18(7), 48-54.

Gable, G. G. (1994). Integrating case study and survey research methods: An example in information systems. *European Journal of Information Systems*, 2 (2), 112-126.

Gill, T. G. (1995). Early expert systems: Where are they now? *MIS Quarterly*, 19(1), 51-81.

Gordon, W. L. and Key, J. R. (1987). Artificial intelligence in support of small business information needs. *Journal of Systems Management*, 38(1), 24-28.

Gorry, G. and Scott Morton, M. (1971). A framework for management information systems. *Solan Management Review*, 13(1), 55-70.

Heikkila, J., Saarinen, T. and Saaksjarvi, M. (1991). Success of software packages in small business: An exploratory study. *European Journal of Information Systems*, 1(3), 159-169.

Houben, G., Lenie, K. and Vanhoof, K. (1999). A knowledge-based SWOT analysis system as an instrument for strategic planning in small- and medium-sized enterprises. *Decision Support Systems*, 26(2), 125-135.

Khan, E. H. and Khan, G. M. (1992). Microcomputers and small business in Bahrain. *Industrial Management & Data Systems*, 92(6), 24-28.

Lai, V. S. (1994). A survey of rural small business computer use: Success factors and decision support. *Information & Management*, 26(6), 297-304.

Levy, M., Powell, P. and Yetton, P. (1998). SMEs and the gains from IS: From cost reduction to value added. *Proceedings of IFIP WG8.2 Working Conference, Information Systems: Current Issues and Future Changes*, Helsinki, December, 377-392.

Levy, M., Powell, P. and Galliers, R. (1999). Assessing information systems strategy development frameworks in SMEs. *Information & Management*, 36(5), 247-261.

Li, S., Kinamn, R., Duan, Y. and Edwards, J. (2000). Computer-based support for marketing strategy development. *European Journal of Marketing*, 34(5-6), 551-575.

Lin, B., Vassar, J. A. and Clark, L. S. (1993). Information technology strategies for small businesses. *Journal of Applied Business Research*, 9(2), 25-29.

Naylor, J. B. and Williams, J. (1994). The successful use of IT in SMEs on Merseyside. *European Journal of Information Systems,* 3(1), 48-56.

Pearson, J. M. and Shim, J. P. (1994). An empirical investigation into decision support systems capabilities: A proposed taxonomy. *Information & Management*, 27(1), 45-57.

Ray, C. M. (1994). Small business attitudes toward computers. *Journal of End User Computing,* 6(1), 16-25.

Raymond, L. (1982). Information systems in small business: Are they used in managerial decisions? *American Journal of Small Business*, 5(4), 20-26.

Raymond, L. (1985). MIS success in small business. *MIS Quarterly*, 9(2), 37-52.

Raymond, L. (1987). Validating and applying user satisfaction as a measure of MIS success in small organizations. *Information & Management*, 12(4), 173-179.

Raymond, L. and Bergeron, F. (1992). Personal DSS success in small enterprises. *Information & Management*, 22(5), 301-308.

Sanders, G. L. and Courtney, J. F. (1985). A field study of organizational factors influence DSS success. *MIS Quarterly*, 9(1), 77-93.

Chapter IX

Computer Security in Small Business–An Example from Slovenia

Borut Werber
University of Maribor, Slovenia

INTRODUCTION

This chapter presents the results of an investigation conducted in Slovenia from November 1999 until January 2000, focusing on some basic computer security problems and use of information technology (IT) and information systems (IS) in 122 small Slovenian businesses. The average number of total employees was 5.7, including the owner of the small business. In some countries, businesses of this size are also called 'very small businesses.' According to that, this chapter is dedicated to small business owners/managers or those dealing with small businesses. In the first section I present the main reason for this research and discuss some previous research dealing with small business use of IT and computer security practice. In the following section I define small business and the methodology that I used for data collection and analysis. The results were based on interviews given by the owners or managers of these companies. In the results section the overall purpose of this study is presented. The aim of the research was to assess why some Slovene small businesses do not use IT, how IT and IS are used in small businesses, what kind of security measures are used, how many and what kind of problems they had with computer hardware and software, and how they managed to solve those problems. I compare the results with some similar research in other countries.

Additionally, I tested if computer security practice factors are in correlation with intensive use of IS in general, because in the literature available there was no research dealing with this. Based on the survey and the literature, recommendations have been given how to better operate the business IS (backup procedures, use of Uninterruptible Power Supply [UPS], computer virus policy and so forth) to prevent dangerous data loss for small companies and others working in connection with them.

BACKGROUND

Back in 1991, after Slovenia separated from Yugoslavia and the establishment of small businesses was in full progress, I found that in Slovenia there was little research on small business, especially on computer use. In 1992 I conducted preliminary research on IT use in small Slovene businesses (Werber and Zupancic, 1993) and found out that there is enough IT available, but it was not used in an adequate way. At that time, I also established a friendship with some small business owners and collected information about their problems with computer use in their businesses. In most cases, owners asked for assistance when their data was lost or their hardware or software did not work as expected. When I searched the international literature, I found that there was very little research in small business in the computer security field. Then, the 'year 2000' computer problem came and I conducted research on how small Slovene businesses were prepared for it (Werber et al., 1999). Once again, I was surprised at how little understanding there was among small Slovene business owners about the year 2000 computer problem and how they planned to solve this problem. In most cases, they planned to purchase new PCs in the last months of 1999. That was when I first had indications that the information available for computer security in small Slovene businesses was not adequate. Searching the international literature again, this time especially on computer security in small businesses, I was surprised to find very few articles dealing directly with this problem.

In Slovenia, with less than 2 million inhabitants, small business is as an essential part of the economy as in other countries. Small business accounts for approximately 94% of all businesses and employs 34% of total employment. In the last six years, there have been 40,000 new positions created in the small business sector, most of them (34,246) created by small business and independent entrepreneurs (SBW, 15/1999). These facts, and the interest of small business owners, encouraged me to conduct this research.

Small Business Characteristics

In general, small companies lag behind large businesses in the use of IT due to a special condition commonly referred to as resource poverty. This condition is characterized by several constraints on financial resources, a lack of in-house expertise and a short-term management perspective imposed by a volatile competitive environment. On the other hand, small business can be more innovative as opposed to large organizations because they are less bound by bureaucracy and cumbersome organizational systems, and are more flexible and able to respond to changing customer needs. Because of scarce financial resources, most small businesses tend to choose the lowest cost IS and often underestimate the amount of time and effort required for IS implementation. Hence, small businesses face a greater risk in IS implementation than larger businesses (Thong et al., 1997).

Because of the unique characteristics of small business, there is a need to examine whether models of IT and IS adoption developed in the large business context can be equally applied to small business. The skills, time and staff necessary for planning are not major issues in large business, yet these same issues represent most of the difficulties in small business. As such, organizational theories and practices that are applicable to large business may not fit a small business (Thong, 1999).

The risk for small business is even bigger because they usually use older and more obsolete hardware and software than large companies. Further, they almost never have their own IS professionals who are able to analyze the impact of security strategy on their IS. They therefore strongly depend on IS-related expertise from outside. Such outside expertise and assistance is usually inadequate and not used until the lack of security causes its first problems (Thong, 1999).

Small Business and Computer Security Practice

The history of hackers and viruses goes back to the 1960s and 1970s, when 'techno-freaks' used weaknesses in AT&T's telephone system to make unlimited long distance calls. In the 1970s, when the first PCs put computing within the reach of individuals, a computer underground began to form which produced the first computer hackers (Kyas, 1997).

Over 1,300 new macro viruses were detected in 1997 compared with about 40 in 1996. Much of the increase is attributed to the targeting of Microsoft products. Business managers fear security threats from viruses as a major security issue today (Post and Kagan, 2000).

Small businesses generally have fewer resources available to devote to IT, and they rarely have their own separate IT department or a computer professional. They also lack the expertise and resources required to effectively implement them. In Slovenia, incorporating security as a part of computer usage is already neglected in larger firms (Hudoklin and Šmitek, 1993), and even more neglected in small businesses. Similar results are found in a survey (Kuhnhold, et al., 2000) of 63 large German firms from TOP 700. Results show that there is a gap between the awareness of security and the lack of counter measures that are engaged in big German industrial companies as well as in other countries.

However, the possibilities of accidental or deliberately caused damage are the same in the large and in the small firm. Possible reasons for data loss can be divided up as a result of human factors and other factors (Vijayaraman and Ramakrishna, 1993). Human loss of business data can occur by accident or deliberately through the loss of software, data, spare copies, documentation, through deletion of data and software or through poor realization of changes in data, software and documentation. Another reason can also be system error or loss, as a result of electricity and computer viruses. Other types of damage that can be included are fire, flood and so forth as a result of natural causes (weather or disasters).

Increased computer security problems come from many sources: the expanded use of IS, the Internet, e-mail applications and the adoption of Microsoft products. An additional factor is the reluctance of business firms to either acknowledge or admit that they were electronically victimized. As the demand and implementation of virus protection software continues to escalate, so does the cost. A large financial institution from the USA reported that a virus attack in 1997 cost the firm $2.3 million in lost transactions over a three-day period (Post and Kagan, 2000).

When talking about Internet security, however, one fact that is often overlooked is that a company's computer system faces serious risks even if it is not on the Internet. For example, a study carried out by Ernst & Young in the U.S. in 1994 found that of the companies questioned, half had suffered financial losses because of problems with data security in the last 12 months. More than two-thirds of these cases were caused by the company's own staff, half of them accidentally (Kyas, 1997). Typical examples of the latter were:
- Inadequate or nonexistent backup
- Introducing viruses via people's own diskettes
- "I only wanted to see what would happen if..."
- Operating errors (accidentally deleting data, and so forth)

While these scenarios can apply to any company, whether on an external communications network or not, getting on the Internet significantly increases the chance of becoming the victim of a deliberate attack.

A survey by the National Computer Security Association in May 1995 found that companies on the Internet were subject on average to eight times as many attacks as those that were not on the Internet. It found that while only 3% of companies not on the Internet suffered from hacking, the figure for those on Internet was 24%. Other risk factors were data links with other companies and having an infrastructure that allows staff to dial into the company's network by modem. A 1994 study by the "Counter Intelligence and Security" section of the U.S. Department of Defense examined these figures further. The main finding was that over 80% of attacks on internal data systems from the outside used the Internet as the way in (Kyas, 1997).

Even in Slovenia, firms are not exempt from computer 'pirates.' Recently, we could read in the newspapers that several large Slovene companies were listed on a black list of computer network server addresses. They were being used by American computer 'pirates' for hiding their tracks of Spam mails (also named as Unsolicited Commercial Email (UCE) or "junk email") for Internet gambling, pornography advertising and so forth. Spam is flooding the Internet with many copies of the same message, in an attempt to force the message on people who would not otherwise choose to receive it. Most Spam is commercial advertising, often for dubious products, get-rich-quick schemes or quasi-legal services. Spam costs the sender very little to send–most of the costs are paid for by the recipient or the carriers rather than by the sender. Email Spam targets individual users with direct mail messages. Email Spam lists are often created by scanning Usenet postings, stealing Internet mailing lists or searching the Web for addresses (Spam.Abuse.Net , 2001).

There are also cases where small business network servers were intruded and used without authorization.

Lack of security is being perceived as the most important inhibitor for developing e-commerce capabilities. This is because confidentiality and security issues are more important because of the confidence and support that people must have to even begin to use e-commerce (Deschoolmeester and Hee, 2000).

Many of the costs associated with a disaster are either intangible or difficult to estimate. Hence, many organizations do not fully understand the costs of computer-based IS disasters, and consequently, do not bother either to take preventive measures or do contingency planning against disasters. There are basically two kinds of responses that are available to businesses against IS disasters: (1) prevention avoidance and/or reduction in probability, and (2) contingency planning. Before any responses can be contemplated and implemented, it is important for businesses to be aware of the potential of IS disasters and what was found to be the prime reason for businesses not being prepared for the disasters (Vijayaraman and Ramakrishna, 1993).

RESEARCH APPROACH AND METHODOLOGY

Small business researchers often define small business differently. The criteria used, depending on the nature of the business and industry involvement, can also vary. Most authors use the total number of employees as a criterion for research analysis. Sometimes this is combined with such financial indicators as total annual sales, operating capital or total assets. Employee criteria can range up to 50 (Palvia et al., 1999; Lawrence et al., 2000) or to 100 employees (Thong, 1999). In an empirical investigation into the size of small businesses, Osteryoung et al. (1995) examined the Small Business Administration (SBA) employees' definitions for small business and found that there is strong evidence that the 500 employee cutoff used by SBA for separating "small" firms from "large" firms in the manufacturing industry is meaningless and of no value in making a distinction between firms with different characteristics. If an employee number based on the distinction between small and large firms must be made, a cutoff at either 25 or 50 employees would be preferred to the 500 employee cutoff (Osteryoung et al., 1995).

In this study, the criteria for defining a small business were adopted from the Business Company Law of Slovenia (Kocbek and Puharic, 1993). A small business is one that satisfies at least two of the following: it has 50 employees or less, fixed assets of 0.5 million ECU or less and annual sales of 1 million ECU or less.

The aim of my research was to find out what kinds of security measures are used in small businesses to prevent data loss? What is the amount of hardware and software used? Is there a correlation between the extent of these measures and the level of use of IS in small business?

To test these assumptions, I set up six hypotheses:

H1 There is a positive relationship between the used security measures and intensive use of IS.

H2 There is a positive relationship between the used security measures and the extent of use of hardware.

H3 There is a positive relationship between the used security measures and use of the Internet.

H4 There is a positive relationship between the used security measures and small business owner IT knowledge.

H5 There is a positive relationship between the used security measures and the years of small business owner job experience.

H6 There is a difference between the used security measures and the gender of the small business owner.

Similar to Buckland (1995), I decided to use opinion research. To collect the data, an interview guide was developed which included several demographic questions and questions related to IT, IS and security problems. Although I was experienced in the use of mailed questionnaires, this time I decided to opt for the interview technique because I wanted to be sure that the participants understood the meaning of all questions. I was interested also in businesses without computer support. If I would use mailed questionnaire, the quantity of answers would be larger but the quality of answers would be less since it is almost impossible to compose all questions to be understandable for all participants. Also, I could not determine how many non-respondent businesses actually do not use computer equipment. These were the two most critical points when the research is done by mailed questionnaire. The interview was tested in 12 selected small businesses. Several contacts with respondents helped to improve the accuracy and relevance of the interviews. Interviews were conducted between November 1999 and February 2000 by myself and in part by voluntary third-year MIS part-time students at the University of Maribor. Interviews were held with randomly selected owners or managers of 136 small businesses with less than 50 employees and less than 280 million SIT (cca. 1 million ECU) in annual sales. Businesses were randomly selected around the students' residences.

RESULTS

One hundred and thirty-six interviews were conducted. Fourteen of them were not usable because the interviewed businesses exceeded the maximum criteria in different areas (annual sales, number of questions with no answer, business type–computing firm–and so forth). Thus, the sample consisted of 122 small businesses. Respondents who supplied data came from a wide variety of business backgrounds and sizes. The average number of total employees was 5.7 including the owner of the business. After grouping respondents according to the position in the organization, most of them were owners (63%), part-owners (16.4%), relatives (8.2%), managers (3.3%) or other executives (9%). In the sample, most organizations (25%) were sale oriented, 21% were manufacture oriented, 20% were service oriented and 10% were wholesale oriented. All others represented 24% of the sampled businesses. The average existence time of the small businesses was 5.7 years.

Businesses Without Computers

Out of 122 businesses, 28 (22.9%) did not use computer equipment. According to the respondents, the main reasons for this were the lack of computer knowledge and financial resources. Most of the businesses without computers (64.3%) were production oriented. The formal education of respondents in businesses without computers was lower than the formal education received by other respondents. To statistically test these results, I conducted the Chi-Square test of independence. The null hypothesis was defined as "There is no statistically significant difference in formal education of business owners between firms with computer equipment and those without computer equipment." I merged the collected data into three groups: 1) primary and secondary school, 2) college degrees, and 3) graduate and postgraduate degrees. I marked businesses without computers with zero "0" and others with one "1." The results showed (Pearson Chi-Square = 9.539 at df = 2, asymp. sign. = 0.008) that our calculated value was greater than the table value, so I rejected the null hypothesis at the $p=0.05$ level of significance. There was a significant difference in the formal education of respondents in businesses with or without computers. I can conclude that in businesses without computer equipment, I will on average find more owners with lower formal education than in businesses without computer equipment. This assumption confirmed results of several other studies (Thong, 1999; Henson, 1995; Buckland, 1995; and so forth), where the formal education of the owner was found to be an important factor for computer adoption in small businesses. In many cases, this was in combination with computer education and level of computer use by the owner.

Businesses with Computers

The average number of computers was 3.5 per organization (one PC per 1.6 employees). In most cases PCs and network servers are used as well as working stations in some. None of the firms interviewed had minicomputers or a mainframe.

The oldest PC still used in two of the sampled firms was from 1989. Most firms from the sample purchased computers after 1995, when Microsoft released the Windows 95 operating system, that are still in use. Therefore, it is not surprising that most businesses (84%) use some version of the Windows system. From various other operating systems, 14% of the firms still use DOS and 2% other systems such as Linux or Novell.

Small businesses in our sample have on average 4.7 years of computer experience and 0.4 network servers. Forty-five percent of businesses use a local network and 15.8% have an intranet connection via a modem. Has the computer become indispensable in small businesses? Almost half of the respondents (47%) think that their businesses could not operate without a computer (Figure 1). Only 2.2% of the businesses could operate without a computer without any problems. I can conclude that in present times there is almost no successful small business without computer support.

Out of 94 businesses with computer equipment, 70 (73.6%) have a

Figure 1: How businesses operate without a computer

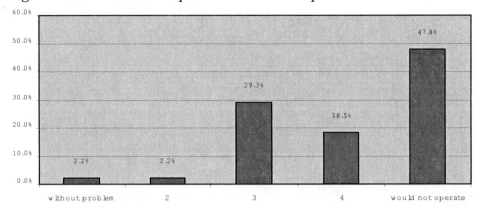

modem, 25 (26.3%) have arranged customer payment with credit cards and 21 (22.1%) use a "bar-code" system for product identification. Due to the fact that 35% of businesses in our sample come from the retail or wholesale field, 75% of them had arrangements with banks for credit card payments for customers and in 63% the "bar-code" system was used.

Thirty-three (34.7%) businesses have a UPS for emergency power supply, in case of power reduction.

Comparison with Other Results

After I compared our results with results of other countries, the results were encouraging. It appears in some instances that Slovene small businesses are not much different from small businesses in developed countries.

In comparison with data for year 2000 in USA and Australia (Burgess and Schauder, 2001) where the percent ages of businesses with PCs were 83% and 84%, the results of this study showed 77.1% of Slovenian small businesses used PCs. On the other hand, more Slovenian firms in the study had Internet access 70.2% (Figure 2), when the results from USA and Australia are 51% and 60%. Slovenian small businesses mostly use the Internet for e-mail (68.1%), followed by information gathering (62.8%) and business advertising (29.8%). A study of Brazilian small businesses from 1997 (Lébre La Rovere, 1998) found that only 22% of small businesses had access to the Internet.

Research in Singapore (Thompson and Tan, 1998) from 1996 shows that there were 69.7% mixed size business (75% with more than 300 employees) with Internet access. The results also showed a significant relationship between Internet adoption and size of firm. Sales over the Internet in Singapore were 29.1%, in comparison with this Slovenian research where they were at level of 10.6%.

In research of small and medium enterprises (SMEs) from Great Britain

Figure 2: Small business usage of the Internet

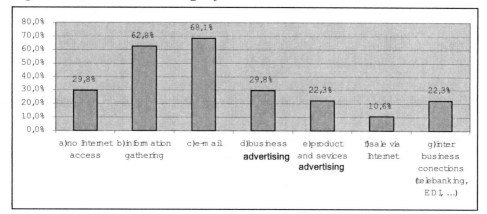

Table 1: Comparison of Internet use

Way of Internet use / Number of employees	Slovenian survey Up to 50	(Lawrence et al., 2000) Up to 49	(Kurbel, 1998) From 1 to 1000+
Information gathering	56.4%	77%	90.6%
Communication (including e-mail)	68.1%	63%	
Advertising of business	29.8%	35%	83.4%
Advertising of products and services	22.3%	34%	76.3%
Sale via Internet	10.6%		34.8%
Electronic business with banks	22.3%	30%	43.6%

(Lawrence and Hughes, 2000), the Internet use by the companies surveyed was 79%. Considering companies with 1-49 employees and 50-250 employees separately, the survey found that there were slightly different levels of Internet use in each of those groups. Table 1 provides a comparison of some of these findings.

The survey results from my research show that 45.3% of small businesses use computer networks (intranet), and an additional 15.8% have data sharing via modem. Results from Great Britain are similar (Lawrence and Hughes, 1997), where 41% of small businesses use an intranet.

Problems with Computer Use

Only 16% of businesses did not encounter any problems with computer equipment. More than half (59%) of the businesses experienced one to three computer hardware problems and 25% experienced more than three problems. Similar results were also exhibited for software problems. Fifty-one percent of the businesses experienced between one to three software problems, 32% experienced software problems more than three times and only 17% did not have any problems with software. Due to the high number of problems with hardware and software, it would be expected that businesses would arrange for an insurance agreement with some insurance office. Only 22% of the firms used an insurance agreement for hardware. In the study of small American business by Vijayaraman and Ramakrishna (1993), 76.1% had some insurance coverage for hardware and software loss. One reason for this may be that there is a three-year guarantee on new computer equipment.

Fifty-eight percent of businesses had not lost any business data yet (Figure 3). However, 17% did lose data at least once, 14.9% lost data twice and 9.6% three or more times. If almost every second business lost some business data at one time or another, how did they get it back?

Out of 45 businesses, 40% re-entered the lost data and 60% retrieved the data from the backup copy. The main reason for the loss of business data is shown in Figure 4. The main reason was hardware failure (21.3%), followed by employee errors (14.9%) and software error (10.6%). Viruses were found in 6.4% of the cases. In one case, business data was lost because the computer was stolen.

It is reasonable to expect that businesses make backup copies of their business data at one time or another. The question now was what type of backup media was used? The results are shown in Figure 5. Some businesses used two different backup procedures (backup on floppy disc and CD). Due to this, the percentage sum in Figure 5 is greater than 100. In most cases (66%) floppy discs were used for backup copies; in 39.4% copies were made on CD,

Figure 3: Number of times businesses lost their business data

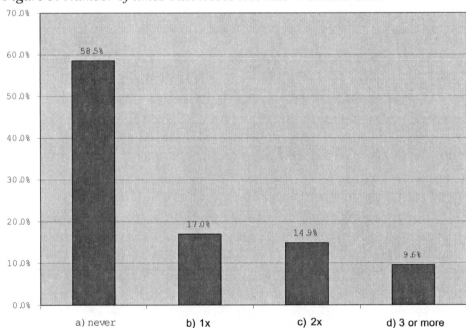

Figure 4: The main reason for the loss of business data

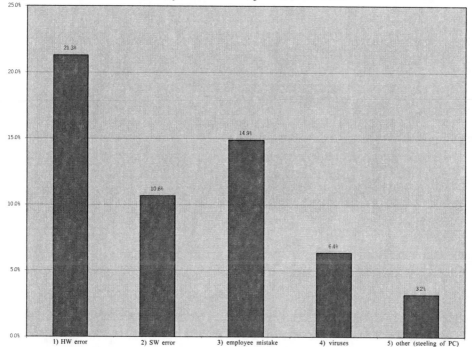

ZIP disk or other backup specialized tools; and 26.6% made backup copies on a second hard disc. The most frightening results came from the 6.4% total of businesses where no backup copies were made at all!

Having backup copies of business data is a good idea, but the question now is, do business owners check the applicability of these copies? More than half (63%) of the businesses checked applicability of their backup copies, 30.4% did not check and 6.5% did not have any backup copies. The last statistic of users with no copy available is different from the previous 6.4% because two businesses did not answer this question.

On average, 3.4 software packages or applications were counted in the tested small businesses. Common office software packages like Microsoft Word, Microsoft Excel or similar were counted as one package. Most of the businesses used retail (68.1%) and purchase applications (63.8%); 56.4% used general ledger applications; 38.3% use applications for salary, leave and illness of employees; and 31.9% use specific business applications. The majority of businesses (79.8%) used common office software packages. Only 23.4% of businesses used a type of package for application development (Access, Visual Basic and so forth), and 11.7% had applications for decision support.

Figure 5: How small businesses store copies of business data

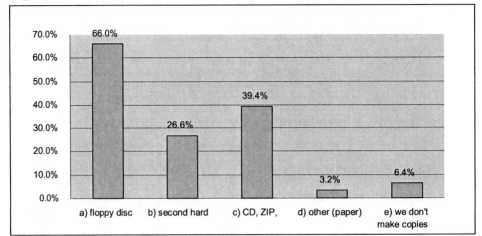

Factor Analysis–Principal Components Analysis

Factor analysis attempts to identify underlying variables, or factors, that explain the pattern of correlations within a set of observed variables. Factor analysis is often used in data reduction (principal components analysis) to identify a small number of factors that explain most of the variance observed in a much larger number of manifest variables (SPSS, Norušis, 1994).

I proceeded with factor analysis (SPSS, Norušis, 1994) using principal component analysis as the extraction method from all valid responses. Among other results, four factors describing intensive use of IS and four factors describing security measures were found. To understand results let us use a simple example. Suppose we want to measure people's satisfaction with their lives. We design a satisfaction questionnaire with various items; among other things we ask our subjects how satisfied they are with their hobbies (item 1) and how intensely they are pursuing a hobby (item 2). Most likely, the responses to the two items are highly correlated with each other. Given a high correlation between the two items, we can conclude that they are quite redundant.

One can summarize the correlation between two variables in a scatterplot. A regression line can then be fitted that represents the "best" summary of the linear relationship between the variables. If we could define a variable that would approximate the regression line in such a plot, then that variable would capture most of the "essence" of the two items. Subjects' single scores on that new factor, represented by the regression line, could then be used in future data analyses to represent that essence of the two items. In a sense we have reduced the two variables to one factor. Note that the new factor is actually a linear combination of the two variables.

The example described above, combining two correlated variables into one factor, illustrates the basic idea of factor analysis, or of principal components analysis to be precise. If we extend the two-variable example to multiple variables, then the computations become more involved, but the basic principle of expressing two or more variables by a single factor remains the same (SPSS, Norušis, 1994).

There is no general definition of the level of intensive IS use in the literature. To be able to analyze the correlation between intensive IS use and the realization of security measures, I decided to use number of software packages or applications and the existence of data exchange with other businesses, similar to research by Henson (1995). In order to place the tested businesses into a group with a higher intensity of IS use, the business must use at least four software packages or applications, of which at least one must be for business application and one for data exchange with other businesses.

As was expected, the result of the correlation conducted with the SPSS statistic software package shows (Tables 2-3) that there is a correlation between businesses with more intensive IS use and others when I analyzed used security measures. All hypotheses except H5 that test the years of the small business owners' job experience were accepted.

After recording the answers of participants, I placed them into two groups according to the correlation among them (not less then 0.3) and according to the problem they discussed. Factor "security-f1" was one of two factors merged from seven questions with the extraction from 0.668 to the smallest 0.297. The questions regarding data loss (0.815) and number of hardware failure (0.604) had the strongest impact. That means that out of seven questions, we would make the biggest difference on result if we changed the answers of these two questions. On the other hand, changing of results of other questions would have minor effect on the results represented as factor "security-f1." We could also say that in general the factor "security-f1"

Table 2: Correlation–security measures, available hardware and use of Internet

Correlations

		security-f1	HW-F1	Internet-f1
security-f1	Pearson Correlation	1,000	,310*	,397*
	Sig. (2-tailed)	,	,003	,000
	N	92	92	92
HW-F1	Pearson Correlation	,310*	1,000	,544*
	Sig. (2-tailed)	,003	,	,000
	N	92	94	94
Internet-f1	Pearson Correlation	,397*	,544*	1,000
	Sig. (2-tailed)	,000	,000	,
	N	92	94	94

*. Correlation is significant at the 0.01 level (2-taile .

represents answers of small business owners who experienced data loss and hardware failure.

It can be concluded that a statistically significant positive correlation exists among these factors and therefore, with a certain probability it can be expected that businesses with more hardware equipment (0.310) and more intensive use of the Internet (0.397) will have more security problems than other businesses. According to these results, small business managers with no bad experiences with hardware failures or Internet use connected troubles should expect them sooner or later if they use more hardware and have more Internet activity. In most cases this is in correlation with time. Arrangements that are necessary for emergency restores of hardware and software (because of those potential threats) must be planned.

Security factor 4 was extracted from three questions regarding how they store business data (0.867), checking the applicability of backup copies (0.841) and the use of anti-virus software (0.567). We could say that the factor "security-f4" represents businesses that use backup copies, did check them and used anti-virus software.

Respondent characteristics related to formal education and self-estimation of computer knowledge–f1. and age and years of experience–f2. Factor "Respondent characteristics-f1" represents businesses with owners with higher formal education and higher self-estimated computer knowledge. Factor "Respondent characteristics-f1" represents businesses with older owners with more business experience.

It can be concluded (Table 3) that a correlation exists between security factor 4 and other listed factors. The results show that with certain probability, we can expect less problems with restoring loss of data in firms where owners/managers have a higher level of education (-0.398), in businesses with more intensive IS use (-0.442) and more hardware (-0.453). On the other hand, we can expect more lost data in businesses with older owners/managers with more years of experience not related with computer use (0.369) or if they are females (0.406). So once again, education was found as one of the important factors for more intensive IS use. I can conclude, as in several other studies (Thong, 1999; Henson, 1995; Buckland, 1995; and so forth), that the higher the formal education of the owner, the better the self-estimation of computer knowledge and because of that, better arrangements will be made for computer security measures in small business. As a result, less data will be lost because of inadequate backup procedures. I did not expect that owners with more years of experience (H5) would use less computer hardware, software and security measures. The point here is in *computer* experience. If owners have a lot of work experience, but no computer experience, they will not know the possibilities for their business in relation to computer support. In most cases, this occurs in very small family businesses until younger relatives start to participate in business development. It is similar in the case of female owners. Previously, the male population was more occupied with computers then females–but that is changing rapidly. Because female owners currently do not get enough opportunities to gain experience with computers (there were no computer courses 10 years ago in Slovene formal education), they need extra education and information on the possibilities and opportunities of computer use in small business.

Discussion

In general it can be stated that most of the small businesses in Slovenia, while struggling with their competition and trying to survive, neglect the importance of security measures, especially in the field of computer risk.

From the literature, it is evident that computer security risk is greater when businesses use PCs, the Internet and Microsoft products. Almost all Slovenian firms use PCs, most of them have Internet access (70.2%) and in general, they use the Microsoft Windows operating system (84%). Therefore, it is not surprising that only 16% of the interviewed businesses do not have any experience with hardware breakdown, and only 17% were without software problems. While most of the PCs used were purchased in the last three years because of the year 2000 problem (Werber et al., 1999), I can also expect that businesses without hardware and software failure can expect to experience it soon. Do they use equipment for the prevention of disaster loss? Only 34.7% of businesses have Uninterruptible Power Supplies for emergency power

Table 3: Correlation–security factor 4 and other factors

Correlations

		security-F4	respondent character-istics-F1	respondent character-istics-F2	respondent sex	Intensive IS use-F1	HW-F1
security-F4	Pearson Correlation	1.000	-.398**	.369*	.406**	-.442	-.453**
	Sig. (2-tailed)	.	.007	.0.13	.006	.002	.002
	N	45	45	45	45	45	45
respondent character-istics-F1	Pearson Correlation	-.398**	1.000	-.001	-.097	.223*	.316**
	Sig. (2-tailed)	.007	.	.994	.351	.031	.002
	N	45	94	94	94	94	94
respondent character-istics-F2	Pearson Correlation	.369*	-.001	1.000	.040	-.304**	-.342**
	Sig. (2-tailed)	.013	.994	.	.703	.003	.001
	N	45	94	94	94	94	94
respondent sex	Pearson Correlation	.406**	-.097	.040	1.000	-.221*	-.159
	Sig. (2-tailed)	.006	.351	.703	.	.032	.127
	N	45	94	94	94	94	94
intensive IS use-F1	Pearson Correlation	-.442**	.223*	-.304**	-.221*	1.000	.457**
	Sig. (2-tailed)	.002	.031	.003	.032	.	.000
	N	45	94	94	94	94	94
HW-F1	Pearson Correlation	-.453**	.316**	-.342	-.159	.457**	1.000
	Sig. (2-tailed)	.002	.002	.001	.127	.000	.
	N	45	94	94	94	94	94

**. Correlation is significant at the 0.01 level (2-tailed)
*. Correlation is significant at the 0.05 level (2-tailed)

supply in case of power reduction.

Forty-two percent of businesses lost their business data at least once. Of them, 40% entered the data once again and 60% retrieved data from a backup copy. In most cases, data is stored on floppy disc (66%), 30.4% did not check the applicability of the backup copies and 6.5% did not have any backup copies. The most common errors were hardware failure, employee error and software error. When comparing the portion of Internet access (70.2%) and 60.6 % of businesses that use some anti-virus software, the results are unsatisfactory. The lack of comparable data is increasing generally, yet these results cannot be compared since results from other similar research of small businesses security measures were not found.

In general, it can be assumed that the state of security measures used in Slovenian small business is not adequate. When talking to owners of small businesses, it is often heard that they change their attitude towards a security strategy only after business data is lost. Similar results were found in the study of small business in the U.S. (Vijayaraman and Ramakrishna, 1993). The correlation with intensive use of IS and the used level of security measures was also tested and the assumption was confirmed. It was stressed many times and also verified in the research that security measures used are in correlation with intensive use of IS and knowledge available in small firms. Again, it can be concluded that knowledge and information are most important for small businesses.

RECOMMENDATIONS

To improve the status of computer security in small businesses, owners/managers and employees must be more extensively educated and informed before they are confronted with business data loss. This issue must be more intensively investigated also in small businesses and not just in large firms (Post and Kagan, 1999; Kuhnhold et al., 2000) where the status is also not much better. In the research conducted by Reimenscschneider and Mykytyn (2000), executives in "small" businesses with seven to 400 employees ranked the most important issues for managing IT and ranked security in 32nd of 36 listed ranks.

Businesses would welcome government initiatives for computer security adoption in small businesses similar to Singapore or EU countries (Lébre La Rovere, 1998; Papazafeiropoulou and Pouloudi, 2000). The utilization of the Internet and electronic commerce would grow faster if the user could be sure what law is in force. This is as well a problem regarding the liability of digital signature in the business, especially from an international viewpoint (Kuhnhold et al., 2000). If the digital signature would be recognized and defined in international business law as a legal instrument, then the number of small businesses using electronic commerce or other ways of trading would increase because of easier ways of trading and information sharing, and also because of lower risk. Until this problem is solved all business documents of high importance must be printed and provided with a signature on paper because digital signature isn't relevant in the current law.

Small business owners should not hesitate to use help from computer specialists, paid by the government for small business consulting. There are many courses, meetings and training courses organized by government organizations for small businesses, but they do not spread enough information about these in public.

Small businesses must recognize three theoretical basic security 'sets of tools': (1) management policy, (2) anti-virus software and (3) backup procedures. The effectiveness of these tools also has to be measured against their costs and the potential damage because of a lack in computer security (Post and Kagan, 2000).

Prevention, as a response to IS disaster threats, should involve:
- investment in hardware such as surge protectors, fireproof vaults, UPS and so forth;
- investment in software for backup, virus detection, data encryption, and so forth;
- developing policies and procedures for computer use–such as backup practices, password access, documentation practices, software testing in isolation before installing on a network and so forth.

Contingency planning, as a response, should involve:
- maintaining slack resources (in some cases it is better to have reserve PCs to use in case of failure);
- making arrangements for loan equipment (some computer services or businesses offer loan of hardware in case of failure);
- buying adequate coverage in insurance which covers hardware, software and data loss as well as business loss (in Slovenia there is only the possibility of hardware insurance);
- service contracts with vendors (if a contract exists then the service time and possible hardware loan in time of service can be arranged);
- reciprocal arrangements with other businesses in the area of IS system use (this is possible only if the IS and software is compatible with partners' IS and software (Vijayaraman and Ramakrishna, 1993).

All of the involved subjects and parts of the business process that are necessary to perform business operations, and can intentionally or unintentionally cause a disaster, should not be forgotten.

Hardware and software are on the minds of small business owners when they take steps to prevent business data loss. However, is this enough? They can have expensive equipment and security software, but without the permanent use of it, there are no benefits. Slovenian hardware and software dealers informed us that when buying new hardware or software, small business owners rarely ask to test it. They should demand automatic backup systems that are incorporated in software solutions to prevent possible damage in case of emergency. Employees should also be educated and trained in the field of computer security. Before being forced to use a security system, it should be checked and tested at least once. Since Slovenia recently started to sell surplus electrical power to nearby countries, it is witnessing several short periods of reduction. Many computers are switched off and break network connections when there are no UPSs. The environment is changing from year to year, and the new weather conditions (hurricane, tornado and flood in new places) are emerging. Are we prepared for that? Computer viruses are not spreading locally. Even in small countries such as Slovenia, anti-virus protection is necessary especially if small businesses are connected to the Internet. There should be a strict line between business and private pleasure, so that no unchecked software or virus-infected diskettes will be used in small business IS. Network servers should be more strictly programmed (using a firewall) to prevent unauthorized login or other ways of unauthorized use of servers. In some cases, well-selected passwords can prevent data loss.

Last but not least, even in the academic sphere, more attention should be given to security problems in small business computer usage. Programmers in the future should posses all the necessary knowledge to develop not only visibly pleasing graphic interfaces, but also secure software with integrated possibilities for automatic backup.

CONCLUSION

This investigation focused on the use of some computer security measures in very small businesses in Slovenia. Despite Slovene small business being well equipped with hardware, software and not far behind developed countries in use of Internet connections, I cannot be satisfied with security measures used in small firms. As in developed countries, Slovenia is not safe from virus attack possibilities and computer intruders, so the importance of security measures in Slovene small businesses must not be neglected.

Results of statistical tests show that there exists a positive correlation between security measures used in small business and intensive use of IS. Factors such as amount of hardware and the use of Internet are increasing the probability of data loss. On the other hand, the greater the owner's formal education and self-estimation of computer knowledge, the higher is the probability of successful used security measures and retrieval of lost data. Small business owners' age and years of work experience and gender were in negative correlation with used security measures. We can conclude that in most cases, older and more job experienced owners, especially women, do not practice use of computer equipment and computer security measures as much as younger, mostly male owners. Because I did not find any other research dealing with this problem, I cannot test if the situation is similar in other countries–but I can assume that there should be no major differences. If so, this chapter is a good starting position for further research in the field of computer security measures used in small businesses.

REFERENCES

Buckland, B. (1995). *Testing the Role of Knowledge Barriers in the Diffusion of Information Technology Within and Among Small Businesses*, Dissertation. UMI Dissertation Services.

Burgess, S. and Schauder, D. (2001). Web site development options for Australian small businesses. *Proceedings of Managing Information Technology in a Global Environment–2001 Information Resources Management Association International Conference*, 957-961, May 20-23, Toronto, Ontario, Canada.

Deschoolmeester, D. and Hee, J. (2000). SMEs and Internet: On strategic drivers influencing use of the Internet in SMEs. In Klein, S., O'Keefe, B., Grièar, J. and Podlogar, M. (Eds.), *Proceedings of 13th Bled E-Commerce Conference, E-Commerce: The End of the Beginning*, 754-769, Slovenia, June 19-21.

Hudoklin, A. and Šmitek, B. (1993). *Quantitative Measuring of Risk Threats of Computer-Supported Information System* (published in Slovene language). Organizacija in kadri, Kranj 26, 180-184.

Henson, J. M. (1995). *Factors Determining the Level of Computerization in a Small Business: An Empirical Examination.* Dissertation. UMI Dissertation Services.

Kocbek, M. and Puharic, K. (1993). *Law on Business Companies.* Newspapers Institution Official Paper of Republic Slovenia.

Kuhnhold, M., Pernul, G. and Herrmann, G. (2000). IT–Security in TOP700 industrial companies in Germany. In Klein, S., O'Keefe, B., Grièar J. and Podlogar, M. (Eds.), *Proceedings of 13th Bled ECommerce Conference, E-Commerce: The End of the Beginning*, 147-161, Slovenia, June 19-21.

Kyas, O. (1997). *Internet Security: Risk Analysis, Strategies and Firewalls.* International Thompson Computer Press.

Lawrence, J. and Hughes, J. (2000). Internet usage by SMEs: A UK perspective. In Klein, S., O'Keefe, B., Grièar J. and Podlogar, M. (Eds.), *Proceedings of 13 th Bled ECommerce Conference, E-Commerce: The End of the Beginning*, 738-753. Slovenia, June 19-21, 738-753.

Lébre La Rovere, R. (1998). Diffusion of information technologies and changes in the telecommunications sector. *Information Technology & People*, 11(3), 194-206.

Norušis, M. (1994). SPSS advanced statistics. *Handbook for Statistic Software Package SPSS*, 6, 1.

Osteryoung, J. S., Pace, D. and Constand R. (1995). An empirical investigation into the size of small businesses. *The Journal of Small Business Finance*, 4(1), 75-86.

Papazafeiropoulou, A. and Pouloudi, A. (2000). The government's role in improving electronic commerce adoption. In Hansen, H., Bichler, M. and Mahrer, H. (Eds.), *Proceedings of the 8th European Conference on Information Systems ECIS 2000–A Cyberspace Odyssey*, Austria, July 3-5, 709-716.

Post, G. and Kagan, A. (2000). Management trends in anti-virus strategies. *Information & Management*, 37, 13-24.

SBW, The Chamber of Commerce and Industry of Slovenia. (1999). *Slovenia Business Week*, April 12(15). Retrieved from the World Wide Web: http://www.gzs.si/eng/news/sbw/default.htm.

Spam.Abuse.Net. (2001). Campaign against Spam mail. Retrieved from the World Wide Web: http://spam.abuse.net/whatisspam.html.

Thong, J., Yap, S. and Raman, S. (1997). Environments for information systems implementation in small businesses. *Journal of Organizational Computing and Electronic Commerce*, 7, 253-78.

Thong, J. (1999). An integrated model of information systems adoption in small businesses. *Journal of Management Information Systems*, (15)Spring, 187-214.

Werber, B., Jere, U. and Zupancic, J. (1999). The year 2000 problem in small companies in Slovenia. In Wojtkowski et al. (Eds.), *Proceedings of the Eight International Conference on Information Systems Development: Methods and Tools, Theory and Practice*, 313-325, August 11-13, Boise, Idaho.

Werber, B. and Zupancic, J. (1993). Application of information technology in small business in Slovenia. In Stowell et al. (Eds.), *Proceedings of the United Kingdom Systems Society Conference on Systems Science: Addressing Global Issues*, 493-504, July 27-30, Paisley, Scotland.

Vijayaraman, B. and Ramakrishna, H. (1993). Disaster preparedness of small businesses with microcomputer-based information systems. *Journal of Systems Management*, June, 28-32.

Part II

Small Business, the Internet and Electronic Commerce

Chapter X

Factors Inhibiting the Collaborative Adoption of Electronic Commerce Among Australian SMEs

Kristy Lawrence
University of Tasmania, Australia

INTRODUCTION

While Electronic Commerce has been touted as the new way in which businesses around the world will operate, there is little research that focuses on small and medium-sized enterprises and the effects that such radical transformation of traditional business processes and practices will have on these small entities. This chapter reports on a practical study undertaken within Australia that focused on small and medium-sized enterprises (SMEs). The specific focus of the study was born out of numerous government reports, which emphasized the advantages of Electronic Commerce and the potential of collaborative, or industry-based practices, to encourage the adoption of Electronic Commerce technologies among these enterprises. The Tasmanian wine sector was investigated in order to identify issues that may inhibit the development of collaborative, industry-wide Electronic Commerce adoption programs. Three issues of significance to these small and medium organizations were identified as: 1) Strategic Orientation and Alignment of members of the sector; 2) Industry Responsibility exhibited by members of this sector; and 3) The Business Case for technology integration.

BACKGROUND

Governments worldwide are beginning to understand and appreciate the potential that Electronic Commerce (E-commerce) holds for advancing national growth and facilitating wealth creation.

According to Kalakota and Whinston (1993, p.3), Electronic Commerce can be defined according to four different perspectives:

1. **Communications perspective**–*Electronic Commerce is the delivery of information, products/services, or payments via telephone lines, computer networks, or any other means.*

2. **Business Process perspective**–*Electronic Commerce is the application of technology toward the automation of business transactions and work-flows.*

3. **Service perspective**–*Electronic Commerce is a tool that addresses the desire of firms, consumers, and management to cut service costs while improving the quality of goods and increasing the speed of service delivery.*

4. **Online perspective**–*Electronic Commerce provides the capability of buying and selling products and information on the Internet and other online services*

Whatever the definition adopted, one thing is generally agreed upon– Electronic Commerce is a business concept, based upon new systems of information and communication, that has the potential to completely revolutionize the way business is undertaken (Department of Industry, Science, and Tourism, 1998).

Many recent publications from Australian federal and state government bodies suggest that Electronic Commerce is, and will continue to be, a priority for all Australians (Department of Industry, Science, and Tourism, 1998; National Office for the Information Economy, 1998; Department of Foreign Affairs and Trade, 1997). Such publications suggest that E-commerce has the potential to transform both national and global economies more rapidly than the industrial revolution, resulting in a major shift in the way we live, learn, and work:

> *Looking to the near future, the Commonwealth envisages an Australia where the process of work, commerce, learning, social interaction, and Government have been transformed by information technologies; in which all Australians are able to take part in the opportunities brought home by the global information economy. Through participation in the information economy, Australia's economy and national wealth grows strongly, providing business opportunities, quality of work, and jobs for more and more Austra-*

lians. Through the adoption of Electronic Commerce and the efficiencies (including lower transaction and marketing costs) allowed by information technologies, businesses increasingly take Australian ideas, goods, and services to markets all over the world, enhancing Australia's competitiveness in the global economy of the twenty-first century (National Office for the Information Economy, 1998: 6).

There exists an increasing perception among governments worldwide that Electronic Commerce is beginning to fundamentally alter the nature of business systems and industry structures. Countries and firms that fall behind run genuine risks of being uncompetitive in the future, while those nations that are 'early adopters' will be well placed to attain major productivity gains and improve international competitiveness (Department of Industry, Science, and Tourism, 1998).

However, the extent to which the Australian economy will benefit from such transformations depends on its willingness to adopt Electronic Commerce innovations and take advantage of the efficiency gains and opportunities for growth they present (National Office for the Information Economy, 1998).

Despite publications suggesting that "*International benchmarks consistently place us among the top countries in the world in terms of adoption and use of information and communications technology*" and that "*We are well regarded internationally for our facilitative and often innovative approach to the information economy*" (National Office for the Information Economy, 1998: 5), there appears little actual implementation of Electronic Commerce among Australia's largest group of business entities–small to medium-sized enterprises (SMEs) (see, for example, National Office for the Information Economy, 1999, 2000; and Andersen Consulting, 1998).

According to the Australia Bureau of Statistics (1999), small businesses are defined as those businesses employing less than 20 people, with medium-sized businesses being defined as those employing 20 or more people, but less than 200.

Extensive research has been undertaken in an attempt to identify reasons as to why Australian organizations, specifically small and medium-sized organizations, appear more reticent in their moves to integrate Electronic Commerce solutions into their businesses than large organizations. A synopsis of some of the most common issues pertinent to SMEs with relation to Electronic Commerce is provided in Table 1.

Governments have become aware of the distinct lack of E-commerce adoption among SMEs in Australia (National Office for the Information

Economy, 2000), and are beginning to understand that E-commerce adoption in large 'mega-corps' is a completely different matter than E-commerce adoption among SMEs. This awareness is significant due to the simple fact that approximately 85-90% of all Australian businesses are SMEs, representing a vast component of Australian industry which may potentially miss out on the benefits of these innovations if their specific issues are not addressed.

Government has recognized that the future success of Australian business in the area of Electronic Commerce requires a cooperative effort on the part of all levels of government, the private sector, and the general community (Alston, 1998). As a result, many local, state, and federal government entities are now actively involved in the push to advance the adoption, implementation, and use of electronic commerce technologies within business. Many projects have been developed throughout the country to facilitate and urge the uptake of Electronic Commerce.

One recent strategy of government has been developed in an attempt to overcome the individual E-commerce adoption difficulties of SMEs, such as lack of resources and infrastructure, by encouraging like-organizations to cooperate with each other. One direction of government bodies has been to push a cooperative and collaborative approach to the introduction of electronic commerce, which involves encouraging the adoption and incorporation at a group, or industry level. This thrust follows the generally held view

Table 1: Factors inhibiting SME adoption of Electronic Commerce technologies (Source: Adapted from Lawrence (1997), Clarke (1997), Lawrence and Keen (1997), Monash University (1996), National Office for the Information Economy (2000))

• *Limited recognition of business case for adoption*
• *Inertia and resistance to change*
• *Technology phobia*
• *Lack of easy-to-use, cost-effective software*
• *Lack of 'critical mass' behind E-commerce adoption*
• *Immaturity of telecommunications and IT infrastructure*
• *Limited resources available for E-commerce implementation (time, funds, skills)*
• *Concerns of Internet leading to uncontrolled growth*
• *Satisfaction with current business arrangements*
• *Fear of alienating intermediaries*
• *Belief that their products or services do not lend themselves to E-commerce*

that organizations operating in similar environments should be able to effectively collaborate on an E-commerce implementation plan from which all members will gain benefit (Department of Industry, Science, and Tourism, 1998; National Office for the Information Economy, 1998; Stickel, 1988).

While collaboration between firms that are located in different phases of the value chain is quite a well-studied problem (Stickel, 1998), the type of organizational alignment which forms *horizontal* alliances to allow collaboration on the collective production of goods, services and the adoption of innovative practices have received little attention in the past (Volkoff, Chan et al., 1999). It is these horizontally collaborative adoption practices which are now being encouraged in order to facilitate the adoption of electronic commerce among Australia's SME sector.

While industry-wide cooperation and government policy are undoubtedly effective when it comes to speeding the acceptance of a new technology (Editor, 1997), little research has been undertaken in an attempt to identify factors which may either facilitate, or inhibit the development of collaborative partnerships between these horizontally placed and traditionally competing firms.

In view of the lack of data available which indicates the potential acceptance of such collaborative approaches to technology adoption among SMEs, this study investigates issues of relevance to organizations operating within traditional (horizontal) competitive structures, which are subsequently faced with the prospect of operating collaboratively for the proposed betterment of themselves and their industry.

BRIEF OUTLINE OF STUDY

Kumar and van Diesel (1996) suggest that rational and economic arguments coupled with technical feasibility are not sufficient to consummate the collaborative alliance. Subsequently, this research investigates whether the realization by individual organizations that cooperative practices can result in increased cost savings and the development of innovative practices throughout the industry is sufficient to allow the establishment of collaborative ventures between these one-time competitors.

The specific question posed by the research can be stated as:

"What issues of significance to SMEs, have the potential to negatively influence projects designed to facilitate the collaborative adoption of Electronic Commerce within Australian industry sectors?"

In order to provide insight into the above question, the case study method was employed, where a single-case study involving multiple sub-units was engaged (Yin, 1994). For the purposes of this research, one Tasmanian industry sector, representing the single case, was selected from state government reports which suggested heightened prospects for this industry from the adoption of Electronic Commerce technologies (Tasmanian Department of Treasury, 1997).

The Tasmanian wine industry was identified as having the potential to reap extensive benefits from the introduction of Electronic Commerce technologies and concepts. It has been suggested that this industry could incorporate E-commerce to make better use of the value-adding opportunities and economies of scale apparent within this sector in order to increase its national and international competitiveness. However, this sector consists of a very large proportion of small and medium-sized enterprises that appear reticent to adopt such technological solutions. The Tasmanian wine industry consists of over 100 organizations operating within different facets of the grape-growing and wine-making value chain ranging in size, function, and years in operation. These organizations (included as sub-units within the case study) were identified as prospective collaborative adopters of electronic commerce procedures and technologies, but were relatively inexperienced with regard to technology adoption.

Due to the relatively small number of organizations operating within this industry, and the proximity of these businesses to the researcher, it was possible to approach all members of the sector for the purposes of sub-unit selection. Resultantly, all members directly involved in the grape-growing and wine-making processes were contacted by telephone or personalized letter and approached about becoming participants within the research project. Organizations that indicated interest in the research were sent specific details of the project and an indication of the extent of their expected involvement.

Initial interest by members of the industry sector resulted in a total of 57 explanatory letters being sent to prospective participants of the study. However, due to issues of availability of the members, a total of seven case organizations were selected as actual participants in this qualitative study.

These seven organizations represent three organizational size differentials operating within this industry. Two small businesses, two medium businesses, and one large organization were included in the study to provide comparison. A number of members of one representative industry association and one state government department were also included in the study in order to provide a non-business perspective on issues affecting the industry. Table 2 provides a list of these businesses and the position of the chief interviewee within this organization (names disguised for purposes of confidentiality).

Table 2: Businesses included in study and relevant organizational representative

Organization	Participant/s
Small Business A	Owner/Manager
Small Business B	Owner/Manager Marketing Manager
Medium Business A	Owner/Manager
Medium Business B	Vineyard Manager
Large Business A	General Manager
Industry Association A	Government Representative Executive Officer Vice President
State Government Department A	Industry Development Officer

All data collection was undertaken within an iterative cycle of both collection and analysis over a period of 18 months. Within this research project, semi-structured interviews were undertaken with a number of representatives of the case organization. As a complementary source of data, each interview was undertaken at the site of the organization, thus allowing opportunities for limited direct observations of organizational processes and procedures, environmental conditions, and the actions of the participants within their natural contexts. Such observations were used as sources of evidence at subsequent data analysis stages. In addition, documentation provided by the participant organization, in addition to publicly available documentation, was obtained as an additional source of data to inform the research. Figure 1 graphically illustrates the iterative process of data collection and analysis which was undertaken in an attempt to provide insight into the research question.

At the completion of the data-collection and analysis phases of the research, three themes were identified as playing a significant role in inhibiting the development of a 'collaborate-to-compete' environment within this Tasmanian industry sector, with particular reference to technological innovation and implementation. These were:

1. *strategic orientation and alignment*–pertaining to the internal strategies of those small and medium-sized organizations;
2. *industry responsibility*–pertaining to the collaborative culture of those small and medium-sized organizations, and their traditionally competitive nature; and
3. *business case*–pertaining to the organizations' perceptions and use of the benefits of Information Technology, specifically Electronic Commerce, applications.

Figure 1: Iterative process of data collection and analysis

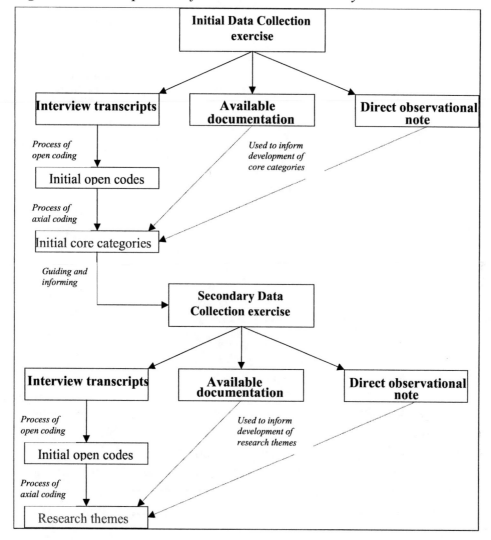

DISCUSSION OF THREE THEMES

The previous section of this chapter identified the analytic development of three themes which have relevance to the research question, *"What issues of significance to SMEs have the potential to negatively influence projects designed to facilitate the collaborative adoption of Electronic Commerce within Australian industry sectors?"*

These three themes, graphically represented in Figure 2, represent the lack of strategic orientation of, and alignment between, members of this sector; the lack of industry responsibility exhibited among members; and the

Figure 2: Three core themes derived from iterative process of data collection and analysis

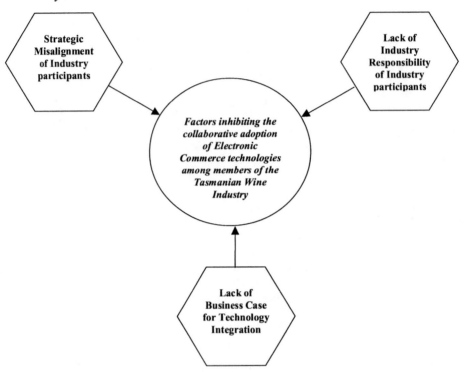

perceived lack of a business case to substantiate investments in electronic commerce technologies. Each of these three themes is significant in terms of their inhibiting influence on projects aimed at introducing market-based (horizontally collaborative) technological implementations within this industry sector. Table 3 indicates the presence of these themes, and their associated sub-categories, within the seven case organizations included in this study.

STRATEGIC ORIENTATION AND MISALIGNMENT

The first significant issue identified in this study, with relation to the research question, was the distinct lack of strategic orientation of firms operating within this sector, and the misalignment of strategic goals among members of the sector. This lack of strategic orientation of the firms operating within the Tasmanian wine industry is significant in that to effectively introduce collaborative practices, all members must exhibit shared goals and objectives. The existence of shared goals and objectives

Table 3: Presence of themes and associated sub-categories among organizations

Case/ Category	Strategic Misalignment		Industry Responsibility		Business Case	
	Internal organizational strategies	External strategic pressures	Collaborative culture	Channel conflict	Tradition	Business benefit
Small Business A	Y		Y	Y	Y	Y
Small Business B	Y		Y	Y	Y	Y
Medium Business A	Y	Y	Y	Y	Y	Y
Medium Business B	Y		Y	Y	Y	Y
Large Business A	Y	Y	Y	Y	Y	Y
Industry Association A	Y	Y	Y	Y		Y
State Government Department A	Y	Y	Y	Y	Y	Y

cannot be seen among those SME organizations operating within this sector. Instead, data from this study indicates that these organizations prefer to work in isolation from each other, and endeavour to reinforce their independence from one another.

"We have chosen this path, and whether it is for the good or not, it really doesn't matter, in the end we're still here, we still own ourselves" (Small Business B).

This individualism counters the development of industry-wide goals and shared objectives, which are required if this industry sector is to apply collaboratively based adoption programs.

In addition to wishing for the maintenance of their independence, rather than consolidation for industry returns, these SMEs appear not to desire an increase in their own existing market share or to obtain strategic or competitive advantage for their products. Those SMEs included in the study appear content to maintain their existing practices and current market share, without entering into highly uncertain nationally and internationally competitive market practices.

"If you look around there is nothing that looks like that we are just interested in growing grapes. It's tourism, it's a lifestyle, it's an interest in the future for a showplace sort of thing, and it's a combined effort with everything that creates a good life with wine surrounding it" (Small Business A).

"We only produce every now and then and we make wine out of it. Sometimes the birds end up getting it, sometimes there is just not enough of the crop to bother about it. Some years the wallabies, possums, and birds leave enough for us, then we will make a little bit of wine. It's more of something we'd sell at the cellar door, nothing that would ever be commercial" (Small Business B).

The above quotes, taken directly from interviews, indicate the lack of strategic orientation among these firms. This, coupled with the way in which these businesses wish to maintain their independence from one another, and resistance of the development of shared goals and objectives, has the effect of inhibiting the development of any project designed around collaborative participation. As a result, the *collaboratively based* introduction of electronic commerce technologies, which are commonly seen as *strategic investments* by small firms, would encounter difficulties if applied in this type of industry sector.

INDUSTRY RESPONSIBILITY

The second theme developed from data obtained from those organizations participating in this study relates to the lack of industry responsibility or the care and accountability of these members to others operating within their environment. This theme identifies the lack of collaborative culture currently existing within this industry sector, and indicates how this, coupled with open conflict apparent between members, has the potential to significantly inhibit the development of collaborative market-based technological implementations. For such projects to be effective, the atmosphere of collaboration must be one of necessary mutual respect, tolerance, and trust between collaborators.

"They all have their gigantic ego heads that won't allow, for instance, if you were going to sell some wine overseas and you didn't have enough but you know of another vineyard who is struggling and has wine to sell but they don't have a way to export, instead of saying 'no, we don't have any on us,' you could say 'well, I don't have any, but I know of a good wine and I can get him to send you a bottle' and we could end the wine together. But they don't do that. There's no camaraderie, no collaboration between any of them" (Small Business A).

"All of these people are trying to destroy us, we're not going to be part of it. I still think we should be part of it, because the best things you can do with your enemies is be friendly with them, so you know what they are dong. The further you stay away from them the more they can do to you without you knowing" (Small Business B).

Such lack of responsibility shown to others within the same sector would result in each organization working in a strongly independent and opportunistic fashion, with attempts to establish the best deal for themselves, rather than establishing the best outcomes for the sector as a whole. Such behavior would necessarily inhibit the effective implementation of these technologies that have the potential to increase the efficiency and effectiveness of the entire industry.

BUSINESS CASE FOR INFORMATION TECHNOLOGY ADOPTION

The third theme identifies issues of particular relevance to the research, which pertain specifically to each individual's perception toward Information Technologies. These organizations have extremely limited experiences with Information Technologies outside those developed for production-enhancement purposes. Technological implementations for administration and logistical functions are minimal or non-existent within the majority of these firms. This lack of personal experience, coupled with inconsistent and often-exaggerated negative information obtained from sources outside their operating environment, reinforces their reliance on traditional manual-based mechanisms for conducting business. Resource limitations such as available capital and time to undertake research and evaluation of available technology, coupled with the preference for traditional mechanisms of business, inhibits these organizations from becoming aware of the potential benefits to be gained from introducing electronic commerce-based tolls and techniques into their operating environment. This lack of recognition further inhibits the development of a business case to substantiate the significant investments that would be involved in the introduction of such techniques.

"I'm just doing the bookkeeping on the computer. I'm not computer literate enough to do the rest of it" (Small Business A).

"[Information Technology] doesn't seem of that much relevance though, fax is just as easy in my opinion. What technology is needed? In business circles I don't see anything that would turn me on..." (Medium Business B).

"I've seen very little on the Internet, but it doesn't seem very stimulating...I really couldn't care if the e-mail and the Internet takes years and years..." (Small Business A).

"Our core business is producing high-quality wine... We don't use e-mail or the Internet because our role in being a small company is selling, ...[dealing with technology] is not one of our core functions–it tends to be put aside" (Small Business B).

With regard to the research question, this lack of an effective business case to support technological implications would prove to be a significant inhibiting factor to any project aiming to introduce non-production-oriented technologies into the working practices of these businesses. Because there is no business case, these SMEs, which are influenced heavily by day-to-day survival, would not be willing to spend their resources on seemingly non-core activities such as these new technological implementations.

CONCLUSION

This chapter has reported on a study that was undertaken within one Australian industry sub-sector with the purpose of identifying issues that exist among the SME members that may have the potential to inhibit the development of industry-wide Electronic Commerce adoption programs.

Three areas of significance to the research question have been identified as: 1) the lack of strategic orientation of the individual SME members of the sector, and the misalignment of these firms' goals for the future; 2) the lack of industry responsibility exhibited by members of this sector for others operating within a similar environment; and 3) the lack of an established business case to support future integration of technological solutions. Each of these themes has been described with an indication of how these issues may inhibit the development of collaboratively based adoption programs.

While government reports may espouse the virtues of Electronic Commerce adoption and suggest the pooling of resources and strategies among SME communities in order to increase the level of adoption, this study indicates that there are significant factors which, unless addressed effectively, have the potential to significantly inhibit the introduction of projects aimed to introduce collaboratively based electronic commerce practices within this industry sector.

The identification of issues that exist among the SME environment which have the potential to inhibit the development of collaboratively based projects is significant. The significance becomes apparent when it is recognized that it is these issues, specific to SMEs and the environment they operate in, that need to be addressed if organizations operating within an SME community, similar to the one described briefly in this chapter, are to take full advantage of the possibilities enabled by the effective implementation and use of Electronic Commerce technologies.

REFERENCES

Alston, R. (1998). *Major Research Project on E-Commerce*. Retrieved from the World Wide Web: http://www.richardalston.dca.gov.au. Australia.

Andersen Consulting. (1998). eCommerce: Our future today. *A Review of E-Commerce in Australia*.

Clarke, R. (1997). *What's Holding up EC in Australia?* Xamax Consulting.

Australian Bureau of Statistics. (1999). *Small and Medium Enterprises: Business Growth and Performance Survey Report Number 8141.0*. Canberra, Australia.

Department of Foreign Affairs and Trade. (1997). *Putting Australia on the New Silk Road: The Role of Trade Policy in Advancing Electronic Commerce*. Canberra, Commonwealth of Australia.

Department of Industry, Science, and Tourism. (1998). *Getting Business Online*. Canberra, Australia.

Department of Industry, Science, and Tourism. (1998). *NEWS: A Project to Get Smaller Enterprises On-Line*. Canberra, Australia.

Editor. (1997). The beauty of being Belgium is skin-deep; though competition has held back the growth of electronic money elsewhere, collusion may not be a better answer. *The Economist*, 17.

Kalakota, R. and Whinston, A. B. (1996). *Electronic Commerce: A Manager's Guide*. Addison-Wesley.

Kumar, K. and van Diesel, H. G. (1996). Sustainable collaboration: Managing conflict and cooperation in interorganizational systems. *MIS Quarterly*, September, 279-297.

Lawrence, K. L. (1997). Factors inhibiting the utilization of Electronic Commerce facilities in Tasmanian small to medium-sized enterprises. *Australasian Conference on Information Systems*, Adelaide, Australia, University of South Australia.

Lawrence, K. L. and Keen, C. D. (1997). *A Survey of Factors Inhibiting the Adoption of Electronic Commerce by Small and Medium-Sized Enterprises in Tasmania*. WP97-01, Department of Information Systems, University of Tasmania. Australia.

Monash University. (1996). *Advice on Electronic Commerce Programs for Small to Medium-sized Enterprises*. Centre for Electronic Commerce.

National Office for the Information Economy. (1998). *Towards an Australian Strategy for the Information Economy: Preliminary Statement*, Canberra, Australia.

National Office for the Information. Economy (1999). *E-Australia: Australia's ECommerce Report Card*. Department of Communications, Information Technology and the Arts. Australia.

National Office for the Information Economy. (2000). *Small Business Index: Survey of Computer Technology and E-Commerce in Australian Small and Medium Business*. Australia.

Stickel, E. (1988). *An Economic Analysis of Collaboration between Competing Firms in a Heterogeneous Market Environment*. Unpublished Manuscript.

Stickel, E. (1998). Electronic commerce and collaboration between competing firms. *Australian Journal of Information Systems* (Special Issue– Electronic Commerce).

Tasmanian Department of Treasury. (1997). *State Budget 1997-1998*. Tasmania, Parliament of Tasmania.

Volkoff, O., Y. E. Chan, Y. E. et al. (1999). Leading the development and implementation of collaborative interorganizational systems. *Information & Management*, (35), 63-75.

Yin, R.K. (1994). *Case Study Research: Design and Methods*. Sage Publications.

Chapter XI

Web Initiatives & E-Commerce Strategy: How Do Canadian Manufacturing SMEs Compare?

Ron Craig
Wilfrid Laurier University, Canada

INTRODUCTION

Two important forces are at work today in the Canadian and global economies. First is the traditional force of small and medium-sized enterprises (SMEs). Statistics Canada reports SMEs account for more than 60% of Canada's private sector employment and 40% of gross domestic product. Second, Information Technology (IT) and the Internet continue to change the way businesses and individuals work, shop, and/or relax. In particular, the Internet and Electronic Commerce (EC) are heralded as a great opportunity for business, consumers, and governments. The impact on SMEs is somewhat uncertain and still emerging. Some argue the Internet levels the playing field, giving smaller firms greater opportunity to compete against larger firms. Others argue that, since SMEs generally have fewer resources available for IT or other initiatives, they could be left behind. In addition, because of their size, SMEs have minimal control or influence over such external forces.

In this chapter the progress of smaller and medium-sized manufacturers in the use, and potential use, of the Internet and EC is investigated. Do they lead or lag larger firms? Is an EC strategy important for them, and what reasons do they see for pursuing it? Are firms that pursue an EC strategy more successful than those that do not?

Statistics Canada defines small businesses as having annual sales in the $30,000 to $5 million range. In this study, firms with sales less than or equal to $5 million were classified as small. Firms with sales in the $5 million to $30 million range were classified as medium in size, and above $30 million were classified as larger. The Canadian manufacturing sector comprises firms primarily engaged in the physical or chemical transformation of materials or substances into new products (either finished or semi-finished). There are 22 major industry groups in Canada, with 238 industries (based on the North American Industry Classification System).

BACKGROUND

EC is used here in the broad sense, dealing with all aspects of business (including communication, information sharing, marketing, purchasing, logistical coordination, and payments). It is driven by both improved and new business models facilitated by information technology advances and the Internet.

Obtaining consistent information concerning national and global Internet commerce is difficult, and there is often hype mixed in with reality. It is clear that business-to-business (B2B) dominates business-to-consumer (B2C) activity. Statistics Canada (2001) reports that in 1999 Canada accounted for almost 7% of worldwide Internet commerce (CDN $195 billion globally). The value of sales received over the Internet rose by 73.4% in 2000, with 80% being business to business. By 2004, it is predicted that global Internet commerce will increase to CDN $3.9 trillion, with Canada's share being CDN $151.5 billion.

Canada was recently ranked fourth in 'e-readiness,' a measure of the extent to which a country's business environment is conducive to Internet-based commercial opportunities (Economist Intelligence Unit, 2001). Leading the rankings was the U.S., followed by Australia, and the UK. At a national level, it is recognized that one of the key issues currently facing Canada is facilitating the transition of existing SMEs into successful e-businesses (Canadian E-Business Opportunities Roundtable, 2001).

SMEs face both challenges and opportunities with EC. Challenges include strategy determination and implementation, new/revised forms of business models and competition, successful technology adoption, and the pace/cost of change. Should a particular business use EC, and if so, when and how? At a basic level, the Web allows local firms to vastly extend their reach, and send a much richer (content-wise) message to others (Evans & Wurster, 1999). There are opportunities to leverage corporate assets (tangible and intangible) in new ways, define new channels for communication and sales, and move toward virtual integration of the entire supply chain network. Yet the history of IT projects shows there are many difficulties and failures. The latest Standish Group (2001) data on IT projects shows 28% succeeded, 49% were challenged, and 23% failed.

EC, as an application of IT, is subject to the same excessive exuberance as exhibited with previous technology advances. Figure 1 depicts an 'EC Reality Model,' adapted from Feeny's (1997) 'IT Reality Model.' EC hype goes beyond the current capabilities of IT and EC, focusing on potential capabilities and outcomes. While it may become reality in the future, at present it is impossible. Beyond the hype, there is the current reality of EC–these are the bundle of products and services currently available, albeit not necessarily yet practical or affordable for most organizations. The domain of 'Useful EC' consists of those products and services that are affordable for most organizations, providing a reasonable return on investment. Finally, there is the 'Strategic EC' area, which can provide a significant contribution to organizational achievement, including substantial competitive advantage. Because of resource issues, one would expect the pool of 'useful' EC to be smaller for SMEs than for larger firms.

The practical application of EC is undeniable, as is the strategic use of IT for competitive advantage. It appears that the hype is gradually being sorted from the reality and practicality, as 'dot.com' firms with no sustainable cashflow or profits disappear, and the worlds of 'bricks' and 'clicks' converge. Yet, strong statements continue to be made, such as, "The period from 2000 to 2002 will represent the single greatest change in worldwide economic and business conditions ever, and most of the impact will occur during the next 18 months. If companies (and countries) do not change their assumptions and strategies during the next 12 months,

Figure 1: EC Reality Model

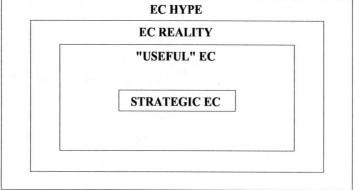

they will almost certainly fall behind and probably be left behind" (Means & Schneider, 2000). Within this context, can SMEs survive or even thrive?

Strategic EC falls into the strategy domain, while Useful EC fits with tactics. The traditional strategy development approach is delineated by Fry & Killing (2000). Technology changes the environment, facilitating new approaches to utilizing the physical (Porter & Millar, 1985) and virtual (Rayport and Sviokla, 1995) value chains, and creating major disruption to historical power balances. The physical value chain model describes a series of value-adding physical activities connecting a company's supply side with its demand side. As originally proposed, the value chain model treats information as a supporting element of the value-adding process. Mimicking the physical value chain is the virtual value chain, where value is added with and through information. The virtue value chain identifies five ways of adding value via information: gathering it, organizing it, selecting it, synthesizing it, and distributing it.

While traditional strategy frameworks are still very useful, new approaches to thinking about and using them are required. In particular, technology provides a means of leveraging all the assets of a firm, including physical, financial, processes, organizational, customer, supplier, and managerial. 'Value Dynamics' (Boulton et al., 2000) recommends firms design, invest in, and manage their entire portfolio of assets. Their view of assets include traditional hard assets (plant, equipment, inventory, money) plus soft assets (customers, suppliers, employees, organization). Business models are based on assembling the proper balance of assets to create the greatest value for shareholders and other stakeholders. Information technology facilitates new and improved business models, of which EC is an important development.

One can think in terms of an EC Importance Grid (Figure 2), similar to the 'IT Strategic Grid' (Applegate et al., 1999). EC has both operational and strategic implications, and this grid can be applied to each. A firm in the low/low quadrant would not be highly dependent on EC for either operational functioning or strategic positioning. The resource implications are that relatively few resources would be expended now, or in the future, on EC, and one would not expect senior management to spend much time, if any, on EC planning. In contrast, a firm in the high/high quadrant is dependent on smooth functioning of current EC applications, and would be planning to extend applications for future competitive advantage. Management in this type of firm would spend considerable time on EC planning, and the resource implications would be significant. Understanding an organization's grid position is critical for developing an appropriate EC management strategy.

EC can also be considered within the framework of the Technology Adoption Lifecycle (Moore, 1995; Rogers, 1995), which explains how communities respond to discontinuous innovations (see Table 1 and Figure

3). Firms will adopt EC for different reasons, and at different times within the lifecycle. Innovators comprise the smallest group, followed by early adopters and laggards. The early majority and late majority comprise the largest segments. While the framework is useful for considering why and when firms adopt EC, its limitations are seen if EC is only considered as a technology. Fundamentally, EC is a different approach to business, and is facilitated by IT. While new forms of IT will appear, and older forms die off, EC will continue to grow as part of the common business model.

Complementing the technology adoption lifecycle is the technology maturation cycle. New technologies go through an invention, development, refinement, and commercialization process. During the commercialization phase of successful technologies, the basic product is enhanced by a set of complementary products and services that enable the target customer to assimilate and use the technology. From the SME perspective, this "whole product" is more likely to be available and affordable much further along the maturation curve. They usually do not have the resources to support implementations requiring substantial technical skills and

Figure 2: EC importance grid

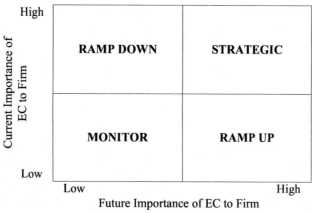

Future Importance of EC to Firm

Table 1: Technology adoption lifecycle

Group	Alternative Name	Motivation	Approx. %
Innovators	Technology Enthusiasts	Technology "High"	1-3%
Early Adopters	Visionaries	Competitive Edge	5-15%
Early Majority	Pragmatists	Productivity/Efficiency	30-40%
Late Majority	Conservatives	Conformity	30-40%
Laggards	Skeptics	Compliance	10-20%

Figure 3: Technology adoption lifecycle

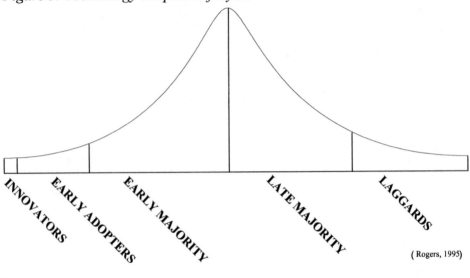

(Rogers, 1995)

investment. In contrast, larger firms have the financial and technological support resources to take on riskier projects earlier in the cycle. They also have the incentive, in terms of developing competitive advantage over other large firms. A more light-hearted, yet still realistic, view of this cycle is the Gartner Group's 'Hype Cycle' (Figure 4), which ties in with the Reality Model of Figure 1.

Most academic EC research has focused on larger firms and high growth startups. Among SMEs, retailers and service providers have been studied more than manufacturers. The Canadian Federation of Independent Business (Whyte, 2000) found that, while an increasing proportion of SMEs are using the Internet, they are slow to adopt EC. Whyte concludes that servicing customers and marketing are the keys to success. Government can help by improving the national telecommunications infrastructure (easier access, high bandwidth), ensuring a fair EC tax policy, improving government Internet services, and reducing legal barriers.

Mackay et al. (2001) studied key factors affecting EC adoption in small British Columbia firms. Drawing upon the Theory of Planned Behavior (Ajzen, 1991), they found management support had the greatest influence on intention to adopt EC, followed by internal pressure and perceived benefits.

Barua et al. (2000) investigated a three-phase model of EC. E-Business drivers (IT applications, processes, e-business readiness) impact operational excellence measures (including % online business, % online procurement, % customer service provided online, order delivery time), which impact financial measures (including revenue/employee, gross profit margin, ROA). Results of

Figure 4: Technology hype cycle

(Gartner Group)

studying some 1,200 firms in the U.S. and Europe (a mix of retailers, manufacturers, wholesalers, and distributors), showed firms with increased financial performance had significantly better operational excellence performance and higher levels of investments in E-Business drivers. In particular, smaller firms (100 or fewer employees) saw much higher percentage gains in financial performance with e-business, relative to larger firms.

Dandridge and Levenburg (1999) investigated Internet use of firms with fewer than 25 employees, finding a subset (young, with growth expectations) actively using the Internet as a marketing tool. Jentzsch and Miniotas (1999) recommend SMEs examine their value chain to determine the most effective use of the Internet. Poon (1999) outlines the state of small business Internet commerce. He found the Internet used mainly for communication and information exchange. Poon presents a "maturity model" based on business processes and EC application (technology) complexity.

Pelham (2000), although not an EC study, investigated performance factors in small manufacturing firms. He found market orientation had the strongest positive relationship with performance measures, and the most influential market orientation elements were fast response to negative customer satisfaction information, strategies based on creating value for customers, immediate response to competitive challenges, and fast detection of changes in customer product preferences. It is easy to see how the Web can be used by smaller firms to enable and support these performance factors.

STUDY PURPOSE & SURVEY METHODOLOGY

This was an empirical study of Ontario manufacturers. Data was collected as part of a larger annual survey of manufacturers in southwestern Ontario

(Canada's manufacturing center), during the final two months of the year. Firms were sampled from a database compiled from several directories (Scott's Ontario Manufacturers Directory, Dun & Bradstreet's Canadian Key Business Directory, and local Chambers of Commerce Business Directories). This ensured as complete a population listing as possible, from which a random sample was taken. The sample was representative based on location, industry, and size. Respondents were senior executives of these firms. With a survey size of approximately 350, the '99 survey had a response rate of 50.6%, while the '00 survey was 45.0%. Firms were categorized based on sales: smaller (< $5 million), medium ($5 - $30 million), and larger (> $30 million).

EC "readiness" and attitude were studied by comparing:
(1) proportions with Web sites,
(2) whether or not EC was viewed as strategic,
(3) actual and anticipated use of EC,
(4) reasons for EC.

Two research questions studied the link between EC strategy and firm performance:
(1) Is there a performance difference between manufacturers who see or do not see an EC strategy as important?
(2) Are there performance differences between different sized firms, all viewing EC as important?

Results were aggregated by size. Chi-square statistical independence tests were completed, and further analysis used difference of proportions (1-tailed t-tests). In several cases, sample sizes were too small to conduct meaningful tests. For example, a three-way classification of Table 5 (Reasons for EC)–based on firm size, strategic view of EC, and reasons–would have resulted in many small cell sizes.

RESULTS & DISCUSSION

A minimal indicator of a firm's interest in, and potential involvement with, EC is given by whether or not they have a Web site. One would expect the presence of an organizational Web site to increase with firm size (larger size equates to greater resources), and this was confirmed (0.001 level of significance). Results are shown in Table 2. While a minority of smaller firms (44%) had a Web site, this was still a considerable group. In contrast, 89% of larger firms had Web sites. In terms of technology adoption, smaller firms lagged considerably (on average) with Web site development, while larger firms led. Firms without Web sites were asked if they would have one within the coming year ("Plan to Soon" row). When this is taken into consideration ("1 Year Projection" row), the gap narrows, yet still persists.

Overall, it is evident that Web sites are by now well along the adoption curve, that smaller firms have been slower (on average) to develop them, and that smaller firms have a larger 'laggard' group. For SMEs as a group, a majority (60%) have had Web sites for some time.

When asked whether EC was an important strategy for their firm (Table 3), no statistically significant differences were found (based on firm size). However, there were two trends: (i) the proportion of firms indicating EC as important increased with size, and (ii) the proportion of firms unsure about this decreased with size. Almost half of the smaller respondents indicated EC was important, rising to more than two-thirds for larger firms. Conversely, almost one in five smaller firms were not sure about the importance of EC to their business, while this dropped to almost one in 20 for larger firms. Given the tremendous impact B2B and B2C commerce is forecast to have, it is surprising that many firms (of all sizes) indicated it was not of strategic importance. Evidence to be examined later in this chapter shows that, while smaller firms are slower to implement supplier electronic connection, the trend is positive.

One year later (Table 4), it is seen that the percentage of firms using EC lags considerably the percentage earlier, indicating EC as an important strategy (Table 3). Even factoring in those indicating EC plans for the coming year ('1 Year Projection' row), SMEs will still lag in adoptions, while for larger firms the gap is eliminated. Though not statistically significant, there is an observable trend of increasing EC use with increasing firm size. Overall, this suggests EC adoption is not as far along the curve as Web site use. SMEs are still in the 'Early Majority' phase, while larger firms now have the 'Late Majority' coming on-stream.

Respondents were also asked how their business will use EC in the next few years, based on a list developed from the literature. Table 5 shows their responses, for both surveys. Two things stand out: in most cases, firm size made little difference

Table 2: Presence of Web site ('99 survey)

	Smaller	**Medium**	**Larger**	**Total**
Yes	43.8%	79.7%	89.1%	72.7%
No	56.3%	20.3%	10.9%	27.3%
Plan to Soon	25.0%	8.7%	3.6%	11.6%
No Plans	31.3%	11.6%	7.3%	15.7%
1 Yr. Proj.	68.8%	88.4%	97.7%	84.3%
Total #	48	69	55	172

(where statistically significant differences exist, these are indicated), and there was no single dominating reason for firms to use EC. Each specific reason was selected by firms of all sizes, while the average number of reasons selected increased with size. There are also interesting differences between the two surveys, suggesting an ongoing maturation process as firms learn more about EC and are able to separate hype from reality.

Overall, the most frequently selected uses focused on sales growth–either through new markets or increased sales with current customers. A Web presence can be particularly beneficial for smaller manufacturers whose reach has been limited, and they had high expectations in the 1999 survey. Comparing the two years, the trend is to lower expectations about accessing new markets, and a continued emphasis on current customers. While this could be because new markets are becoming saturated, it is more likely that firms are realizing it is easier to increase business with current customers.

Integration backward to suppliers was of concern to few small firms, while it was important for larger ones. For medium-sized firms, this became more important in 2000. This agrees with the current concern for supply chain management and optimization. Larger firms are important participants in supply chains, while smaller firms usually are not. Over time, though, electronic connection of supply chain participants will continue to expand.

Table 3: E-commerce important strategy for firm ('99 survey)

	Smaller	Medium	Larger	Total
Yes	48.9%	53.7%	67.3%	56.8%
No	31.9%	31.3%	27.2%	30.2%
Unsure	19.1%	14.9%	5.5%	13.0%
Total #	47	67	55	169

Table 4: Use of e-commerce ('00 survey)

	Smaller	Medium	Larger	Total
Yes	21.1%	31.1%	48.3%	35.0%
No	65.8%	57.4%	32.8%	50.3%
1 Yr. Proj.	34.3%	42.6%	67.3%	49.6%
Total #	38	61	58	157

Gaining access to information about the market and competition (market intelligence) was another frequently indicated reason. Rubin (1999) studied how small businesses can use the Web for competitive intelligence about competitors, industry trends, and customer opinions. All sizes of firms saw the Web facilitating this, although the trend is downwards for smaller and medium-sized firms.

One aspect of customer relationship management (CRM) is dealing with customer complaints. In both surveys, the percentage of firms mentioning this reason increased with firm size. Comparing the two years, there was an increase for medium-sized firms, and a decrease for smaller firms.

This market orientation of many respondents aligns with the performance findings of Pelham (2000) described earlier: fast response to customer complaints, responding to competitive challenges, early detection of customer product changes, and an emphasis on a growth/differentiation strategy (rather than a low-cost strategy). Use of the Web and EC provides a means of supporting these actions.

Interestingly, cost competitiveness was not a reason given by that many firms, and its importance decreased in the 2000 survey (especially for smaller firms).

Table 5: Reason for electronic commerce (% indicating)

Reason	Smaller		Medium		Larger	
Survey Yr:	'99	'00	'99	'00	'99	'00
Access to New Markets	64.5	36.7	46.9	28.0	45.1	26.4
More Business from Current Customers	48.4	46.7	44.9	58.0	45.1	54.7
Market Intelligence	38.7	20.0	53.1	34.0	35.3	37.7
Access to New Technologies	29.0	16.7	18.4	26.0	25.5	20.8
Customer Complaints (d)	22.6	16.7	24.5	34.0	39.2	37.7
Cost Competitiveness (c)	22.6	3.3	22.4	18.0	29.4	24.5
Speed New Products to Market (c)	22.6	6.7	22.4	14.0	17.6	24.5
Integration Forward (Retail)	19.4	6.7	22.4	24.0	27.5	37.7
Integrate Markets & Technologies	19.4	10.0	22.4	28.0	21.6	26.4
Jump Market Barriers	19.4	3.3	32.7	14.0	15.7	11.3
Integration backward to Suppliers (a, c)	16.1	16.7	28.6	36.0	47.1	43.4
Block Competitors' Moves	12.9	3.3	8.2	8.0	9.8	5.7
Trade/Government Help	12.9	3.3	10.2	4.0	3.9	1.9
Total #	n = 31	n = 30	n = 49	n = 51	n = 51	n = 53

(a) significant @ .00 level ('99 survey)   (c) significant @ .05 level ('00 survey)
(b) significant @ .00 level ('00 survey)   (d) significant @ .10 level ('00 survey)

Further analysis of data in the '99 study looked at performance measures, cross tabulating these with perceived importance of an EC strategy (Table 3). Analysis consisted of one-sided t-tests for the difference of proportions. Three surrogates of performance were employed:

(1) Firm is financially better off this year.

(2) Firm expects to be financially better off next year.

(3) Confidence in the future (this is a good time to invest).

Table 6 shows the results within the three sizes of firms ('Yes' gives proportion viewing EC as strategic; 'Gap' equals difference with firms not viewing EC as strategic). For smaller and medium-sized firms, this gap is always positive, while for larger firms it varies.

In terms of the two previously stated research questions, results support the hypothesis that SMEs can benefit from EC. Comparing performance within each size grouping, there were statistically significant differences in four of the nine measure/size pairs (asterisked cells). In another two of the pairs, the direction suggests better performance for firms viewing EC as strategically important. Comparing firms considering EC strategic, on a size basis, one significant difference was found–for the first measure (firm financially better off this year), between smaller and larger firms. Simply comparing differences among the three size groups, the direction for the first and third measures suggests an inverse relationship between size and performance. For the second measure, the results are inconclusive.

Overall, the findings are positive, suggesting that SMEs can gain dispropor-tionately from EC. This supports the CREC study conclusions (Barua et al., 2000).

Table 6: EC strategy important vs. performance (proportion agreeing)

Performance Measure:		Smaller	Medium	Larger
Firm Financially Better Off	Yes	0.83	0.72	0.59
	Gap	0.26*	0.22*	(0.24)
Expect Better Next Year	Yes	0.74	0.72	0.76
	Gap	0.03	0.22*	0.12
Confidence in Future	Yes	0.83	0.80	0.75
	Gap	0.21**	0.00	(0.07)

 * statistically significant @ .05 level

** statistically significant @ .10 level

CONCLUSIONS

Early in this chapter, four frameworks were presented: the EC Reality Model, the EC Importance Grid, the Technology Adoption Lifecycle, and the Technology Maturation Cycle. Each of these can be applied to EC and SMEs.

For the EC Reality Model, this study suggests firms are developing a better understanding of the actual benefits to be obtained from EC. Reality is being separated from hype. In particular, firms are becoming more focused with their reasons for EC. They are also becoming more realistic about potential benefits from EC (as evidenced by the decreasing importance of accessing new markets, and the continued importance of deriving more business from current customers). This study confirms that the pools of Useful EC and Strategic EC options appear to be more limited for SMEs than for larger manufacturers (larger firms gave more reasons, and were more likely to already be involved in EC).

There is considerable evidence suggesting firms can fit into any of the four EC Importance Grid quadrants while still being successful. Comparing firms considering EC as strategic with those that did not, stronger performers were found in both groups. Yet, for SMEs, a higher proportion of strong performers were found in the group considering EC strategic (providing a positive response to the first research question: Is there a performance difference between manufacturers that do or do not see an EC strategy as important?). Since these are manufacturers, with physical products, the physical side of their operations (plant, equipment, and people) are important. The virtual value chain can supplement the physical, but cannot replace it. So the current effect of EC does not yet appear to be significant for many manufacturers, particularly the smaller ones. While the world is changing, it is happening gradually. EC is maturing, and moving along the maturation curve. Firms will need to monitor their position on the grid and make necessary adjustments at the appropriate time.

In terms of the Technology Adoption Lifecycle, larger firms clearly led SMEs. They had Web sites earlier than most SMEs, were more likely to see EC as an important strategy, were more likely to be using EC currently, and their reasons for using EC were broader. With their greater resources, and in-house IT capabilities, larger firms are better positioned to undertake adoption of technologies at an earlier point in the lifecycle. Size can make a difference! As technology matures, becomes less expensive, and the 'whole product' infrastructure expands, more SMEs will be able to expand their EC initiatives. With limited resources, not many SMEs can afford to be on the 'bleeding edge' of EC.

Comments received indicated that some small firms felt they lacked technical understanding and resources to evaluate and implement a Web site and undertake

EC initiatives. It appears that unless the owner/manager is really interested in the technology, the firm was not pressing ahead (which aligns with the findings of Mackay et al., 2001). Further investigation would be appropriate. "Resource poverty" has always been associated with smaller firms, and this is particularly relevant in the information technology area.

In response to the second research question–Are there performance differences between different sized firms, all viewing EC as important?–weak support was found suggesting that SMEs have more to gain from EC than larger firms. A higher proportion of them were stronger performers, compared to larger firms.

There were several limitations with this study. Results are representative of a particular region, rather than the entire country, at a single point or two in time, in a changing environment. The past two years have seen a period of strong economic growth in Canada, which could mask weaknesses in particular firms. This study relied on responses from senior managers, rather than observed measurements. Furthermore, differences found suggest, but certainly do not prove, causality. Nevertheless, the study provides a snapshot of what manufacturers within Canada's industrial heartland are doing, and planning to do, with EC.

REFERENCES

Ajzen, I. (1991). The theory of planned behavior. *Organizational Behaviour and Human Decision Processes*, 50(2), 179-211.

Applegate, L. M., McFarlan, F. W. and McKenney, J. L. (1999). *Corporate Information Systems Management: The Challenges of Managing in an Information Age* (5th Ed.). New York: McGraw-Hill.

Barua, A., Konana, P., Whinston, A. and Yin, F. (2000). *E-Business Value Assessment. Working Paper.* Center for Research in Electronic Commerce. Retrieved September 28, 2000, from the World Wide Web: http://cism.bus.utexas.edu/.

Boulton, R. E. S., Libert, B. D. and Samek, S. M. (2000). *Cracking the Value Code: How Successful Businesses Are Creating Wealth in the New Economy*. New York: Harper Business.

Canadian E-Business Opportunities Roundtable. (2001). *Fast Forward 2.1, Taking Canada to the Next Level*. Retrieved June 6, 2001, from the World Wide Web: http://www.ebusinessroundtable.ca/english/documents/ff2.pdf.

Dandridge, T. C. and Levenburg, N. M. (1999). Small firms and the Internet: new insights on frequency and type of use. In *Proceedings of the 13th Annual National Conference*, United States Association for Small Business and Entrepreneurship, San Diego, USA.

Economist Intelligence Unit. (2001). *The Economist Intelligence Unit/Pyramid Research E-Readiness Rankings*. Retrieved June 8, 2001, from the World Wide Web: http://www.ebusinessforum.com/index.asp?layout=rich_story&doc_id=367.

Evans, P. and Wurster, T. S. (1999). Getting real about virtual commerce. *Harvard Business Review*, 77(6), 84-94.

Feeny, D. F. (1997). Introduction–Information management: Lasting ideas within turbulent technology. In Willcocks, L, Feeny, D. and Islei, G. (Eds.), *Managing IT as a Strategic Resource*, 17-28. New London: McGraw-Hill.

Fry, J. N. and Killing, J. P. (2000). *Strategic Analysis and Action* (4th Ed.). Scarborough, Ontario: Prentice-Hall.

Jentzsch, R. and Miniotas, A. (1999). The application of e-commerce to a SME. *Proceedings of the 10th Australasian Conference on Information Systems*, 435-447. Wellington, NZ.

Mackay, N., Gemino, A., Igbaria, M. and Reich, B. (2001). Empirical test of an electronic commerce adoption model in small firms. *Proceedings of the Annual Conference of the Administrative Sciences Association of Canada Information Systems Division*, 14-22. London, Canada.

Means, G. and Schneider, D. (2000). *Meta-Capitalism: The E-Business Revolution and the Design of 21st-Century Companies and Markets*, 15. New York: John Wiley & Sons.

Moore, G. A. (1995). *Inside the Tornado: Marketing Strategies from Silicon Valley's Cutting Edge*. New York: Harper-Business.

Pelham, A. M. (2000). Market orientation and other potential influences on performance in small and medium-sized manufacturing firms. *Journal of Small Business Management*, 38(1), 48-67.

Poon, S. (1999). Small business Internet commerce–What are the lessons learned? In Romm, C. and Sidweeks, F. (Eds.), *Doing Business on the Internet: Opportunities and Pitfalls*, 113-124. Springer.

Porter, M. E. and Millar, V. E. (1985). How information gives you competitive advantage. *Harvard Business Review*, 63(4), 149-160.

Rayport, J. F. and Sviokla, J. J. (1995). Exploiting the virtual value chain. *Harvard Business Review*, 73(6), 75-85.

Rogers, E. M. (1995). *Diffusion of Innovations* (4th Ed.). New York: The Free Press.

Rubin, R. S. (1999). Searching for competitive intelligence on the World Wide Web: A small business perspective. *Proceedings of the Small Business Institute Directors' Association Conference*, San Francisco, USA.

Standish Group. (2001). *GLOB of the Week*. Retrieved April 10, 2001, from the World Wide Web: http://www.pm2go.com/.

Statistics Canada. (2001). *Electronic Commerce and Technology 2000*. Retrieved June 26, 2001, from the World Wide Web: http://e-com.ic.gc.ca/english/documents/ecom_ict_2000.pdf.

Whyte, G. (2000). E-commerce–Meeting the SME challenge. *Presentation to the E-Business Capabilities in Canada Summit*, Ottawa, February. Retrieved June 26, 2001, from the World Wide Web: http://www.cfib.ca/legis/national/5064.asp.

Chapter XII

The Role of SMEs in Promoting Electronic Commerce in Communities

Celia Romm and Wal Taylor
Central Queensland University, Australia

INTRODUCTION

The primary emphasis of much of the literature on electronic commerce (EC) is on its global nature. The literature is replete with examples of companies that, over a relatively short period of time, made a successful transition from a local, small business, to a global enterprise, with customers and suppliers based all over the world. The literature in EC, both in the popular media and the learned journals, attributes this phenomenon to the fact that with access to the Internet, many businesses can sell globally without having to make an investment in "bricks and mortar."

The rhetoric that EC is free from constraints of geography is, however, contradicted by a growing evidence that, particularly for small and medium enterprises (defined in this chapter as "organizations with less than 500 employees"), business on the Internet is not necessarily as profitable and risk free as it is supposed to be. Establishing an EC "shop-front" may be a relatively painless exercise, but having prospective customers notice that shop-front, having them actually transact with the virtual business, and setting the business so that it successfully copes with the demands of a virtual customer base are all challenges that most small and medium enterprises (SMEs) find difficult to meet.

Given these comments, the question arises whether SMEs should consider national or global business as the main reason for getting themselves 'EC enabled.' In a number of articles by Steinfield and Whitten (1999), and Steinfield et al. (1999a, 1999b), the authors mount the opposite argument, namely, that SME's should, in the first instance, consider their local communities as their target market, rather than attempt to transact outside their immediate region. To support this proposition, Steinfield and Whitten (1999) propose a number of advantages that can accrue to both SMEs and their communities from engaging in EC in the local rather than the global arena.

In the following sections, we present some of the rationale on which Steinfield and Whitten's (1999) thesis is based and discuss the major arguments in relation to the advantages to SMEs from engaging in local EC rather than global EC business. In the context of this chapter, we discuss local EC particularly as it pertains to regional, rural, or remote communities. We use this discussion as the basis for our own Action, Reaction, Integration (ARI) model, which considers the role that SMEs can play in promoting Internet technologies in their communities. We conclude the chapter by outlining the implications from the ARI model to further research on the uptake of EC technologies by SMEs.

BACKGROUND

A review of the literature on the uptake of EC technologies by companies reveals that this practice is seen as associated with the following advantages.

Advantages to Companies

1. Cost reduction through the ability to exchange information and transact rapidly and cheaply with existing suppliers and customers (Malone, Yates and Benjamin, 1987);
2. Cost reduction through the ability to engage in relatively rapid and cheap searches for new customers and suppliers (Miller, Clemons and Row, 1993; Wigand and Benjamin, 1995);
3. Cost reduction as a result of bypassing the intermediaries in the retail distribution value chain (Wigand, 1997);
4. Lower sunk and operating costs through savings on buildings and salaries, given that the virtual business does not "take space" and does not need to be "open" at particular times (Steinfield and Whitten 1999);
5. Access to a larger market with the consequent result of volume discounts on production inputs (Steinfield, 1999a).

Advantages to Customers

1. Potential to offer better service to customers through brokerage facilities that enable customers to locate items that meet their requirements for both cost and quality (Malone et al., 1987);
2. Potential to adapt products and services (mass customization) to customers' unique needs (Malone et al., 1987);
3. Potential to make rapid changes to product mix and prices in response to feedback from customers (Steinfield and Whitten, 1999);
4. Potential to offer customers additional, complementary products through hyper-links on the company's Web site (Steinfield et al., 1993);
5. No limit to access to the business (7 days a week, 24 hours access) or to amount of information provided by the business to its customers (Steinfield and Whitten, 1999).

THREAT TO SMES FROM THE INTERNET

Given that most of the advantages that are associated with engaging in EC are advantages that virtual businesses have over 'bricks and mortar' ones, the implied conclusion from the discussion in the previous sections is that Internet-based retailers have the potential to undercut the prices of local retailers, particularly those offering products that are readily available on the Internet (for example, non-perishable, easily transportable products).

Local businesses can respond to this threat by establishing a presence on the Internet, thereby attempting to re-capture market niche lost to virtual businesses. Interestingly, empirical research into the motivation to establish an on-line presence and the specific strategies undertaken by SMEs once they have such presence (Gallagher, 1997; Steinfield et al., 1990a) indicates that expanding beyond the immediate location is the major motive underlying SMEs decision to establish a Web presence. Indeed, the empirical evidence seems to suggest that a year after SMEs establish their Web shop-front, they still have a limited focus on local business and consider national and global business the major justification for this initiative (Steinfield et al., 1990a).

But is this expectation realistic?

Given that the success rate of start-ups on the Internet is relatively low (*New York Times*, July 26, 1999), the expectation that a presence on the Internet by SMEs will lead to an expanding, profitable business is dangerous. Indeed, given the heavy investment of time and money required to establish and maintain a Web shop-front, SMES need to be careful in adopting these new technologies.

Given the high rate of failure for Internet-based businesses, the fact that SMEs are tempted to invest in Web shop-fronts may be considered as a threat posed by the Internet. In regional, rural, and remote communities, the threat to SMEs from the Internet can result from one of the following:

1.   Large Internet-based companies can compete on price, product range and delivery with local businesses by "siphoning away" their business through economies of scale.
2.   By relying on international suppliers, large Internet-based companies are likely to transact less with locally based SMEs, hence taking even further business away from SMEs, particularly in regional, rural or remote communities.
3.   By targeting national and international Internet customers and neglecting local customers, SMEs are opting for a risky business strategy that is, likely to increase the adverse effects of the Internet on their business (Steinfield and Whitton, 1999).

POTENTIAL DAMAGE TO COMMUNITIES

To make matters worse, the majority of businesses in regional, rural and remote communities are SMEs, which means that the adverse effects of the Internet on SMEs are likely to result in a host of social costs in those communities. As indicated by Steinfield and Whitten (1999), these social costs may include:

1.   job losses, particularly in relatively unskilled areas (for example, sales clerks, stockists);
2.   decreased attractiveness of the local community due to the loss of specialized businesses and professional services (for example, government services, banks);
3.   loss of products and services unique to the region (for example, services related to the culture, religion of the population);
4.   loss of tax income from businesses, resulting in further deterioration in the quality of the public services available to the community.

THE PROPOSED SOLUTION

Steinfield and Whitten (1999) propose that the best way that SMEs, particularly in regional, remote, and rural communities, can cope with the threat of the Internet is by establishing a "hybrid presence" on the Internet. This strategy combines a 'bricks and mortar' business with an EC capability.

More importantly, the authors insist that locally based SMEs should use both the physical and the virtual aspects of their business to target local rather than national or international business. The authors indicate that by adopting this strategy, locally based SMEs can gain competitive advantage in several crucial ways, including:

1. **Trust**–One of the most dominant issues mentioned in the EC literature as a major impediment to diffusion of EC is customers' lack of trust in the virtual business (Bollier, 1995; Coates, 1998). This lack of trust can be expressed in a reluctance to provide credit card details on the Internet and apprehension about the Internet business delivering the promised merchandise and/or service. Obviously, these issues would not apply if the customers transacted with businesses with a physical presence familiar to them. In other words, if a locally based business establishes a Web presence but targets its local customers, it will be building on the existing trust that they have in the business, rather than having to establish this trust from the outset.

2. **Consumer needs and behavior**–Consumers have several preferences that can be advantageous to locally based SMEs, which complement their physical business strategy with a virtual one. The physical facet of the business can reduce the perceived risk of customers by giving them an opportunity to return faulty merchandise. A store-based computer can assist customers to search the Internet (with guidance and help from the store personnel) for a specific product that they need and which may not be available in the store. The store can then place an order and have it delivered to the customer with guidance on how to use or maintain the merchandise (Klein, 1998). Thus, the Internet can save customers' time and effort by speeding and optimizing the search and decision-making processes that ARE major components of purchasing.

3. **Services and applications that capitalize on complementarities between the physical and the virtual**–There are a number of ways in which a physical and virtual business can combine to add value to each other. Many customers prefer to browse the Internet but then "feel" the product before purchasing it either on-line or in the physical store. Customers may select the product on-line but then enjoy bargains that are provided by the physical store. The physical store can provide additional advice on related products, the place to obtain information about installation and maintenance, and a preferred option for complaints and return of faulty merchandise.

4. **Local Knowledge**–Perhaps the area where the locally based virtual business has the most pronounced relative advantage is in knowledge of

the local environment. Local knowledge can enable SMEs to use a dialect or key words that are meaningful to their customers, make use of members of the community to endorse products and to design a whole marketing strategy (including the design of the Web site) to make IT culturally sensitive. All of these strategies would obviously be impossible for a national or international virtual business.

HOW CAN SMEs CAPITALIZE ON THEIR RELATIVE ADVANTAGE?

Given that Steinfield and Whitten's (1999) recommendation is for SMEs to embrace EC but with a local rather than a national or an international focus, the question arises whether SMEs are in a position to do this. In other words, this recommendation is underpinned by the assumption that SMEs are based in communities where there is a high level of diffusion of Internet technologies and, hence, enough potential customers to nurture EC-enabled businesses. This assumption may be true for some regional, remote or rural communities in some countries, but definitely not for all. In fact, for many SMEs, particularly in less developed parts of the world, the solution that Steinfield and Whitten recommend is not feasible simply because the level of diffusion of Internet technologies in their communities is very low.

The issue of low level of diffusion of Internet technologies in communities and how to overcome it is addressed by a relatively new research area called "community informatics" (CI). In contrast to much of the IT literature on diffusion, CI focuses on diffusion of IT in communities, with special emphasis on regional, rural or remote communities. As such, this body of literature is considered most appropriate for the topic of this chapter.

As indicated by Gurstein (1999), CI links economic and social development at the community level with emerging opportunities in such areas as electronic commerce, community and civic networks and tele-centers, electronic democracy, self-help, advocacy and cultural enhancement. As such, this term brings together the concepts of IT and information systems with the concept of community development.

As an area of research, CI can be regarded as the body of theory underlying one of the most exciting phenomena of the last decade, namely the diffusion and use of Internet technologies within communities. The Smart Communities movement, as it is often referred to in the popular press (Canadian Government, 1998; Nordicity, 1997), is a social reality not just in North America and Europe, but also in Asia, Australia and the Middle East. There are also large-scale CI projects in South America and Africa.

One of the most important themes in the literature on CI is the search for effective means for diffusing IT within communities. In this context several success stories are frequently quoted. The first of these, the Missouri Express Project, was established in Missouri in 1993. This project aimed to connect 80 communities in rural Missouri through Community Information Networks (CINs) (Pigg, 1998). The approach underlying this project was based on a wide variety of IT applications intended to create vibrant sustainable regional economies through targeting business and formal educational processes.

One of the early attempts to identify issues that can help remote communities benefit from CI was initiated by Gurstein (1999). In his discussion of the CI Project in rural and remote communities in Cape Britton, Nova Scotia, which he initiated and led, Gurstein mentioned the following as potential advantages of CI for remote communities: (1) overcoming distance insensitivity; (2) achieving local ownership and management of local information; (3) making tele-work possible; (4) enabling local nuance in the processing of information; (5) promoting flexibility for small-scale distributed production; and (6) obtaining economies of dis-aggregation.

In the same study, Gurstein identified three strategies for CI as an enabler of community economic development: (1) using it as a 'marketing tool' for small business; (2) using it as an 'enabler' for the mobilization of a wider range of resources for community economic development; and (3) and using it as a 'distributed networker' for the emergence of new networks and economies of 'dis-aggregation.'

In a recent review of the Access Indiana project which funded the establishment of 28 community networks in rural communities in Indiana, Rosenbaum and Gregson (1998) listed the following as factors that contribute to the success of CI projects:
- integration into the routine life of the community;
- local content for local needs;
- linkage to local government, schools and social services; and
- processes that ascertain long-term sustainability.

Gurstein's work (1996, 1999) also heralded the beginning of the search for factors that may hinder the successful diffusion of IT within communities. Based on his findings, Gurstein indicated that less than successful CI projects were associated with the failure to link the projects with local economic activity and to unite community efforts behind strong leadership. In this context, Gurstein (1999) saw the use of CI as a double-edged sword. While it could facilitate community development, it could also be associated with discord within the community resulting from the differential effect on various community stakeholders.

Another study that attempted to identify factors that hinder successful diffusion of IT within communities was undertaken by Scott, Diamond and Smith (1997). This study was based on the first and largest CI project in Australia. It involved the establishment of 450 public access points across three Australian states. The most important shortcoming of this project was that its facilities were under-utilized. The authors saw the fact that the project was based on public rather than private access points as the major reason for its limited success. They recommended that in the future, public-funded CI projects should strive to encourage private access points (through local ISPs) and invest in raising community awareness of Internet technologies through promotion and training activities.

A recent paper by Kling (1999) alerted researchers to the need to develop theoretical tools that would assist in understanding and eventually overcoming obstacles to diffusion of IT within communities. Perhaps in response to this call, another recent paper (Romm and Taylor, 2000) outlined a model of diffusion of IT within a CI context. The model builds on the literature on diffusion of IT in organizations, highlighting the unique issues that need to be addressed when diffusing IT in communities as opposed to work organizations.

Building on previous work by Markus (1994) and Romm, Pliskin and Clarke (1997), the authors mention the following factors as critical to successful diffusion of IT within a CI context:

- **Technology**–Given that CI focuses on the whole community, including its less computer literate members, it is important that technological constraints, namely the degree to which technologies are seen as "user friendly," are taken into account when CI projects are undertaken.
- **Motivation**–The degree to which individuals within the community are motivated to participate in CI projects is crucial to the success or failure prospects of these projects. Consequently, from a practitioner perspective, a lot of attention should be given to understanding the unique motivation of subgroups within the community (different age groups, socioeconomic groups and so forth).
- **Task**–If members of the community cannot see how the technologies can be of use to them, they are not likely to adopt them. From a practitioner perspective, a lot of attention should be given to understanding the tasks that members of the community wish to undertake and how these can be facilitated by IT.
- **Environment**–This variable would translate as changes to the social and economic environment in which the community as a whole is operating. For example, living in a remote area such as Cape Breton, Nova Scotia

(as reported by Gurstein, 1999) would work as an incentive for community members to embrace Internet technologies as a means for marketing their unique products. From a practitioner perspective, a lot of attention should be given to understanding the external environment in which the community is operating and using IT to increase the comparative advantage of the community within its environment.

- **Politics**–This variable refers to the degree to which the community as a whole is characterized by harmonious relationships between its members. It would also translate into the extent to which the members of the community support their leaders in their effort to diffuse the new technologies. From a practitioner's perspective, this variable would suggest that practitioners should be sensitive to conflicts within the community and endeavour to resolve them as a means for facilitating the diffusion of IT.
- **Culture**–This variable would suggest that the culture of the community to which the new ITs are being introduced has to be compatible with the goals of the project in order for the project to succeed. From a practitioner's perspective, this would suggest a "culture analysis" of both the community values and the values embedded in the IT to be diffused.

TOWARD A MODEL OF DIFFUSION OF EC IN COMMUNITIES

One of the aspects missing from the CI literature is a discussion of the strategic issues of CI. Questions such as, what activities should be initiated by CI project managers, in which order and for what purpose, are not discussed in the literature much. This is both a theoretical and a practical shortcoming, as many communities and agencies that are involved in CI projects desperately need guidance in this area.

The ARI model that is described in the following sections was developed to address this issue. The model is descriptive and prescriptive in nature in that it describes "best practice" in CI. The model is not expected to be used as a basis for empirical research. In the following sections we present the model and then use case data to demonstrate its major components.

The ARI model was developed in the context of the following constraints:

- CI projects may start from a very low baseline, namely a community whose diffusion of IT is minimal.
- There are exogenous and endogenous factors that motivate the community to embark on a CI project.

- Certain steps have to be undertaken to close the gap between the relatively low baseline at the beginning of the project and the desired high level of IT diffusion at its end.
- Assumptions that are derived from the literature about endogenous and exogenous factors that shape the diffusion process are part of the ARI model.
- The model is descriptive and prescriptive, rather than predictive. Its emphasis is on recommending a course of action that is analytically sound, rather than predicting an outcome based on an empirical experiment.

  The ARI model is based on the following assumptions:
- The model is based on three major building blocks, Action, Reaction, Integration. In addition, it incorporates a number of endogenous and exogenous factors from the literature on diffusion of information systems.
- The Action (A) component is defined as activities (or projects) intended to increase **demand** for IT products and services. The Reaction (R) component is defined as activities intended to increase **supply** of IT products and services. The Integration (I) component is defined as activities intended to integrate the demand for and supply of IT products and services through **aggregation** of either demand or supply or both.
- Ultimately, the goal of CI projects is to aggregate demand and supply for IT goods and services, as their aggregation will result in an upward spiral of increase in both demand and supply, establishing a self-sustaining "market" for IT products and services.
- Of the two factors (supply and demand), demand is easier to manipulate by external agents. Therefore, for the purpose of the ARI model, it is defined as the "Action " phase and describes the set of intervention activities that should take place first.
- The ARI model refers to the manipulation of supply for IT products and services as the "Reaction" phase based on the assumption that it would be more difficult to manipulate it in a community context unless a demand for IT products and services already exists. In other words, it would be difficult to convince industry to provide a community with Internet-based products and services (particularly a remote community or one placed in a developing country), unless there is already a body of customers willing to buy the products and services.
- The ARI model refers to the aggregation of demand and/or supply of IT products and services as "Integration" phase because this set of activities represents a level of integration involving the first two. The model also assumes that aggregation will not be possible to achieve unless a minimum level of both demand and supply for IT goods and services has been established.

- The ARI model assumes that the three components, "Action," "Reaction," "Integration" (or demand, supply, aggregation) will drive each other, ultimately producing a mutually dependent upward spiral effect where all three continue to increase over time.

Finally, the ARI model assumes that to sustain a CI project over time, the leaders of the project will have to maintain a "balanced portfolio" of "Action," "Reaction" and "Integration" activities, intended to reinforce each other.

Figure 1: The basic components of the ARI model

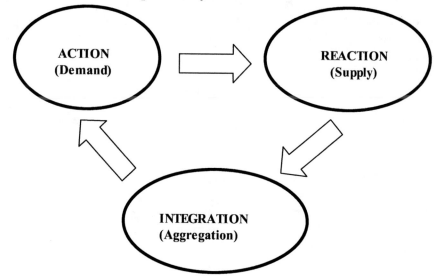

Figure 2: The ARI model

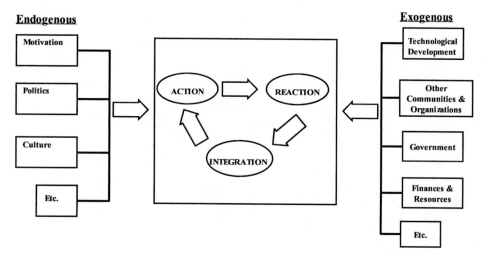

THE ROCKHAMPTON CASE STUDY

In the following sections, the major components of the ARI model are demonstrated with examples from a series of CI projects undertaken in Central Queensland in and around the city of Rockhampton.

Rockhampton is the capital of Central Queensland, Australia, a region that is five times the size of the UK. The city, which has a population of about 60,000, is the commercial center for a regional, rural and remote population of about 190,000.

The suit of projects that constitute the case study was initiated as a joint effort by the Rockhampton City Council (RCC) and Central Queensland University. The goal of these projects was to increase the diffusion of Internet technologies in the city and the region as a vehicle for promoting the use of EC by the community. SMEs that constitute the major commercial group and the major employer in the city played an important role in this process.

Phase 1

Projects Intended to Promote Demand for IT Products and Services
During 1998 and early 1999, two projects that were intended to promote awareness of Internet technologies were initiated. These included: "The Rural Youth project," which provided public access points for youth in a dozen of Central Queensland's small rural communities, and the "Indigenous Networks project," intended to promote awareness and provide public access to the Internet to 15 Aboriginal communities in Central Queensland.

Projects Intended to Promote Supply of IT Products and Services
During 1988 and early 1999, several developments that signalled an increase in the supply of Internet products and services took place. These included a marked increase in the number of ISPs in the city (from two to seven), and a significant increase in the number of Web design companies. Another important development was the establishment of an Internet café by one of the largest ISPs and an aggressive campaign by the local banks for residents to take advantage of the banks' newly developed Internet banking packages.

Projects Intended to Promote Aggregation of Demand and Supply
The most important project representing aggregation of demand and supply during this period was launched in late 1999 by the largest ISP

in the city. The project was a commercial portal, supported by an extensive database of businesses in the city and accompanied by an on-line news bulletin with information about the city's major attractions and events. The portal was developed on a very low budget and had a very low "hit rate" but was still an important attempt to create a platform where Internet-based businesses and customers could interact as one market.

Phase 2

Projects Intended to Promote Demand for IT Products and Services
The first project intended to promote demand for Internet products and services was the "Distributed Telecenter," consisting of a network of telecenters based in rural communities around the city of Rockhampton. The "heart" of the project was a major facility, the Rockhampton Community Informatics Center, based in the city's business center and offering members of the community affordable access to computers, on-line services and video-conferencing. While the initiative for these projects came from the university, the actual funding came from local, state, and federal government. Another project, also conceived in 2000, was "SeniorConnect." This project was supported by the City Council and was intended to introduce senior citizens in the city to Internet technology.

Projects Intended to Promote Supply of IT Products and Services
During late 1999 and early 2000, several developments that signalled further increase in the supply of Internet-based products and services took place. The first was an announcement by the City Council that it would establish a number of "kiosks" around the city shopping centers where a range of services (paying of fees, obtaining licenses and so forth) could be accessed on-line. At about the same time, several companies dedicated to Internet training moved into the city, establishing alliances with some of the major ISPs and computer retailers. These companies offered a range of training courses, particularly on how to use the new services (telebanking, the city council's kiosks) and how to engage in Electronic Commerce.

Projects Intended to Promote Aggregation of Demand and Supply
In early 2000, COIN, the most ambitious of this suit of projects, was initiated, again as a joint partnership between the Rockhampton City

Council and Central Queensland University. The project (entitled "COIN" for community informatics) established an "evolving" Web site for the city, with a linked "hierarchy" of e-mail lists and chat groups. The project was intended to be a platform for businesses and community groups to interact with each other and engage in electronic commerce activities. In addition to modest financial contribution from the university, it was supported by the local Chamber of Commerce, with strong representation to the local ISPs, Web design companies and computer retailers, all of whom were, of course, SMEs. Table 1 categorizes the CI projects undertaken in terms of the major components of the ARI model.

FUTURE TRENDS

The objective of this chapter was to consider the impact of the Internet on SMEs, particularly in regional, rural and remote communities, and the possible contribution that they can make to the diffusion of EC in their communities. As indicated in the previous sections of this chapter, SMEs' involvement with EC is a complex matter. The Internet can be a threat to SMEs, particularly those in regional, rural and remote areas, but it can also be a blessing.

The determining factor on whether the Internet will be a curse or a blessing for SMEs is the level of Internet diffusion in their communities. If the base level for Internet technologies in the community is relatively high, namely there is enough of a customer-base to support and nurture SMEs, then the strategy that is proposed by Steinfield and Whitten (1999) should be recommended. SMEs should be encouraged to undertake a "hybrid" business strategy combining a 'bricks and mortar' business with an Internet shop-front. In this particular situation, SMEs should also be advised to focus on the local market, where they have distinct relative advantages, rather than target

Table 1: Categorization of case data in terms of the ARI model

	Action	Reaction	Integration
Phase 1	Rural Youth	ISPs	Commercial Portal
	Indigenous Communities	Web Designers	
		Internet Banking	
Phase 2	Distributed Telecenter	Kiosks	COIN
	Senior Connect	Internet Training	

regional, national or international markets. These will come for some businesses at a later point in time, but should definitely not be seen as the major justification for getting the business EC enabled or the major marketing strategy once the Internet presence is established.

As for SMEs operating within an environment where the diffusion of Internet technologies is very low, namely SMEs that are based in regional, remote or rural communities, their strategy cannot be the one recommended by Steinfield and Whitten (1999). Instead, as demonstrated in the previous sections of this chapter, a strategy intended to increase the diffusion of Internet technologies in the community will have to be initiated first, with major involvement from SMEs and from both public and not-for-profit agencies (such as local, state, and federal government).

CONCLUSIONS

There are a number of conclusions that can be drawn from the ARI model in terms of the role of SMEs as promoters of EC technologies in their communities.

First is the issue of the **timing** of intervention activities. The ARI model suggests that even though activities that promote demand and supply for IT goods and services should be undertaken simultaneously, demand-related activities should take precedence and should be initiated first. The reason for this recommendation is that if SMEs are to play a leading role in getting their communities EC enabled, there has to be a commercial reason for them to proceed. There has to be a big enough market of potential customers willing to transact with them on-line. If such a customer base does not exist, it would be difficult and highly misleading to encourage SMEs to establish a Web presence, as it can be a costly and high-risk strategy for them.

Second is the issue of **priorities**. The ARI model suggests that activities that promote aggregation of demand and supply should be seen as the ultimate goal of intervention strategies in communities. The reason for this recommendation is that aggregation strategies have the potential to "drive" further demand and supply in the community. In other words, introducing major aggregating projects (such as a portal) into a community will establish "growth dynamics," creating further incentive and justification for SMEs to be involved in the 'EC enabling' of their communities. Note, that SMEs can play important roles in providing products and services that support both community demand (training of members of the community in Internet-related skills) and the supply side of the ARI model (selling Internet-related products and services).

Third is the issue of possible overlaps. Does the recommended timing of intervention activities mean that unless a minimum level of demand has been reached, no activities involving the manipulation of supply or aggregation of both supply and demand should take place?

Obviously the answer to this question is no. The fact that a community is at a low level of diffusion, and most efforts are focused on increasing demand for IT products and services, does not mean that activities that are intended to increase supply of these products and services should not be undertaken. Similarly, even though a minimum level of both demand and supply is probably necessary for aggregation to occur, it is possible, as the Rockhampton case study demonstrates, to envisage both low level (the commercial portal project) and high level (the COIN project) aggregation of supply and demand.

Finally, given that the ARI model combines the elements of Demand, Supply and Aggregation with a range of endogenous and exogenous factors, the most important research questions that emanate from it are associated with the exact nature of the relationship between these sets of factors.

The following sets of questions could be the basis for a future research agenda in this area:

- What is the impact of endogenous factors such as motivation, politics and community culture on SMEs' likelihood to establish an Internet presence? Do these factors have different impacts in communities that are initially high or low on level of diffusion for Internet technologies? Does the impact that these factors have change over time?
- What is the impact of endogenous factors such as technology, other organizations and communities, government and financial resources on SMEs' likelihood to establish an Internet presence? Do these factors have different impacts in communities that are high or low on level of diffusion for Internet technologies? Does the impact that these factors have change over time?
- How do these factors impact on the basic building blocks of the model, namely the demand, supply and aggregation of IT products and services? Are the effects the same or different for communities with high levels of diffusion for Internet technologies? Are they the same for communities in different national cultures?

These and other empirical questions that relate to the role of SMEs in promoting the use of EC in their communities can be explored by employing a combination of qualitative and quantitative research methodologies. Such investigations can uncover the interplay between issues like who should initiate EC diffusion projects, who should lead such projects and who should contribute the resources to make them possible and sustainable in the long term. Based on such research, preferably within and across cultures, it would be possible to test the propositions of the ARI model and, consequently, to determine the role that SMEs can and should play in diffusion of EC in their communities.

REFERENCES

Boller, D. (1995). *The Future of Electronic Commerce: A Report of the Fourth Annual Aspen Roundtable on Information Technology.* Washington, DC: Aspen Institute.

Canadian Government. (1998). *The Smart Communities Program.* http://smartcommunities.ic.gc.ca/smart/indexen.htm.

Coates, V. (1998) *Buying and Selling on the Internet: Retail, Electronic Commerce.* Washington, DC: The Institute for Technology Assessment.

Gurstein, M. (1996). *Managing Technology for Community Economic Development in a Non-Metropolitan Environment.* UNESCO International Conference on Technology Management, Istanbul, Turkey.

Gurstein, M. (1999). Flexible networking, information and communications technology, and local economic development. *First Monday,* 4(2).

Klein, L. (1998). Evaluating the potential of interactive media through a new lens; search versus experience goods. *Journal of Business Research,* 41(2), 195-203.

Kling, R. (1996). Social relationships in electronic forums: Hangouts, salons, workplaces and communities. Section IV. In Kling, R. (Ed.), *Computerization and Controversy: Value Conflicts and Social Choices.* San Diego, CA: Academic Press.

Kling, R.(1999). What is social informatics and why does it matter? *D-Lib Magazine,* 5.

Malone, T., Yates, J. and Benjamin, R. (1987). Electronic markets and electronic hierarchies: Effects of information technology on market structure and corporate strategies. *Communications of the ACM,* 30(6), 484-497.

Markus, M. L. (1994). Electronic mail as a medium for managerial choice. *Organization Science,* 5(4), 502-527.

Miller, D., Clemons, E. and Row, M. (1993). Information technology and the global village corporation. In Bradley, S., Hausman, J. and Nolan, R. (Eds), *Globalization, Technology and Competition: The Fusion of Computer Sand Telecommunications in the 1990s,* 283-307. Boston, MA: Harvard University School Press.

Nordicity. (1997). *Community Experiences with Information and Communications Technology-Enabled Development in Canada.* International Development, Research Center, Canadian Government.

Pigg, K. (1998). *Missouri Express: Program Implementation Assessment.* Missouri University.

Romm, C., Pliskin, N. and Clarke, R. (1997) Virtual communities and society: Toward an integrative three-phase model. *International Journal of Information Management,* 17(4), 261-270.

Romm, C. and Taylor, W. (2000). Community informatics: The next frontier. In Khosrowpour, M. (Ed.), *Challenges of Information Technology Management in the 21ˢᵗ Century. Proceedings of the Information Resources Management Association,* 1167-1169. Hershey, PA: Idea Group Publishing.

Rosenbaum, H. and Gregson, K. (1998). *A Study of State-Funded Community Networks in Indiana.* Indiana Department of Education, Center for School Improvement and Performance.

Scott, M., Diamond, A. and Smith, B. (1997). *Opportunities for Communities: Public Access to Networked IT.* Canberra: Department of Social Security.

Steinfield, C., Caby, L. and Vaille, P. (1993). Internationalization of the firm and the impacts of videotext networks. *Journal of Information Technology,* 7, 213-222.

Steinfield, C. and Whitten, P. (1999). Community-level socio-economic impacts of electronic commerce. *Journal of Computer-Mediated Communication,* 5(2).

Steinfield, C., Mahler, A. and Bauer, J. (1999a). Electronic commerce and the local merchant: Opportunities for synergy between physical and Web presence. *Electronic Markets,* 9(1).

Steinfield, C., Mahler, A. and Bauer, J. (1999b). Local versus global markets in electronic commerce: Towards a conceptualization of local electronic commerce strategies. In Bohilin, E., Brodin, K., Lundergren, A. and Thorngren, B. (Eds.), *Convergence in Communications and Beyond.* Amsterdam: Elsevier.

Wigand, R. (1997). Electronic commerce: Definition, theory and context. *The Information Society,* 13, 1-16.

Wigand, R. and Benjamin, R. (1995). Electronic commerce: Effects on electronic markets. *Journal of Computer Mediated Communication,* 1(3).

Chapter XIII

Strategies for Consultancy Engagement for E-Business Development–A Case Analysis of Australian SMEs

Shirley Bode and Janice Burn
Edith Cowan University, Australia

INTRODUCTION

It is estimated that there are 1,004,200 private sector small businesses in Australia, of which almost 900,000 were non-agricultural businesses, and 104,500 in the agriculture, forestry and fishing businesses (DEWRSB, 1997). It is also estimated that Small and Medium Enterprises (SMEs)[1] employ 51% of the private sector workforce (SBDC, 1999) and so make a substantial contribution to the nation's economy and employment. This pattern is not unique to Australia but reflected in many developed and developing economies around the world. In general, therefore, SMEs have been strongly encouraged by government to embrace the new e-business environment and expand their global reach with enhanced productivity. However, the relationship between SMEs and e-business has been found to be an uncomfortable fit. SMEs have been reluctant to adopt electronic commerce principles and practices in their day-to-day business transactions (Beer, 1999; DIST, 1998; Shern, 1998; SBI, 1998; Yen, 1998) for a wide variety of reasons.

One reason can be traced to early forms of e-commerce, principally Electronic Data Interchange (EDI). EDI transactions were not particularly suited to the SME environment as they were expensive and involved the use of proprietary software which could not be used with other business partners (DIST, 1998; Rose et al., 1999; Turban et al., 1999). A number of SMEs that embraced this technology felt "locked into" a system that did not provide them with any real economic benefit (DIST, 1998; Iacovou et al., 1995).

An OECD report "Enhancing the Competitiveness of SMEs in the Global Economy: Strategies and Policies" (2000) found that the penetration rate of the Internet in the Australian SME sector is only 25% (see Figure 1). According to a report by the Institute of Small Business Research, SMEs have been cautious in their uptake of electronic commerce as it is seen as complex and not perceived as relevant to their organization (ISBR, 1998). Indeed considerable confusion exists within the SME community in regard to the definition of e-commerce or e-business.

Another factor that presented a barrier to the early uptake of e-commerce by the SME sector was the size and scope of SMEs. The majority do not employ IT managers or specialists. The lack of information technology staff within the SME sector has been identified as one obstacle for the wholesale adoption of e-commerce strategies and technologies (Cragg & King, 1993; Thong, Yap & Raman, 1996; Yap, Soh & Raman, 1992). In the SME sector, IT decisions and operational factors tend to be relegated to the realm of the Accountant, Manager or Owner-Operator and are mostly seen as a peripheral

Figure 1: Internet penetration in the small business sector in selected OECD countries (OECD, 2000)

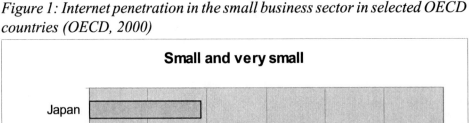

and sometimes annoying business factor (Prakash, 1998; Shern, 1998; DIST, 1998). Consequently, many SMEs tend to rely on external consultants to design and implement Websites and in so doing often outsource their e-business strategy.

Many SMEs do not engage in strategic planning for their business. Small businesses, in particular, tend to focus on day-to-day survival, including dealing with immediate issues that may impact on their business, such as profits, taxation and other areas of compliance (Centre, 1996; DIST, 1998a). This focus inhibits general business planning and would also inhibit planning the introduction of electronic commerce policies and practices.

In spite of the above barriers, research has found that SMEs' access to, and use of, the Internet has increased over the last few years. The Yellow Pages Small Business Index, for example, found an increase of small business connected to the Internet from a low of 5% in 1995 to 34% in 1998, which constitutes one-third of all small businesses using computers. In medium business (defined by the Yellow Pages Small Business Index as up to 200 employees), the Index found in 1998, that two-thirds were connected to the Internet.

The questions addressed in this chapter are:
1. Do SMEs have explicit e-business strategies prior to development of a Website?
2. Are Website consultants engaged through a formal engagement process, aligning business and Web development strategies?
3. To what extent do SMEs feel their individual e-business needs are understood and met by Website design consultants?

In an attempt to answer the above questions, this chapter incorporates a multiple case analysis of 10 Western Australian online SMEs which contracted Website design consultants to produce their sites. The SMEs chosen were established retail businesses and each utilized the services of different Website design consultants.

WEBSITE DESIGN CONSULTANTS AND SMES

Definition of Website Design Consultants

In this chapter Website design consultants are defined as consultants offering a 'total electronic commerce solution' to potential SME clients. For example, common claims made by Website design consultants on their Web pages include:
*   "[We] offer complete Internet solutions for Western Australian business–we are here to serve you!"
*   "We cater primarily for those people who need real Websites. You know, the ones with content!"

- "We understand that managing the transition to e-commerce requires specialist knowledge–both business and technical... [we] have the resources and expertise to make the jump to e-commerce. Talk to us about developing a practical online strategy for your business."

Other common terms for Website design consultants include, 'Website developer,' 'Internet developer' and 'Web page designer' (Cormier, 1999; Falkenstin, 1996). In this study the consultants suggested they could offer the case SMEs e-business strategic management, Website design, hosting and marketing advice.

The Relationship Between Website Design Consultants and SMEs

The success or failure of an SME engaging a Website design consultant involves a number of issues. Firstly, it may be the SME's first attempt at engaging an external consultant and the SME may lack the relevant knowledge and experience required for successful engagement. Secondly, Website design consultants are often SMEs themselves, and in the current climate of accelerating growth in the e-business area, Website design consultants are often business start-ups and consequently, may lack experience in negotiating successful contracts. Finally, consultants tend to view SMEs as one-off jobs and may consequently lack commitment to the project:

"Small firms were viewed as one-shot opportunities, offering no potential for establishing a long-term relationship. Consultants...would sell the small firms software and hardware, put together a network and move on to the next company" (McCollum, 1999).

Thong and Yap's (1996) research examined external expertise and management support for the implementation of Information Systems in small business. Their findings suggest that, while top management support is one important factor, high quality external expertise is critical to successful IS implementation in the small business sector. Gable (1989, 1991) identified a number of issues that SMEs need to consider when engaging the services of a consultant. These included the amount of time and effort the SME contributes to the project and the maintenance of a clear understanding of the role of the SME and the role of the consultant. Gable (1989) developed a 12-phase model of consultant engagement to clarify the role of a SME in selecting a consultant (see Figure 2).

Gable's model can be categorized into three distinct areas: *preliminary evaluation*, *engagement process* and *post-engagement follow-up*.

Gable's 12-phase model seeks to identify the steps required for successful consultant engagement. It is implicit in this model that each step should be followed in order to increase the potential for engagement success.

Figure 2: Twelve-phase model of consultant engagement. (Adapted from Gable (1989))

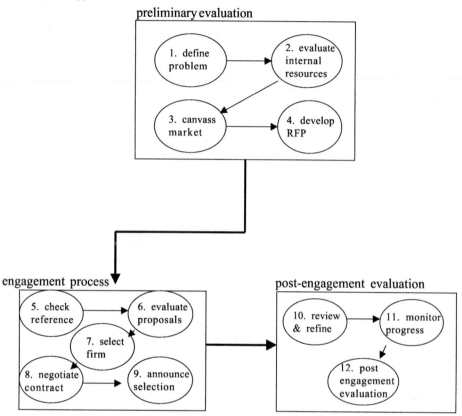

Gable, in a later study, introduced the concept of the 'pro-active client role in small business' and identifies areas where consultants failed to adequately meet key steps in the 12-phase model (Gable, 1991). In conjunction with this, Gable assesses the impact of client involvement in consultant engagement finding that "effective engagement requires that the problem is well defined and an appropriate consultant is selected with the problem in mind." He then identifies three areas where SMEs can improve their consultant engagement process:

- assess client and consultant compatibility (Phases 5, 6, 7 & 8);
- identify and address specific organizational roles (Phases 1, 2, 11 & 12) and accommodate evolving project objectives (Phases 11 & 12).

Although Gable's studies focus on first-time computerization, it is felt that this model is applicable to Australian SMEs' engagement of Website design consultants. It is the intention of this study to use Gable's model as a guide in understanding SME consultant engagement processes.

INTERNET STRATEGY

Prior to consultant engagement, an SME should have a clearly defined Internet strategy. Current research shows that another important factor in the success of online enterprises is their ability to align business processes with Website strategy (Angehrn, 1997; Poon, 1995; Cragg, 1998; Bergeron, et al., 1998; Lawrence & Chau, 1998).

Cragg (1998) identified four components of Internet strategy that may be useful for SMEs to consider when engaging in online commerce (see Table 1). The four components are *goals, content, process* and *functional.*

The *goals* component of an Internet strategy is sub-categorized into primary and secondary goals. Cragg indicated that the benefit of incorporating primary and secondary goals would be a method for SMEs to recognize potential economic benefits, and to indicate "…that increased sales can only be considered as one indicator of success."

The *content* dimension of an Internet strategy identifies the main uses of an SME's Website. This component enables an SME to clarify what the site started with, its current major uses, what the site is for and future plans for the site.

Table 1: Cragg's Internet strategy (Cragg, 1998)

Goal	Example
primary	to reach an international market
secondary	to market site to potential customers
Content	
started with	email, catalogue, order form
major use	marketing/promotion
WWW site for	product distribution
future plans	introduce new functions
Process	
led by	owner/manager
whose initiative	internal
built	external
Function	
functions of site	business-to-business, business-to-consumer

The *process* component is basically a method to identify whether the initiation and leadership of the strategy was from the CEO level or further down the chain of command, and whether the site was built utilizing internal or external expertise.

Finally, the *functional* component of Internet strategy examines the functions of the Website. This could incorporate B2B e-commerce, B2C e-commerce or the implementation of a method for increasing and retaining customers.

This model is used, in conjunction with Gable's model, as a tool to evaluate the level of SME involvement in the development of an Internet Strategy and how this may impact on the success of the SMEs venture into Internet commerce.

THE STUDY

The research design and methodology for this study is qualitative in nature and based on an *interpretivist* perspective. "The objective of interpretive research is to piece together people's words, observations and documents into a coherent picture expressed through the voices of the participants" (Trauth & Jessup, 1999, p.26) and as Fisher states, "It [the interpretivist approach] does not seek to identify or test variables but to draw meaning from social contexts" (Fisher & Arnott, 1998, p.216).

Use of the interpretivist approach is to enable the researcher to make sense of the people and organizations involved in the research project and to develop theory via an inductive process whereby, "immersion in the details and specifics of the data to discover important categories, dimensions and interrelationships; begin by exploring genuinely open questions rather than testing theoretically derived (deductive) hypotheses" (Patton, 1990, p.40).

Because the research was interpretive and designed to examine the experiences, ideas and opinions of a small number of SMEs which had direct experience in consultant engagement for their first entry into e-business, it is not expected that this study is generalizable to the entire population of SMEs. The purpose was to examine and comprehend major issues facing Australian SMEs, consultant engagement and e-business, which would lead to further research on a larger scale.

Case Studies

To find an appropriate research methodology for this project, a review of the literature on research methods in information systems, electronic commerce and SMEs was conducted. It was decided that theory building using a multiple case project approach would be utilized. As electronic commerce, particularly in Australia, is still in an emergent phase, it was felt that the case research methodology would be most appropriate:

Case research is best utilized when the goals of the researcher and the nature of the research topic influence the selection of a strategy. Case research is particularly appropriate for   certain types of problems: those in which research and theory are at their early, formative stages (Benbasat, 1987, #56).

A review of the literature into research methodologies highlighted the usefulness of the case methodology in new and relatively new fields (Benbasat et al., 1987; Carroll et al., 1998; Poon & Swatman, 1997; Rose, 1991; Stake, 1994; Yin, 1994).

Case studies have a long history of use in the IS field. There are multiple definitions of case project research and they cover a wide range of research methods, from single in-depth case studies to multi-site, multi-method studies.

Benbasat et al. define case studies as:

A case project examines a phenomenon in its natural setting...The boundaries of the phenomenon are not clearly evident at the outset of the research and no experimental control or manipulation is used...The case project researcher may have less a priori knowledge of what the variables of interest will be and how they will be measured (Benbasat, 1987, #56, p.370).

Sample

The cases were chosen via a deliberate theoretical sampling plan (Minichiello et al.,1995). The basic premise of theoretical sampling implies that participants are chosen deliberately to suit the parameters of the research. In this study the parameters included online Australian SMEs whose Websites were designed by a Website design consultant. As Burgess states, "Theoretical sampling…involves researchers in observing groups with a view to extending, modifying, developing and verifying theory" (Burgess, 1984, #80). Minichiello et al. (1995) add that theoretical sampling must be relevant to the evolving data. They further suggest that theoretical sampling requires 'purposeful' selection of informants that "have been identified as relevant categories in the literature" (p.163). To facilitate this study the researcher collected online small business contacts from four Internet directory sites: www.aussie.com.au, www.ozsearch.com.au, www.perthwa.com.au and www.webwombat.com.au. The SMEs were chosen based on the following criteria:

- <5 employees (micro category);
- <20 employees (small category);
- <100 employees (medium category);
- retail business;
- Websites capable of electronic transactions;
- Website designed by an external consultant and
- business located in Australia.

From this, 10 online SMEs were identified and their Websites assessed based on a model of Website activities (see Table 2). The Website activity model was synthesized from Internet usage surveys and interviews conducted by several researchers (ISBR, 1998; Poon & Swatman, 1997; Small Business Index, 1998).

Background Information

Table 3 presents the background information of the case SMEs.

Table 2: Website activity model

	Use of Site	Communication	Promotion	E-Transactions
SME #1	Educational products supplier	email for client queries	local, national & international customers	Order online via email order form – products available in a variety of languages. Pre-payment requirement
SME #2	Clothing retailer	email for client queries	local, national & international customers	Order products via email order form. Prices not included in catalogue.
SME #3	Giftware	email for client queries; email for supplier communication	local, national & international customers	Full electronic transactions via shopping cart technology, credit card enabled.
SME #4	Music retailer	email for client queries; online newsletter & calendar of events	local, national & international customers	Searchable database of music. Orders placed via a Secure Transaction Server using credit card or International money order.
SME #5	Boating retailer	email for client queries	local, national & international customers	Product catalogue with email/fax backorder information.
SME #6	Car retailer	email for client queries, newsletter	local & national customers	Searchable database of makes & models – links to car manufacturers.
SME #7	Reticulation supplier	email for client queries	local & national customers	Searchable database – secure online e-transactions via credit card.
SME # 8	Giftware retailer	email & newsletter (subscription only) for clients	local, national & international customers	Online catalogue, secure online e-transactions via credit card.
SME #9	Lingerie retailer	email for client queries	local & national customers	Online catalogue, secure online e-transactions via credit card.
SME #10	Sport & Leisure retailer	email for queries – mailing list, calendar of events	local customers.	Information of products & services, special offers, email/fax-back forms for purchases.

The data collection method consisted of in-depth interviews with owners/managers of the SMEs located in both metropolitan and regional areas. Each of the participants was interviewed in person and the interviews took between 40 minutes to one hour. The interviews were semi-structured and based on the major issues identified by Gable's 12-phase model (Gable, 1989b, #140) while also allowing additional issues to be raised by the interviewees.

Table 3: Background information of case SMEs

SME	Founded	Staffing	Increase in annual sales turnover directly related to Website	Date Website started
SME #1 Educational products supplier	1995	2 full-time 2 part-time	15%	November 1998
SME #2 Clothing retailer	1997	1 full-time 2 part-time	0	May 1999
SME #3 Giftware retailer	1980	3 full-time 1 part-time	15%	November 1998
SME #4 Music retailer	1971	14 full-time	20%	1996
SME #5 Boating retailer	1956	25 full-time	0	1998
SME #6 Car retailer	1994	27 full-time	300%	1997
SME #7 Reticulation	1963	5 full-time 2 part-time	0	March 2000
SME #8 Giftware retailer	1999	2 full-time	15%	July 1999
SME #9 Lingerie retailer	1994	1 full-time	10%	June 1999
SME #10 Sport & Leisure	1931	10 full-time 20 part-time	15%	1998

RESULTS AND ANALYSIS

The interview data was analyzed using a matrix as proposed by Miles and Huberman (1994). The purpose of this method of analysis is to enable the data to be analyzed visually, and the data from the cases to be easily compared and contrasted, and themes and patterns identified. The data was then further analyzed using Gable's 12-phase model for consultant engagement.

Table 4 illustrates how closely the SME case studies adhered to the guiding principals of the 12-phase model (Gable, 1989) for consultant engagement.

Consultant Engagement

None of the case SMEs utilized each of the steps in Gable's model (see Table 4). SME #1 completed six steps and partially completed two, and SME #3 completed six steps; the remaining SMEs completed five or less steps. Only one SME canvassed the market and developed a request for proposal prior to using the consultant (Step 4). Although, interestingly eight of the SMEs stated that in hindsight they would have canvassed the market and asked for full quotations: "...in hindsight I would have looked around more and found someone more capable and experienced..." (SME #1); and "The manager was a gent in his '50s and seemed to have good business sense, but the lads who designed the site well...it's absolutely shocking. When I first saw them, I thought, 'My kids are older than them.' They

Table 4: SMEs and Gable's (1989) 12-phase model

Gable's 12-phase model	1	2	3	4	5	6	7	8	9	10
1) Define the problem	•	•	•	•	•	•	•	•	•	•
2) Evaluate internal resources	•	•	•	•	•	•	•	•	•	•
3) Canvass the market									•	
4) Develop RFP									•	
5) Check references	partially		•		partially				partially	
6) Evaluate proposals										
7) Select firm	•	•	•	•	•	•	•	•	•	•
8) Negotiate a contract	partially		•	informal						•
9) Announce selection										
10) Continuing review of responsibilities	•	•	•	•			•	•		
11) Continuing monitoring & control	•	•				•	•			
12) Post-engagement evaluation	•	•								

Table 5: Method of choosing Website designer

SME	Method of choosing Website designer
#1	Internet Service Provider (ISP)
#2	ISP
#3	Psychic
#4	Can't remember
#5	Friend
#6	Friend
#7	Business associate
#8	Friend/work colleague
#9	Request for Proposal (RFP)
#10	Yellow Pages

were shocking, absolutely shocking–we got burnt badly; next time we'd be far more careful" (SME #6).

In terms of the three strategic areas of Gable's model (see Figure 2) the SMEs were strongest in the first area *preliminary evaluation,* and weakest in the final area *post-engagement evaluation.*

Table 5 indicates where the SMEs found their Website designers.

Seven of the SMEs relied on recommendations from friends, colleagues or their ISP, trusting that the recommendations were appropriate. Only one SME developed an RFP and obtained several quotes. Three SMEs viewed the refereed sites suggested by the consultant, but did not contact either of the sites for a verbal or written confirmation SME #4 "got a feel for them" during informal discussions. SME #3 did check the consultant references and found them to be:

> "…good, they were excellent…she is smart and certainly knows her computer stuff backwards…the unfortunate thing is her business acumen is in the toilet…she's not aware of what someone needs in business and it's like we're speaking two different languages" (SME #3).

Again, several of the SMEs stated that in hindsight they would have requested either verbal or written references from the consultants' client sites.

Six of the SMEs did not have a formal written contract with their consultants, although SME #1 had negotiated a verbal contract in relation to pricing for the design of their site. The verbal contract was not adhered to, and when presented with the final bill, SME #1 stated: "…that was a real shock, because I told him from the beginning I had a really strict budget and it was blown right out…." SME #3 had a written contract with their consultant and stated:

> "Yes there was a formal contract; it included a budget which got blown out, it included a timeframe which didn't work; to be honest I think the contract was a complete waste of time because nothing in it has been stuck to…" (SME #3).

It is believed that a formal written contract with agreed penalty clauses outlining the roles of both parties, requirements for the sites, pricing, timeframes and contract variations would have been useful for the SMEs when engaging a Website design consultant.

SMEs #1 and #3 had engaged in a process of review with their consultants, whereas the others had not. Interestingly, all SMEs had, or were in the process of, severing the consultant/client relationship. SME #1 and SME #3 had employed .5 FTE staff to maintain and update their sites, while SME #2 intended to conduct future updates in-house and SME #4 had allocated the task to internal staff. For all the SMEs this decision was not merely a cost-cutting exercise; all felt they lacked control over the site and could manage the site better internally:

> "…it's quite annoying to find you can't ring up someone and say 'Hey, this isn't working, what are you doing about it?' You've got to call an account manager and he doesn't have a technical background, he'll say, 'Oh fine, I'll go off and consult with someone else,' but then that person won't call you and the original person will call

back and then you might have questions you need clarifying and it becomes quite frustrating at times. As a result we now take care of the content of the site" (SME #4).

Pricing and Service

In the analysis of the data, pricing and service were recurrent themes for all the SMEs, and the importance of clarifying the role of consultant and client was very clearly highlighted. In several of the cases, it appeared that the SMEs passively trusted the consultant to produce results at minimal cost. Gable stated that the "misconceived view of the client role" (1991) is one of the prime reasons for the breakdown of the client/consultant relationship.

Nine of the SMEs felt that they had been overcharged and did not receive value for money from their Website design consultants. SME #1 had discussed a budget with the consultant and was unaware that changes to the site would incur additional charges "..but that's when the money came into it and it ended up costing for every little tiny change and that's until we got the bill and said 'Hey this is much more than what you said'; I told him we had a really strict budget and it was just blown right out...."

SME #2 linked pricing and service provision several times throughout the interview: "...if I've got to constantly be telling them what to do, I think paying $90 an hour is a bit ludicrous" and "I don't think I got value for money...basically I think they charged me an hourly rate for the work that they did, the fact that they had no ideas of their own should have been taken into account when billing me."

SME #5 felt that pricing was inflated and service from the consultant inadequate: "...I feel we were ripped off, it's like buying a bicycle with no wheels...."

Interestingly, only two of the SMEs voiced their concerns with the consultants, and as can be seen from the comment of SME #2 above, assumptions regarding billing were made but not explicitly drawn to the consultant's attention to enable any potential rectification.

This lack of feedback from the client to the design consultant confirms Gable's (1991) statement. This is further highlighted in comments made by several of the SMEs in regard to a perceived lack of follow-up service provision. SME #1: "It was me contacting him rather than him coming out at the end and going through it and saying, 'Right, this is it, it's final,' and saying, 'are you happy?' It didn't close up at all." SME #2: "I haven't heard from them since May and it's now July..if it was me, you know, a week or two later I would have phoned and said 'how's it all going?'"

Consultant Experience

One of the client concerns identified by Gable in his analysis of consultant engagement is that consultants often appear to have minimal relevant experience. He stated that this can be overcome if selection of a consultant were guided by his 12-phase model. The SMEs in this study lend support to this statement as they did not adhere strongly to the guidelines of Gable's model and very clearly felt that their consultants lacked essential experience.

For example, SME #2 believed their consultant was technically competent, but lacking in original ideas. "I don't think they have any ideas of their own. I think they are very good technically, but I don't think either artistically or marketing wise that they are particularly well clued up." SME #1 stated, "We gave them our catalogue, we thought they'd come up with something whizzbang but they copied exactly what we had done. We could have done that ourselves...they gave us the basis but that was all, there wasn't any extras...we fed them the ideas."

The development and evaluation of an RFP, Steps 4 and 6 in Gable's model, may have clarified for the SMEs exactly what they were seeking from a Website design consultant. In conjunction with the RFP, the preparation of a firm contract (Step 8) may have assisted in circumventing these problems.

Cragg's Internet Strategy

Of the 10 SMEs studied, only one of them actually planned the implementation of their Website. The others relied on ad-hoc ideas, thoughts and hopes for their sites. SME #1 had ongoing discussions between the partners of the firm to generate ideas and future plans based on their original goals of reaching an international market and increasing overall profits. SME #2 stated that they did not have a written plan, "just ideas, obviously I'd like to develop it to other things." The plan developed by SME #3 was written after discussions with business colleagues and several consultants, but quickly became a superfluous document. The written plan was not adhered to and the site development became an "evolutionary process."

When interviewed, the SMEs could verbally identify their primary and secondary goals, but were less clear in regard to content strategy. All the SMEs had future goals for their sites but had not formulated a structure for ensuring their ideas were captured, that plans and timeframes developed or that future costs were identified.

Cragg's (1998) Internet Strategy model clearly identified four key areas that businesses should adhere to in order to increase e-business success, *Goals, Content, Process and Function*. The SMEs in this study were unable to articulate their e-business strategies and had assumed that the consultants would provide a strategic focus for them. Although all of the SMEs were at different stages in e-business implementation, all of them had a common goal of achieving an increase in sales and customers.

SME #1 felt that they had achieved their first goal of reaching an international marketplace: "We're pleased with the response we're getting from people all over the world." They did not, however, feel that they had achieved the second goal of increased profits: "…the fact that we're not getting any follow up is really disheartening; at the moment I wouldn't rate it an economic success."

SME #2 on the other hand felt strongly that they had not achieved their primary goal of establishing mail order, "sales off that have been minimal." Yet their secondary goal of reaching a wider audience was seen as quite successful: "We've had about 200 requests for catalogues off the site in two months which is pretty good; people are walking around with our catalogues." SME #2 also stated that they had achieved the contents strategy of marketing/promotion of the Website. This was seen by SME #2 as an intangible measure of success and that economic success would follow once the Website had been reassessed and redesigned internally.

CONCLUSION

There are many factors affecting the success of SMEs entering the world of e-business and this chapter focused on two possible factors. Firstly, consultant engagement for Web design was investigated using Gable's 12-phase model for consultant engagement, and secondly e-business strategies were explored to identify the main intended uses of the Website adapted from Cragg's Internet Strategy model.

From this a framework for consultancy engagement has been developed to guide Australian SMEs toward a more successful e-business implementation strategy. Prior to consultant engagement, a SME needs to have a clear idea of their Internet goals and the strategies required for achieving those goals.

Framework for Consultancy Engagement

1. *Locating a Website Design Consultant*
- Internet Service Provider (ISP)
- Business associates/colleagues
- Family/friends
- Online directories of Website design consultants
     www.aussie.com.au

www.ozsearch.com.au
www.perthwa.com.au
www.webwombat.com.au

2. *Planning*
- Goals–identification of primary and secondary goals
- Use of Website–marketing; sales; promotion
- Match the Internet plan with business plan
- Keep a written record of plans and goals
- Allocate a start-up budget and an ongoing maintenance & development budget

3. *Canvas the Market*
- Research the market
- Approach several potential consultants for quotes and advice
- Check consultant background–view previous work; request references
- Check consultant's experience and qualifications

4. *Contract*
- Negotiate a contract for service–obtain advice from your local Small Business Development Corporation on contract negotiation
    www.sbdc.com.au
    www.business.gov.au
- Include clauses for termination of the contract; project timeline; fee variations & payment mechanisms

5. *Control & Monitor Progress*
- Are timeframes being met?
- Maintain regular contact to obtain feedback on project milestones
- Receive regular verbal or written reports on status of project
- Be prepared to deal with and resolve obstacles

6. *Post-Engagement Evaluation*
- Does the Website meet your expectations?
- Do all the links work?
- Does each page of the site download quickly?
- Consider ongoing relationship with consultant for future maintenance and/or development of site

Frequently during the course of this study, a small business owner indicated that they lacked sufficient understanding on e-commerce to really specify what was required. Far more information sessions are required where practical workshops introduce the concepts of e-commerce with hands-on experimentation. These workshops should not be driven by vendors or consultants, but rather by government and academics. There is a real need to cut through the hype of "e-business" and demonstrate how SMEs can turn these opportunities to their own advantage.

ENDNOTE

1 There is no definitive model of a small or medium enterprise in Australia. The Yellow Pages Small Business Index defines a small business as having up to 19 full-time employees and a medium business as having between 20 and 200 employees; these figures do not include agricultural businesses (Small Business Index, 1998). The Small Business Development Corporation (SBDC) of Western Australia definition of small business is less than five employees in a micro-business, less than 20 employees in the non-manufacturing sector and less than 100 employees in the manufacturing sector. For the purpose of this chapter, 10 small enterprises were chosen for case analysis in the micro and small business category.

REFERENCES

Angehrn, A. (1997). Designing mature Internet business strategies: The ICDT model. *European Management Journal*, 15(4), 361-369.

Beer, (1999). Little response to e-commerce from small business. *Australian Financial Review*.

Benbasat, I., Goldstein, D. K. and Mead, M. (1987). The case research strategy in studies of information systems. *MIS Quarterly*, 360-386.

Bergeron, F., Raymond, L., Gladu, M. and Leclerc, C. (1998). The contribution of information technology to the performance of SMEs: Alignment of critical dimensions. *6th European Conference on Information Systems Proceedings*, France.

Burgess, R. G. (1984). *In the Field: An Introduction to Field Research*. London: Allen & Unwin

Carroll, J. M., Dawson, L. L. and Swatman, P. A. (1998). Using case studies to build theory: Structure and rigour. *Proceedings of the Ninth Australasian Conference on Information Systems*, NSW.

Cormier, K. (1999). Netstorming: Website development strategies. *Strategic Finance*, 80(11), 64-67.

Cragg, P. B. (1998). Clarifying Internet strategy in small firms. *Proceedings of the 9th Australian Conference on Information Systems*, NSW.

DIST. (1998a). *NEWS: A Project to Get Smaller Enterprises Online.* Canberra: Department of Industry, Science and Tourism.

Falkenstin, S. (1996). Why you should outsource the creation of your Website. *Pennsylvania CPA Journal*, 67(5), 9-12.

Fisher, J. and Arnott, D. (1998). An example of the analysis of qualitative case study data in information systems research. *Proceedings of Ninth Australasian Conference on Information Systems*, NSW.

Gable, G. G. (1989). Consultant engagement for first-time computerization in small and medium enterprises. *Proceedings of the 3rd Pan Pacific Computer Conference*, Bled, Yugoslavia.

Gable, G. G. (1991). Consultant engagement for computer system selection: A pro-active client role in small businesses. *Information and Management*, 20, 83-93.

Iacovou, C., Benbasat, I. and Dexter, A. (1995). Electronic data interchange and small organizations: Adoption and impact of technology. *MIS Quarterly*, 19(4), 465-485.

ISBR. (1998). *Small Business Opinion Survey.* Perth: Institute for Small Business Research.

Lawrence, K. L. and Chau, S. T. (1998). Capable but inactive: The Tasmanian electronic commerce experience. *Proceedings of the 9th Australian Conference on Information Systems*, NSW.

McCollum, T. (1999). Tailored solutions for growing firms. *Nation's Business*, June, 87, 42-44.

Miles, M. B. and M. H. A. (1994). *Qualitative Data Analysis: An Expanded Sourcebook.* Newbury Park, CA: Sage Publications.

Minichiello, V., Aroni, R., Timewell, E. and Alexander, L. (1995). *In-Depth Interviewing Principles, Techniques, Analysis* (2nd Ed.). Melbourne: Longman.

Patton, M. (1990). *Qualitative Evaluation and Research Methods* (2nd Ed.). Newbury Park, CA: Sage Publications.

Poon, S. and Swatman, P. M. C. (1997). Small business use of the Internet: Findings from Australian case studies. *International Marketing Review*, 14(4-5).

Prakash, A. (1998). *Electronic Commerce for Small Business*. Retrieved July 17, 1999, from the World Wide Web: http://www.iko.com.au.

Rose, H. (1991). Case studies. In Allan, G. (Ed.), *Handbook for Research Students in the Social Sciences*. London: The Falmer Press.

Small Business Index. (1998). *Small Business Index: A Survey of E-Commerce in Australian Small & Medium Businesses*. Melbourne: Yellow Pages.

Shern, S. (1998). *Internet Shopping: An Ernst & Young Special Report*. USA: Ernst & Young.

Stake, R. E. (1994). Case studies. In Denzin, N. K. and Lincoln, Y. S. (Eds.), *Handbook of Qualitative Research*. Newbury Park: CA: Sage Publications.

Thong, Y., Yap, C. and Raman, K. (1996). Top management support, external expertise and information systems implementation in small business. *Information Systems Research*, 7(2), 248-267.

Trauth, E. and Jessup, L. (1999). Understanding computer-mediated discussions: Positivist and interpretive analyses of group support system use. *MIS Quarterly*, 2-83.

Turban, E., McLean, E. and Wetherbe, J. (1999). *Information Technology for Management* (2nd Ed.). New York: John Wiley & Sons.

Yen, V.C. (1998). An integrated planning model for electronic commerce. *Proceedings of the Effective Utilization and Management of Emerging Information Technologies Conference*, Boston, MA.

Yin, R. K. (1994). *Case Study Research Design and Methods* (2nd Ed.). Newbury Park, CA: Sage Publications.

Chapter XIV

Building the Professional Services E-Practice

Dieter Fink
Edith Cowan University, Australia

INTRODUCTION

Information Technology (IT) has played an important role in the professional services sector for many years. Professional firms such as accountants, lawyers and management consultants have used IT to increase internal efficiencies, and the expertise gained has enabled some of them to offer IT-related professional advice to their clients. Over time, IT has increased in sophistication and we have now entered the Internet or electronic age (e-age) where the letter 'e' precedes commerce, business, government, learning and so forth. The emergence of the World Wide Web (Web) on the Internet has created even greater scope for professional firms to manage their internal affairs more efficiently and effectively, and to improve client services.

The purpose of this chapter is to provide small professional services practices with an understanding of how to enter the e-age by building an e-practice. It proceeds by mapping the progress that needs to be made in moving from a previous stage of organizational development to one that is suitable for the 'virtual age.' In the transition to the mature stage of development, they need to re-engineer their practices to offer online services and to maximize their intellectual capital through technology-enabled knowledge management.

The chapter will focus on firms that are of a small to medium size because they constitute the greatest number in the professional services sector and reflect unique challenges. Much of the content is based on research carried out into small and medium accounting firms. However, the findings and discussions may have validity for other service disciplines such as law, management consulting and financial advice because they are similar. They are characterized by a partner-oriented organizational structure in which highly trained professionals offer their services to clients at relatively high fees.

STAGES OF GROWTH

Since the introduction of computer technology into organizations in the 1960s, there have been numerous attempts to develop models of IT maturity. Amongst the earliest of these was that of Nolan (1973), subsequently refined and extended (Nolan, 1979). These 'stages of growth' models are premised on the idea that organizations pass through notional 'stages' of maturity or sophistication with respect to the way they use and manage IT to support and facilitate business activities, processes and operations. Such models of maturity may be used for descriptive or prescriptive purposes. They serve an important function to consider issues concerning the management and organization of the IT function as the organization progresses to greater sophistication in its use of IT.

In the e-age, the model developed by Venkatraman for the virtual organization (Venkatraman, 1995, referenced in Sieber and Griese, 1998) has previously been applied to chart the progress of professional accounting services firms (see Sieber and Griese, 1998). The term 'virtuality' was defined as " the ability of the organization to consistently obtain and coordinate critical competences through its design of value-adding business processes and governance mechanisms involving external and internal constituency to deliver differential, superior value in the marketplace" (Sieber and Grise, 1998, p. 170, quoting Venkatraman and Henderson, 1994). Based on this definition, three dimensions of the virtual organization model were identified in Venkatraman's (1995) model, namely market experience, competence leverage and work configuration. Within each of the dimensions, three evolutionary stages of virtual organizing are represented as an extension of Business Process Reengineering (BPR), a recreation of the organization and a recreation of value. This model is used to observe the evolution of the 'e-practice' and is reproduced in Figure 1.

As seen from Figure 1, an organization would evolve through three stages for each of three dimensions. The first stage is termed 'extension of BPR' which means that business processes are re-engineered in order to achieve modern performance expectation of speed and service. IT would be a strong enabler of this. During the second stage, 'recreation of the organization,' existing organizational structures and cultures are reviewed and challenged as to their appropriateness in the e-age. An obvious example is the move from a hierarchical

Figure 1: The structure and evolution of the e-practice (Venkatraman, 1995)

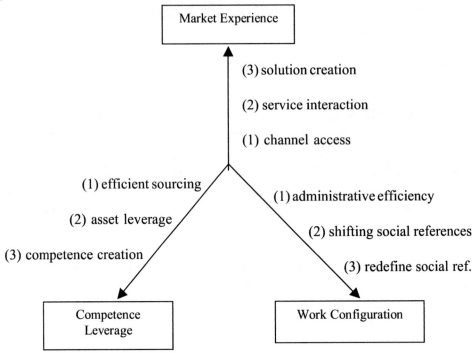

(1) Extension of BPR (2) Recreation of the organization (3) Recreation of value

to a flat organizational structure. In the third stage of 'recreation of value,' organizations would be searching for innovative and new ways of gaining competitive advantages. They can achieve this by adding new values to their products and services, thereby attracting new customers and/or increasing business volumes with existing ones.

The three stages of evolution described above are carried out in three dimensions which are work configuration, competence leverage and market experience as shown in Figure 1. Within the first named dimension, the organization changes the way work is carried out. Initially, it focuses on administrative efficiency (through BPR as highlighted above), followed by changing the interaction (termed social references) among its employees. The second dimension is 'competence leverage' which refers to better management of knowledge and skills. The stages within this dimensions are: obtaining the relevant competencies (termed sourcing), integrating (leveraging) them and creating new competencies, which is associated within the creation of values as discussed in the previous paragraph. The third dimension of 'market experience' covers the delivery of products and services. In the first stage, electronic channels are introduced, and this is followed by increased service interaction and offering solutions rather than ad hoc advice to customers.

To observe relevance and adoption of Venkatraman's model in practice, interviews were conducted with five small public accounting firms. These firms were members of the Institute of Chartered Accountants in New Zealand and were located in the city of Christchurch. Each firm was operating autonomously which provided them with the authority to develop their practices according to local requirements. The research was carried out by interviewing those senior members in each of the firms who possessed an organizational view of how professional intellect was managed. During the interviews information was gathered for the three dimensions of the model shown in Figure 1, namely work configuration, competence leverage and market experience.

The evolutionary progress of the majority of firms could be placed into the first stage, namely the extension of BPR. They recognized the importance of networking their professional staff (administrative efficiency in work configuration dimension), provided a limited amount of knowledge services to their clients (channel access in market experience dimension) and relied on vendor-supplied software for their Knowledge Management (KM) systems (efficient sourcing in competence leverage dimension). Only one firm had made some progress towards the second stage of evolution. It had developed a sophisticated in-house KM system (the asset leverage stage in competence leverage) and had shifted social references in the work configuration dimension.

The interviews not only attempted to establish the progress that firms had made in their evolution but also the changes that might occur in stages not yet reached. A discussion of all the stages outlined in Figure 1 follows. As indicated above, the first stage (extension of BPR) was observed in the case studies completed. The next two stages (recreation of the organization and recreation of value) have not been empirically verified because the firms had not reached them. However, the interviews conducted provided insight into how these stages may emerge in the future. The following discussion is presented in a 'generalized' form to provide generic guidance to small professional services firms in their quest to become an e-practice.

Stage 1: Extension of BPR

Work configuration (administrative efficiency): To improve administrative efficiencies, practices rely on a range of Information and Communications Technology (ICT). Extensive e-mail and groupware technologies facilitate dissemination of knowledge between firm members, calendaring and scheduling software provide efficient group activity and task management capabilities, and e-forms and workflow systems are available to provide guidelines on the conduct of assignments. The beginning of Knowledge Management systems are observed in the form of vendor-supplied practice management software used to store experiences gained in the conduct of client assignments.

Competence leverage (efficient sourcing): Unlike data and information, which are readily stored in organizational information processing systems, knowledge is largely stored in peoples' minds and undergoes constant changes. The challenge for firms is to convert this tacit knowledge into explicit knowledge by putting it into a structured form in organizational repositories which can be accessed and utilized by other members in the firm. The availability of suitable knowledge repositories avoids employees 're-inventing the wheel' when confronted with situations similar to those that have been experienced and resolved in the past.

Market experience (channel access): Channels for the delivery of knowledge services to clients is provided by e-mail systems. Since most clients can be contacted by e-mail, it is possible to supply them with knowledge and to interact with them electronically. The former category includes notices and advice on matters such as legislative changes, while for the latter, firms are able to send documents to the client for perusal and approval, and receive them back in the form of e-mail attachments.

Stage 2: Recreation of the Organization

Work configuration (shifting social references): From an organizational culture perspective, an effective service organization requires a change in attitude from individualism to 'caring and sharing.' In western culture, knowledge is regarded as a competitive advantage. Giving this up is not always readily accepted and some form of resistance can emerge. However, there are grounds for optimism in this respect as indicated by Tapscott (1999): "My research indicates that the interactive experience enabled by the Net is creating a new youth culture which values independence, innovation, knowledge sharing and collaboration–all very different values from those of their TV generation parents, who grew up in the age of mass communications, mass production, mass marketing and hierarchical organizations" (p. ix).

Competence leverage (asset leverage): Even though software vendors encourage firms to make suggestions for the improvement of their products, firms desire to move towards internally developed KM systems. For example, threaded discussions are seen as desirable but require the creation of intranet bulletin boards on which staff can follow discussions on topics such as the progress of an assignment or respond to queries arising from changes in legislation. The firms are also eager to capture and structure the content of e-mail discussions for storage in custom-developed knowledge repositories.

Market experience (service interaction): There are opportunities for practices to provide a greater degree of technology-enabled client knowledge services. To enhance service interaction, clients can be offered access to knowledge repositories within the firm. "The key issue in technologies for support KM is whether or not to structure the knowledge before the time of use or to provide structure in real time through search and interpretation" (Davenport and Klahr, 1998, p. 201). It appears as if firms prefer the first approach since this ensures that knowledge is structured to fit into the context in which the client would be using it.

Stage 3: Recreation of Value

Work configuration (redefine social references): The move towards an e-practice requires further redefinition of social references. Changes in work configurations are required in which 'intellectual Webs' replace partner- and client-oriented teams. A Web hierarchy is designed "to accomplish a particular project and disband when the project is completed. They are appropriate when knowledge is dispersed among many specialists, who must provide a coordinated solution to a complex customer problem" (Quinn et al., 1996, p. 79).

Competence leverage (competence creation): Professional firms should consider forming inter-firm networks because they have become a modern mode of organizing economic activity and provide a locus of learning and innovation. They are particularly valuable when there are high levels of uncertainty brought about by rapid changes within the firm and the environment. When uncertainty is high, organizations interact more, not less, with external parties to access knowledge and resources (Powell, 1998). They are an effective means to increasing inhouse skills or getting the job done without acquiring such skills.

Market experience (solution creation): A further opportunity to provide solutions-oriented services to clients exists in the form of knowledge brokering (Davenport and Klahr, 1998). Professional practices have access to, and extensive experience in, a wide range of industries and clients, and have developed the ability to link past knowledge of solutions to new problems. Knowledge brokering provides an opportunity to utilize these strengths and create further value in the delivery of client services.

During the evolution to an e-practice, small firms have to evaluate the advantages of using the Internet. For professional service firms, two significant opportunities can be identified. One is to offer Web-based online client services, and the other is to use Internet and other technologies to develop Knowledge Management systems. These opportunities are reflected in Figure 1 as 'market experience' and the combination of 'competence leverage' and 'work configuration' respectively. They are discussed in the following sections.

OPPORTUNITIES FOR THE SMALL E-PRACTICE

The Web has become a dominant phenomenon in commercial life because it "provides a new, function-rich, high-capacity and nearly ubiquitous infrastructure for business. It enables firms to enrich products with information, knowledge and services for unique competitive advantage" (Tapscott, 1999, p. vii). As indicated above, this enables firms to provide online services to clients. The main reasons why professional firms may want to deliver online services to their clients are the following (adapted from Davenport and Klahr, 1998):

- To constrain and preferably reduce the growing cost of customer support. With an increasingly complex and competitive business environment, clients demand more attention and a competitive price.
- *To encourage client self-sufficiency by reducing the demand for lower levels of services which may be uneconomical to provide.* One way to achieve this objective is to provide clients with ready access to the firm's knowledge base.
- *To retain and preferably expand their market share.* Information and Communications Technology is seen as providing a competitive edge through cost reduction and/or developing a market niche by adding value to products and services.

The main advantage for clients is that the Web provides access to a large range of potential service providers and types of services. Previously they would have had contact with a limited number of service providers and would know less about the range of services available. The Web provides the potential to find and utilize services that offer the highest value to them. However, a less stable relationship between the two may emerge because of the greater choice in services and providers available. Furthermore, bad experiences or poor services may become more public through being broadcasted on the Web, while before, problems were kept 'inhouse' and remained largely restricted to the client and his/her service provider.

Second, the reasons why firms may desire to implement KM systems are primarily centered around the following (adapted from Davenport and Klahr, 1998):

- *The transfer of knowledge to other members of the firm.* Firms comprise individuals and teams who, during the conduct of carrying out client assignments, accumulate knowledge. A KM system has the potential for disseminating this knowledge, thereby increasing the amount of in-firm learning and the quality of professional practices.
- *The retention of knowledge within the firm.* This can be lost when expert staff 'walk out of the door.' Knowledge that has been codified provides a permanent store of knowledge that can be made available to newcomers.

- *The desire to quantify and thereby maximize the firm's intellectual capital.* This is knowledge capital wealth that the firm possesses, and consists of tacit and explicit knowledge.

Under KM, knowledge assets are managed in a series of processes that can be identified as those of knowledge identification, coding, storage, usage and maintenance. The processes are facilitated by the use of modern IT such as intranets, group support systems and data warehouses, but also require a supportive organizational environment and the introduction of new 'values' (for example, value of care) to guide relationships and conduct.

ONLINE SERVICES TO CLIENTS

In a recent study, Evans and Volery (2000) established what experienced business service providers, who included consultants and counsellors, regarded as opportunities that exist for providing professional services on the Internet. The participants, who came from five countries, identified them as intelligence, consulting, counseling, relationship networks, education and training. Of these services, online education and training were not highly regarded by participants in Evans and Volery's study and can therefore largely be ignored by the e-practice.

The inherent features of the Web should be exploited to deliver the kinds of client services identified above. The Web has the capability of providing continuous service by offering access to information around the clock and globe in multiple languages. Furthermore it can do this in a static or interactive mode. The former is suitable for the provision of intelligence while the latter supports consulting and counseling services. A Web site can also contain links to other Web sites and thereby facilitate relationship networking.

A discussion of the services and the form they may take currently when delivered over the Web follows. The latter is based on a recent review of Web sites of accounting firms in Western Australia representing the two major accounting bodies, namely the Institute of Chartered Accountants in Australia (ICAA) and Certified Practicing Accountants in Australia (CPAA). The number of accounting firms operating in Western Australia was around 80 according to their listings in the Yellow Pages phone directory. Of the 80 firms, 16 firms had a Web presence at the time of the study, which was carried out in the second half of 2000. Of the 16 firms, 11 could be regarded as being small practices because they only had one to two partners and had only a Perth (the capital of Western Australia) office location.

Intelligence

This essentially involves the gathering of information and making it available to clients in a form suitable for decision-making. The emergence of the Web, however, has contributed to an information overload being experienced. Evans and Volery's (2000) research indicated that business clients find it difficult to establish, first what is a good Web site and second, what is good information. The opportunity, therefore, exists for the service provider to 'add value' to information so that clients can use it 'intelligently' in their own context.

The quantity, quality and currency of material provided are entirely under the control of the firm. The research showed that the larger the firm, the more extensive the material provided online. There existed a wide variety in the content that is made available. Some firms provided access to intelligence available from external sources while others had compiled it themselves. The currency of the material seemed to be achieved through the publication of newsletters.

Consulting

Where information is too general to solve a particular problem, it has to be customized for the client. This activity is regarded as consulting. While traditionally this is done in face-to-face meetings, online consulting services are emerging over the Internet. A well-known example is Ernst & Young's (EY) Web site Ernie (http://ernie.ey.com) which provides an online consulting service targeting high-growth SMEs. It is subscription-based and password protected, and features a database, e-mail and an electronic newsletter. The e-mail provides a question-and-answer dialog in which clients request advice and EY respond with opinions, solutions and custom-made answers. Research indicates that Web-based consultancy, however, is still in its infancy (Katz, 1998, referenced in Evans and Volery, 2000).

The survey showed that while firms' Web sites referred to a broad range of professional consulting services, these generally could only be obtained offline by contacting the office or individuals. Quite a few of the firms made available checklists in such areas as super-annuation and lease payments. Online interactive access to consulting services was provided by one medium-sized firm on their Web site and one small firm through a link to an external site (named 'doctor ebiz'). The former assists clients in developing electronic channels while the latter helps small businesses succeed online.

Counseling

Counseling is where the counsellor guides and assists the client to discover solutions to problems. This can be achieved through a number of strategies. For example, the firm can assist the client in structuring the problem, identify and recommend problem-solving approaches that may be suitable or act as a mentor. According to Evans and Volery (2000), a well-known online counseling service for small business is SCORE (http://www.score.org) in the United States of America. There are approximately 11,000 business counsellors that can provide counseling on a broad range of business topics. Local counsellors, who can meet with clients face-to-face or through e-mail, are available to supplement this service. The service is free and confidential. There were no online counseling services among the Web sites examined in this study.

Relationship Networking

Networking is important because it establishes relationships between clients and facilitates exchanges of ideas and information. For example, it can bring a small business into contact with organizations that have the required resources such as finance, people, skills and so forth to complete a project. Networking often overlaps with consulting and counseling activities. A well-known online networking site is 'First Tuesday' (http://www.firsttuesday). It got its name from the fact that businesses used to meet on the first Tuesday of every month. This now takes place online on the Internet through discussion forums, an e-mail newsletter and an online swap shop for office space.

The survey conducted showed that links to other sites were provided in only a few cases. They tended to be to Web sites that were regarded of high quality professional nature (for example, Australian Stock Exchange, Business Review Weekly), useful (for example, Universal currency converter) or specialized (for example, 'doctor ebiz').

Web Site Management

In their study, Evans and Volery (2000) established that, to ensure that the Web site achieves its client service objectives, it needs to be effectively managed. This can be interpreted in a number of ways. First, the site should utilize synchronous technology (e-mail) and asynchronous technology if at all possible. In the study of Western Australian Web sites, it was found that larger firms tended to provide office addresses only and no names of individuals. Typically the location addresses, telephone and fax numbers of offices were given as well as common e-mail addresses. The use of the 'contact us' feature was popular so that a prospective client could fill in details about him or herself and e-mail this to the office. This gives the office the opportunity to respond to the contact made. For the medium and small firms, office addresses as well as names of individuals are generally provided. Professional staff could be contacted through the office or directly.

Second, the Web site should be 'friendly' to use. This requires that the client can easily and quickly find his/her way around the site and material can be downloaded conveniently and smoothly. The study showed that access to information was provided by the use of menus that typically reflected items that gave details about the firm (for example, location), services offered, people and publications.

Access to details was obtained mostly in two to three levels which reflects good Web site design. A few sites had a search facility and one site provided a help function on navigating the site. One medium-sized practice displayed Chinese instructions, presumably aimed at potential overseas clients.

Third, links should be provided to enable clients to get access to Web sites of offices or services that may exist in other offices of the service provider. The larger and most of the medium-sized firms had offices in other Australian centers as well as overseas. The Web sites provided information about the Australian offices and, in the case of the international affiliation, a hot link to the overseas Web site.

THE NEED FOR KNOWLEDGE MANAGEMENT

An important issue for the professional firm is the effective use of IT to maximize its intellectual capital, the term commonly used to express the knowledge-based equity that firms possess (International Federation of Accountants, 1998). For example, IT can be used to digitize existing paper-based notes and to inter-network the minds of knowledge professionals. Effective KM relies not on one type of technology but on a number of diversified technologies (Ruggles, 1998). In the context of the e-practice, KM can be facilitated by an IT framework as depicted in Figure 2.

The infrastructure of the IT framework essentially consists of a messaging architecture for communications and the sharing of information and knowledge among professional staff and possibly clients. It is the primary technology beneath e-mail but allows calendaring and scheduling, workflow and collaborative functions such as groupware. The knowledge repository provides a store for unstructured and semi-structured knowledge created by users through e-mail attachments, electronic forms, images and voice messages. They can serve as data warehouses to be interrogated through data mining tools.

As discussed earlier (see stages of growth), small and medium-sized professional firms have successfully adopted e-mail as a key technology but vary in their adoption of other forms of KM technology. Among the more straightforward, currently used technologies are groupware, calendaring, scheduling and workflow software; they facilitate the dissemination of knowledge, group activity and task management. On the other hand, threaded discussions require the creation of intranet bulletin boards on which staff can follow discussions on topics. They do not appear to be commonly in use.

Some familiarity with knowledge repositories is emerging in the firms studied through the use of 'notes' posted in client databases. These databases are currently supplied by external vendors as part of practice management software. As is the case with all prewritten software packages, vendors will only develop specialized features that appeal to a broad user base. Professional firms therefore need to decide on a strategy to increase the availability of KM features within software packages provided to them. They can act as an industry group to persuade vendors to develop genuine KM systems or develop internal ones to lessen their reliance on externally provided systems.

The effective utilization of IT for KM has to be accompanied by other developments. A critical one is the implementation of procedures to convert tacit into explicit knowledge. Van Krogh (1998) refers to this activity as the public justification process, which is described as follows. "The first steps in knowledge creation, 'sharing tacit knowledge' and 'creating concepts' hinge on the individuals being able to share their personal true beliefs about a situation with other team members. At this point, the whole process of creating knowledge becomes dramatically different: *justification becomes public*. Each individual is faced with the challenge of justifying his true beliefs in presence of others, and precisely this process of justification makes knowledge creation a highly *fragile process*" (van Krogh, 1998, p. 135).

According to van Krogh (1998), there are four major barriers that could hinder the public justification process. Professional firms will have to develop new approaches and change attitudes to overcome these hurdles.

*   *Legitimate language.* Appropriate terminology needs to be developed that enables personal knowledge to be expressed in language known and acceptable to team members and the firm.
*   *Stories and habits.* The firm needs to be supportive of and accept individualistic behavior in the communication of knowledge. These may include stories of failed attempts or habits that appear questionable.

Figure 2: Information technology framework for Knowledge Management (Davis, 1998)

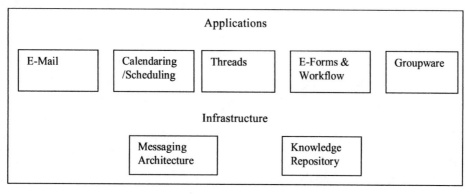

- *Formal procedures.* Formality in the knowledge justification process can produce successful solutions to complex tasks but also work against the process because of the suppression of individual beliefs and behavior.
- *Company paradigms.* These are expressed as visions, missions and core values. Individuals, however, may find it difficult to justify personal beliefs that are not in accordance with the ruling paradigm.

CHALLENGES AHEAD

The move towards the e-practice requires a redefinition and shift of social references that currently exist. First, changes in work configurations are required in which 'intellectual Webs' replace partner- and client-oriented teams. Second, attitudes have to move from individualism where 'knowledge is power' to one that encourages and rewards giving up and sharing knowledge with others. For example, internal promotion could be made conditional on staff, demonstrating their willingness and effectiveness in transferring knowledge to other staff by holding training sessions, project reviews and so forth. This would ensure that knowledge passes from experienced senior staff to junior staff. Firms, however, have to learn to accept that personal knowledge can be unique and personal beliefs may not always be in accordance with the ruling paradigm.

The move to the e-practice furthermore provides the opportunity to develop entrepreneurial versus the administrative capabilities of firms. For example, greater service interactions with clients can be achieved through online client support. The expansion of entrepreneurial activities, however, introduces business risks because activities are inextricably linked to changes that may occur within clients' organizations (Lin, 1998). For example, technology-enabled knowledge services reduce contextual and non-verbal communication cues, and clients may broadcast their dissatisfaction to the world via the Internet rather than to the firm in the traditional ways. Furthermore, clients may become less reliant on the firm since they gain greater control over the source of products and services. With the emergence of the Internet-based economy, power may shift from service provider to service consumer.

Small professional service firms experience high levels of uncertainty brought about by rapid changes within their firms (for example, the emergence of KM) and their environment (for example, the challenges posed by the Internet). When uncertainty is high, organizations interact more, not less, with external parties to access knowledge and resources (Powell, 1998). Inter-firm networks have become a modern mode of organizing economic activity in which the network has become a locus of learning and innovation. They can be a learning tool to increase inhouse skills or be a means to get the job done without acquiring such skills. Small firms need to develop suitable alliances.

CONCLUSIONS

The move to an e-practice has the potential to provide professional services firms with substantial internal and external benefits. The greater transfer of knowledge within practices leads to improvement in professional performance and an increase in intellectual capital. Technology enables client services to be invigorated by the addition of new forms of value. Knowledge-enhanced products and services provide the means to consolidate existing client relationships as well as increase the frequency of interactions between service providers and consumers. However, more research needs to be conducted to determine how best the opportunities of the e-age can be realized.

The above developments are particularly promising for small and medium-sized professional practices. Effective KM together with advancements in online services may, in the future, enable them to challenge the domination by the large practices that rely on their physical presence around the globe to provide services to their international clients. Small and medium-sized firms can overcome their lack of economies of scale and physical resources by creating virtual knowledge assets and processes. They will be able to offer their specialized and niche services to a wide range of clients either directly through the Internet or through inter-firm collaboration. The potential exists for the local office of these firms to become their global office.

REFERENCES

Davenport, T. H. and Klahr, P. (1998). Managing customer support knowledge. *California Management Review*, 40(3), 195-208.

Davis, M.C. (1998). Knowledge management. *Information Strategy: The Executive's Journal*, Fall, 11-22.

Evans, D. and Volery, T. (2000). Online business development services for entrepreneurs: An exploratory study. *ICSB World Conference*, Brisbane.

International Federation of Accountants. (1998). *The Measurement and Management of Intellectual Capital: An Introduction*. Retrieved from the World Wide Web: http://www.ifac.org.

Katz, J. A. (1998). *Distance Consulting: Potentials and Pitfalls in Using the Internet to Deliver Business Development Services to SMEs, A report to the Donor Committee on Small Enterprise Developments*. Open Society Institute, October 27.

Lin, L. (1998). The impact of electronic commerce on marketing of services: A proposal of research models. *Marketing and Research Today*, August, 93-102.

Nolan, R. L. (1973). Managing the computer resource: A stage hypothesis. *Communications of the ACM*, 16(7), 399-406.

Nolan, R. L. (1979). Managing the crisis in data processing. *Harvard Business Review*, March-April, 115-126.

Powell, W. W. (1998). Learning from collaboration: Knowledge and networks in the biotechnology and pharmaceutical industries. *California Management Review*, 40(3), 228-240.

Quinn, J. B, Anderson P. and Finkelstein S. (1996). Managing professional intellect: Making the most of the best. *Harvard Business Review*, March-April, 71-80.

Ruggles, R. (1998). The state of the notion: Knowledge management in practice. *California Management Review*, 40(3), 80-89.

Sieber, P. and Griese, J. (1998). Virtual organizing as a strategy for the "big six" to stay competitive in a global market. *Journal of Strategic Information Systems*, 7, 167-181.

Tapscott, D. (1999). *Creating Value in the Network Economy*. A Harvard Business Review Book.

Von Krogh, G. (1998). Care in knowledge creation. *California Management Review*, 40(3), 133-153.

Venkatraman, N. and Henderson, C. (1994). Avoiding the hollow: Virtual organizing and the role of information technology. September 23. Retrieved from the World Wide Web: http://Web/bu/SMG-SRC/projects/virtual.html.

Venkatraman, N. (1995). The IS function in the virtual organization: Who's wagging whom? *Panel 10 of the Sixteenth International Conference on Information Systems*, December 10-13, Amsterdam.

Chapter XV

How a Procedural Framework Would Assist SMEs in Developing Their E-Business Strategy

Anthony Stiller
University of the Sunshine Coast, Australia

INTRODUCTION

While Small-to-Medium Enterprises (SMEs) in Australia have an excellent opportunity to take advantage of the growth of e-commerce in Australian and the Asia Pacific region by reducing the effects of Australia's relative isolation to Asian and world markets, a large number of managers choose not to take advantage of the opportunity to reach both the local and global markets because they do not know how to go about developing a strategic e-business and marketing plan. While there is plenty of literature provided by government agencies, business interest groups and commercial Web development houses, there is no procedural framework available for SME managers to follow when designing their e-business plan and revenue model so they can remain in charge of the process and not be pushed into a particular template designed by a consultant to suit their hardware and software platform.

One method to increase adoption rates by SMEs and to give them an opportunity to participate in the benefits that can be derived from e-commerce is to provide them with a procedural framework that sets out in a very detailed manner the steps they need to follow. The framework should give SME owners control over the entire process until they are at the stage to either develop their own online presence, or have sufficient information to take to a Web consultant who can develop a model which reflects the e-business strategy and is in harmony with the traditional business and marketing plan.

CONTEXT AND BACKGROUND

The definition for a Small-to-Medium Enterprise in Australia (as set out in The Yellow Pages Small Business Index, 2000) identifies a small business as one which has 'up to 19 full-time employees including the proprietor if he or she is part of the workforce [and] medium-sized business employing between 20 and 200 full-time persons.' The Australian Bureau of Statistics (ABS) has identified another category of business operators within this sector, the 'Very Small Business' (VSB) which employs fewer than five employees (ABS, 2000). Since this sector of industry employs approximately 50.2% of the total Australian workforce of the 9,141,800 people (ABS, 1999) and contributes significantly to the supply of goods and services, one would expect a high level of uptake of information technology, namely using the Internet for business-to-business (B2B), business-to-consumer (B2C) and business-to-government (B2G) technology to assist in the reduced costs and efficiencies normally associated with electronic commerce.

While the adoption of Internet technology by SME's has increased from 29% to 56% in the period from 1997/1988 to 1999/2000, and the use of a Web site or home page has also increased proportionally over the same period from 6% to 16% (ABS, 2000), SMEs using the Internet to carry out e-commerce accounts for only 0.4% of total sales (ABS, 2000). A survey by the National Office for the Information Economy (NOIE) of a random sample of 1,196 small businesses and 300 medium businesses from six industry sectors (manufacturing, building/construction, wholesale/retail, transport/storage, finance/property/business services and recreational/personal/other services) across each of the six states and two territories of Australia identified some remarkable findings as to why SMEs are not adopting e-commerce technology (NOIE, 2000).

Major reasons (NOIE, 2000) for not adopting e-commerce include:
- A concern that the use of the Internet for e-commerce could lead to uncontrolled growth
- Satisfaction with current business arrangements
- Uncertainty about the quality and availability of products, and about delivery and supply arrangements
- Fear of alienating intermediaries

- Concern about not having enough understanding of technology to be able to manage and direct the adoption of e-commerce, and about how these skills would be assessed
- Time and expense
- A belief that the business products or services did not lend themselves to the Internet.

Adding to the concern of SMEs outlaying financial and human resources to the development and implementation of an online strategy are the statistics contained in an article by Geer (2001), stating that "there is only a 2% conversion rate of a customer buying on the Web...and that there really needs to be work before the magnificent projected numbers that Juniper, Forrester and other advertising watchers are predicting by 2003 or 2004." While Greer identifies factors such as security and trust as major reasons why customers stop from completing a transaction, these issues should have been addressed by the SME when developing their e-strategy to ensure customer requirements have been satisfied.

SMEs are being subjected to articles from major newspapers, journals and books on electronic commerce, advertising from computer consultants and sales firms, government agencies and within their own industry groups spelling out the virtues and in many instances, the necessity for being an adopter of e-commerce. For the SME this can become rather confusing and presents conflicting views as to what an e-business strategy is or what an e-commerce adoption model means. With so many SMEs not even having a basic business and marketing plan, an e-commerce consultant's statement (Sussis, 2000)–"as businesses move into significant e-businesses, good planning strategies, design and implementation become more and more essential"–adds to the confusion for the SME and simply compounds the problem, as little or no further explanation is given on what steps they need to take in working through each of these concepts.

SME managers obtain their information from various sources, and while the information contained is relevant and of a quality, it focuses on particular aspects of e-commerce, business management and technology treating them as separate entities rather than a unit where each relies on the other. Examples include:

- E-commerce and business management textbooks and reference material set in formal education courses at universities, Technical And Further Education (TAFE) Institutes and private providers
- Web site information downloaded from e-commerce consultants and sent through email subscription lists
- Handbooks and training courses offered through industry advising organizations, trade groups and government departments

For the SMEs that undertake formal education or read textbooks recommended by universities in electronic commerce courses, the confusion is further compounded when they read statements by Adam, Dogramaci, Gangopadhyay and Yesha (1999) that "Business models provide general rules for companies to adhere to when implementing new initiatives." This is good news and gives some guidance; however, I have already established that many SMEs have little or no understanding of e-commerce concepts, terminology, best practice principles, the World Wide Web and how to develop an e-business strategy, let alone how to purchase, use and gain maximum benefit from the technology.

In order to take advantage of e-commerce opportunities, a number of questions need to be raised, including;

1.   Who does the SME turn to for strategic planning advice?
2.   How can I do business across the Internet?
3.   After spending all this time and money, what will be my net rate of return on investment?
4.   What happens if my business grows too fast and I cannot cope with the expansion?

In addressing the issue of using Internet technology, 61% of SMEs that took part in the Small Business Survey said they "would benefit from training in the Internet and e-commerce" (NOIE, 2000). Through such an education program, SMEs could then see the benefits by developing an e-business strategy that addresses their particular business needs rather than adopt an off-the-shelf total business solution or simply take the advice and direction of a consultant, since "relatively few small and medium businesses connected to the Internet believe that the Internet is useful for buying and selling or paying for products" (DCITA, 1998).

A study, conducted by Arabatzis and Rovolis (1999) for the European Commission Enterprise DG, aimed at improving SMEs access to electronic commerce in the European Union, stated:

"After an analysis of success indicators for Web sites (traffic achieved, turnover increase, cost savings, new customers acquired), it was found that the type of the Web sites play a crucial role for business success. Companies whose Web site plays a vital part in their operations are the most successful. In contrast, Web sites that are a first step in exhibiting an Internet presence do not appear to have any positive impact on a business's success."

Unfortunately, more emphasis is placed on developing a Web presence rather than developing the e-business strategy which complements the business and marketing strategy. "The adoption of online technologies does not replace business processes (such as ordering, supply and delivery) but has the potential to change the way these processes are performed and improve a firm's profit margin" (DISC, 1998).

IMPLEMENTING A PROCEDURAL FRAMEWORK

The online community is becoming more sophisticated in accessing and using the Internet for business-to-business (B2B), business-to-consumer (B2C), consumer-to-consumer (C2C) and business-to-government (B2G) communication and transactions. The Australian Government acknowledges that "the rate of change in electronic commerce is rapid because the technology is evolving quickly, new business models are being created and an ever-increasing variety of business interests are arising. Therefore the policy settings for getting business online need to be re-evaluated at least every six months" (DISC, 1998). SME owners should also re-evaluate their position within the marketplace on a regular basis as they look to their future and take ownership of their business operations.

One way to assist in this process is for SMEs to follow a procedural framework which is cyclical in nature and can be reviewed at regular intervals so as not to miss out on online opportunities. The following procedural framework, proposed by the author, encompasses various e-commerce and best practice principles while remaining flexible to meet the individual needs of the SME, their e-environment and customer demand.

SME Business and Strategic Plan

The most important first step for any SME within an organization is to have a clearly identified and workable business and strategic plan whether they are in the traditional or virtual business environment. Earle and Keen (2000) state that "We can't see any option for a firm except to take a fundamental look at the basics of the new business landscape and define the business model to address them... Its business model remains focused on bricks and mortar with its Web site a secondary channel, but it will still need to address channel harmony."

Issues that an SME may want to consider when developing their strategic business and e-business plan include:

- What is the nature of our current business operations?
- Who are our customers and business partners?
- What are our products and/or services, and what benefits do our customers get from our organization?
- How do we perform a strengths, weaknesses, opportunities and strengths analysis (SWOT) on current and perceived business opportunity?
- How do we define the geographical boundaries in which the business should compete?
- Who is our competition and what products and/or services do they offer?
- What is the nature of the market in local, interstate and in a global perspective?

Figure 1: Procedural framework

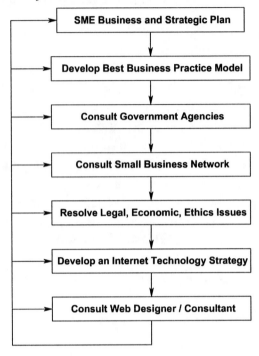

- How can our products and/or services be distinguished from the competition?
- What steps do we need to implement to ensure we remain competitive?
- What steps do we need to take to investigate future expansion?
- What organizational mix will our organization need for now and in the future?
- Do we have the innovative skills including any training plans should the organization implement to take advantage of the Internet?
- What detailed resources, targets and actions are required in order to achieve the e-business strategies and goals?
- Who do we turn to for help and assistance?

Develop a Best Business Practice Model

Once the business and strategic plan has been developed, the SMEs' attention becomes focused on operational issues for implementing the plan. Cox (1997) states that "there is no single answer to the question of what is operational 'best practice' because of the contingent nature of the world within which companies operate," and while Fitz-enz (1997) explains that "the principal shortcoming of best-practice stories is that they focus on yesterday's problems and solutions," SMEs can learn from best practices case studies and adopt the most appropriate practices to suit their business strategy.

A best practice model, as defined by the Department of the Treasury (1999), is one that "provides guidance to business on the standards and practices which they should adopt in the area of business-to-consumer commerce" and could easily be expanded to meet the requirements for other e-commerce activities so that "consumers are adequately protected and have confidence in making online transactions."

For SMEs wanting to adopt Internet technology and expand their 'bricks and mortar' business plan to an e-business strategic plan, they will need to develop an e-commerce model that matches their business and marketing strategy.

Electronic commerce literature identifies a number of distinct business or adoption models from which an SME can choose when designing and developing their e-commerce strategy. The use of models to assist in the development of an e-strategy has its benefits as well as limitations, and Harding and Long (1998) advise us that while "models can help us to clarify, broaden and deepen our analysis and thinking and to organize, manage and manipulate reality in our minds ... models should not be used as tools in analysis and never as ends in themselves."

The danger of adopting a model is that the SME could modify the nature of the business to fit the model instead of developing or refining a model to suit the needs of the business. To complicate matters, electronic commerce textbooks used by education and training organizations offering courses in this area specify varying numbers and names for their models and how they should be applied within the business setting.

Examples from the selection of textbooks used by universities in electronic commerce courses at undergraduate and post-graduate courses below highlight the added confusion for the SME when confronted by consultants who have studied a particular textbook and structures the adoption models on those principles.

1. Lawrence et al. (2000) identify the key strategies brought from management techniques such as planning, controlling, monitoring, adjusting and managing quality, but do not elaborate how these key management strategies relate to e-business strategies. Emphasis is placed on the commercial interface aspects of Web design by using one or more combinations of the *seven* adoption models of poster/billboard, online yellow pages, cyber brochure, virtual storefront, subscription, advertising, 3.5.7, auction/reverse auction, affiliation and portal models.

2. Treese and Stewart (1998) argue that there are four Internet business strategies that can be used, either as a single entity or in a combination. Their emphasis is on customer relations and they identify channel master, customer magnet, value chain pirate and digital distributor as key strategies when using their three-step approach of selecting a

strategy, designing the commerce value chain and implementing an evolving solution to meet the needs of the enterprise.

3. The *Eight* Rules for e-Business outlined by Kalakota and Robinson (1999) give some guidance to the SME when considering e-business integration by identifying key flexible business structural design strategies in place to ensure they are in a position to detect emerging trends faster than their competition by challenging the traditional business models by focusing on the customer's needs and requirements.

4. Turban, Lee, King and Chung (2000) agree that e-commerce is 'interdisciplinary,' involving marketing, computer sciences, finance, economics, management information systems, management, business law and ethics, accounting and auditing, consumer behavior, psychology and other disciplines. Their 'Strategic Planning Cycle,' an alternative methodology put forward by Ware et al. in the '*Seven-Step Model*' for clarifying goals and expectations, fails to offer a procedural framework which can be readily adapted by the SME to combine best practices in management, electronic commerce adoption models and Internet technologies.

5. The 'e-Commerce Strategy Model' proposed by Whitley (2000) states that "e-Commerce has the potential to redefine corporate strategy as opposed to being a component within the implementation of that overall strategy (and) needs to be accepted throughout the business and to pervade the tactical decision-making process."

6. Adam, Dogramaci, Gangopadhyay and Yesha (1999) provide a *general framework* for e-commerce business model adoption and note that models are still being formulated and developed because e-commerce is still at an early stage; but as a field, the customer, vendor, retailer and the financial institution are key players in the development of legal and policy strategies.

7. Frick and Lill from the GartnerGroup (2000) present "*Ten Imperatives for E-Business Success*" based upon the success of organizations that have adopted e-commerce. In their article they point out that 'while there is great promise in the new economy, there is also great risk.' The rules are:
    • Never plan further than 24 months out.
    • Do not attempt to develop an e-business strategy of the full business strategy.
    • Use separate strategies according to industry, geography and culture.
    • During analysis, give weight to internal and external processes.
    • Obtain total buy-in from the board.
    • Deliberately execute alternatives to buy, spin off or transform business model.
    • Play by the "new rules."

- Enhance or destroy distribution channels based on their true power and value.
- Establish a metrics program that measures the true effectiveness of the e-business initiative.
- Speed and ruthless execution are everything.

While there is confusion amongst the various writers as to the number of models, a central theme emerges based on the requirement of the SME to research, plan, seek advice and take action if they are to participate in and benefit from the digital economy. The best practice model will emerge from out of the planning and development stages and may, or may not, resemble any of the strategies presented by any one writer, or may in fact be a combination or re-engineering of sections of various model components. Whatever meets the needs of the SME's business operations is the most appropriate model.

Consult Government Agencies

Australian Federal and State Government agencies have a vast amount of information, advice and assistance for the adoption of Internet technologies as this has become one of the Federal Government's key objectives to assist as many SMEs go online.

Areas of assistance that SME may be seeking:

1. Awareness of available training for electronic commerce and how their business could benefit.
2. Specific technology training on how to use Internet technologies.
3. Financial assistance to get established.
4. Taxation policies when conducting trade and commerce across borders.
5. Government assistance is seeking out and making international trade connections.
6. Rural and regional relief, especially in the area of telecommunications and bandwidth requirements.
7. Questions relating to transport within and external to Australia.

While many of the issues listed above may have a significant Federal Government impact, there are also State Government initiatives that SMEs can utilize when implementing their e-business strategies.

The following list of online Web sites that could be useful to Australian SMEs in the adoption and diffusion of Internet technologies, while not exhaustive, are representative of the type and level of support and assistance that is, already available to the SME free of charge:

1. Australia Online, where SMEs can search a database for companies that have similar products and/or services. http://www.austrade.gov.au/AOD/index.asp.
2. Ausinfo has been established by the Federal Government for the dissemination of information on finance, operations and services. http://www.dofa.gov.au/infoaccess/.

3.   Ausindustry is a National Research Web site providing business organizations with information on research and development grants, tax concessions and business information on customers, products and services, media releases and publications, what's new and links to other government agencies. http://www.ausindustry.gov.au/.

4.   Australian Governments' Business Entry Point is a Web site providing the latest news items, case studies, information based on topics and a search facility for services across Australia on a whole range of relevant issues. http://www.business.gov.au/.

5.   The National Office for the Information Economy with information on the Federal Government's strategy on implementing and promoting Internet adoption. It holds research papers and findings on issues related to the information economy. http://www.noie.gov.au/.

Consult Small Business Network

The Internet has assisted in bringing homogeneous organizations and related industries together through the wide use and availability of email, newsgroups, newsletters, video conferencing and online education programs for such areas as finance, business procedures and how to apply for grants when special initiative projects are advertised.

As well as gaining information from Internet-based Web sites, SMEs are encouraged to join local industry groups to discuss specific issues that relate to their geographical area such as telecommunications; services; transport; how they are affected by local, state and federal laws; and rules and regulations. At such meetings, SMEs could establish partnerships complementing each other, offering to the online and off line customer a value-added service.

The use of portals as a gateway or entry point for people and business organizations looking for goods and/or services has not been embraced to a large extent by businesses of similar industry groups or industries located within a local geographical area. SMEs could increase their presence and advertising awareness through the use of a B2B portal "accessed only by member enterprises, specializing in business commodities and materials" or a 'vortal' where industries are part of a "value chain beginning with raw materials and ending with finished products" (Schneider & Perry, 2001).

Resolve Legal, Economic and Ethics Issues

Business law and ethics takes on a new significance when operating on the Internet, as organizations have to comply with the laws in their country of origin as well as those associated with international law, as their Web site can be accessed from anywhere in the world. Businesses operating through a Web site are more open to scrutiny by rival competitors since their text, graphic images, audio and/or video is open to public viewing, whereas within a traditional 'bricks and mortar' business operation, it becomes more difficult to scrutinize.

Key issues the SME will have to address when operating a virtual business include:

1. Consumer protection, in light of local and global electronic commerce, because of the difficulties consumers may have trying to enforce their rights (especially when trying to find information on the ownership, contact details, conditions of sale, and return of goods and/or services) due to poor Web site design. The Treasury Department has released a set of guidelines in its publication, United Nations Guidelines for Consumer Protection titled, "Consumer Protection in Electronic Commerce–Principles and Key Issues" (1999), which are based on the principles put forward by the United Nations Guidelines for Consumer Protection. (http://www.ecommerce.treasury.gov.au/html/build.htm).

2. The Australian Competition and Consumer Commission (ACCC) has released guidelines for businesses so that they do not engage in anti-competitive behavior, unfair practices, country of origin claims, conditions and warranties, product liability, authorization and notification, with the aim of providing an environment for "the promotion of a fair and competitive operating environment for small business" (http://www.accc.gov.au/).

3. The National Office for the Internet Economy has released a number of publications, speeches and media releases advising business owners, particularly in relation to Internet operations, on issues such as privacy and the use of information gathered on people who visit their Web site, the use of cookies and the possibility of gaining information from a person's computer and using it against their wishes or knowledge (http://www.noie.gov.au/projects/consumer/privacy/index.htm).

4. As SMEs take-up electronic commerce, they will have to work within the legal and regulatory framework for electronic transactions, intellectual property, online content or services, consumer protection and infrastructure regulations as set out under legislative arrangements located on the National Office for the Internet Economy Web site, with its objective being to increase customer confidence (http://www.noie.gov.au/projects/ecommerce/legal_framework/ecomlego.htm).

5. For SMEs importing and exporting goods and/or services internationally, their business operations will need to comply with the rulings coming out of the Australian Taxation Office International Tax Division (ITD), which is responsible for issues arising from cross-border transactions. ITD's aim is to achieve a fair allocation of income and expenses between taxing jurisdictions (http://www.ato.gov.au/level2.asp?placement=AS/BS).

Develop an Internet Technology Strategy

Although ownership of computers by SMEs is relatively high at 84% (NOIE, 2000), this does not mean that the technology is suitable for online transactions, Web site maintenance, provides a secure environment for databases, operates at a desirable speed for data upload and download from an Internet Service Provider (ISP) and/or supports the software for electronic commerce. With only 44% of SMEs surveyed in the Small Business Index saying that they rely on computer technology to do their business (NOIE, 2000), an awareness program will need to be carried out for SMEs to assist them in finding new ways to use this technology.

An Internet Technology Strategy goes beyond awareness to actually doing business online. In The Yellow Pages Index table on How the Internet is Used–By Size, 84% of small business and 98% of medium business owners stated that "the most common form of Internet usage was for email," while they also indicated that 11% of small businesses and 17% of medium business used the Internet for payment for products and services (NOIE, 2000).

Table 1, compiled by Sweeny Research for the Small Business Index (NOIE, 2000), highlights the potential for growth in the areas of placing and taking orders as well as for paying and receiving payments for products and services, all of which are the essence of electronic commerce transaction processes.

Realizing that there are significant barriers to adopting Internet technology by SMEs, three key initiatives identified in "Australia's e-commerce report card" (DCITA, 1999) being pursued by the Federal Government directly address technology diffusion, that is:

1. Overcome bandwidth limitations
2. Address the incompatibility of proprietary information technology systems and their effect on the efficiency of logistics in the business sector
3. Promote the role of financial institutions in encouraging e-commerce uptake

Investing in information technology infrastructure requires SMEs to consider purchasing technology that can "be scaled and integrated to meet larger requirements of interaction, transaction and transformation dimension initiatives without excessive rework" (GartnerGroup, 2000); however, the selection of information technology will be dependent to the e-business strategy and the electronic business model as the technology is there to support, not drive the business.

In considering an information technology strategy, SMEs will need to consider issues such as:

1. For what purpose will the computer system be used?
2. What will be the hardware requirements for processor speed, memory capacity, modem and other technologies such as video conferencing and multimedia?
3. Standalone or network configuration?
4. What integrated suite of software will be required?

Table 1: How the Internet is used–by size

Which of these would your business regularly use the Internet for?			
	TOTAL	Small Business	Medium Business
To communicate via e-mail	85%	84%	98%
To look for info about products or services	76%	76%	73%
To get reference info or research data	65%	65%	72%
To browse or surf for fun	64%	65%	52%
To access directories such as Yellow Pages	44%	43%	51%
To advertise products or services	43%	42%	52%
To network with other businesses	36%	35%	41%
To monitor markets or competition	31%	31%	34%
To place orders for products or services	28%	28%	31%
To get update info such as timetables, weather	26%	25%	34%
To take orders for products or services	25%	24%	26%
To pay for products or services	19%	19%	19%
To receive payment for products or services	12%	11%	17%

5. Will the Web site be hosted locally or remotely, and what is the need for an Internet Service Provider (ISP)?
6. What will be the cost of doing business online?
7. Security and firewall protection?
8. Virus detection and removal software?
9. Backup and restore procedures?
10. Filtered un-interruptable power supply (UPS)?
11. Technical support?
12. Securing online transactions and electronic payment systems?
13. Selection of information technology supplier and ongoing maintenance requirements?

Sophisticated computer technology and integrated software application software is available for the user on the desktop PC, notebook and mobile computer systems. This is combined with the vast array of peripheral hardware such as scanners, video conferencing cameras, video capturing and editing software, graphic design tools, and inline modems for very fast upload and download of data all at relatively affordable prices. The problem for the SME is that they could get caught up in the technology revolution designing, developing, maintaining and promoting their Web site and lose focus in their core business requirements to use the technology to increase efficiency and productivity to assist their business in being competitive, increase market share and provide customers with greater satisfaction.

Consult Web Designer/Consultant

With the SME in total control of the e-business strategy development and having completed each of the previous steps in the procedural framework, it will be in a position to determine if someone within their own organization has the skills and expertise to develop a Web site, or if it needs assistance from a Web designer or e-commerce consultant to work from the specifications which meet the SME's business needs.

There are few research outputs available to the SME as to what key features it should be looking for when seeking the assistance of a Web designer or engaging an electronic commerce consultant. Factors such as the number of sites developed, the layout and design, the cost of development and satisfaction of other SMEs dealing with that Web designer or consultant are all valid considerations. More research in this area is needed since it is the conversion factor of hits to transactions, online and offline, that is one of the key determining factors as to the viability of carrying on with an e-business presence.

While a review of the literature identifies key elements of an internal development or outsourcing, Web site name, Web browsers, Web site content, language tools, plug-ins, scripting and testing of a Web page for errors, online transaction payment systems, Web site performance and download rates as well as Web site navigation issues, current textbooks and literature do not address the issue relating to the process of choosing a Web designer or a consultant, nor do they address any differences there might be between the roles and functions of a Web designer and that of an electronic commerce consultant.

As there are no standard definitions for a Web designer and for an electronic commerce consultant, SMEs are left to their own devices when selecting a person or a company to implement their e-business strategy, yet this is the visible interface between the potential customer and the organization in their 24/7 virtual store front. An SME is simply left to source a telephone book, search online, talk to other SMEs (and listen to their stories of success and/or failure), look in the newspapers and magazines or seek assistance through a government agency.

Until further research is available as to what characteristics an SME should be looking for when choosing a Web designer or an electronic commerce consultant, questions an SME should ask during the interview and selection process include:

1. Is your focus on the business model or on the use of technology?
2. Do you use templates or can you design a site based on my e-business strategy?
3. Can you make my site secure for online transactions?
4. What search engine-enabling capabilities will be incorporated into my site?
5. Are you in a position to assist with the selection of a domain name and its registration?
6. What Web usability and performance tests do you perform when evaluating a Web site?
7. Can you advise me on Web hosting services, their initial costs and maintenance fees?
8. Do you have a list of clients I could contact?
9. What project management technique do you use with your clients?
10. Can you list the fees and charges for undertaking a Web site project?

The process involved in choosing between building an in-house solution or outsourcing the design and development of the Web site depends on the complexity of the business functions to be performed on the site and the skills and expertise within the organization. Until there is further research carried out in determining the mixture of in-house to outsourcing, the SME has little else to assist them other than to ask questions, review the results and stay in charge of the total e-business strategy project.

CONCLUSION

While Australian SMEs have an excellent opportunity to take advantage of the growth of e-commerce in Australian and the Asia Pacific region, the Small Business Index and other literature have identified key reasons why this is not becoming a reality despite considerable human and financial resources on offer from federal and state governments to entice small-to-medium enterprises to adopt Internet technologies through various awareness, training and incentive schemes. Although SMEs have high levels of computer usage, email access, searching competitor Web sites for information and have or are about to have a Web presence, the adoption and diffusion of this technology to perform online transactions of order placing, order taking and using payment systems is extremely low.

An analysis of the *seven* reasons why SMEs have not engaged in e-commerce reveals concern about uncontrolled growth, satisfaction with current practices, uncertainty about quality and availability of products and services, fear of alienating intermediaries, not able to understand the technology, time and expense of adopting e-commerce and a belief that their products and/or services were not appropriate for e-commerce. Each of the reasons is valid when the SME is unaware of how doing business electronically can assist them in doing business efficiently and profitably, the potential for business opportunities and expansion into new markets, and the benefits of value adding to the products and/or services to meet the needs of the customer.

The implementation of a procedural framework for SMEs when developing their e-business strategy removes their concerns for not having an operating procedure to follow; keeps the SME in control of the whole project and direction for the organization; addresses the key issues when operating in a global economy such as the regulatory framework, legal and ethical issues; and equips them to compare the costs of transactions to revenue generated through the Internet technology adoption.

REFERENCES

Afuah and Tucci. (2000). *Internet Business Models and Strategies, Text and Cases*. USA: McGraw-Hill Irwin.

Aabatzis and Rovolis. (1999). Best business Web sites. *European Commission Enterprise DG*. Heletel Ltd. Retrieved from the World Wide Web: http://www.heletel.gr.

Consumer Affairs Department. (2000). *Best Practice Model & Tools for Business*. Canprint, Australia. Retrieved from the World Wide Web: http://www.ecommerce.treasury.gov.au/.

Cophra and Meindl. (2001). *Supply Chain Management: Strategy, Planning, and Operation*. Prentice Hall, USA.

Davidson and Griffin. (2000). *Management Australia in a Global Context*. Singapore: John Wiley & Sons.

Department of the Treasury. (1999). *Building Consumer Confidence In Electronic Commerce: A Best Practice Model for Business*. Aussie Print, Australia. Retrieved from the World Wide Web: http://www.treasury.gov.au/ecommerce.

Deloitte Touche Tohmatsu. (2000). *The New Economy in Asia: Fact or Fiction?* Retrieved from the World Wide Web: http://www.deloitte.com.

DISC. (1998). *Getting Business Online*. Australia: Green Advertising.

DCITA. (1999). *E-Commerce Beyond 2000*. Commonwealth of Australia. Retrieved from the World Wide Web: httpwww.dcita.gov.au.

DCITA. (1999). *Australia's E-Commerce Report Card*. Commonwealth of Australia. Retrieved from the World Wide Web: http://www.dcita.gov.au.

DCITA. (1998). *Taking the Plunge*. Commonwealth of Australia.

DIST. (1998). *Getting Business Online.* Commonwealth of Australia. Retrieved from the World Wide Web: http://www.noie.gov.au/publications/noie/sme/gbo.pdf.

Earle and Keen. (2000). *From .com to .profit. Inventing Business Models that Deliver Value and Profit.* USA: John Wiley & Sons.

Fellenstein and Wood. (2000). *E-Commerce, Global E-Business, and E-Societies.* USA: Prentice Hall.

Frick and Lill. (2000). *Ten Imperatives for E-Business Success.* GartnerGroup. Retrieved from the World Wide Web: http://www.gartner.com.

Hennessey, J. (2001). *Global Marketing Strategies* (5th Ed.). Houghton Mifflin Company, USA.

Hockey, J. (2000). *Building Consumer Sovereignty in Electronic Commerce. A Best Practice Model for Business.* CanPrint Communications, Commonwealth of Australia. Retrieved from the World Wide Web: http://www.treasury.gov.au.

Huff, W., Parent, Schenberger and Newson. (2000). *Cases in Electronic Commerce.* (International edition). USA: Irwin McGraw-Hill.

IBM. (1999). *E-Commerce Roadmap, Successful Strategies for E-Commerce.* Retrieved from the World Wide Web: http://www.ibm.com.

Kalakota & Robinson. (1999). *e-Business: Roadmap for Success.* USA: Addison-Wesley Longman.

Geer, K. (2001). *How to Convert Visitors to Customers' Smart Business Magazine*, Business 2.0.

Lawrence, Corbitt, Fisher, Lawrence and Tidwell. (2000). *Internet Commerce Digital Models for Business* (2nd Ed.). Singapore: Wiley & Sons.

Lee, Seddon and Corbitt. (1999). Evaluating the business value of Internet-based business-to-business electronic commerce. *Proceedings of the 10th Australasian Conference on Information Systems.*

McConnell International. (2000). *Risk E-Business: Seizing the Opportunity of Global E-Readiness.* Retrieved from the World Wide Web: http://www.mcconnellinternational.com.

Merklow, M. (1999). Designing your e-commerce site for service. *E-Commerce Outlook, Internet.com Corp*, USA. Retrieved from the World Wide Web: http://www.Internet.com.

National Best Practices Newsletter. (1997). *Issue 11, Australian National Training Authority.* Retrieved from the World Wide Web: http://www.kdc.com.au/bp_issues/bp11.htm.

NOIE. (1999). E-commerce beyond 2000. *Small Business Index.* Commonwealth Department of Communications Information Technology and the Arts, Australia.

NOIE. (2000). *Survey of Computer Technology and E-Commerce in Australian and Medium Business*. Telstra Corporation Limited, Australia.

Peilly, G. (2000). *E-Business Dimension Model: The Information Dimension*. GartnerGroup.

Pettey, C. (2000). *Gartner Says Three E-Marketing Models Will Control the B2B Market by 2005*. Gartner Interactive.

Plant, R. (2000). *eCommerce Formulation of Strategy*. USA: Prentice Hall.

Preece, J. (2000). *Online Communities Designing Usability, Supporting Sociability*. Great Britain: John Wiley & Sons.

Samuelsen, R. (2000). The five business models of e-commerce. *eVine Online*. Retrieved from the World Wide Web: http://www.searchz.com.

Schulman, J. (2000). *E-Business Dimension Model: Transformation Dimension*. GartnerGroup.

Schneider and Perry. (2000). *Electronic Commerce*. Course Technology, Canada.

Schneider and Perry. (2001). *Electronic Commerce*. Second Annual Edition, Course Technology, Canada.

Sussis, D. (2000). *A Useful e-RoadMap*. e-Consultant. Retrieved from the World Wide Web: http://commerce.Internet.com/e-consultant/print/0,,9571_363881,00.html.

Treese and Stewart. (1998). *Designing Systems for Internet Commerce*. USA: Addison-Wesley.

Turban, Lee, King and Chung. (2000). *Electronic Commerce. A Managerial Perspective*. International Edition. USA: Prentice Hall.

Vanakkeren and Cavaye. (1999). Factors affecting entry-level Internet technology adoption by small business in Australia: An empirical study. *Proceedings of the 10th Australiasian Conference on Information Systems*.

Viehland, D. (1999). New business models for electronic commerce. *17th Annual International Conference of the Association of Management/International Association of Management*, San Diego, California, USA.

Ward, Griffiths and Whitmore. (1994). *Strategic Planning From Information Systems*. Great Britain: John Wiley & Sons.

Whiteley, D. (2000). *e-Commerce Strategy, Technologies and Applications*. Cambridge: McGraw-Hill.

Wortzel and Wortzel. (1997). *Strategic Management in a Global Economy* (3rd Ed.). USA: John Wiley & Sons.

Yeh, Pearlson and Kozmetsky. (2000). *Zero Time Providing Instant Customer Value–Every Time, All the Time*. USA: John Wiley & Sons.

Chapter XVI

Management's Contribution to Internet Commerce Benefit–Experiences of Online Small Businesses

Simpson Poon
Charles Sturt University, Australia
The University of Hong Kong, Hong Kong

INTRODUCTION

The importance of management and Information Technology (IT) success had been repeatedly identified in small business IT studies (for example, DeLone, 1988). When measuring information satisfaction among small firms, top management involvement was found to be one of the most important factors (Montazemi, 1988). The quest for the role of management involvement in Information Systems (IS) success in small firms continued into the 1990s. For example, Yap, Soh and Raman (1992) studied a group of Singaporean small firms using earlier findings and discovered that CEO involvement was positively related to IS success. CEO involvement such as attending project meetings, involvement in information requirement needs analysis, reviewing consultants' recommendations and project monitoring are important to IS success. Thong, Yap and Raman (1996) pointed out that although management support was important, in cases where internal IS expertise was lacking, specialist knowledge (for example, engaging IT consultants in projects) was important to success. An in-depth study on motivators and inhibitors for small firms to adopt computing identified managerial enthusiasm as a key motivator (Cragg, 1998). The overseeing role of management during system implementation was found to be important to success. Management support was also found to be an important factor for IT success in the case of personal computing acceptance (Igbaria, Zinatelli, Craig and Cavaye, 1997). All of these studies suggested that management involvement was critical to IS success regardless of cultural background.

Although these studies focused on small businesses, their definition of 'small firms[1]' varied greatly in terms of size and turnover. I highlight this because the IT infrastructure and investment of a 'large' small business (that is, with 100 or more employees) is very different from one that only has 10 or less employees. This difference might have accounted for the varying view of how important the role of management is compared to, say, external consultants. In a very small firm, the role of management is crucial because the CEO (or owner) is the key, if not the only, decision-maker. Without the very active push/participation of the CEO, no IS project can even get started. However, in a firm of 100 employees, there is likely to be someone (for example, the IT manager) who is responsible for IT development, and senior management only needs to endorse projects. Either way, the backing of management must be available for success.

In this day and age, IT applications are no longer just about in-house business software applications or local area networks. Today's IT issues are invariably linked to the Internet and Internet Commerce applications. *Is there any difference between traditional IT applications and e-commerce? Can we apply what we have learned from earlier small business IT experiences to e-commerce? Does the largely external nature of e-commerce systems mean that management needs to play a different role than in the past?* These and many other questions need to be properly addressed. The aim of this study was to explore the answers to some of these questions and bridge the knowledge gap between traditional small business IT systems (such as Accounting, Inventory Management, and so forth) and Internet Commerce systems. The results may help management to rethink how they can secure Internet Commerce benefit, and avoid activities that are non-effective.

INTERNET COMMERCE AMONG SMALL BUSINESSES

The Internet has fundamentally changed how business can and will be conducted. Statistics are pointing to increased adoption of Internet Commerce by large and small companies alike (www.yellowpages.com.au). Given the amount of resources available, large companies have created very sophisticated Internet Commerce systems (for example, those by major software vendors, publishing and information service firms). However, small firms have also benefited from Internet Commerce even with relatively little resources compared to a large firm (for example, an E-Business group).

Internet Commerce in this chapter is defined as *the use of the Internet and associated technologies (for example, WAP), as well as applications built upon this infrastructure to solicit, carry out and support various aspects of business activities of all levels*. This deliberately broad definition supports my belief that Internet Commerce should not only cover selling and transactional activities as in the case of traditional Electronic Data Interchange (EDI) systems. The major difference between Internet Commerce and traditional inter-organisation systems in the former is not (and should not be) limited to process-to-process business activities but also human-to-human, human-to-business communications.

Governments around the world are increasingly keen to ensure small firms adopting Internet Commerce (for example, http://www.oecd.org/dsti/sti/it/ec/index.htm). The reason for this is because most economies have a high percentage of small- and medium-sized enterprises (SMEs), some up to 95% or more. Small business success directly affects the economic health of a country.

Since the mid-1990s, more studies are focusing on Internet Commerce among small businesses. Some are surveys on small businesses' Internet usage patterns (for example, Abell, 1996; Barker, Fuller and Jenkins, 1997; Fink, Griese Roithmayr and Sieber, 1997; Poon and Swatman, 1996), some into sales and marketing activities (for example, Auger and Gallaugher, 1997; Bennett, 1998; Poon and Jevons, 1997) and others on user experiences (for example, Barker, 1994) and usage strategy (for example, Cragg, 1998). We now know that small businesses are adopting very different approaches to Internet Commerce as compared to large firms (Quelch and Klein, 1996). However, there is still insufficient understanding on how management can effectively help a small firm to gain benefit through Internet Commerce.

Because of the still little-known linkage between the influence of management and the experience of Internet Commerce success, I decided to apply the known effects of management influence from earlier studies to develop a number of propositions. The intention of these propositions was to examine if similar observations could be found in the case of Internet Commerce. The outcomes would help management of SMEs to pursue a correct course of action to take advantage of Internet Commerce for strategic advantage.

MANAGEMENT'S ROLE AND INTERNET COMMERCE BENEFIT

Although it is known that the role of management is instrumental to IT success among small businesses, it is not sure if we can expect the same in the case of Internet Commerce. Presumably there will be similarities because the Internet can be considered a form of IT. However, there are differences between many Internet-based systems and traditional IT systems such as the focus on external and inter-organizational activities rather than internal activities. Also, the openness, non-proprietary nature and easy accessibility make the Internet the most scalable and affordable IT infrastructure for SMEs to-date. Because of this, measurements used in earlier studies (Montazemi, 1988; Yap et al., 1992; Thong et al., 1996)–such as the number of PCs used, the existence of systems analysts and the number of internal applications–are likely to be less relevant, with the exception of management involvement. In fact, I created new indicators such as ability to convince members of the supply chain to use Internet Commerce, apply Internet Commerce with innovation and ability to create new business initiatives to examine their predictability of Internet Commerce experience.

THE STUDY

I set up a study to investigate the effects of management on Internet Commerce benefits. Apart from adapting some earlier measurements such as management push for project development, new indicators relevant to Internet Commerce such as convincing firms on the supply chain to adopt Internet Commerce were also used. A set of seven propositions was developed and the rationale of each of them is explained in the following sections. A research model depicting the relationship between each of the propositions and its influence on perceived Internet Commerce benefit gained is shown in Figure 1.

Push for Internet Connectivity

Management, as a driving force for technology adoption, has been repeatedly identified as key to IS success in small firms (DeLone, 1988; Martin, 1989). As such, I decided to investigate how management drives for Internet connectivity have resulted in actual benefits. Some studies (for example, Yellow Pages Australia, 1997) have suggested that one of the reasons why small firms are not using Internet commerce is because management does not see the need to use the Internet in the first place. Given the

Figure 1: A research model proposing management influences on Internet comerce benefit

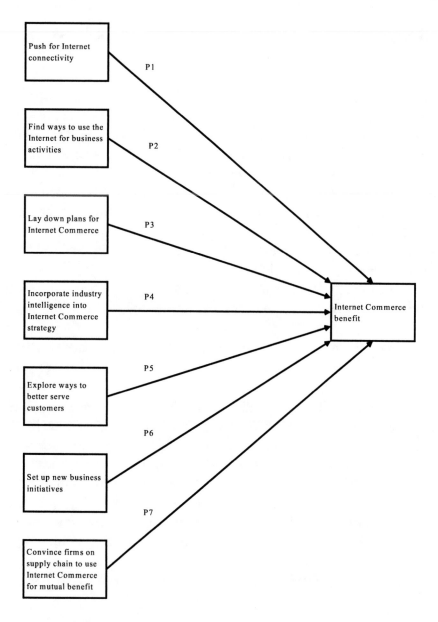

importance of management initiative (or enthusiasm) to IT success (DeLone, 1988; Martin, 1989), I endeavoured to re-confirm if this was also true for Internet Commerce adoption. I formulated Proposition 1 as below.

Proposition 1: Small firms, in which management pushes for Internet connectivity, experience more benefit.

Actively Find Ways to Use the Internet for Business Activities

As Internet Commerce really means using Internet technology to support business activities, how to do so effectively should be a key to success. Consequently, it is important for the user to carefully align business strategy with technology deployment. However, among the literature I found which studied how small businesses could benefit from IT, none examined the correlation between active usage and increased benefit. Logically, the more actively management experiments with Internet Commerce, the more experienced management becomes in taking business advantage of such technology. Therefore, I speculated that those who actively explore using Internet Commerce to support business activities would experience more benefit. I formulated Proposition 2 follows.

Proposition 2: Small firms, in which management is active in exploring how to apply Internet Commerce, experience more benefit.

Lay Down Plans for Internet Commerce Implementation

Once a small business starts to have a rough idea of how the Internet can be used for business activities, logically, the next step for management is to lay down a plan (sometimes with external help) to implement an Internet Commerce strategy. Cragg (1998) studied Internet strategy of small firms and found that management often steered the strategy development process. This concurs with findings from earlier IT studies (DeLone, 1988; Martin, 1989; Montazemi, 1988; Thong et al., 1996). I formulated Proposition 3 to test whether there was any evidence of this leading to experiencing more benefit.

Proposition 3: Small firms, in which management lays down an implementation plan for Internet Commerce, experience more benefit.

Incorporate Industry Intelligence into Internet Commerce Strategy

Apart from having an Internet Commerce strategy, what the strategy is based on determines its quality. Industry intelligence is an important input to Internet Commerce strategy because it keeps the strategy relevant. A small business can use many economical and yet effective ways to gather industry intelligence such as publicly available information online and sources within its business networks (Hershey, 1984). By incorporating quality industry intelligence into the Internet Commerce strategy formulation process, it should enhance the chances of gaining more benefit.

Therefore, I postulated that if management of a small business incorporates industry intelligence when setting Internet Commerce strategy, it would benefit more from Internet Commerce than firms which do not. I set up Proposition 4 follows.

Proposition 4: Small firms, in which management incorporates industry intelligence when formulating Internet Commerce strategy, experience more benefit.

Explore Ways to Better Serve Customers

For small businesses, Internet Commerce seems to be more useful in supporting customer than supplier relationships (Poon and Swatman, 1999). Poon and Swatman suggested that this might be due to the highly customer-focused nature of most small firms. Because of this, it seems logical to assume that small firms which actively explore ways to better serve their customers would experience more benefit from Internet Commerce. I formulated Proposition 5 to explore if this speculation is sustainable.

Proposition 5: Small firms, in which management actively explores ways to better serve customers, experience more benefit.

Set Up New Business Initiatives Based on Internet Commerce

Apart from using Internet Commerce to improve existing business processes, innovative small firms may actually set up new business initiatives to take advantage of what Internet Commerce can offer. There are examples of traditional bookshops setting up virtual book clubs over the Internet, auctioneers setting up virtual auction sites to sell goods and traditional stock brokers setting up online broker firms. These companies have taken an extra step to not just use the Internet to support existing businesses, but new business paradigms which may be quite different.

Whether setting up new business initiatives will help a firm to experience more benefit from Internet Commerce has rarely been confirmed. Because of this, I formulated Proposition 6 to examine whether setting up new business initiatives after adopting Internet Commerce would lead to more benefit.

Proposition 6: Small firms, in which management sets up new business initiatives through Internet Commerce, experience more benefit.

Convince Firms on the Supply Chain to Use Internet Commerce for Mutual Benefit

When large manufacturing and retail firms first adopted EDI technology, they were quick to diffuse the technology to suppliers and customers (Iacovou, Benbasat and Dexter, 1995; Webster, 1995). For an inter-organizational system to succeed, it must have strong commitments from both upstream and downstream of the supply chain. In the case of EDI, large firms were often found to be pressuring small suppliers and customers to adopt their technology. In such power relationships, large firms often got what they wanted–but the price to pay was the lack of full commitment from the other end. This often led to a decrease in benefit over time.

Based on earlier EDI experiences, I formulated Proposition 7 to examine whether convincing others to use the Internet helped to bring about benefit.

Proposition 7: Small firms, in which management attempts to convince businesses on the supply chain to use Internet Commerce, experience more benefit.

MEASURING EXPERIENCE OF INTERNET COMMERCE BENEFIT

The ideal way to measure benefit from technology adoption is to measure the change in financial performance. However, I experienced considerable difficulties in collecting financial figures from small firm management. This is shared by the obvious lack of financial analysis in earlier small business IT studies (see DeLone, 1988; Montazemi, 1988; Thong et al., 1996; Yap et al., 1992). My alternative was to measure benefit based on management's experience and perception. Although this is not as 'quantitative' as financial figures, I hoped such a measurement would give me some qualitative understanding in the absence of hard figures. A five-point Likert scale (5– most positive experience, 1–least positive experience) was used for the four benefit indicators which were:

- being more competitive than other non-online competitors;
- improved business performance;
- improved supplier/customer relationship; and
- current benefit to be continued.

Each of the seven propositions was measured against the four indicators above and any significant differences noted.

RESULTS AND DISCUSSION

A survey instrument containing questions related to the seven propositions was developed and sent to 224 small businesses via email. These small companies were already online with an email address and a Web page. The sample was collected from search engines which listed small businesses which were interested in trading with other firms and online directories (for example, www.austrade.gov.au). For the former, I targeted search engines such as www.aussie.com.au to look for companies which did not look like a large company based on their descriptions. The sample consisted of firms from different business sectors (IT, Media and Publishing, Business and Professional Services, Tourism, Manufacturing, Retail and Wholesale); however, they were not broken down into equal portions. No firm from the Internet sector (such as Internet Service Providers and Web page developers) was included because their responses were likely to bias the result. Among the replies collected, 67 were usable and this gave a 30% response rate. I acknowledge that the number of responses is small in comparison to large-scale studies, but I believe the result is still useful for an exploratory study. Every effort was made to have the questionnaire reach a member of the senior management. This was done by carrying out investigations to find out the email address of the CEO or a member of the management team.

The role of the respondents includes Director (48%), Owner (17.4%), Managing Director (16%), Manager (8.7%) and Partner (4.3%). This means 95% of the responses were from a member of the senior management–an important condition to ensure their answers reflected the management perspective.

For all the seven propositions, a statistical method called T-test was used to examine if the two groups within the sample, those who did what was suggested in the proposition and those who did not, exhibited any significant difference in their experiences of gaining benefit from Internet Commerce. The T-test was used because through visual examination of the sample distribution curve, normality could be assumed. Such visual examination process was recommended by the statistical analysis package SPSS (in its Windows Help file), which was used to carry out all the statistical analysis in this study.

Push for Internet Connectivity

Table 1 shows that those firms which management pushed for Internet connectivity (87% of the sample did so) had more positive experiences. The difference between the two groups is significant across all four indicators. By observing the last row in Table 1 labelled *T-test (2-tailed p-value)*, one can see all four values are less than 0.05, with the one in the last column labelled *Current benefit to be continued* equal to 0.000. What all these figures mean is that there are significant differences between the two groups in terms of experiencing Internet Commerce benefit when measured across the four benefit indicators. The most significant difference lies in the future view of Internet Commerce suggesting that management that pushed for Internet Commerce implementation was confident of the benefit to be continued. Based on the result in Table 1, I can suggest with at least 95% confidence that Proposition 1 is a correct predictor of Internet Commerce benefit based on user experience and perception.

I acknowledge that this might have been a self-fulfilling prophesy, being that those who pushed for adoption would naturally hope that Internet Commerce benefit will continue. Nonetheless the result re-confirms similar claims made in earlier small business IT studies. This also suggests that if management is not able to take the first step to acquire Internet connectivity, then it is unlikely for the firm to experience significant benefit, even if someone else in the firm gets them online.

Actively Find Ways to Use the Internet for Business Activities

My proposition that suggests firms that actively find ways to use the Internet for business activities have better experience from Internet Commerce does not seem to hold true among the respondents. Eighty-eight percent of the respondents admitted they actively found ways to use the Internet for their business activities, but the experience of the two groups remained

Table 1: Mean scores between firms whose management pushed for Internet connectivity and those who did not (*p = .05, **p = .01)

	More competitive than non-online competitors	Improved business performance	Improved supplier/ customer relationship	Current benefit to be continued
Pushed for Internet connectivity	3.5	3.3	3.3	4.3
Did not push for Internet connectivity	2.4	2.0	2.0	2.3
T-test (2-tailed p-value)	.032*	.016*	.015*	.000**

similar. One possible explanation is that once online, most firms would find ways to use the Internet anyway. The difference between those who actively did so and those who did not is insignificant. The T-test result is shown in Table 2. It is also possible that simply 'finding' ways to use the Internet for business without implementing a good business strategy is insufficient for differentiation. What the result suggests is that once online, small business management must understand that looking for ways to use the Internet for business activities is a competitive necessity, not an advantage. Although the result also indicates that those who did not do so were not worse off, the future for them can be less favorable in the longer term.

Lay Down Plans for Internet Commerce

Although earlier studies point out the importance of management involvement in IT planning, it seems that this alone may be insufficient to guarantee benefit (see Table 3). This is again unexpected given that management involvement in planning has proven to be critical to IT success. One explanation is that the level and the type of involvement may need to be further clarified. For Internet Commerce projects, management sitting in on planning meetings might not be sufficient. Also simply providing 'general guidance' in planning is insufficient when working with a rapidly changing business paradigm. It is important that management works with a multi-disciplinary team including technical experts and Web page designers among others for success. Another way to interpret the result is that it maybe too early to determine the effect of management planning. This is reflected by the fourth benefit indicator (current benefit to be continued) which exhibits a weak significant difference. Despite the lack of statistical differences, the mean

Table 2: Mean scores between firms which management had found ways to use the Internet for business activities and those who did not (*p = .05, **p = .01)

	More competitive than non-online competitors	Improved business performance	Improved supplier/ customer relationship	Current benefit to be continued
Found ways to use the Internet for business	3.4	3.2	3.1	4.1
Did not find ways to use the Internet for business	3.3	2.7	3.2	4.0
T-test (2-tailed p-value)	.844	.408	.935	.875

Table 3: Mean scores between firms whose management laid down plans for Internet Commerce and those who did not (*p = .05, **p = .01)

	More competitive than non-online competitors	Improved business performance	Improved supplier/ customer relationship	Current benefit to be continued
Laid down plans for Internet Commerce	3.5	3.3	3.2	4.3
Did not lay down plans for Internet Commerce	3.1	2.8	3.0	3.6
T-test (2-tailed p-value)	.211	.218	.528	.034*

scores for all four benefit indicators are higher for small firms that did lay down plans. Again, laying down a plan for Internet Commerce is a competitive necessity instead of a competitive advantage.

Incorporate Industry Intelligence into Internet Commerce Strategy

The effect of incorporating industry intelligence into strategy formulation has been important to the traditional planning process. Two-thirds of the respondents claimed to have incorporated industry intelligence into their strategy formulation process for Internet Commerce. Therefore, it is surprising that the result in Table 4 shows that there is no significant difference between the groups. It is possible that the nature of Internet Commerce rendered traditional industry intelligence less relevant. Scrutinising what type of industry intelligence a firm is gathering and how it incorporates into its Internet Commerce strategy may provide some explanations. Since Internet Commerce models change very quickly, intelligence that was useful in the past may not contribute much to future competitiveness. It may be simply a case of selecting the 'right' type of intelligence and applying appropriate analysis techniques which matter.

Explore Ways to Better Serve Customers

Quality customer service is a key to the success for small businesses because serving returning customers generally costs less than looking for new customers. If a small firm is operating with limited resources, then using Internet Commerce to help service both new and returning customers is important. Among the respondents, 83.6% indicated they had explored ways to better serve their

Table 4: Mean scores between firms whose management incorporated industry intelligence for strategy formulation and those who did not (*p = .05, **p = .01)

	More competitive than non-online competitors	Improved business performance	Improved supplier/ customer relationship	Current benefit to be continued
Incorporated industry intelligence for strategy formulation	3.6	3.3	3.3	4.2
Did not incorporate industry intelligence for strategy formulation	3.1	2.8	2.8	3.9
T-test (2-tailed p-value)	.186	.135	.159	.357

customers (see Table 5). Although there is limited evidence that those respondents who explored ways to better serve customers had experienced improved business performance, it is uncertain whether they were better off than their non-online competitors or whether the current benefits would continue. Because non-manufacturing small businesses interact more with customers than suppliers, the result of the third indicator (improved supplier/customer relationship) may have been diluted by the 'supplier' component.

Although both groups of respondents were exploring ways to better serve customers, interacting with customers online (for example, customer support, product delivery) can be a steep learning experience and customers might not be ready for it yet. Consequently, the benefits gained from such efforts were not yet realized.

Set Up New Business Initiatives Based on Internet Commerce

A browse on the Internet will show that many businesses come into existence because of the Internet. To take full advantage of Internet Commerce, a small firm may have to transform itself to make its business 'Internet Commerce compatible.' The result in Table 6 presents strong support for this observation. Among the respondents, 61.2% expressed that they had set up some kind of new business initiative. Interpreting this with the results from previous propositions, this is the observation. *A small firm can explore, lay down a plan for and gather information on how to deploy Internet Commerce, but only those who actually set up new business initiatives tailored for the*

Table 5: Mean scores between firms whose management explored ways to better serve customers and those who did not (*p = .05, **p = .01)

	More competitive than non-online competitors	Improved business performance	Improved supplier/ customer relationship	Current benefit to be continued
Explored ways to better serve customers	3.5	3.3	3.2	4.2
Did not explore ways to better serve customers	3.0	2.2	2.7	3.6
T-test (2-tailed p-value)	.330	.025*	.308	.193

Table 6: Mean scores between firms whose management set up new business initiatives and those who did not (*p = .05, **p = .01)

	More competitive than non-online competitors	Improved business performance	Improved supplier/ customer relationship	Current benefit to be continued
Set up new business initiatives	3.9	3.7	3.4	4.3
Did not set up new business initiatives	2.6	2.2	2.7	3.7
T-test (2-tailed p-value)	.000**	.000**	.045*	.038*

Internet will experience distinct benefits. This means setting up totally new business initiatives around Internet Commerce. This concurs with the common observations among the most successful E-Businesses (for example, Yahoo!, Amazon.com, among others). Another approach is to radically transform existing business activities based on sound Internet Commerce principles. This means adopting a so-called 'clicks and mortar' approach. Examples of this approach include E-enabled Supply Chain Management systems, Customer Relationship Management systems and Enterprise Resource Planning systems.

Convince Firms on the Supply Chain to Use Internet Commerce for Mutual Benefit

Among the many studies of IT in small firms, this factor was not considered because those systems studied were internal instead of interorganizational systems. Convincing partner firms on the supply chain to use Internet Commerce can be quite difficult, particularly small firms which do not normally have the power to influence the others. However, streamlining exchanges (both document and information) along the supply chain was so important that in early cases of EDI adoption, some large firms actually provided the technology free for their small suppliers (Iacovou, Benbasat and Dexter, 1995). Among the respondents, 67.2% had managed to convince others on the supply chain to use the Internet to work together. These firms also exhibited more positive experience of gaining benefit (see Table 7).

This confirms that Internet Commerce, like EDI systems in the past, can only bring benefit to users when others on the supply chain are using it as well. Small firms that are planning to adopt Internet Commerce need to start lobbying other firms on the supply chain to go along with them in the process. In other words, a small firm will not gain significant benefit from Internet Commerce if others on the supply chain are not adopting it.

IMPLICATIONS FOR SMALL BUSINESS MANAGEMENT

This study suggests that although management needs to do many things to keep a small firm competitive through Internet Commerce, only a few things make a distinct contribution to success. The THREE key issues management needs to focus on, based on the findings from this study, are:

1. **Push for Internet technology adoption**. The importance of direct intervention by management to start off the IT adoption process is not news; my results re-confirm this is 'Step One' to Internet Commerce success. If management adopts a 'hands-on' attitude to Internet adop-

Table 7: Mean scores between firms whose management convinced others to use Internet Commerce and those who did not (*p = .05, **p = .01)

	More competitive than non-online competitors	Improved business performance	Improved supplier/ customer relationship	Current benefit to be continued
Convinced others to use Internet Commerce	3.8	3.5	3.4	4.4
Did not convince others to use Internet Commerce	2.6	2.4	2.5	3.3
T-test (2-tailed p-value)	.002**	.002**	.010*	.000**

tion, this will sound off a message to the rest of the company that management is serious about the Internet. Leadership-by-example is apparently quite important and those companies that did so in this study found they experienced strong benefit from Internet Commerce. I interpret this as a psychological strengthening effect–a change of attitude of the firm. Others in the firm who are keen to see the adoption of Internet Commerce will be more encouraged to work towards this goal. The effect is significantly stronger than a firm in which management does not do so. The implication of this finding is that if management is not playing a leading role to start the adoption process, then even if the firm is eventually online, the experience of Internet Commerce is significantly less positive.

2. **Set up new business initiatives through Internet Commerce**. Setting up new business initiatives that exploit the characteristics of Internet Commerce can also bring much benefit to a small firm. Compared to other less effective Internet initiatives, such as laying down a plan for implementation, it is the innovation applied by management that makes the difference. The implication of this finding to small business management is that if one wants to gain real benefit from Internet Commerce, one needs to really think long and hard how to develop new business ideas which can be further enhanced through Internet Commerce. Purely creating an 'e-version' of the same thing may not work. For example, purely sending email catalogues to customers instead of the printed version can be cost effective, but it is through a Customer Relationship Management strategy to customize the catalogue to address individual needs which counts. For example, one of the small businesses studied was a traditional printing business that transformed itself to become a Web page designer by focusing more on its design competence instead of its printing operation. Self-evaluation and reflection, together with a sound knowledge of Internet Commerce, forms the most powerful strategy.

3. **Convince those on the supply chain to adopt Internet Commerce**. Internet Commerce is not really useful if the size of the user community is small, particularly on the same supply chain. However, due to different reasons, some parties on the supply chain may not want to adopt Internet Commerce. For example, some members on the supply chain may see allowing others to access their ordering systems as a threat. Others may see rapid exchange of information as erosion of power because information (or the lack of it) is the bargaining chip. Unfortunately, until everyone decides to effectively use Internet Commerce to streamline the

supply chain, no one may gain full benefit from it. In this study, small firms that managed to convince their supply chain partners to adopt Internet Commerce experienced more benefit. The implication for small business management is this: for Internet Commerce, quite different from traditional IT systems, it is other members' adoption that counts for more. Consequently, a small business should, after adopting Internet Commerce, try hard to convince those who do business with them to do so as well. This may not mean setting up a sophisticated supply chain management system but may be as simple as using email to attach order and invoice documents. Given the limited resources (both financial and personnel) a small business has, it is more appropriate to adopt an evolutionary rather than revolutionary approach to major IT investments.

CONCLUSION

Based on earlier studies on small businesses IT success, I set up a study to examine the factors contributing to Internet Commerce success among small business, with specific focus on the role of management influence. I constructed seven propositions to investigate the different ways management of a small firm influenced its Internet Commerce deployment. My finding

Table 8: A summary of the effect of management initiatives on Internet Commerce benefit: "✓" significant, "×" insignificant

	More competitive than non-online competitors	Improved business performance	Improved supplier/ customer relationship	Current benefit to be continued
Push for Internet connectivity	✓	✓	✓	✓
Find ways to use business activities	×	×	×	×
Lay down plan for Internet Commerce	×	×	×	✓
Incorporate industry intelligence	×	×	×	×
Explore ways to better serve customers	×	✓	×	×
Set up new business initiatives	✓	✓	✓	✓
Convince others to use Internet for mutual benefit	✓	✓	✓	✓

Figure 2: The benefit value chain for small business management involving Internet Commerce

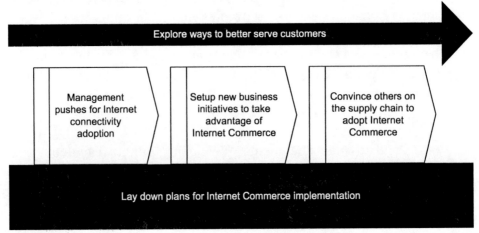

reveals that not all actions taken by management are equal–some have a more significant effect on success than others. The three most critical things management of a small firm should focus on are:

1. push for Internet and subsequently Internet Commerce adoption;
2. set up new business initiatives to take full advantage of Internet Commerce based on strategic re-thinking and planning; and
3. convince members on the same supply chain to adopt Internet Commerce and use it to conduct business with itself.

In conclusion, to fully experience Internet Commerce benefit, small businesses need to take proactive actions to fully exploit Internet Commerce. The relationship of these most important actions is depicted in Figure 2. Moderate actions may not be sufficient because other competitors are doing so anyway. In addition, a firm cannot be inward looking as in the case of deploying traditional IT systems. Given the dynamics and rapidly evolving nature of Internet Commerce, small firm management needs to transform traditional ways of thinking and re-conceptualize on how to create new business models around the capability of Internet Commerce.

ENDNOTE

1 The Australian Bureau of Statistics (ABS) defines small business as:
- businesses employing fewer than 20 employees.

In addition, small businesses typically have the following management or organizational characteristics:

- they are independently owned and operated,
- they are closely controlled by owners/managers who also contribute most, if not all of the operating capital; and
- the principal decision-making functions rest with the owners/managers.

REFERENCES

Abell, W. and Lim, L. (1996). *Business Use of the Internet in New Zealand: An Exploratory Study*. Retrieved from the World Wide Web: http://www.scu.edu.au/ausweb96/business/abell/paper.htm.

Auger, P. and Gallaugher, J. M. (1997). Factors affecting the adoption of an Internet-based sales presence for small businesses. *The Information Society*, 13(1), 55-74.

Barker, N. (1994). *The Internet as a Reach Generator for Small Business*. Unpublished Masters Thesis, Business School, University of Durham, (September).

Barker, N., Fuller, T. and Jenkins, A. (1997). Small firms' experiences with the Internet. *Proceedings of the 20th ISBA National Conference*, Belfast, Northern Ireland.

Bennett, R. (1998). Using the World Wide Web for international marketing: Internet use and perceptions of export barriers among German and British businesses. *Journal of Marketing Communications*, 4, 27-43.

Cragg, P. B. (1998). Clarifying Internet strategy in small firms. *Proceedings of the 9th Australasian Conference on Information Systems*, 1, 98-107. Sydney, Australia.

DeLone, W. (1988). Determinants of success for computer usage in small business. *MIS Quarterly*, 12(1), 51-61.

Fink, K., Griese, J., Roithmayr, F. and Sieber, P. (1997). Business on the Internet–Some (r)evolutionary perspective. In Vogel et al. (Eds.), *Proceedings of the 10th International Bled Electronic Commerce Conference*, 2, 536-555. Slovenia.

Hershey, R. (1984). Commercial intelligence on a shoestring. Gumpert, D. E. (Ed.), *Growing Concerns: Building and Managing the Small Business*, 121-130. Harvard Business Review Executive Book Series. New York: John Wiley & Sons.

Iacovou, C. L., Benbasat, I. and Dexter, A. S. (1995). Electronic data interchange and small organizations: Adoption and impact of technology. *MIS Quarterly*, 19(4), 465-485.

Igbaria, M., Zinatelli, N., Cragg, P. and Cavaye, A. L. M. (1997). Personal computing acceptance factors in small firms: A structural equation model. *MIS Quarterly*, 21(3), 279-305.

Martin, C. J. (1989). Information management in the smaller business: The role of the top manager. *International Journal of Information Management*, 9, 187-197.

Montazemi, A. R. (1988). Factors affecting information satisfaction in the context of the small business environment. *MIS Quarterly*, 12(2), 239-256.

Poon, S. and Swatman, P. M. C. (1996). Small business Internet usage: A preliminary survey of Australian SMEs. *Proceedings of the 4th European Conference on Information Systems*, 1103-1112. Lisbon, Portugal.

Poon, S. and Jevons, C. (1997). Internet-enabled international marketing: A small business perspective. *Journal of Marketing Management*. 13(1-4), 29-41.

Poon, S. and Swatman, P. M. C. (1999). A longitudinal study of expectations in small business Internet Commerce. *International Journal of Electronic Commerce*, 3(3), 21-33.

Quelch, J. A. and Klein, L. R. (1996). The Internet and international marketing. *Sloan Management Review*, 37(3), 60-75.

Thong, J. Y. L., Yap, C. S. and Raman, K. S. (1996). Top management support, external expertise and information systems implementation in small businesses. *Information Systems Research*, 7(2), 248-267.

Webster J. (1995). Networks of collaboration or conflict? Electronic data interchange and power in the supply chain. *Journal of Strategic Information Systems*, 4(1), 31-42.

Yap, C. S., Soh, C. P. P. and Raman, K. S. (1992). Information systems success factors in small business. *OMEGA International Journal of Management Sciences*, 20(5-6), 597-609.

Yellow Pages Australia. (1997). *Small Business Index™: A Special Report on Technology in the Small Business Sector*, August. Retrieved from the World Wide Web: http://www.yellowpages.com.au.

Chapter XVII

Options for Business-to-Consumer E-Commerce in Developing Countries: An Online Store Prototype

Robert Klepper and Andrew Carrington
Southern Illinois University–Edwardsville, USA

INTRODUCTION

Business-to-consumer electronic commerce in the developing world is hampered by a host of technological, cultural, economic, political and legal problems (Davis, 1999; Enns and Huff, 1999; Janczewski, 1992). Viewed from the perspective of consumers, the most fundamental requirement–Internet access–is unavailable to many. For example, Africa has the lowest rate of Internet access in the world–less than 1% in a population of nearly 800 million (Dunphy, 2000). As dramatic as measures of the digital divide may be, one can easily argue that investment priorities in the areas of health and education should rightfully come before investment in a larger Internet infrastructure for Africa or other developing areas of the world (Verhovek, 2000).

Nonetheless, Internet access does exist for the few, and Internet access will grow in the future for a market of literate users in medium and large cities. Certainly this has been the pattern in Asia and Latin America where Internet cafes and kiosks or their equivalent have sprung up offering relatively inexpensive access, even for those who do not own microcomputers or have telephone service in their homes (Davis, 1999; Richtel, 2001).

Viewed from the perspective of business, the ability of businesses in developing countries to absorb and effectively use technology is a potential stumbling block to B2C electronic commerce (Austin, 1990). Many businesses are limited by their environments and by internal resources, skills and management acumen. Nevertheless, some developing country businesses do succeed in making effective use of information technology (Montealegre, 1998), and in some developing areas of the world, such as Latin America, Internet business is growing rapidly (Davis, 1999).

Furthermore, a developing world electronic commerce business that hopes to reach customers in the developed world faces the competitive might of already-established, brand-name e-businesses operating from developed countries. The World Wide Web has not leveled the playing field for small businesses relative to large businesses in most major market segments.

However, in the developing world there are market niches that small businesses can occupy. In some cases these niches are protected from the competition of the giants of online retailing by language. In other cases the niche can be created by geographical distance. In still other instances a small, specialized market segment can be created from the sale of a specialized product category. For example,:

- The world's many languages provide an opportunity to create markets catering to a language group, perhaps in literature and music in languages spoken by too few people to provide a market of interest to large online retailers.
- Developing countries are often at the extremities of global distribution chains for many products. Moving product to locations peripheral to the centers of global commercial power often entails high transportation costs relative to product value. Many such regions exist for various products in Africa, Latin America, Asia, Oceania and the Caribbean.
- Small segments of specialized products exist within many large market segments. For example, the clothing category holds many small segments of ethnic clothing produced by local producers for a local population.

These market niches may be spaces that online stores might occupy if the technical problems and cost of developing and operating such stores is not prohibitive.

In this chapter we consider some of the challenges faced in establishing an electronic commerce store in a developing country. We are particularly concerned with ways of reducing costs that otherwise would be a barrier to entry. Our thinking on this subject had its origins in a project undertaken by the second author, a citizen of Barbados and a masters student in MIS. As part of his degree work, he undertook an independent project under the direction of the first author to develop an online store using free, open source software. His goal was to demonstrate that the software costs of providing business-to-consumer Web-based capabilities for small volume online stores could be reduced by using open source software. The prototype store utilizes the Linux operating system, Apache Web server, the Postgres database, and online forms for the store components composed from HTML, Java applets and the Perl language — all available at no cost. A discussion of some of the technical issues involved in developing the prototype can be found in the Appendix to this chapter.

The online store prototype was a success. Free, open source software can be used to develop an online store. The lessons learned from this exercise led us to place this experience in the larger context of options facing would-be online store entrepreneurs in developing countries and strategies they might use for success in low-cost development of an online store.

ISSUES FOR DEVELOPMENT AND STARTUP OF ONLINE STORES IN DEVELOPING COUNTRIES

In the following discussion we abstract from the larger environment in which an online store effort must be mounted in a developing country–such factors as developing a market for the products of an online store, promotion of a store so that potential customers know of its existence, the political and legal environment, and so forth. We focus narrowly on issues and options involved in developing a store and putting it on the World Wide Web. We further narrow this focus to the kinds of issues to be faced by small and medium-size enterprises (SMEs) in developing countries; large enterprises have very different access to resources. We adopt the widely used definition of an SME as an enterprise with 250 employees or less. The issues we consider are:

- Use of readily available online store templates versus development of a more customized store.
- Hosting of an online store, whether by an Internet service provider (ISP) in a developed country or in one's own home, developing country.
- Payment by customers to the online store business and payment by the business to the service that hosts the store site.
- Technical knowledge and expertise.
- Hardware, software and labor costs.

Prices used in this chapter are those that pertained in mid-2001 and are in U.S. dollars, unless noted otherwise.

Store Templates Versus More Customized Stores

One can quickly develop an online store with a shopping cart using templates at developed world Web sites, for example, at HyperMart (www.hypermart.net) or Yahoo (store.yahoo.com). However, such stores have limitations. First, the ability to customize the store template is severely limited. To help overcome this limitation, most of these services allow the store owner to develop his/her own interface using HTML or FrontPage. Customization could be critical to online store success in niche markets like those referenced in the introduction to this chapter. For example, Vinaja (2001, p. 89) notes that, "...although the Spanish speaking world shares the same language, it is a heterogenous group with many differences..." that factor into the likely success or failure of e-commerce endeavors. Thus, from a developing world perspective, an online store developer still faces problems of software and skills to develop a store if customization is important to store success. Second, most services like HyperMart and Yahoo charge for such stores (the days of free dot-com services are waning). At HyperMart the charge is $40 per month plus shared hosting charges that range from $10 to $90 per month, depending on the power of services required. At Yahoo the charge is $100 per month including hosting for a small store with up to 50 items and $300 per month for a store with up to 1,000 items. Third, customers coming to such stores must find them in the maze of other stores put up on sites like HyperMart and Yahoo. An alternative is to have one's own domain name, which Yahoo and HyperMart will support, but with the additional cost of obtaining and maintaining a domain name. Perhaps the difficulty in differentiating a store and locating a store are reasons for the limited success Yahoo and Amazon have met in attracting stores to their mall shopping sites (Wingfield, 2001).

We checked the availability of online store templates at developing world ISPs in an informal, convenience sample of countries of the developing world. For this purpose we used several Web sites that maintain directories of such services, including thelist.internet.com, herbison.com, yahoo.com and excite.com. The results were:

- Latin American store templates at indigenous ISPs:
  o Yes: Mexico and Argentina
  o No: Bolivia, Ecuador and Peru
- African store templates at indigenous ISPs:
  o Yes: Republic of South Africa
  o No: Botswana, Zambia and Kenya (no indigenous ISPs were found in Chad, the Central African Republic, the Gambia and Senegal)

- Asian store templates at indigenous ISPs:
  - o Yes: India and the Philippines
  - o No: Cambodia
- Caribbean store templates at indigenous ISPs:
  - o Yes: Jamaica
  - o No: Barbados

We conclude that store templates are not now available at many indigenous ISPs, particularly in the less developed of the developing countries.

Of course the absence of store templates can be overcome, at a cost, by custom development of an online store. In many developed countries consulting is available for help in designing and customizing an online store. We called several ISPs and checked magazine advertisements and found rates of about $130 to $140 per hour to be common in the United States. We corresponded with academic colleagues with knowledge of Indonesia, Nepal, Samoa, the Philippines and Brazil. Web site consulting is available in these countries, and charges are much less in these developing world countries — ranging from $5 per hour to $20 per hour. A Jamaican ISP advertises a rate of $39 per hour, the highest rate we encountered in the Web sites we visited in developing countries.

Webstore Hosting

If an online store owner in the developing world wishes to have his/her store hosted in the developed world, he/she can find many companies that offer these services. We checked advertisements in computer magazines and called some local ISPs for prices. Shared Web hosting in which the store is served from a machine shared with other Web sites starts at about $50 per month and ranges up to about $200 per month for smaller stores, depending on the hardware capabilities required by the store and the traffic at the store. Dedicated hosting services in which the store owner rents an individual, dedicated server for the store from the hosting service start at a branded site like Dell's at $200 per month for a small store and $375 for a larger store. These costs go up to thousands of dollars per month for large stores with high traffic volume.

We noted above that some less developed of the developing countries do not have indigenous ISPs. In our informal survey we also encountered indigenous ISPs in some developing countries with no hosting services in Bolivia, Ecuador, Peru, Kenya and Zambia. These ISPs provide Internet access services only. Where hosting services are available, shared hosting is universally available while dedicated hosting is not. Our colleagues report hosting prices in the

$50 to $80 per month range for smaller Web sites in the developing countries with which they are familiar.

If a developing country ISP does not offer hosting services, it may still be possible to implement an online store using a design similar to our prototype. Two computers, not networked together, are involved in the prototype design– one to host the store, the other as the machine to store the backend business data associated with the store. In the prototype this design was used to strengthen security (see the Appendix for details). The two-machine design might also be used to obtain hosting services, if the indigenous ISP agrees to take the online store owner's PC and connect it to the Internet at its site as a Web server in a collocation arrangement. The online store owner has a second machine at his/her premises and dials into the collocated machine periodically to download order data.

Any alternative hosting arrangements in the absence of hosting services from the ISP are probably not feasible. For example, a design in which the online store owner hosts the store from his machine at his premises would involve leasing a line from the local telecommunications company in order to connect to the Internet through a local ISP. Telecommunication costs are generally very high in developing countries and service is not always reliable. Both factors would make an "own hosting" design infeasible.

Security is not a focus of this discussion nor is availability, but it can be noted in passing that both security and availability may be generally better for stores hosted by services in the developed world than in the developing world.

Payment

Payment by a developing world online store owner for online store services, consulting services and Web hosting services obtained from providers in the developed world would be made in the currency of the developed country from which the services are provided and by means, in almost cases, of a credit card or debit card. This can present a formidable barrier to obtaining these services from developed countries for several reasons. First, in developing countries even members of the middle classes may not have a credit card or debit card. Second, even with a credit or debit card, payment of continuing services like Web hosting from a provider in a developed country subjects the store owner to exchange rate risk. The financial melt down in Asia in 1997-98, the Turkish economic upheaval of 2000, the steady erosion of the South African Rand and the continuing economic difficulties of many developing countries around the world suggest that exchange rate risk is not trivial and could, with little warning, subject a developing world online store owner to sharply higher store costs measured in local currency.

Most purchases from smaller online store sites by customers are made by credit card where the transfer of funds is handled through a third-party merchant account service. This raises additional problems for developing country online store owners with stores on developed world hosts–their customers must have credit cards and the store owner must pay additional charges (in foreign currency) for a merchant account.

Technical Knowledge and Expertise

Considerable technical skill and ability is necessary for any IT endeavour of consequence, and certainly this is true of effort to develop, implement and maintain an e-business. This is why studies show consultants to be important change agents in the adoption of information technology in small and medium-size enterprises both in developed (Bode and Burns, 1999) and developing countries (Utomo, 2001).

We noted above that consulting costs for work on e-commerce Web sites is commonly $130 to $140 per hour in the U.S. while costs of consulting in developing countries is most often 5-10% of the U.S. rate. Developing country consulting rates are also low relative to hardware and software costs in those countries, compared to the developed world. Our network of academic colleagues familiar with Indonesia, Nepal, the Philippines, Brazil, the Republic of South Africa and Samoa report that the ranks of consultants doing Web consulting work is heavily populated with recent university graduates and students. While the availability and cost of consulting help may once have been an insurmountable barrier in developing countries, that barrier may be coming down in some countries.

While consulting help is clearly an enabler, it is not the only factor at work in obtaining necessary technical help for e-business efforts of SMEs. A number of studies of e-businesses run by small and medium-size firms show that family members and friends with technical knowledge often play a key role. Valli (2001) found knowledgeable family members to be important in Australian online books stores; Utomo (2001) found the same for IT systems of various kinds in SMEs in Indonesia. Utomo also reports that these family members are often students or recent university graduates who have studied computer science.

Hardware, Software and Labor Costs

A developing country online store owner needs a PC with browser software and a dial-up connection to a local ISP so that necessary data can be downloaded, often by means of a Web browser interface. Larger stores might require a database system on the owner's PC to adequately manage the online business. The necessary hardware and software are available in most developing countries, but at widely varying prices. Some of our knowledgeable colleagues report that unbranded PC prices in their countries are comparable to machines with the same capacities in the U.S., for example, in Indonesia and Nepal. Other colleagues report prices twice those of the U.S., as in Barbados and Samoa. Still others report prices three times as great, as in South Africa. Clearly, government policies including various tariffs and taxes are at work here.

Software can show similar price variation between countries, but not when it is free, open source software downloaded from the Internet. This was the initial inspiration for the online store prototype developed by the second author of this chapter. No matter the country, the software tool costs to a developer of an online store are zero if he/she uses open source software. An offsetting consideration is the greater skill and time necessary to learn and make open source software work with other open source software. Most of the time taken to develop our online store prototype was spent in climbing parallel learning curves on the several open source software packages used to construct the store. However, with the prototype completed, the estimated time to develop a second store with the same software is a fraction of the first. A consultant in a developing country who has multiple online store clients would enjoy almost immediate and significant economies of scale that would, with some competition from other consultants, be passed in large part to the online store owner clients. See the Appendix for data on labor and labor costs for the prototype.

What of support? Unbranded hardware choices might require more frequent repair, but this can be offset by the more ready availability of parts and service for unbranded machines. A colleague with knowledge of Nepal reports that unbranded local machines are not only cheaper to purchase, they are also more serviceable — they can be repaired locally. Branded machines often are sent out of the country for repair and may not be returned inside of three months. In developed countries, support for proprietary, branded software products is readily available, though often at a fee, and is generally well matched to technical level and experience of the user. Support available for open source software is not as good, though it is always available in the form of online developer and user communities on the Internet.

Summary of Development and Startup Issues

Store templates are the fastest, easiest and cheapest way to start an online store, but customisation is severely limited and templates are not available at many developing world ISPs with hosting services. Hiring relatively inexpensive indigenous consulting to develop a customized store is a possibility.

SMEs in many developing countries can choose between Web store hosting by a developed world service provider or an indigenous service provider.

But some developing world countries have no indigenous ISPs and others have ISPs that offer no Web hosting services.

Reliance on developed world services requires payment in the currency of the developed country and involves exchange rate risk for ongoing services like hosting. Payments for purchases by customers are usually made by credit card and are handled through a merchant account, which may involve additional costs. Payment problems and costs may deter SMEs in developing countries from starting online store businesses under such arrangements.

Knowledgeable consultants are important enablers of new IT ventures, including online stores, in both the developed and developing worlds. Evidence suggests that consulting help is available in many developing countries at costs much lower than those in the developed world, and that family members with technical training and knowledge are also an important enabler. Barriers in the form of knowledge and expertise, while not absent, do not appear to be the absolute barriers they once may have been in many developing countries.

Computer prices in developing countries range from prices more or less equal to those in the United States to prices three times as high, depending on government policies. High hardware prices could be a barrier for online stores in some countries. Proprietary software prices can also be higher. The better support available for proprietary software has to be weighed against the zero cost of open source software.

OPTIONS FOR ONLINE STORES AND CONCLUSIONS

In this chapter we consider only a subset of the factors that would impact the feasibility of developing an online store for a SME in a developing country, and those that we consider are largely technical, skill, and payment related. We can see some factors that present barriers and others that involve trade-offs. Conditions are wildly different between developing countries. General conclusions are hard to derive.

In an attempt to capture some of the variation in conditions and range of choice in online stores for SMEs in developing countries, we chose several options for online store development and operation that bracket the range of possibilities that might face SMEs, and we present what might be representative costs of each option for a store of about 500 to 1,000 items. See the options in Table 1. Labor costs are from our online store prototype, as are software and hardware costs (see the Appendix to this chapter). We assume developing country labor is used for store customisation, and the labor rate we use falls within the range of typical consulting rates found in our informal survey of knowledgeable colleagues for developing countries. We include no labor for support or maintenance in on-going operations of a store because we have no data, but these costs will surely be greater for customized stores and for collocated hosting than options without these characteristics. We include no PC costs outside the collocated hosting option, because all options require a PC in the SME to connect to the online store site, and businesses that develop online stores are likely to have a PC already and use it for purposes other than the store, as well. Three-year total costs are the sum of development labor, development software and hardware costs, and three years of hosting costs. Three years was chosen because it might represent the useful life of the server hardware in the collocation option. The costs presented in Table 1 should be understood as very rough approximations of the costs of the options–perhaps more useful for indicating the rank order in costliness of these options than the absolute costs. Of course the reader can adjust any or all of the costs underlying Table 1 to reflect conditions existing in any particular developing country to arrive at his or her own insights into the relative costs of these options.

Costs are higher for the two developed country options because of higher hosting costs, but one should bear in mind that stores hosted in developed countries may have compensating qualities of higher availability and better security. The collocated hosting option in a developing country ISP is nearly as expensive as the two developed country resource options, and if maintenance labor was included, it could well cost as much or more than the developed country options.

Table 1: Selected options for online store development and operation

	Shared hosting – U.S.		Shared hosting developing country	Collocated hosting developing country
	With store template	Customized store	Customized store	Customized store
Development labor cost (developing country consultant)	none	$360	$360	$360
Store development software cost	none	$340	$340	$340
Hosting cost	$300/month	$300/month	$100/month	$200/month
Hardware cost (for collocated hosting)	n/a	n/a	n/a	$800
Server software cost (for collocated hosting)	n/a	n/a	n/a	free, open source
Three-year costs	$10,800	$11,500	$4,300	$8,700

CONCLUSIONS

The prototype online store that was the genesis of this chapter was a useful exercise for understanding the development costs of an online store and the role that open source software might play in keeping those costs lower than they would otherwise be. The prototype experience also confirmed the important role that skilled labor plays in the success of any online store venture and the importance of consulting economies of scale in keeping development costs low.

Our investigation of ISPs in developing countries and their services shows that locally hosted online stores are not possible in some countries. From our communications with colleagues knowledgeable about conditions in various developing countries, it appears that consulting services are available and cost much less than consultants in developed countries. Other researchers point to the importance of technology knowledgeable family members and friends in the success of IT adoption in SMEs, and we would guess that this would be particularly important for on-going maintenance of online stores in developing countries.

No single picture emerges, nor should one expect that it would given the diversity of conditions in the developing world. Online store activity seems to be impossible in some developing countries if reliance on a local ISP is a prerequisite. In other developing countries locally developed and hosted online stores do exist, particularly in the more developed of the developing countries.

In the future several trends will work to favor more local, indigenous provision of online store services. Government initiatives can be taken to hasten some of these, but many will unfold without government intervention:

- Countries without ISPs will develop them. Countries with ISPs will develop more of them, and competition will improve their quality and range of service offerings, including hosting services.
- Store templates and other support services will become available at more developing world ISPs.
- Hardware costs will continue to fall.
- The open source software movement will continue to grow. Knowledge and skills in the use of open source software will expand. Support for open source software will strengthen, especially in online communities.
- The ranks of consultants who can undertake e-commerce projects in developing countries will expand. Knowledge of IT will also expand in the general population, particularly among young people who obtain their knowledge in formal training programs and through their own initiative.

The difficulties of initiating e-commerce in the form of online stores for SMEs in developing countries should not be minimized. They are formidable. But we expect the barriers to diminish and e-commerce activity to expand for SMEs in developing countries in the future.

REFERENCES

Austin, J. E. (1990). *Managing in Developing Countries*. New York: The Free Press.

Bode, S. and Burn, J. (1999). SMEs and the role of consultants in establishing e-businesses: A case analysis. *Proceedings of the Third CollECTer Conference on Electronic Commerce*, Wellington, NZ.

Davis, C. H. (1999). The rapid emergence of electronic commerce in a developing region: The case of Spanish-speaking Latin America. *Journal of Global Information Technology Management*, 2(3), 25-40.

Dunphy, H. (2000). *Report: African Internet Use Too Low*. Retrieved October 31, 2000, from the World Wide Web: http://news.excite.com/news/ap/001030/19/africa-online.

Enns, H. G. and Huff, S. L. (1999). Information technology implementation in developing countries: Advent of the Internet in Mongolia. *Journal of Global Information Technology Management*, 2(3), 5-24.

Janczewski, L. J. (1992). Factors of information technology implementation in under-developed countries: Example of the West African Nations. In Palvia, S., Palvia, P. and Zigli, R. (Eds.), *The Global Issues of Information Technology Management*, 187-212. Hershey, PA: Idea Group Publishing.

Montealegre, R. (1998). Managing information technology in modernizing 'against the odds': Lessons from an organization in a less-developed country. *Information & Management*. 34(3), 103-116.

Richtel, M. (2001). New economy: Access charges are tumbling in Vietnam. *The New York Times, (National Edition)*. March 5, C5.

Utomo, H. (2001). The influence of change agents on IT diffusion: The case of small and medium-size firms in Indonesia. In Palvia, P. and Chen, L. (Eds.), *Proceedings of the Second Annual Global Information Technology Management World Conference*, June 10-12, 176-179. Dallas, TX.

Verhovek, S. H. (2000). Bill Gates turns skeptical on digital solution's scope. *The New York Times, (National Edition)*, November 3, A18.

Valli, C. (2001). An initial study of Australian online bookstores. In Palvia, P. and Chen, L. (Eds), *Proceedings of the Second Annual Global Information Technology Management World Conference*, June 10-12, 82-85. Dallas, TX.

Vinaja, R. (2001). The effects of localization method and personality type on consumers' recall, recognition, perceived quality and attitudes in global e-commerce. In Palvia, P. and Chen, L. (Eds.), *Proceedings of the Second Annual Global Information Technology Management World Conference*, June 10-12, 86-89. Dallas, TX.

Wingfield, N. (2001). Ebay allows sellers to set up 'storefronts' online in bid to expand beyond auctions. *The Wall Street Journal, (USA Midwestern Edition)*, June 12, B8.

APPENDIX: THE ONLINE STORE PROTOTYPE

Server Environment

The server platform for the prototype Web store utilizes the Linux operating system, the Common Gateway Interface (CGI), Secure Socket Layer (SSL) and Apache Web server.

The Linux operating system is a credible rival to other operating systems for mission critical systems. Like Unix, Linux is a multi-user, multitasking system, which is a requirement for Internet commerce. Linux is supported by and continues to enjoy major technological updates and additions by a large community of developers.

Linux supports the use of the Common Gateway Interface in conjunction with specialized Web servers. The CGI protocol allows programs to interact with Web pages and is supported by most Web servers. CGI allows the examination of user input and can generate new input between two hosts on the Internet, and provides third-party authentication of the sender and/or receiver, message confidentiality and integrity.

The Apache Web server is the result of an open source collaborative software development effort that has encouraged contributions and bug fixes by hundreds of programmers around the world. The proof of the success of this freeware product is the fact that it is by far the most popular Web server in the world and is used more frequently in commercial applications than all other Web servers combined.

Security Measures

The security approach taken in our prototype utilizes the security measures available in the Linux operating system, CGI and SSL plus a two-computer design that physically separates the Web server on one machine from the database of customer information and accounts on another machine. The security measures in the prototype include the following: first, the Web server is run as a barebones machine with the minimal, required complement of Linux utility programs. Second, communication between the server and client browser utilizes the Secure Socket Layer protocol. The Secure Socket Layer protocol is an encrypted TCP/IP pathway between client and server. SSL is included in the free RedHat release of Linux. Third, all scripts, applets and files that manage sensitive customer and order information are located in the CGI-bin subdirectory of Linux which has the most restrictive permission levels and thus the most security. Finally, the server machine is physically separated from the backend database machine. Order information is captured in a file on the server machine and is periodically copied from and deleted on the server machine and then copied to the backend database machine. This design, while practical only for a small-volume online store, assures that only a small amount of customer order and credit card information is vulnerable to hacking at any one time.

Design of the Online Store

The design of the prototype online store includes user interface, application logic and data layers.

User Interface Layer

The user interface provides a menu of choices of several product types. After selecting one of these, the user is presented with a number of product subtypes or items. The user can select an item for purchase and add it to a shopping cart. A product search capability is also part of the user interface. Search is accomplished by SQL and a Perl script that searches a Postgres database for items matching criteria entered by the user. The result of a search can be added to a shopping cart. The contents of a shopping cart can be ordered and paid for by credit card. A Perl script is used to obtain and store the order and customer information in files within a secure Linux subdirectory. User interactions with the interface are implemented through Java scripts.

Several tools were used to generate HTML for the user interface including Notepad and FrontPage express. FrontPage is not freeware, but it was used to speed development, with corresponding reductions in labor time. We used some templates available in FrontPage for the frame layout of the prototype, used FrontPage to convert some scanned graphics to thumbnail images that appear on product pages and used FrontPage to test the navigation between pages in the user interface. All of these could have been accomplished by other means that involve no software tool costs, albeit with more knowledge of HTML coding and greater expenditure of time.

Data Layer

There are many backend systems currently available on the market. But most commercial products are expensive. We utilized the freeware Postgres database module for the prototype database. This plug-in module has much of the functionality of expensive proprietary solutions and allows for easy use and maintenance by a Web site administrator.

The data layer consists of a product table for each product in the store as well as tables related to the customer and customer transactions. The complementary forms for the customer, sales orders and order line tables provide the major source of interaction for the user when presented in the user interface.

The prototype database has seven tables: four PRODUCT tables and a CUSTOMER, SALESORDER and ORDERLINE table. Searches on tables by users are restricted to the product tables, and users are allowed browsing access only.

Application Logic Layer

The application logic is driven by several technologies including CGI, the Perl programming language, HTML and Java applets.

Java applets are used to generate the shopping cart buttons. The applets are nearly freeware available from Microburst Internet Technologies. One of the benefits of Java applets embedded in HTML pages is the security that such applets can provide. Java applets are not allowed to access local file systems, and they can be written to limit the ability of client machines to access servers in unauthorized and unintended ways.

Scripts in the Practical Extraction and Report Language (or Perl) were used in the prototype application logic layer to drive the search engine, as well as to create and store customer order files in secure directories on the Linux machine. Table A-1 gives a summary listing of the Java applets and Perl scripts in the prototype and their access levels.

Prototype Development Costs

The prototype involves labor, hardware and software costs. Labor hours and costs are presented in Table A-2. A consultant with an on-going business in online store development would start each engagement with an already developed generic online store application, then modify it for specific clients. This would enable economies of scale and greatly reduced development costs for multiple clients. We make an attempt to approximate the labor effort necessary in the context of economies of scale by presenting a "second time through" estimate of the number of hours to develop and implement a second version of the prototype online store for a similar business situation.

The hardware needs for the prototype online store server machine which hosts Linux and the Apache Web server can be met with a relatively cheap

Table A-1: Applets, scripts and their access levels

Class/Script Name	Description	Access Level
uShopCartBase.class	Applets manager	Class Files
uShopInputButton.class	Input button	Class Files
uShopInputMenu.class	Optional product generator	Class Files
ShopInputStandard.class	Standard form generator	Class Files
uShopMessageWindow.class	Message popup class	Class Files
uShopOrderButtonCGI.class	SSL interface class	Class Files
uShopOrderCGI.class	Customer collection class	Class Files
uShopCart.class	Shopping cart	Class Files
cgiscript.pl	Writes orders to server	Secure Server
AceProg.pl	Search engine driver	Selected Database Tables

commodity PC with 128 megabytes of memory. This would be adequate for an online store with modest transaction volume. Such PCs can be purchased in the United States at the time of this writing for about $800.

Open source and free software used included Linux, Apache Web server, Perl and Postgress. A trial version of the plug-in Java online store applets is free; the commercial version is available at a nominal cost of $200. Although FrontPage was used as an HTML development tool for the prototype, other free software tools would have worked just as well if one were willing to take the time to do the HTML coding. If we include the cost of FrontPage, total software costs are $340.

The total development costs of the prototype for hardware, software and labor was a little less than U.S. $3,000 for the first-time-through effort and an estimated U.S. $1,500 for a second online store, more reflective of economies of scale in online store development. The reader can adjust any or all of the cost components under alternative assumptions of hardware and labor costs and labor hours for a revised estimate of costs under other conditions.

Persons interested in learning more about the free and nearly free software resources used in the prototype can consult the online references presented in Table A-3.

Table A-2: Prototype labor hours by systems development phase (first time through with software learning curve and second time through) and summary labor costs

Development Phase	First Time Through Hours	Second Time Through Hours
Analysis of generic online store needs consistent with freeware approach	28	17
Design of data model, user interface, and database search and update facilities	20	6
Design of client-server interaction	17	2
Build & Test the prototype	89	9
Implementation (including set-up of security)	9	2
Documentation (writing up student project first time through; revise document second time through)	40	4
Total Hours	203	40
Total Labor Cost at $US 9. per hour	$US 1827	$US 360

Table A-3: Online resources for software used in the prototype

Operating System	www.redhat.com
Web server	httpd.apache.org
Perl Language	www.perl.com
Datebase	www.postgresql.org
Online Store Applets	www.uburst.com

Chapter XVIII

Electronic Commerce Opportunities, Challenges and Organizational Issues for Australian SMEs

Mohini Singh
RMIT University, Australia

INTRODUCTION

Australian small businesses are increasingly adopting the Internet and the World Wide Web as a medium of doing business to reach new customers and suppliers, cut costs and expand business. They also use it to enhance communication between buyers and suppliers. This chapter discusses the findings of an exploratory study in Australia that identified the objectives, opportunities and challenges of e-commerce experienced by small businesses that were mostly early adopters of the Internet as a medium of trade. E-commerce issues presented in this chapter include research findings, supported by theory from literature. Electronic commerce opportunities, challenges and organizational learning by small and medium enterprises (SMEs) in Australia indicate that small businesses have created value with e-commerce, although benefits are long term and dependent on a plethora of technological, business and management issues that need to be addressed. Due to the fast-evolving nature of e-business and technological developments that are new to many small businesses, challenges such as managing the expanded flow of information, cross-border taxation, authentication, trust and security, as well as the high costs of acquiring the required technologies and skills, are prevalent. Other challenges of e-commerce range from Web site maintenance to business process re-engineering for an integrated environment. Research findings also highlight the fact that small businesses need formal methods of evaluating the performance of e-commerce to realize the benefits of investment and to further expand their e-commerce venture.

ELECTRONIC COMMERCE

E-commerce generally means doing business on the Internet. It is also referred to as Internet commerce, digital business and online trade. Different authors, depending on the perspective from which it is viewed, have defined electronic commerce differently. According to Watson et al. (1999), electronic commerce is the use of computer networks to improve organizational performance. Turban et al. (2000) define it as the process of buying and selling or exchanging of products, services and information via computer networks including the Internet.

Increasing profitability and market share, improving customer service and delivering products faster are some of the organizational performance gains allegedly possible with electronic commerce. Activities such as the buying and selling of goods and services, as well as transferring funds, utilizing digital communications and all aspects of an organization's electronic interactions with its stakeholders, such as customers, suppliers, government regulators, financial institutions, managers, employees and the public at large, are included in e-commerce. All inter-company and intra-company functions such as marketing, finance, manufacturing, selling and negotiation that use electronic mail, EDI, file transfer, fax, video conferencing, workflow or interaction with a remote computer are components of e-commerce. The rapid adoption of the Internet and the World Wide Web by small businesses as a commercial medium in Australia and other parts of the world is changing the face of business. The Internet has created electronic marketplaces where buyers and suppliers meet to exchange information about prices and product and service offerings, and to negotiate and carry out business transactions (Archer and Gebauer, 2000). Archer and Gebauer are also of the opinion that although electronic marketplaces involve business-to-consumer (B2C) and business-to-business (B2B) systems, growth in B2B is estimated to be five times the value of B2C. Many small businesses are suppliers of products to larger businesses and are important entities of the supply chain.

ELECTRONIC COMMERCE ISSUES FOR SMALL AND MEDIUM BUSINESS ENTERPRISES

SMEs are embracing electronic commerce for many reasons, however, an important reason is to improve competitiveness and to reach out to customers at greater distances. New markets and distribution channels, increased communication and low-cost advertising are easily achieved with e-commerce. Although electronic commerce has been proved to be popular with large business enterprises, small and medium companies can also create value by marketing and selling goods and services electronically (Dublish, 2000). Each company is constrained by the same amount of graphics and design capability that the Internet can deliver, so everyone starts from the same position with their Web sites. This allows small companies to compete directly with larger organizations and acquire a valuable market share (Turban et al., 2000). On the Internet it is easy for small organizations to build and maintain a professional-looking site with innovative services and capture a market share that generally belonged to larger organizations. Smaller businesses, due to their size, have the advantage of being able to implement changes faster and adapt to the demands of Internet commerce better than larger organizations, which are based on more bureaucratic structures. However, as pointed out by Baldwin et al. (2000), for small and medium-sized businesses to achieve success with e-commerce, technology must become widely available to ordinary people and SME's must be prepared to alter their business processes.

Poon and Swatman (1996) classified the benefits of the Internet as a medium of business for SMEs to be direct or indirect. Direct benefits include those relating to measurable cost savings in areas such as communications and marketing, and indirect benefits include shortened communication cycles, and an improved relationship and image. Whinston, Stahl and Choi (1997) and Viehland (1998) described the opportunities of electronic commerce as savings arising from lower procurement and overhead costs, reduced inventory costs arising from electronic ordering and just-in-time delivery, and reduced service costs by providing support via electronic channels. Extended markets for online businesses have resulted in increased revenue by selling to buyers from a wider geographic region. According to the Aberdeen Report (1997), business transactions conducted electronically are completed in less time and at reduced administrative costs. The reduced cost of creating, processing, distributing, storing and retrieving paper-based information is also an opportunity that can be realized from e-commerce. Small organizations can create highly specialized businesses and reduce the time between outlay of capital and receipt of goods and services. Turban et al. (2000) confirmed that e-commerce expands the marketplace to national and international buyers with minimal capital outlay and facilitates contacts with more customers, better suppliers and suitable business partners worldwide, markets to be replaced by buyers.

While business organizations can enjoy the benefits of reduced operating costs, increased revenue and effective information monitoring from electronic commerce, consumers have the advantage of convenient shopping as well as access to information regarding the product and its use. As suggested by Hoffman, Novak and Chatterji (1999), the Web provides the ability to amass, analyze and control large quantities of specialised data to enable 'comparison shopping' and speed the process of finding items. Winner (1997, p.31) added to customer convenience by saying, "People will relish the convenience of buying things on the Net, flocking to stores whose electronic doors are always open and where parking is never a problem."

E-commerce issues discussed in this chapter have been identified from a study that investigated 20 small to medium online businesses. Of these, 17 were 'bricks-and-mortar' organizations that had adopted e-commerce as a new channel of business, and three were 'pure plays' that took advantage of the Internet to set up trade. The research project was exploratory in nature and aimed at identifying e-commerce issues for small and medium enterprises.

RESEARCH METHODOLOGY

For this micro study I adopted an exploratory study method. It involved conducting interviews with small e-business owners. The companies were selected on the basis that they had been identified as significant e-commerce initiatives within the state of Victoria. The names of companies were acquired from documents that listed them as 'electronic commerce success stories' (Phillips, 1998) and from Internet searches. Victorian companies that had a presence on the Internet with online transaction capability were identified from different search engines. Although it was intended to investigate different industry sectors, the 20 case studies are representatives of those organizations with whom interviews could be arranged in the year 1999. Initial contact was made by telephone with the person who headed the electronic commerce project at the organization.

Yin (1994) describes exploratory studies to contain a number of 'what' and 'how many' types of inquiries, which were the types of questions included in the interview tool used to collect data. It comprised five major sections that included questions on the objectives of developing electronic commerce, its opportunities, challenges, technological requirements and its impact on business. With the permission of the interviewees, all interviews were recorded on tape and later transcribed. Findings discussed in this chapter are the outcome of a qualitative analysis of responses acquired from e-commerce project leaders and/or owners of 20 early adopters of e-commerce.

Companies Investigated

For reasons of confidentiality, names of companies investigated are not identified. I have referred to them as Companies A to T listed in Tables 1 and 2. Of these, Companies E, I and T are 'virtual' organizations, while the others are examples of 'bricks-and-mortar' organizations that have adopted the Internet as a new channel of business. E-commerce objectives, opportunities and challenges identified from the research are included in Tables 1 and 2.

E-COMMERCE OBJECTIVES AND OPPORTUNITIES

Many small and medium enterprises in Australia are adopting e-commerce to exploit the potential of new technologies such as the Internet and the World Wide Web. The opportunities and objectives of e-commerce identified from the research project include:

Increased Customer Base

An important advantage of Internet businesses is that they have no defined location, time zone or country. Their Web sites can be accessed 24 hours a day, seven days a week. By offering a '24x7' shop front or 'we never close' customer service, Australian small businesses intend to capture customers from wider geographic regions. Online shopfronts for both national and international customers allow these organizations to offer a wide variety of goods to customers from distant locations, as compared to shoppers in the vicinity of traditional outlets. Expanding business to local, regional and global customers, and offering them convenient shopping hours were important objectives of adopting e-commerce for the organizations investigated.

Increased Sales

For the sample of SMEs investigated, an increase in sales and revenue was achieved with e-commerce. An increase in revenue is usually more significant to smaller organizations as compared to larger ones. For example, a million dollars of revenue could mean a substantial increase in profits for SMEs, but may be insignificant for large businesses. The sale of goods to customers in the Asia and Pacific regions who are out of reach with traditional business was already achieved by some small e-commerce enterprises. Promotion of goods to an increased number of customers and dealing with them in new ways, that is, allowing electronic ordering, online tracking of orders and sales, and offering e-payment methods, escalated sales. Providing additional information about products also led to cross selling and upselling of products that may be complementary or add-ons.

Disintermediation

Disintermediation occurs with e-commerce as the services of middlemen become irrelevant. Research findings indicate that many organizations have managed to transform the market chain, that is, reach out to their customers directly. They have curtailed the role of middlemen such as brokers and dealers. Not having to deal with middle people meant reduced costs for the sellers providing faster service and sometimes more accurate information to customers.

Improved Customer Service

Customer service and support is one of the most promising areas of electronic commerce. Delivering a better customer service and achieving improved customer relations was another important objective of e-commerce identified from this research. Organizations investigated indicated that with online trade they intended to offer their customers access to real-time information about products, services, inventory, product updates and other relevant information. Reaching out to customers directly with correct information and personalized services via the Internet enabled their clientele to make better decisions about their purchases. With e-mail responses to confirm orders and the dispatch of goods, these organizations developed a better relationship with their customers. The supplier is able to communicate directly with the customers, thus a valuable one-to-one relationship is developed. Via e-mail responses, customers are addressed by their names, creating a more personalized service as compared to the general form of greetings offered in traditional stores. With the hyper link capability of Web technology, organizations have been able to provide additional information about new products and services to customers. The Internet's interactive qualities allow for customers' comments and feedback for business improvements, which many small enterprises had begun to capitalise on.

Improved Efficiency and Reduced Costs

The investigated organizations improved efficiency by automating processes that were repetitive, such as sending newsletters, quotes, order and delivery confirmation, product brochures and, in some more developed e-commerce organizations, accounts and advertising. Automated processes result in efficiencies such as reduced paperwork, errors, time and overhead costs. Automated, built-in responses to customers leads to a reduction in the number of employees required by an organization to handle customer queries by phone and fax. Reduced logistics operating costs, and reduced inventory with e-ordering systems and JIT delivery, led to the reduction of overhead costs for many of the small businesses, instead of early adopters of e-commerce; however, it was more prevalent for 'pure plays.' As suggested by Cameron (1997), although the establishment and maintenance of a Web site has costs of its own, the price of using the Web compared to other sales channels is significantly less.

Increased Circulation of Advertisements

Most of the organizations investigated managed to increase the circulation of their advertisements on the Internet at no substantial increase in costs. As an advertising medium, promotion using a Web site results in the sale of 10 times the number of units with one-tenth of the advertising budget and one-quarter of direct-mail expenditures (Cameron, 1997). There is no time lag between publishing information on a Web site and it being accessed by customers. Research findings indicate that most organizations adopted e-commerce initiatives for advertising and marketing, and many were content with using the Internet for brochureware more than selling, which required the development and implementation of other e-processes. Others started their e-commerce with a Web site for marketing and promoting their business, followed by further 'e' developments.

Improved Competitiveness

Irrespective of their size, all online businesses have the same access to potential customers. Small businesses are able to compete with well-established companies that have name recognition, an established infrastructure and purchasing power. Customers accessing online business sites are not aware of the size nor location of the business. Electronic storefronts have allowed smaller organizations to compete with large multinationals by reaching out to the same set of customers. They have also been able to access and implement competitive intelligence used by larger organizations to promote business, and develop new services. New product information and other marketing campaigns used by competitors can be 'tweaked' at little or no cost and with very little time lag. Improved competitiveness was an important objective of e-commerce indicated by most small businesses investigated.

Educated Clients

An important intangible opportunity that resulted from electronic commerce, according to one organization, is the upgraded technology capability and business skills of consumers. To be able to take advantage of electronic commerce, consumers have to have the knowledge to use the Internet and Web technology.

They have to learn to track their orders, understand secure electronic transactions and payments, and other intricacies of electronic commerce. E-commerce encouraged buyers to become technology savvy.

Other objectives and opportunities of e-commerce identified from this research were to become a 'smart and innovative organization,' use data mining and knowledge management to predict demand, and use 'push technology' to win customers. Some less prevalent objectives were improved business relations, improved productivity of salespeople, 'new-found' business partners, a better image and enhanced skills of employees.

ELECTRONIC COMMERCE CHALLENGES EXPERIENCED BY SMALL BUSINESSES

While the opportunities of electronic commerce are undeniable, electronic commerce is new and therefore faces a number of problems. The challenges of electronic commerce identified from this research are:

An Infrastructure for Electronic Payment System

As suggested by Watson et al. (1999), when commerce goes electronic, the means of paying for goods and services must also go electronic. Paper-based payment systems cannot support the speed, security, privacy and internationalization necessary for electronic commerce. Although different electronic payment methods are available in Australia, it is clear from this research that educating consumers and business partners on secure payment systems is necessary to build their confidence and intensify electronic trade. The research highlighted the fact that electronic trade is repressed by the lack of confidence in the methods of payment systems available. As a consequence many of these businesses depended on multi-channel payment methods (checks, cash on delivery, money orders and so forth) to sustain e-commerce.

International Legal Standards

Australian organizations generally close business agreements with a handshake or a signature on a paper contract. Although small businesses could significantly expand business by contributing to various supply chains, many of them missed out on the prospect due to 'fuzzy' e-agreements. They emphasized the need for a set of regulatory frameworks and authenticating policies that online merchants and buyers can turn to if disputes arose. Electronic commerce legal and security frameworks will increase the confidence of online shoppers and businesses to extend trade on the Internet.

Web Site Design and Development

Except for a few that developed their own Web sites, most of the organizations investigated outsourced its development. An important problem identified from this research was that in the process of outsourcing Web site design and development, control was given to outsiders who at times failed to adequately address the objectives of business. It was emphasized that outsourcing Web site designs meant losing creative ideas to competitor organizations taken to them by designers and developers. Another difficulty experienced was keeping up with advanced design tools and technologies. That is, by the time the e-commerce development was completed, a new and better technology for the same purpose was available. Coordination with internal people and ISPs (Internet Service Providers) during the development stage was a problem mostly due to a lack of technology knowledge in-house and the short life span of many ISPs. Striking a balance with rich graphic presentation and download speed, frequently updating and maintaining information, identifying tools for quick search and applying correct logic to e-applications were other problems identified. It was also highlighted that Web sites designed without analyzing the projected users' knowledge of technology, background and needs is a mistake. Small businesses that supplied goods to larger organizations emphasized the need for regular meetings with business partners for uniform formats for transaction data and applications of automated processes.

Technological Limitations

Although technology issues have contributed to other challenges discussed earlier, more specific ones identified were the high costs of integrating business processes, implementing networked services, incompatible software and hardware, and a lack of standards and communication protocols for B2B e-commerce.

It is also worth noting that only a small percentage of organizations investigated had extranets or intranets, therefore issues pertinent to these technologies have not been included in this chapter.

Sociotechnical Issues

The nature and number of jobs at all levels of organization is likely to change as a result of electronic commerce. A number of problems, such as job losses due to a lack of skills and having to take up new responsibilities, led to resistance from employees. The 'old guards' especially felt threatened if their previous skills gained from years of experience were not valued in the electronic environment. Although electronic commerce promises new opportunities, people are still needed to make it work. Therefore, individual feelings and needs must be addressed if the benefits of electronic commerce are to be fully realized. Motivating employees to take up training for improved e-commerce skills is essential. Benefits of e-commerce are sacrificed due to a lack of employee experience and knowledge, which many of the SMEs investigated were coming to terms with.

Evaluating the Performance of E-Commerce

Although most of these organizations achieved some improvements with e-commerce, such as increased sales, they emphasized the need for formal methods of evaluating success. Participants were asked to rate the success of their e-commerce effort, both anecdotally and on a seven-point Lickert scale, with 1 representing "very successful" to 7 representing "failure" on aspects such as earnings or return on the e-commerce investment, making the business known to customers, amount of traffic on their Web sites and dollar value of sales generated online. It was interesting to note from the responses the wide variations in perceptions of success. Most e-commerce ventures thought they were successful, without knowing how to measure success. The most common methods of measuring success by the organizations was placing a counter on their homepages to keep a track of the number of times the homepages were accessed. However, these online businesses ignored the fact that some users access a site but do not buy and some end up at the same site again and again by mistake or due to 'keyword' search. Two of the organizations had implemented 'cookies,' which are a very small text file placed on the users' hard drive by a Web page server. It uniquely identifies a user and tells the server that a user has returned. Although the use of cookies raises privacy and security concerns, they are used to record a user's preferences when using particular sites.

Other challenges experienced by the e-commerce organizations investigated were integrating existing information technology with their e-commerce sites, transferring business from EDI systems onto the Internet and extranets, notifying their consumers that they could do business with them online and determining the best e-channels (e-malls, portals and e-hubs) to promote online business.

Organizational Learning

It is apparent from this research that in Australia the value and potential of e-commerce has been realized by small businesses. It is also clear that although 'bricks-and-mortar' organizations are adopting electronic commerce as a new channel of business, there are others who are taking advantage of the Internet and the World Wide Web to develop virtual businesses. The Internet and the World Wide Web have given small and medium enterprises the advantage of setting up global business with minimal capital. Most small businesses depend on Internet

Service Providers and consultants to set up their electronic business. Online delivered content and promotion of business was hampered due to a lack of skills in-house to continuously refresh Web sites, to add information, and to make it more interesting and interactive. Although many of these organizations expected to achieve much more from e-commerce, all they have managed is a Web presence, due to a lack of knowledge and the high costs of outsourcing.

Although some SMEs have been successful with disintermediation of middle-men such as salespeople, many have not realized the need for re-intermediation of business partners for quick delivery of goods, handling payments, promoting business and discovering new buyers. Re-intermediation refers to the inclusion of the reliance on business partners who may enhance e-business. Forming new alliances with business outlets that allow easy pick up and return of goods sold by online stores leads to enhanced sales and stronger bonds with customers. Successful e-commerce organizations are increasingly forming alliances with other business entities for the delivery of goods, payments and other customer services. New business partnerships with gas (petrol) stations, corner stores and Australia Post are widely discussed and implemented to support e-commerce organizations. New online business alliances are promoting each other's business as well as enhancing e-commerce. One such alliance offers a discount on petrol if the goods are picked up at the nearest service station and a gift voucher for another online business that is regional and sells fruits and vegetables.

Australian e-commerce ventures placed a lot of emphasis on the development of the online business, but human inputs (employee skills) were generally left to the individuals. Supporting the development of employee skills also enhances the organization's intellectual capital, which leads to improved efficiencies and competitiveness in global markets. Continued education is required for success with e-commerce.

RECOMMENDATIONS

Discussion on the following issues, although not prescriptive, will enhance the value of e-commerce to small organizations.

Strategy

A strategy for e-commerce that provides a focus on the business advantage of the venture is required, not only for large organizations, but small and medium enterprises as well. It is also important to link the e-business strategy to the business strategy of the organization. E-business strategy should be both proactive and reactive to customers, new technological developments, the environment and globalization; and it should be flexible. The e-commerce marketplace changes every three to six months, therefore flexibility to allow for the adoption of new developments and changing directions requires strategic plans to be short term and adaptable.

Technology

Security, speed and ease of Web site navigation are important characteristics for successful e-commerce. However, personalization, service orientation and incorporation of new technologies such as mobile phones, data warehousing, data mining and knowledge management are equally important. A good alignment of business and technology is needed for success. If the Internet can be applied to the right niche business, it is guaranteed to be successful.

Legal Issues

The *Electronic Signatures in Global and National Commerce Act* of 2000, otherwise known as the e-sign bill, is designed to promote online commerce by legitimizing online contractual agreements. Under the bill, digital agreements receive the same level of validity as their hard-copy counterparts. The bill also allows cooperating parties to establish their own contracts. Digital signatures, which are electronic equivalent of handwritten signatures, are used to authenticate the participating parties, and ensure the integrity of the message (Rayport and Jaworski, 2001). Small businesses will benefit tremendously as this bill gains acceptance against repudiation and the formation of new e-partnerships. Electronic commerce will be enhanced if the users know that the electronic transaction is secure, orders and payments can be traced and that it is cost effective. The nature of business is such that internationally accepted legal standards are welcomed.

Effective Web Page Design

The quality of the design of the Web page is directly correlated to its success (Cameron, 1997). Effective Web sites are those that can carry valuable information to the consumer. They must be easy to use and navigate, and updated frequently to encourage the user to return. Customers should be able to respond to the service provided either by electronic forms or email. As suggested by Viehland (1998), a successful site should follow a three-click rule, allowing its visitors to find what they are looking for within these three clicks from the homepage. Winning the confidence of consumers to revisit the Web site means creating an atmosphere of continuous innovation. Outsourcing the design of Web sites will require a close coordination between the organization representative and the provider to ensure that the objectives of business are adequately addressed.

New Skills

Education and training bridge the gap between development and successful implementation of new technology (Singh, 2000). Training provides new skills and methods needed to maintain the new Internet-based electronic trade. Considerable time is involved in training a person, which is usually underestimated by many organizations. A trained workforce with appropriate knowledge and skills will better procure the benefits of electronic commerce and avoid resistance to change. It is essential to consider people factors right from the onset of new technologies, and not after implementation, as usually happens. Proper planning of staffing, new job design, training, reward system and gain sharing will help organizations overcome most of the sociotechnical problems.

A Close Link with the Internet Service Providers

In cases where an organization is not well equipped with technical people, it will have to develop a close relationship with service providers. Staff in an organization will not know much about the intricacies of the electronic trade unless they work closely with technical people and technology providers. A close relationship with the e-commerce technology providers, with a high level of trust and understanding that not everything can be spelled out in a contract or specification, is required. A positive relationship with the supplier of technology promotes collaboration in the areas of technical support, backup, training and communication process.

Online Business Promotion

Encouraging the acceptance of electronic trade both within and outside organizations will lead to its success. Without promotion a Web site will be lost in cyberspace. Press releases that present the highlights of the site and focus on information of interest to customers, the most important content, and its benefit to customers and business partners should be highlighted. Although business cards, brochures, stationery, print and TV advertisements are excellent ways of promoting the online business, the e-paradigm is evolving so fast that new models, trading hubs, e-malls, portals and other approaches should be continuously monitored and adopted for further expansion.

Business Process Re-engineering and Linking Back Office Systems to the Web

To maximize the opportunity of rapid information processing with electronic trade, some business processes will have to be re-engineered so that back-end systems are successfully integrated with the Web site. Online stores will then be able to rapidly process information and further reduce costs. Problems of inefficient and ineffective communication with manual order processing and delays caused by human error will also be eliminated. Integrated back-end systems are easily integrated to e-supply chains, which is another opportunity for e-commerce small businesses.

Evaluating the Effectiveness of the E-Commerce Strategy

Determining the effectiveness of the electronic commerce strategy will result in informed decisions about the site and the business approach. Various methods and tools for measuring the effectiveness can be applied. Electronic business effectiveness should take into account intangible benefits as well. Continuous monitoring of electronic commerce will highlight its progress and improve its utilization. Formal evaluation will identify problems for which solutions can be developed to minimize any negative repercussions. The evaluation method put in place should be one that will highlight the apparent financial and non-financial costs and benefits associated with the new business system. Without performance evaluation of electronic commerce, it will take a long time to identify its shortcomings and an equally long time to rectify the problems. Although different methods of evaluations and effectiveness matrices for e-commerce have been suggested by different experts (Rayport and Jaworski, 2001; Schubert and Selz, 2000), business implementation reviews most appropriate to the organization, based on its business case, can be applied.

CONCLUSION

Issues included in this chapter clearly indicate that some small and medium enterprises in Australia have realized the potential of electronic commerce and increased the use of the Internet as a business advantage. Electronic commerce in most organizations is adopted for financial rewards rather than just establishing a Web presence for image building or advertising. However, it is also clear that a lot of support and learning is required for the SMEs to be successful e-commerce ventures.

Early adopters of e-commerce have created loyalty with lucrative customers and business partners, and achieved a competitive advantage. An appropriate human, process and technology architecture for e-commerce is required for creating business value. To enhance e-commerce it is essential for small organizations to concentrate on brand recognition, customer loyalty and service, flexible and short-term strategic plans, worthwhile business alliances, and to focus on profitable e-commerce applications.

To be successful with e-commerce, full commitment of the managers/ owners are required to enforce the changes and create the e-business culture in the organization. E-commerce applications should be fully integrated to avoid 'islands of Web application.' Information sharing, effective communication of ideas and future plans to all employees, and being business focussed and not only technology focussed, will lead to success. As suggested by Wigglesworth (2001), for an e-commerce venture to be successful, it will have to learn to improve and modify continuously. An attitude of 'a Web fairy will come along and make it all better' will not work.

REFERENCES

Aberdeen Group. (1997). Electronic commerce to Internet commerce: The evolution of the Internetworked enterprise. *An Executive White Paper*, October.

Anderson Consulting. (1999). *A Review of E-Commerce in Australia*, April. Retrieved from the World Wide Web: http://www.ac.com/services/ ecommerce/ecom_australia.html.

Archer, N. and Gebauer, J. (2000). Managing in the context of the new electronic marketplace. *Proceedings of the First World Congress on the Management of Electronic Commerce*, McMaster University, Hamilton, Canada (CD ROM).

Baldwin, A., Lymer, A. and Johnson, R. (2001). Business impacts of the Internet for small- and medium-sized enterprises. *E-Commerce & V-Business: Business Models for Success*. Great Britain: Butterworth Heinman.

Cameron, D. (1997). *Electronic Commerce: The New Business Platform for the Internet*. Computer Technology Research Corporation, South Carolina, USA.

Dublish, S. (2000). Retailing and the Internet. *Proceedings of the First World Congress on the Management of Electronic Commerce*, McMaster University, Hamilton, Canada (CD ROM).

Hoffman, D. L., Novak, T. P. and Chatterji, P. (1999). *Commercial Scenarios for the Web: Opportunities and Challenges*. Retrieved from the World Wide Web: http://www.ascusc.org/jcmc/vol1/issues3/hoffman.html.

Phillip, M. (1997). *Successful e-Commerce*. Melbourne, Australia: Bookman.

Poon, S. and Swatman, P. (1997). Internet-based small business communication: Seven Australian cases. *EM-Electronic Markets*, 7(2).

Rayport, J. F. and Jaworski, B. J. (2001). *e-Commerce*. Singapore: McGraw-Hill International.

Singh, M. (2000). Electronic commerce in Australia: Opportunities and factors critical for success. *Proceedings of the First World Congress on the Management of Electronic Commerce*, McMaster University, Hamilton, Canada (CD ROM).

Turban, E., Lee, J., King, D. and Chung, H. (2000). *Electronic Commerce: A Managerial Perspective*. USA: Prentice Hall International.

Viehland, D. (1998). *E-Commerce*. Melbourne: Australian Institute of Charted Accountants.

Watson, R. T., Berthon, P., Pitt, L. and Zinkhan, G. (1999). *Electronic Commerce*. Orland, FL: The Dryden Press.

Whinston, A., Stahl, D. and Choi, S. (1998). *The Economics of Electronic Commerce*. Indianapolis, IN: Macmillan Technical Publishing.

Wigglesworth, K. (2001). ....in the eSpace. *Lecture Notes*, RMIT, Melbourne.

Winner Langdon. (1997). The neverhood of Internet commerce. *MIT's Technology Review*, 100(6).

Yin, R. (1994). *Case Study Research Design and Methods*. New Delhi, India: Sage Publications.

Table 1: Objectives and opportunities of electronic commerce

Case	Objectives and Opportunities
Company A	Increased circulation of advertisements, expanded existing market, reached out to customers at greater distances, reduced costs, reduced the time required to process an order.
Company B	A better relationship with customers, expanded customer base, increased sales.
Company C	Captured markets both nationally and internationally, reduced the need for middle people, traced buying habits of customers, easy demand forecasts.
Company D	Increased business, automated repetitive processes, reduced stock, shifted business-to-business transactions to the Internet.
Company E	Increased sales, expanded customer base.
Company F	Savings on labour costs, automated processes, improved customer relationship by offering 24 hour service, reached out to non-Australian customers.
Company G	Online booking and payment, better account monitoring, reduced the number of middleman, increased business-to-business and business-to-customer linkages.
Company H	Reduced the number of middleman, obtained new distribution channels, expanded business.
Company I	Increased sales and customer base.
Company J	Increased customer base both nationally and internationally.
Company K	Improved customer service, improved business with 'smart technology.'
Company L	Quick and improved transaction records, reduced paperwork, reduced costs.
Company M	Better customer service with 'click, talk, walk', to be competitive, 24-hr shopfront, reduced costs.
Company N	Provide campus services online, better customer service, reduce face-to-face contact, increase the use of remote offices.
Company O	Increase customer base, promote business, competitive advantage, gaining knowledge and technologies.
Company P	Reaching clients at greater distances, quick retrieval of information, amass large amount of information.
Company Q	Capture new customers, exploit new technologies to offer better customer service, offer customised products and services.
Company R	Provision of updated information to customers, improved efficiency, reduced costs thus reduced prices to consumers.
Company S	Wider clientele, apply 'push' technology to increase business, improve business processes, reduce overheads, reduced cost for warehousing, easy marketing, speeds negotiation process, access to international markets, improved lead times.
Company T	No overheads, no cost of warehousing, quick dissemination of information, marketing on the Web.

Table 2: Electronic commerce challenges

Case	Electronic Commerce Challenges
Company A	Integrating e-business into existing business, archive business rules about payments online, develop Web interfaces useable for users, creating Web sites that will be accessed by users and provide them with maximum support, deal with people and new technology issues.
Company B	Letting people know that their business is online, winning the confidence of customers to trade electronically, international payment structure for Australian businesses, dealing with people issues in the organization such as getting them to adopt electronic business.
Company C	Presenting sites in different languages to reach customers in different countries in the region.
Company D	Senior management being less inclined to technology and taking a long time to accept technology initiatives.
Company E	Banks not ready to accept chargebacks for credit cards (credit card companies create fear among users about other payment systems).
Company F	Getting the customers to accept the Internet as a business medium.
Company G	Uncertainty, being able to keep up with rapidly changing technology, need for continuous improvement, appropriate content and Web page design, perceiving and responding to people's sensitiveness.
Company H	Getting the community and the employees to accept the e-commerce culture,
Company I	Support and trust for credit card payments over the Internet, difficult to measure the effectiveness of the site to compare the advertising costs.
Company J	Overcoming security concerns, educating the marketplace to use e-commerce.
Company K	Changing the culture within the organisation and users to do things electronically.
Company L	Obtain senior management support for electronic business, depending on outsiders to make technology decisions, not being able to get the users to accept electronic services.
Company M	To get managers, employees, partners and users interested in electronic commerce. To educate the customers to access the solutions to their questions online.
Company N	Copyright issues for hard copies of electronic material, authentication problems.
Company O	Gaining consumer confidence to use online business, keeping up with technology, making transaction process user friendly, educating employees and customers to accept online business, dealing with resistance to change.
Company P	Assuring users that transactions are secure, encouraging customers to use to use online business, finding ways to promote e-commerce.
Company Q	Establishing online business without affecting existing business, change the culture within the organization to accept online business.
Company R	The need for EC standards for data integrity, contracts with business partners, high costs of setting e-business.
Company S	Incompatible systems with business partners, technical data in different formats since business partners operate on different platforms, sociotechnical issues.
Company T	Secure financial transactions.

Chapter XIX

Training for E-Commerce Success in SMEs

Yanqing Duan, Roisin Mullins and David Hamblin
University of Luton, UK

INTRODUCTION

Rapid developments in Information and Communication Technologies (ICTs), such as electronic commerce (e-commerce), have revolutionized the way that business is conducted. E-commerce refers to the process of buying and selling goods and services electronically involving transactions using Internet, network, and other digital technology. It offers companies tremendous opportunities to improve their business performance in new and innovative ways. However, its huge potential benefit would only be realized by capable managers who can deal with these emerging technologies and implement them wisely. A skills shortage has been categorized as one of the challenges facing global e-commerce by Bingi and Khamalah (2000). The demand for highly knowledgeable and skilled managers and workloads places enormous pressure upon companies to improve or update their current knowledge and skills. This is particularly important in Small and Medium Enterprises (SMEs) as compared with their larger counterparts, as they are often described as "lacking the expertise needed to set up the technologies necessary, despite having a great deal to gain from doing so" (Anonymous, 1998).

Training is often seen as the most effective way to help SMEs to cope with the increasing demand on improving their skills, while not increasing staffing. A pilot project supported by the European Commission's Leonardo Da Vinci Program was set up to address training issues and provide online training and support for SMEs in participating countries. To provide the training in the most needed areas and at the most appropriate levels, surveys and focus group discussions were conducted. Guidelines for the development of the online training system are derived from the findings. This chapter reports the results and summarizes the findings from the empirical studies conducted across five participating countries.

The definition of SMEs varies in different countries. For the purposes of the research, a small and medium-sized business is defined as having between 10 and 249 employees. This working definition is in line with that used by the UK Department for Trade and Industry (DTI) in its SME Statistics for the UK (DTI, 1998), and its Spectrum Business Surveys on the use of Information and Communication Technologies in SMEs (Spectrum, 1999).

E-COMMERCE CHALLENGES FOR SMES

E-commerce and e-business affect the whole business process and cover a wide range of activities. The issues related to the e-commerce challenges within these areas can be examined from different perspectives. From the strategic perspective, Laudon and Laudon (1999) summarized them as:

- The strategic business challenge
- The globalization challenge
- The information architecture challenge
- The information systems investment challenge
- The responsibility and control challenge

From the operational perspective, Bingi and Khamalah (2000) categorized e-commerce challenges along four major dimensions:

1. Economic: Cost justification, Internet access, Telecom infrastructure, Skill shortage.
2. Technical: Security, reliability and protocols, Bandwidth, Integration.
3. Social: Privacy/security, Cultural diversity, Trust, Absence of "touch/feel."
4. Legal: Intellectual property right, Legal validity of transactions, Taxation issues, Policing/regulation.

Despite the widespread use of numerous electronic tools, SMEs are described as the slowest sector to embrace e-commerce (Mehling, 1998; Poon and Swatman, 1999). For many small businesses, e-commerce seems like a confusing nightmare. They are not able to react to the rapid changes brought about by this emerging technology, but on the other hand they are scared to be left behind and therefore eager to embrace the technology (Hobson, 2000). The fear of being left behind was also recognized by focus group discussions conducted by the authors (Mullins et al, 2000).

Cragg and King (1993) discover that the strongest inhibiting factors for small firms' implementation of information technologies are lack of IS knowledge, lack of managerial time, poor support and limited financial resources. Corbitt (2000) argues that if management is not made aware of new and enabling technology, then it is not surprising that they are unwilling to adopt e-commerce. Timmers (2000) also concludes that a lack of awareness and understanding is one of the reasons for hesitation among many companies about committing any major effort to e-commerce.

Research by Spectrum (1997, 1998, 1999), which is a series of Benchmarking Studies commissioned by the UK DTI aimed at measuring UK's progress towards the Information Age, shows that most SME managers are not aware of the opportunities presented to them by e-commerce and Internet business. The surveys by Spectrum indicate that closely linked to awareness, understanding and acceptance of the information society is a distinct lack of skills, and lack of skills is perceived to be the most significant barrier to uptake of ICTs (Auger and Gallaugher, 1997; Database Network, 1998; Duan and Kinman, 2000).

A critical task which all SME managers will face is how to respond to the e-commerce challenges. The initial challenge is to address the current lack of appropriate skills. These can be broadly defined in two areas: technology understanding and ability to facilitate successful technology implementation through appropriate strategic thinking and business planning. Therefore, there is a need for better education and support for SME managers to ensure successful adoption and running of their e-business activities.

SMEs are normally portrayed as having a lack of appropriate skills and are in need of training (Gaskill et al. 1993). Some research has recognized that lack of IT training is a major problem (Anonymous, 1998; Doukidis, 1994; Riemenschneider and Mykytyn, 2000; Robert, 1998). Although lack of proper training and support is not a specific problem associated with e-commerce adoption in SMEs, it is becoming more prominent for e-commerce success, as managers not only need to become equipped with technical awareness and understanding, but more importantly, with its profound business implications. A great deal of evidence from the literature appears to suggest that there is a gulf between the level of skills and knowledge required for e-commerce success and the current level of skills which managers possess. To reduce the gap, effective training and education is paramount. However, to provide training in the most effective way and, at the most, appropriate level, better understanding of what SME managers really need is deemed critical.

In summary, e-commerce poses many challenges to SMEs; one of them is the greater demand on managers and workers in terms of updating their knowledge and expanding their skills. Helping SME managers to understand the opportunities and challenges brought by e-commerce and to act upon them represents a challenge for all concerned. Lack of expertise and skills has been found as one of the inhibitors for adopting e-commerce in SMEs. Issues related to training and education in SMEs need to be carefully examined and investigated. The study described in the following section demonstrates an attempt to address the skill challenge in SMEs by providing effective training and education.

A PAN-EUROPEAN STUDY ON E-COMMERCE TRAINING NEEDS

To investigate the current training provisions and identify the managers' perceived training needs for adoption and implementation of e-commerce, a study was conducted with SMEs (10-249 employees) across five European countries, including Germany, Poland, Portugal, Slovak Republic and the United Kingdom (UK). Questionnaire survey, focus group and interview methods were adopted for the study with the questionnaire survey as the predominate method, and focus groups and interviews as the complementary methods to clarify survey findings and provide more in-depth views on the issues concerned. As a follow-up, and in an attempt at a more in-depth investigation of the questionnaire survey results, a series of structured interviews and focus group discussions were conducted among project partners. Using a structured interview meant that partners did not need to sacrifice the benefits of a standardized form of responses and that they could hope to obtain more objective, unbiased data. Focus group discussions, on the other hand, can effectively support the analysis of a variety of contexts, and generally tend to yield more "creative" answers.

To ensure that the results are comparable with results produced in other countries, a standard set of questions proposed by the University of Luton was adopted. Although the primary objective of the survey was to identify the training needs, other relevant information also needed to be collected and examined. The questionnaire was designed to gather information in the following areas: company and respondent's profile, current use of Internet, EDI and e-commerce, employees' understanding and perception of ICTs, current training provision and managers' satisfaction, needs for ICT training in terms of areas, levels and modes of preferred training delivery. Most of the questions related to identifying training needs. Levels and methods were designed to have pre-defined options with a choice of adding the respondent's own specification. The detailed description of the data collection techniques and the subject selection for focus groups and interviews is described in the study partners' sections later.

Table 1 summarizes all the activities conducted by project partners, and the following sections describe, in more detail, the work conducted in participating countries.

UK Survey and Focus Groups

Survey questionnaires were sent to 950 SMEs in the UK. The companies were chosen randomly from the FAME database. UK FAME (Financial Analysis Made Easy) is a CD-ROM-based database containing detailed information on UK companies for research and marketing. Eighty-seven responses were received (9.2% response rate) of which 81 were usable.

Focus group discussions were also adopted to complement the survey method. The approach to the focus group was through a short introductory meeting about e-commerce. The group was then informed of the phases the discussion would follow. A total of eight groups consisting of about 10 people each formed the focus groups for a discussion about e-commerce problems and training needs. The members of the group were all SME employees enrolled in an 'Introduction to the Web' course which runs for four hours a week over six weeks and considers practical and managerial issues. They all had different levels of knowledge about e-commerce and were all from different industrial sectors. The discussion was recorded and later analyzed from the perspective of the use of language and issues raised during the discussion.

Polish Survey, Focus Group and Interviews

The translated questionnaire was distributed among a number of local businesses. The Polish partner also obtained the assistance of the Katowice Chamber of Commerce and Industry that acted as an intermediary with SMEs in the Katowice area. The Polish team decided to employ a questionnaire-based interview, which is classified as a standardized and structured technique involving a direct communication process. The use of a questionnaire helps standardize the research situations and, as a rule, guarantees a satisfactory degree of structural

Table 1: Summary of the research activities by participating countries

	Survey		No. of focus groups	No. of interviews
	Usable responses received	Response rate		
Germany	34 (1000)	3.4%		
Poland	30 (200)	15%	1	10
Portugal	64 (552)	11.6%	1	
Slovak			1	25
UK	87 (950)	9.2%	8	

homogeneity of data acquired. This, in turn, facilitates further processing of information and makes it possible to convert the results into quantitative data.

Portuguese Survey and Focus Group

The questionnaire was sent, by mail, to 552 small and medium enterprises with less than 250 workers, located in Portugal. They were selected from a list of Portuguese small and medium enterprises, ranked by IAPMEI (which is an association of the Portuguese SMEs) as "The Best of Portuguese SMEs in 1998." The manufacturing sector was the main target, but other sectors, for example, marketing, services, wholesale and construction, were also used. A total of 69 usable responses were collected through the survey.

One focus group discussion was organized involving five managers that are currently enrolled in the MBA course at the Management Department of Universidade Nova de Lisboa. They were from the manufacturing and service industries.

Slovak Republic Interviews and Focus Group

A group totalling 25 SMEs was selected for the process of analysis of the current state of implementation of information technologies and usage of Internet in SMEs in the Slovak Republic. To aid the selection, the assistance of the National Agency for Development of SMEs in the Slovak Republic was sought. One of its activities is in support of business development in small and medium enterprises. The aim within the selection of the group of 25 SMEs to be interviewed was to choose a group of SMEs, which vary in size and cover the whole area of the Slovak Republic.

The focus group comprised representatives from five companies from Bratislava. These representatives were given a presentation of the project goals and expected outputs, then their opinions were sought on such areas as education, the problems which, from the SMEs' point of view, can be expected in the implementation and usage of the training materials developed by the pilot project and the possibilities of testing, evaluating and using the training and support systems produced by the project.

German Survey

The survey was conducted in the German language. The questions were therefore translated and some aspects (for example, management positions) were adapted to differences in business culture. The survey questionnaires were addressed to the top management of 1,000 SMEs in Germany.

A notable difference in research methodology could be seen in the fact that the SME selected to participate in the survey had up to 500 employees while the British survey was addressed to SMEs between 10 to 249 employees. This difference could not be avoided because the company address databases in Germany generally define SME in this way and other data was not accessible. The regional allocation of the questionnaires sent out embraced the German postal ZIP-code areas starting with the numbers 3 and 4. These regions comprise very populated areas and large cities as well as rural areas, but not especially noted technology centers in the south of Germany. The selected companies should therefore be representative of the vast majority of German SMEs. There is no obvious evidence that a diverse regional dissemination could have had systematically different results. The questionnaire was sent out to 1,000 SMEs with 34 usable returns.

FINDINGS AND DISCUSSIONS

It is not necessary to provide detailed results of the studies conducted in all five participating countries in this chapter, but it is important to highlight the most valuable findings and implications based on the evidence collected through surveys, focus groups and interviews. The findings are discussed in terms of:

- Current training provision
- Training and support needs
- Level of training required
- Preferred ways of training delivery

Current Training Provisions

If training is important to the use of ICTs including e-commerce, do the companies provide adequate training for their employees? Table 2 shows some results on current training provision in participant companies from four countries. In terms of training provision, 36% of firms in the UK, 53% in the Slovak Republic and 58% in Germany indicated that they never or rarely train their employees. Most of the companies provide training occasionally and less than 10% provide training frequently in all four countries. Although the implementation of ICTs requires a high level of skills and extensive knowledge, training provision in SMEs still needs to improve.

The assessment of the training the companies have already received is generally satisfactory. The final question in Table 2 identifies the managers' perception of the importance of training in relation to the successful implementation of ICTs. It indicates that the majority of the respondents in the surveyed countries believe training is important with over 30% of them thinking that it is essential. This provides evidence that training plays an essential role in the successful implementation of ICTs.

Training and Support Needs

Table 3 displays the results of the identified training needs of ICTs, especially Internet, EDI and e-commerce. Although there are some variations among the five countries, it is evident that managers in general would like to receive training in all relevant areas. The majority of respondents indicated their training needs in e-commerce, Internet, EDI and related business issues. In more detail, on average, 82% would like to have training on e-commerce/business, 83% on Internet, 77% on the strategic and managerial issues on the use of ICTs, 75% on general knowledge of ICTs and their use in SMEs, 72% on business Web page writing and 72% on EDI. As expected, e-commerce is ranked as a top priority for training, which may reflect the SME's strong willingness to embrace the technology. The least needed areas highlighted are

Table 2: Current training provision

	UK	Germany	Poland	Portugal
Do you provide training for your employees on ICTs?				
1. No training	15%	26%	23%	16%
2. Rarely	21%	32%	30%	7%
3. Occasionally	37%	26%	30%	58%
4. Quite often	21%	6%	10%	17%
5. Frequently	6%	3%	7%	0%
Providers of training				
1. Experts within the company	57%	25%	42%	42%
2. IT training companies	56%	16%	42%	29%
3. Technology suppliers	47%	55%	58%	33%
4. Specialist consultant	31%	16%	13%	17%
5. Academic institutions	13%	10%	4%	1%
6. Government organizations	3%	6%	4%	0%
Satisfaction with training received				
1. Very dissatisfied	2%	0%	0%	0%
2. Dissatisfied	3%	6%	4%	9%
3. Moderately satisfied	46%	32%	58%	46%
4. Satisfied	48%	45%	29%	25%
5. Very satisfied	1%	0%	9%	0%
Perceptions on the importance of training in relation to the successful implementation of ICTs				
1. Essential	36%	32%	40%	46%
2. Very important	31%	42%	30%	25%
3. Quite important	31%	26%	30%	28%
4. Not very important	2%	0%	0%	0%
5. Not at all important	0%	0%	0%	0%

teleworking (55%), video conferencing (60%), mobile communications (57%) and CD-ROM and electronic storage (58%). It seems that some SMEs show lower interest in applying these advanced technologies at the present time. According to Spectrum's survey, SMEs are not yet convinced that the cost can be justified by the benefits (Spectrum, 1999).

The literature review suggests that a lack of e-commerce skill is more prominent in SMEs than larger organizations. Therefore the survey was also designed to ask more detailed questions on training in this area. Table 4 depicts the results for training needs in different aspects of e-commerce.

As the implementation of e-commerce will have a profound impact on the overall business process in a company, business issues should always come before the technical issues. Most importantly, "a clear strategy for an e-commerce solution is the key to the door of success" (Cunningham, 1998) as e-commerce takes more than the technology (Turban et al., 2000). Companies need to treat e-commerce as a strategic business decision, not just a technology decision (Golderg and Sifonis, 1998). This issue is clearly reflected in the managers' needs for training and support by the survey. Table 4 shows that on average, the most demanded area for e-commerce training and support is "business strategies for successful e-commerce" (54%), followed by "manag-

Table 3: Identified training needs in different areas

Areas for ICTs training	Training needed					
	UK	Germany	Poland	Portugal	Slovak	Average
1. General knowledge of ICTs and its use in SMEs	79%	71%	79%	86%	60%	75%
2. Strategical and managerial issues on the use of ICTs	77%	81%	75%	91%	60%	77%
3. E-commerce	86%	74%	75%	94%	80%	82%
4. EDI	67%	45%	74%	87%	86%	72%
5. Business Web page writing	70%	68%	81%	88%	53%	72%
6. Internet	82%	81%	81%	93%	80%	83%
7. Intranet and extranet	62%	48%	67%	83%	54%	63%
8. Multimedia	53%	61%	81%	80%	54%	66%
9. Networking	51%	68%	77%	86%	67%	70%
10. E-mail and fax	63%	71%	71%	87%	74%	73%
11. CD-ROM and electronic storage	61%	55%	51%	78%	46%	58%
12. Video-conference	46%	65%	59%	78%	54%	60%
13. Mobile communications	51%	52%	53%	77%	54%	57%
14. Teleworking	40%	68%	63%	77%	26%	55%

ing e-commerce operations" (38%) and "security" (38%). In terms of training on technical issues, 37% of respondents would like to have training on hardware/software and 25% on legal and tax issues. Compared with traditional IT training, which is mainly concerned with technical aspects of information systems, training in e-commerce needs to address not only technical skills, but more importantly business issues related to performance analysis, strategy development and implementation. It is evident that managers are aware that the appropriate e-commerce strategy and management is vital for any business and should be considered as the most important area for training and support. These findings are also confirmed by focus groups conducted by the authors (Mullins et al., 2000) that show that strategic issues are very important for SMEs, but managers are not sure what strategy they should follow due to a lack of knowledge. It is not surprising to find that even if the right strategy has been implemented, managing e-commerce operations is also considered a vital area which needs further support. E-commerce is not a one-off event. Effective measures should be implemented to ensure its continuing effective operation.

Level of Training Required

In terms of training levels for those who have indicated the need for training, survey results show that most respondents would like to be trained at the beginner and intermediate levels, although the levels vary according to the training areas and countries (see Table 5). For example, in the UK 41% of training on e-commerce is required at the beginner level, 43% at the intermediate level and 16% at the advanced level, while just 16% of training on the general knowledge of ICTs is required at the beginner level, 67% at the intermediate level and 23% at the advanced level. Business Web page writing required training from the beginner level (47%) to advanced level (21%). This may reflect the variability in Web page writing skills among SMEs. In Germany, 65% of training on e-commerce is required at the

Table 4: E-commerce training needs

Current training and support needs for e-commerce	UK	Germany	Poland	Portugal	Average
1. Business strategies for successful e-commerce	43%	61%	50%	62%	54%
2. Managing e-commerce operations	38%	35%	20%	58%	38%
3. Electronic market analysis	35%		27%	35%	32%
4. Hardware/software	27%	32%	57%	32%	37%
5. Security	23%	45%	30%	54%	38%
6. Legal and tax implications	19%	19%	30%	32%	25%
7. E-commerce and banking	14%	29%	20%	25%	22%

beginner level, 26% at the intermediate level and 9% at the advanced level, while 36% of training on the general knowledge of ICTs is required at the beginner level, 59% at the intermediate level and 5% at the advanced level. In Portugal, 39% of training on e-commerce is required at the beginner level, 33% at the intermediate level and 14% at the advanced level, while 33% of training on the general knowledge of ICTs is required at the beginner level, 43% at the intermediate level and 16% at the advanced level. Although the training needs for video conferencing, intranet and extranet are not significant, the level for those who need training is more focused at the beginner and intermediate levels. The areas which require more advanced levels of training are e-mail and mobile communications. Again, the high proportion of low level of training required confirms other research findings (for example, Chappell and Feindt, 1999) on the lower awareness and knowledge of ICTs among SMEs.

Preferred Ways of Training Delivery

Training can be delivered in different ways. How would the managers like to be trained? Table 6 shows some results from the survey. It suggests that the most preferred way of receiving training is on site by external resources (48%), followed by off site training by training organizations (37%). Computer-based self-training delivered by CD-ROM comes as the most preferred self-training method (24%). This may reflect the research finding by Riemenschneider and Mykytyn (2000) which indicates that smaller firms could investigate newer forms of IT training, such as computer-based training (CBT) or even an intelligent CBT system that contains expert-like capabilities to guide the trainee. It appears that Web-based self-training through the Internet is least popular, especially in Poland. Considering the hurdles, such as limited bandwidth and slow speed of Internet access, it is no surprise that managers would like to have off-line training with CD-ROM. However, it is anticipated that online training, particularly at the advanced level, will become more popular with improvements in Internet access speed. It is also possible that the lower enthusiasm for the Web-based training method is closely linked with the lower level of computer literacy among SME managers.

CONCLUSION

Rapid changes in information and communication technologies have brought enormous opportunities as well as challenges. To handle the challenges effectively and turn the opportunities into real benefits, managers in SMEs need to be equipped with new skills and better knowledge. Companies that are successful in traditional business transactions will be affected if they are left behind. This

Table 5: Level of training required

Areas for ICTs Training		Training needed at beginner level			Training needed at intermediate level			Training needed at advanced level		
		UK	Germany	Portugal	UK	Germany	Portugal	UK	Germany	Portugal
1.	General knowledge of ICTs and its use in SMEs	16%	36%	33%	61%	59%	43%	23%	5%	16%
2.	Strategical and managerial issues on the use of ICTs	22%	60%	33%	67%	36%	40%	11%	4%	19%
3.	E-commerce	41%	65%	39%	43%	26%	33%	16%	9%	14%
4.	EDI	39%	57%	39%	42%	36%	39%	19%	7%	22%
5.	Business Web page writing	47%	62%	44%	32%	29%	37%	21%	10%	19%
6.	Internet	33%	40%	24%	50%	52%	59%	17%	8%	16%
7.	Intranet and extranet	44%	33%	24%	44%	67%	57%	12%	0%	19%
8.	Multimedia	46%	42%	33%	36%	42%	56%	18%	16%	11%
9.	Networking	36%	38%	21%	45%	43%	52%	19%	19%	26%
10.	E-mail and fax	12%	27%	25%	53%	50%	45%	35%	23%	30%
11.	CD-ROM and electronic storage	22%	71%	19%	53%	24%	50%	25%	5%	31%
12.	Video-conference	58%	88%	53%	29%	6%	36%	13%	6%	11%
13.	Mobile communications	31%	35%	23%	42%	55%	45%	27%	10%	32%
14.	Teleworking	38%	63%	54%	38%	31%	32%	14%	6%	14%

Table 6: Training delivery methods

Preferred delivery methods for ICTs training		UK	Germany	Poland	Portugal	Average
1.	On-site training using external resources	42%	35%	43%	70%	48%
2.	Off-site training by training organizations	31%	52%	47%	26%	39%
3.	On-site training by internal expert	36%	23%	37%	14%	28%
4.	Computer-based self training delivered by CD-ROM	37%	29%	17%	14%	24%
5.	Computer-based self-training materials downloaded through the Internet	15%	29%	20%	9%	18%
6.	Web-based self training delivered through the Internet	21%	16%	7%	14%	15%

chapter highlighted challenges faced by modern business managers to establish the skills and knowledge as one of the barriers for e-commerce adoption and implementation in SMEs, to emphasize the paramount demand placed upon the skills possessed by managers and most importantly to identify the training needs with a pan-European study. The findings emerging from this study indicate that lack of skills is one of the major inhibitors for e-commerce adoption in SMEs. Managers believe that effective training is very important or essential for the success of e-commerce, but most SMEs only provide occasional training for their employees. The most needed training areas for e-commerce are e-commerce strategy development, managing e-commerce operations and Internet security. The majority of respondents indicate they would like to be trained at beginner or intermediate levels. The most popular human training method is on-site training using external resources and the most preferred computer-based training method is self-training delivered by CD-ROM.

The survey findings offer helpful guidelines for the design and development of further training and support system for SMEs. Considering that SMEs' managers normally lack available funds and have time restrictions, it is believed that the use of Web-based training and advisory systems would be a less expensive and more flexible approach to improve their skills. The findings also provide valuable information to policy makers, SMEs' training organizations, SME consultants, as well as academic researchers.

ACKNOWLEDGMENT

The authors would like to acknowledge the following people for their contribution to the chapter by data collection. They are Prof. U. Rossler and Prof. R. Berning in Fachhochschule Bielefeld (Germany), Prof. H. Sroka and Dr. S. Stanek in Karol Adamiecki University of Economics (Poland); Prof. V. Machado and Dr. J. Araujo in New University of Lisbon (Portugal), Prof. P. Podhradsky in Slovak Technical University (Slovak Republic), Prof. A. Lavrin and Prof. R. Raschman in Technical University of Kosice (Slovak Republic) and Dr. P. Burrell in South Bank University (UK). Research reported in this chapter forms an important part of a pilot project TRICTSME which is supported by the commission of the European Communities under the Leonardo da Vinci Program.

REFERENCES

Anonymous. (1998). E-commerce for SMEs. *Accountancy*, 122(1259), 52.

Anonymous. (1998). June poll results: Readers' view: Training needed. *Nation's Business,* 86(8), 66.

Auger, P. and Gallaugher, J. M. (1997). Factors affecting the adoption of an Internet-based sales presence for small businesses. *The Information Society*, 13(1), 55-74.

Bingi, P. and Khamalah, J. (2000). The challenges facing global e-commerce. *Information Systems Management*, 17(4), 26-34.

BMG Research. (1998). Internet penetration. *A Summary Report by BMG Research for Business Links Bedfordshire*, February.

Chappell, C. and Feindt, S. (1999). Analysis of e-commerce practice in SMEs. *KITE Project Report*.

Corbitt, B. J. (2000). Developing intraoganizational electronic commerce strategy: An ethnographic study. *Journal of Information Technology*, 15, 119-130.

Cragg, P. B. and King, M. (1993). Small-firm computing: Motivators and inhibitors. *MIS Quarterly*, 17(2), 47-59.

Cunningham, M. (1998). Business strategies for e-commerce. *Inform*, 12(10), 10-15.

Dalton, G. (1999). E-business evolution. *Information Week*, (737), 50-66.

Database Network. (1998). European Internet sales to reach $2,000 billion by 2001. *Database Network Journal*, 28(6), 21

Doukidis, G. I., Smithson, S. and Lybereas, T. (1994). Trends in information technology in small businesses. *Journal of End User Computing*, 6(4), 15-25.

DTI. (1998). *Statistical Bulletin URN 98/92*, July.

Duan, Y. and Kinman, R. (2000). Small manufacturing business: Meeting decision support needs. *Journal of Small Business and Enterprise Development,* 7(3), 272-284.

Gaskill, L. R., Van Auken, H. E. and Manning, R. A. (1993). A factor analytic study of the perceived causes of small business failure. *Journal of Small Business Management*, 31(4), 18-31.

Goldberg, B. and Sifonis, J. G. (1998). Focusing your e-commerce vision. *Management Review*, 87(8), 48-51.

Hobson, S. (2000). Making an e-fit. *Conspectus*, August, 20-21.

Mehling, M. (1998). Small businesses are eager to sell wares on the Web. *Computer Reseller News*, 794(May), 87-94.

Laudon, K. C. and Laudon, J. P. (1999). *Essentials of Management Information Systems* (3rd Ed.). New Jersey: Prentice-Hall Inc.

Mullins, R., Duan, Y. and Hamblin, D. (2000). An analysis of factors governing the use of e-commerce in SMEs. *Proceedings of the First World Congress on the Management of Electronic Commerce*, January, 19-21. Hamilton, Canada.

Poon, S. and Swatman, P. (1999). An exploratory study of small business Internet commerce issues. *Information & Management*, 35, 9-18.

Riemenschneider, C. K. and Mykytyn Jr., P. P. (2000). What small business executives have learned about managing information technology. *Information & Management,* 37, 257-269.

Robert, J. (1998). Small-business IT hangups. *Computer Reseller News*, 774(February), 19.

Spectrum. (1997). International benchmarking study. *Information Society Initiatives*. Spectrum and DTI Publications.

Spectrum. (1998). International benchmarking study. *Information Society Initiatives*. Spectrum and DTI Publications.

Spectrum. (1999). International benchmarking study. *Information Society Initiatives*. Spectrum and DTI Publications.

Timmers, P. (2000). *Electronic Commerce: Strategies and Models for Business-to-Business Trading*. Chichester, England: John Willey & Sons Ltd.

Turban, E., Lee, J., King, D. and Chung, H. M. (2000). *Electronic Commerce: A Managerial Perspective*. Upper Saddle River, NJ: Prentice Hall, Inc.

About the Authors

Stephen Burgess is a Senior Lecturer in the School of Information Systems at Victoria University, Melbourne, Australia. He has a Bachelor's degree in Accounting and a Graduate Diploma in Commercial Data Processing, both from Victoria University, Australia; an MBus (Information Technology) from RMIT, Australia, and a PhD at Monash University, Australia, in the area of small business-to-consumer interactions on the Internet. His research and teaching interests include the use of IT in small business, the strategic use of IT and B2C electronic commerce.

***

Shirley Bode is a Research Associate and PhD student in the School of Management Information Systems at Edith Cowan University (ECU) in Perth, Western Australia. Her research interests relate to SMEs, consultant engagement and Internet strategy, particularly in relation to business-to-consumer electronic commerce. She has been published in a number of refereed publications and has presented her research at several international conferences.

Giacomo Buonanno received his Laurea (cum laude) in Electronic Engineering in 1988 and his PhD in Computer Science and Automation Engineering in 1993, both from Politecnico di Milano. He received his MBA from the Scuola di Direzione Aziendale–Università Bocconi in 1991. He is an Associate Professor in the Istituto di Tecnologie of the Università Carlo Cattaneo–LIUC. He was also an Assistant Professor at the Politecnico di Milano, Dipartimento di Elettronica e Informazione, until 1998. His current research interests include Information System and ICT impact in SMEs. He is a member of the IEEE and the IEEE Computer Society.

Janice Burn is Foundation Professor and Head of the School of Management Information Systems at Edith Cowan University (ECU) in Perth, Western Australia, and World President of the Information Resources Management Association (IRMA). She previously held senior academic posts in Hong Kong and the UK. Her research interests relate to information systems strategy and benefits evaluation in virtual organizations, with a particular emphasis on cross-cultural challenges in an e-business environment. She is recognized as an international researcher with over 100 refereed publications in journals and international conferences. She is on the editorial board of five prestigious IS journals and participates in a number of joint research projects with international collaboration and funding.

Andrew Carrington is a graduate of the University of the West Indies and holds MBA and MIS degrees from Southern Illinois University–Edwardsville, USA. He is currently a Software Engineer with Fastechnology Inc. In the future he plans to return to his home country of Barbados to form an information technology services business.

Ye-Sho Chen, PhD, is a Professor of Management Information Systems in the Department of Information Systems and Decision Sciences, E. J. Ourso College of Business Administration, Louisiana State University. He is the Associate Director of the International Franchise Forum at LSU. He currently teaches and conducts research in the fields of knowledge management, business intelligence, and electronic commerce in franchising and small business.

P. Pete Chong, PhD, is currently an Associate Professor of MIS at Gonzaga University, Spokane, Washington. His primary research interest has been in the area of information usage analysis and its application in business.

Ron Craig is a Professor of Business at Wilfrid Laurier University and Area Coordinator of the Operations & Decision Sciences Group. He holds a PhD and MASc in Management Sciences, and a BASc in Chemical Engineering, all from the University of Waterloo. His research interests are in the areas of small business and technology management. Co-founder of a computer peripheral manufacturer prior to joining Laurier, Professor Craig also served more recently as the university's first IT Officer.

Yves Decady is currently working as a Statistician and Policy Analyst for Environment Canada. He completed his PhD in Business from Carleton University in 2000. His research interests include the analysis of complex survey data and multiple response data analysis.

Monica Diochon earned a BA from St. Francis Xavier University and an MBA from Dalhousie University, then she worked in the small business sector prior to her teaching appointment at the Schwartz School of Business and Information Systems at St. Francis Xavier University. Inspired by her work experiences in the small business field, she completed a PhD at Durham University (UK) in the field of entrepreneurship and returned to the Schwartz School. Currently, she is a member of the Canadian research team that is examining how new enterprises emerge. She is also doing further research on the use of information technology among small business in eastern Canada.

Yanqing Duan is a Senior Research Fellow at Luton Business School, University of Luton. She received her PhD from Aston Business School, Aston University. Her principle research interest is the development and use of intelligent systems (on-line and off-line) for supporting business and management, especially business decision making, marketing planning, and e-business strategy development and implementation. She is also interested in the design and the development of Web-based intelligent systems for training purposes.

Linda Duxbury is a Professor in the Eric Sprott School of Business, Carleton University, Ottawa, Canada. She received an MSc in chemical engineering and a PhD in Management Sciences from the University of Waterloo. She has published widely as both an academic and practitioner in the area of work-life balance, career development, supportive work environments, adoption of technology and the impact of company size on human resource management.

Dieter Fink, PhD, is an Associate Professor in the School of Management Information Systems at Edith Cowan University (ECU). He is the current Director of the Small and Medium Enterprise Research Centre at the university. Prior to joining ECU he worked as a Manager Consultant for Arthur Young & Co (now Ernst & Young) and as a Systems Engineer for IBM, both in South Africa and Australia. Dr. Fink has held a visiting academic position in a number of countries, including Germany and New Zealand. He has published widely in the areas of IT and SMEs, IT security and audit, and strategic IS planning.

David Hamblin is Professor of Manufacturing Management and Acting Dean of Luton Business School. His research interests include managing performance in extended manufacturing enterprises, particularly in the aerospace and automotive sectors.

M. Gordon Hunter is an Associate Professor in Information Systems in the Faculty of Management at The University of Lethbridge. Dr. Hunter has previously held academic positions in Canada, Hong Kong and Singapore, and visiting positions in the USA and New Zealand. He has a Bachelor of Commerce degree from the University of Saskatchewan in Canada. He received his doctorate from Strathclyde Business School in Glasgow, Scotland. He has extensive experience as a systems analyst and manager in industry and government organizations in Canada, and is an Associate Editor of the *Journal of Global Information Management*. He is the Canadian World Representative for the Information Resource Management Association. He serves on the editorial board of the *Journal of Global Information Technology Management* and the *Journal of Information Technology Cases and Application*. Dr. Hunter has conducted seminar presentations in Canada, the USA, Asia, New Zealand, Australia and Europe. His current research interests relate to the productivity of systems analysts with emphasis on the personnel component, including cross-cultural aspects, and the effective development of information systems.

Robert Justis, PhD, is the Director of the International Franchise Forum at LSU. He is a Professor in the Management Department and the Entrepreneurship Institute, E. J. Ourso College of Business Administration, Louisiana State University. He specializes in the development and start-up of franchising and entrepreneurial organizations. In addition, Dr. Justis has developed and presented franchising programs in Brazil, Mexico, China, Australia, Japan, Korea, Singapore, the Philippines, Malaysia, France, Finland and Switzerland. He is recognized as an expert in franchising and entrepreneurship around the world and has served on the National Steering Committee of the Small Business Administration for five years. He was also a Founder of the Society of Franchising and the Small Business Institute Directors' Association (SBIDA). He is the author of *Managing Your Small Business* (Prentice-Hall, Inc.), *Dynamics of American Business* (Prentice-Hall, Inc.), *Strategic Management and Policy* (Prentice Hall Inc.) and *Basics of Franchising*. His most recent textbook, *Franchising* (co-authored with Richard Judd), is published by South-Western Publishing Co. and is the best selling textbook in the field.

Russell Kinman is the Former Head of the Department of Business Systems in the University of Luton Business School. His research interests include decision systems and management education.

Robert Klepper is Professor of Computer Management and Information Systems at Southern Illinois University–Edwardsville, USA. His recent publications include articles on electronic commerce, organizational culture and information technology assimilation, and IT outsourcing. He is the author of *Outsourcing Information Technology Systems and Services*, published by Prentice-Hall.

Kristy Lawrence currently holds a Lecturing position within the School of Information Systems, at the University of Tasmania, Australia. Her research and teaching interests deal with electronic commerce and electronic business, with a specific emphasis on how these technologies can be adopted among small and medium-sized enterprises.

Roisin Mullins is a Lecturer in Business Information Systems at Luton Business School. She has a MSc in User Interface Design. Her research interests are in the design and development of an intelligent Web-based training system for implementing information and communication technologies (ICTs) in SMEs. She is also interested in modelling the mechanisms of action of intelligent agents in multimedia and Web-based systems.

Simpson Poon is Chair Professor of Information Systems at Charles Sturt University, Australia. He is also a Visiting Professor at the University of Hong Kong. Dr. Poon earned his PhD in Information Systems from Monash University, Australia. He was the Founding Director of the Centre of E-Commerce and Internet Studies at Murdoch University, Australia. Dr. Poon has been an e-business consultant and has worked with both government and business organizations in Australia and Asia. He has published widely in the area of e-business in both academic and professional journals.

David Pugsley completed a BBA degree at Acadia University, before receiving his chartered accountant (CA) designation. Prior to teaching he gained experience as an auditor, technology consultant and tax professional. He was involved in the project management, installation and training for a number of accounting information system projects and has experience as a network administrator. Currently teaching in the Schwartz School of Business and Information Systems, he has a strong interest in information technology. His research areas focus on student transition to professional accounting careers, the use of information technology by small business, as well as the impacts and potential of enterprise resource planning systems for business.

Aurelio Ravarini is Assistant Professor of Information System Management at Cattaneo University (LIUC), Italy, since 2001. His research work concerns business information management, with an emphasis on the organizational impacts deriving from the business application of information technology, and a focus on small and medium enterprises applications. He has been teaching Informatics Fundamentals and Information System Management at the Faculties of Business Economics and Management Engineering in LIUC, and at the Faculty of Language and Literature in the Catholic University of Milan, Italy.

Celia Romm is a Foundation Professor of Information Technology at Central Queensland University and an Honorary Professor at Fujian Radio and TV University, the People's Republic of China. She received her PhD from the University of Toronto, Canada (1979). She has been a lecturer, consultant and visiting scholar in Israel, Japan, Germany, Canada, the USA and Australia. Dr. Romm's current research interests include: community informatics, electronic commerce, computer-mediated communication, and IT/IS education. She has published three books: *Electronic Commerce: A Global Perspective* (published through Springer, London, in 1998), *Virtual Politicking* (published through Hampton Press, USA, in 1999) and *Doing Business on the Internet–Opportunities and Pitfalls* (published in 1999, by Springer, London and to be published in China by Tianjin People's Publishing House in 2001). In addition, Dr. Romm published more than ninety papers in refereed journals and chapters in collective volumes, as well as presented her work in over 60 local and international conferences.

Donatella Sciuto has been a Full Professor of Computers at Politecnico di Milano, Italy, since 2000. In 1988 she earned a PhD in Electrical and Computer Engineering at the University of Colorado. Her research interests cover methodologies for testability analysis and testable design of complex digital systems, methodologies for hardware/software co-design of embedded systems, and methodologies for low power estimation and design. She has published in the major journals within these fields. She has been teaching Computers and Advanced Computer Architectures at Politecnico di Milano and Information System Management at the Faculties of Business Economics and Management Engineering in LIUC.

Mohini Singh is a Senior Lecturer in E-Business at RMIT University, Australia. She earned her PhD from Monash University in the area of New Technology Management. Her publications and presentations are in the area of Management and Implementation of New Technologies and Electronic Commerce. Dr. Singh was the Founding Director of the Electronic Commerce

Research Unit at Victoria University, Melbourne. She has successfully completed funded research projects in the area of e-commerce, and presented and published widely both locally and internationally. Her current research focus is on electronic commerce management and business issues, evolving e-business models, e-commerce effectiveness metrics and e-business relationship management.

Anthony Stiller is a Lecturer in Information Systems at the University of the Sunshine Coast, Queensland, Australia. His research and practical experience as a consultant has led to both theoretical and practical advances in electronic commerce, and in particular, the development of a procedural framework for small-to-medium enterprises to follow when developing their e-business strategy. He is also involved with industry in the development of information systems that support their business model, security and control, workflow and customer resource management. He is a regular contributor and reviewer of papers at refereed conferences, journal articles and book chapters as well as a Member of the International Board of Editors for the *Journal of Information Technology Education*.

Marco Tagliavini has a degree in Computer Science from Milan University and a Masters in IT from the CEFRIEL Research Center in Milan. He has been teaching Computer Science and Information Systems for both Cattaneo University in Castellanza (since 1993) and the Catholic University in Milan (since 1998). His research concerns the management of information systems and Internet-based technologies, focusing on the peculiarities of small and medium enterprises. He is CEO and Partner of a consultancy firm which focuses on the strategic, technical and organizational planning of eBusiness projects.

Arthur Tatnall is a Senior Lecturer in the School of Information Systems at Victoria University, Melbourne, Australia, and Director of its Electronic Commerce Research Unit. He holds Bachelor's Degrees in Science and Education as well as a Master of Arts in which he explored the origins of business computing education in Australian universities. His PhD involved a study in curriculum innovation where he applied innovation translation theory to investigating the manner in which Visual Basic was adopted into the curriculum of an Australian university. His research interests include the management of technological innovation and change, project management and information systems curricula.

Wal Taylor is attached to the COIN Internet Academy, which is a collaborative community informatics research activity between the Faculty of Informatics and Communication at Central Queensland University and the Rockhampton City Council. He has 30 years experience in community economic development in rural and regional areas at both practitioner and management levels in the public sector. He has been recognized for his work with a range of community awards and is the Rockhampton Citizen of the Year for 2001. His current research interest is the role of IT in communities in regional urban settings.

Angel Tse is a Master's of Management Studies student at the Eric Sprott School of Business, Carleton University. Her master's thesis deals with computer use in small businesses and is being completed under the supervision of Dr. Linda Duxbury.

Borut Werber is a Teaching Assistant of Information Systems in the Faculty of Organizational Sciences at the University of Maribor, Slovenia. In 2000, he received his PhD from the University of Maribor in the area of MIS. Previously he was working for one year as an Information Systems Analyst on the reengineering of a small Slovene firm. In the last 10 years, he has authored several accounting and book-sale database applications for small firms and participated in developing a part of an IS application for the University of Maribor. He is author or co-author of two computer-programming manuals and several articles presented at international conferences in the USA, Canada, Great Britain and Eastern Europe.

Barry Wright is an Assistant Professor in the Schwartz School of Business and Information Systems at St. Francis Xavier University. He is a graduate of Queen's University with a PhD in Management. His research interests include: leadership issues, small business use of information technology and spirituality in the workplace. He has provided a variety of training and research consultations to Canadian organizations, including Sobeys Canada Inc., Bank of Montreal, Price Waterhouse, Swim Canada, Royal Oak Mines, the MacLeod Group and the Insurance Council of Canada. He has worked in executive development for several years with both the Queen's *Executive Program* and Queen's *Program for Public Executives*. In addition, he provides individual executive 'coaching' for several senior managers across Canada.

Mark (Xianzhong) Xu, PhD, is senior lecturer at the Portsmouth Business School. His specialist areas are in strategic intelligence management, Executive Information Systems and e-Business strategy. He supervised a research project on business environment scanning and information refining. He has publications in international conferences and some leading journals such as the *International Journal of Information Management* and the *Journal of Information Systems Management*.

Index

Symbols

80/20 principle 127

A

"abandoned" projects 48
ABI/Inform 1
action 210
actor-network theory 87, 89
actual coverage ratio 69
adoption 19
advanced 120
advertisements 322
agency theory 119
application logic layer 313
application manual 77
application service providers (ASP) 120,
    134
ARI model 210, 217
association analysis 129
attitude 120
Australia 316
average cost per coverage unit ACpCUi 70

B

B2B portals 270
back office operation system 129
barriers 5, 24
beginner 120
benchmarks 135
bespoke 148
best business practice model 266
business case 184, 189
business practice 98
business service providers 253
business units 121
business-to-consumer electronic commerce
    299

C

Canada 20, 193
case 92
case analysis 227
case study 183, 220
challenges 1, 10, 316
cluster analysis 129
cognitive dissonance theory 51
collaborative 178
collective knowledge 131
commerce benefit 279
communication system 129
communities 209
community informatics (CI) 214
company 92
compatibility 86
competence leverage 250
complexity 86
computer-assisted technology 28
computer security practice 156
computer technology 19
consultancy engagement 227, 241
consulting 254, 303
content validity 145
cooperative 181
costs 308
counseling 254
cross-sell analysis 129
culture 7
customer relationship management 294
customer/product profiles 126

D

data layer 313
data mining 129
decision support systems (DSS) 140
decision tree analysis 129
define 25

definition 3, 79, 262
definitions 3
developing countries 7, 300
developing economies 119
developing world 299
development costs 313
diffusion theory 85
DSS 140
Dvorak keyboard 91

E

e-business 227
e-business strategy 262, 326
e-commerce adoption model 263
e-commerce challenges 335
e-practice 246
e-readiness 194
e-sign bill 327
e-strategy 263
early adopters 197
early majority 197
EC importance grid 196, 205
EC reality model 195, 205
EC strategy 194
effectiveness 64, 120
efficiency 64, 120
electronic commerce (e-commerce) 13, 178,
    179, 209, 316, 334
electronic commerce defined 179
electronic payment system 323
encroachment 124
enrollment 90
escalating commitment 51
essentialism 87
evaluation grid 67, 72
evaluation of ICT 65
evolution 248
exclusive territories 120
exploratory study 319
extension of BPR 249
external environment 6
extranet for business-to-business (B2B)
    collaboration 129

F

factor analysis 167
focus group 337

framework 52, 120
franchise community 119
franchise development system 128
franchise knowledge repository framework
    132
franchise support system 128
franchisee 119
franchising 118
franchisor 119
franchisor headquarter 121
franchisor headquarter management
    system 128
franchisor-franchisee relationship 120
front office operation system 129

G

Gable's model 230
global business 210
government support 8
group behavior 120
growth 98
growth strategy 119

H

hype cycle 198

I

ICT investment level ILi 67, 70
ICT manager 64
implementation 32
in-house 148
individual behavior 120
industry averages 135
industry responsibility 184, 188
information and communication technolo-
    gies (ICTs) 334
information sophistication 22
information systems 156
information systems development out-
    comes 48
information technology 1, 98, 120, 156,
    246
innovation 83
innovation diffusion 83
innovation translation 83, 91
innovative capacity 98

innovators 197
integration (ARI) model 210
interessement 90
'internal' dependency 104
internal reliability tests 145
international franchise association (IFA) 124
international franchising 119
Internet 4, 13, 279
Internet commerce 281
Internet for business-to-consumer (B2C) 129
Internet service provider (ISP) 301
Internet strategy 232
Internet technology strategy 272
interpretive approach 102
interpretivist perspective 233
interview methods 337
interviews 103, 156, 249, 319
intranet for intra-enterprise collaborations 129
inventory control system 56
IS check-up 65
IS coverage level CLi 67, 69
IS development trend 67, 76
IS evaluation grid 77
IS management 64
IS strategic alignment 72
IS utilization coefficient 69
issues 1

K

KAMIG 132
knowledge 120

L

labor costs 305
laggards 197
late majority 197
local 210
long interview technique 103
longitudinal survey 26

M

management information system (MIS) 140
management involvement 279
manufacturers 193
market experience 250
market segmentation analysis 129
master 120
maximum level of possible automation, MLPA(i) 69
media certification 120
micro business 4
minimum acceptable level of automation, MALA(i) 69
MIS implementation 23
mobilization 90
motivation 120

N

narrative inquiry method 54
national computer security association 160
negative information 48
networking 255
novice 120

O

observability 86
off-the-peg 148
online services 246
online store 299
online store Prototype 311
open source software 301
opportunities 5, 316
optimization model 141
organizational impact level OILi 67
organizational issues 316

P

payment 304
perceived effects 39
personality profiles 126
plug-in module 312
potential coverage ratio 69
practical application 67
pricing 239
problematization 90
procedural framework 261
professional 120
professional services 246

profile 146
project 301
'promoter' approach 100
prospective franchisees 121
prototype 301
purposeful sample 102

Q

questionnaire 77
questionnaire survey 337
QWERTY keyboard 91

R

reaction 210
recreation of the organization 250
recreation of value 251
relative advantage 86
research 1
resource scarcity 119
respondent characteristics 170
rural small businesses 9

S

satellite small businesses 118
security measures 156
security practice 158
security-f1 169
service 239
seven-step model 268
site profiles 126
Slovenia 156
small and medium enterprises (SMEs) 2, 4,
    63, 178, 209, 227, 261, 316, 334
small business
    1, 19, 49, 83, 98, 140, 156, 209,
    279
small business administration (SBA) 118
small business development centers 118
small businesses defined 180
sociology of translations 87
song book 54
stakeholder 109
startup issues 306
STATA 27
store templates 306
strategic alignment 64

strategic alignment assessment 67
strategic EC 195
strategic orientation and alignment 184
strategic orientation and misalignment 186
strategic planning 229
success factors 5
suppliers/government contact management
    system 129
survey 25, 140, 199, 287
survival of the franchisor 124

T

technical knowledge 301
technological innovation 83
technology adoption lifecycle 196, 205
technology maturation cycle 205
ten imperatives for e-business success 268
training 32, 334
training and support needs 341
training delivery 344
training levels 343
training provisions 340
trialability 86

U

UFOC 136
unsolicited commercial email (UCE) 160
useful EC 195
user 148
user interface 312

V

viruses 158
vortal 270

W

Web hosting 303
Web initiatives 193
Website design consultants 229
Webstore hosting 303
what if model 141
work configuration 249
working knowledge 120
workplace and employee survey (WES) 26